T0355461

The *Chevron* Doctrine

The *Chevron* Doctrine

ITS RISE AND FALL, AND THE FUTURE

OF THE ADMINISTRATIVE STATE

Thomas W. Merrill

HARVARD UNIVERSITY PRESS

Cambridge, Massachusetts
London, England
2022

Library of Congress Cataloging-in-Publication Data

Names: Merrill, Thomas W., author.
Title: The Chevron doctrine : its rise and fall, and the future of the
    administrative state / Thomas W. Merrill.
Description: Cambridge, Massachusetts : Harvard University Press, 2022. |
    Includes bibliographical references and index.
Identifiers: LCCN 2021036942 | ISBN 9780674260450 (cloth)
Subjects: LCSH: Judicial review of administrative acts—United States. |
    Administrative law—United States—Interpretation and construction. |
    Separation of powers—United States. | Judicial discretion—United States. |
    Administrative discretion—United States.
Classification: LCC KF5425 .M47 2022 | DDC 342.73/06—dc23/eng/20211109
LC record available at https://lccn.loc.gov/2021036942

For Kim

Contents

The *Chevron* Doctrine

Introduction

JAMES FREEDMAN ONCE OBSERVED that the American administrative state has long been afflicted by recurring crises of legitimacy.[1] These crises typically follow upon an expansion of the federal government. Expansions typically mean creating new agencies or conferring new powers on existing agencies. And given that the Constitution says nothing about administrative agencies, other than a few passing references to the heads of departments, it is perhaps not surprising that those opposed to the expansion of federal authority—or just made uneasy by it—respond by raising questions about the legitimacy of the administrative state.

The latest crisis of legitimacy appears to have been triggered by efforts of the Obama Administration to tackle climate change and immigration reform by expanding existing administrative authority.[2] Agitation about the legitimacy of these efforts led to dark warnings that America is governed by a "deep state," and, at least among conservative legal commentators, took as its most prominent target something called "the *Chevron* doctrine."[3] The doctrine is named for a Supreme Court decision handed down in 1984, *Chevron U.S.A. Inc. v. National Resources Defense Council, Inc.*[4] After gradually consolidating its grip for over thirty-five years, the *Chevron* doctrine became a matter of intense controversy at the tail end of the Obama Administration. Conservative judges and lawyers—including two of the Justices named to the Supreme Court by President Trump—have argued that *Chevron* must be overruled or at least significantly modified. Liberal judges and lawyers—including the Justices named to the Court by Presidents Clinton and Obama—generally think *Chevron* should remain undisturbed or perhaps only modestly reformed. Both sides attribute great significance to the outcome of this debate.

What exactly is the *Chevron* doctrine? It refers to a standard that courts apply in determining whether an administrative agency has correctly interpreted the statute under which it operates. The doctrine says a court is always to proceed in two steps. First, if the court finds Congress provided a "clear" or "unambiguous" answer to the meaning of the statute, the court must enforce that understanding. But if the statute does not provide a clear answer—if it is ambiguous or silent—then, as a second step, the court is to enforce the agency's interpretation, as long as it is "reasonable." This is the gist of the *Chevron* doctrine, at least as commonly formulated. In the scores of decisions that invoke the doctrine, the Court has varied some of the terminology, but the basic "two-step" standard of review remains the same.

So what is the big deal? Terms like "clear" (versus "unclear") and "reasonable" (versus "unreasonable") are vague, and conceivably the *Chevron* two-step does not impose any real barrier to courts accepting or rejecting the agency's view of the law in any particular case. A number of studies have attempted to determine whether the *Chevron* doctrine has made any difference in terms of the outcomes of judicial challenges to agency interpretations. The general picture that emerges is that the doctrine has made at most only a modest difference in terms of the "win rate" of agencies in getting their interpretations accepted by the courts. Agencies seem to have won about 55–65% of these challenges before *Chevron,* and maybe something like 65–75% of these challenges after *Chevron.*[5] This is not a trivial change, but it is difficult to know for sure whether it is attributable to the two-step doctrine. After all, it is possible that courts are more inclined to apply the seemingly deferential two-step standard if they decide to affirm an agency decision, and less inclined to apply it if they decide to reverse.

The picture is especially murky in studies that examine the fate of the *Chevron* doctrine in the Supreme Court.[6] The Supreme Court authored the *Chevron* decision in 1984, but it took some time for all Justices to accept what this book calls "the *Chevron* doctrine" as an all-purpose metric to apply in reviewing agency interpretations of law. Even in recent years, the Court has found reasons not to apply the doctrine when it seemingly should apply—as when the Roberts Court upheld a controversial interpretation of the Affordable Care Act (Obamacare) and said the issue was too important to decide under the *Chevron* standard.[7]

At the level of the courts of appeals, which sit just below the Supreme Court and hear the vast majority of challenges to administrative decisions, the evidence suggests that the *Chevron* doctrine is associated with a small increase in deference to interpretations by agencies.[8] To be sure, the overall picture is complex. Different courts of appeals apply the two-step doctrine at different rates, and some agencies fare better under the doctrine than others.[9] And there is always the concern about selection effects—that the *Chevron* doctrine is used more often to uphold a decision and less so to set one aside. Even a modest uptick in deference to agencies means that the doctrine is important, although it might not by itself justify an entire book on the subject.

The significance of the *Chevron* doctrine, however, goes beyond its effect on the overall win rate of agencies in court. First, the doctrine may have changed the distribution of wins and losses in ways that are unfair to persons who, for whatever reason, fail to engage the sympathies of judges. As we will see, the legal doctrine that prevailed before the *Chevron* doctrine (and that persists today in certain contexts) required courts to consider a variety of factors in determining whether a particular agency interpretation is proper. The *Chevron* doctrine, in contrast, is simplicity itself. Step 1: Is the statute unclear? Step 2: Is the agency interpretation reasonable? For busy judges confronted with complex questions of statutory interpretation, the *Chevron* doctrine offers a way to resolve the case by saying, if the statute seems unclear, the agency wins. In his last opinion addressing the *Chevron* doctrine before he retired, Justice Kennedy said he was troubled by what he perceived to be the "reflexive deference" accorded to agency interpretations by lower courts based on "cursory analysis."[10] If this perception was correct, it means some persons may have been treated unfairly by agencies, or at least in ways that are inconsistent with what Congress intended, because they could not persuade a court to take the legal question seriously.[11]

Second, and as a mirror image of the first, the *Chevron* doctrine may have changed the way agencies behave. Donald Elliott, who previously served as general counsel of the Environmental Protection Agency, has argued that the *Chevron* doctrine made agencies more aggressive in interpreting their statutory mandate in novel ways.[12] Under the doctrine, he has maintained, agencies began to see less need to go to Congress to secure new statutory authority because they could simply reinterpret existing law to reach the desired result. A recent survey of agency employees seems to confirm Elliott's observation on this score.[13] The *Chevron* doctrine may also have changed the balance of authority within agencies. Before the doctrine was established, agency lawyers wielded great authority, based on their presumed ability to predict how courts would interpret the agency's statute. After the doctrine was established, the power of lawyers receded, and that of scientists and other nonlegal experts surged to the fore. Elliott regards this as good thing, and he may be right. But these are highly significant developments, however one views them.

Finally, and perhaps most fundamentally, the *Chevron* doctrine seems to validate a dramatic shift in power in our system of constitutional government. The two-step standard of review, taken at face value, seems to say that primary authority to interpret ambiguous agency statutes—and virtually every statute is unclear or silent on many points—has been transferred from courts to agencies. Courts since the days of Chief Justice John Marshall have been thought to have authority "to say what the law is."[14] *Chevron* seems to take a big chunk of that authority and transfer it to agencies, now widely regarded as part of the executive branch. This is significant because courts in matters of statutory interpretation generally act as "faithful agents" seeking to carry out the will of the Congress. The *Chevron* doctrine downplays the role of Congress's faithful agent, the courts, and elevates the roles of executive agencies, which are not so faithful because they are subject to oversight by the President, who often has different views about policy than did the enacting legislature. This has profound implications for how we think of the role of Congress under our system of government. The conventional view is that Congress is the prime mover in establishing policy, and the role of the agencies is to implement that policy, under the supervision of the courts. The *Chevron* doctrine seems to validate a different view, that agencies are a coequal source of policy change, and Congress can constrain the agencies only by adopting limits—in "clear" language—on what agencies can do. Considered in this light, the *Chevron* doctrine may countenance one of the largest transfers of political power in our history, from Congress to the executive. One might think this would require a constitutional amendment, not a decision of the Supreme Court.

The *Chevron* doctrine, then, is understandably controversial. Like other controversial issues in our polarized age, it has given rise to some very polarized views. Two recent books, both vigorously argued, provide a sense of the debate that has broken out over the doctrine.

From the anti-*Chevron* side, we can take as an illustration a recent book by Peter Wallison entitled *Judicial Fortitude: The Last Chance to Rein in the Administrative State.*[15] Wallison depicts the American constitutional system as sliding toward administrative authoritarianism, as Congress passes the buck by enacting vague delegations of power to agencies, which are then allowed to interpret these delegations so as to expand their power even more. The result is a collapse in the Constitution's system of checks and balances, with emboldened agencies sapping the economic vitality of the country and threatening individual liberty. He despairs of directly convincing Congress to resume its rightful role as the nation's primary policymaker. The only solution he sees is to overrule the *Chevron* doctrine, and require courts to engage in independent interpretation of every statute enacted by Congress. This, he argues, would check the power of agencies and, by blocking the expansion of the administrative state, force Congress to resume its constitutional function of enacting legislation to deal with pressing social and economic problems. Given Congress's superior representation of the diverse interests of the people, and the limits on its capacity to legislate, this would free the economy from stifling overregulation and protect individuals from encroachments on their liberty by an imperious bureaucracy.

On the pro-*Chevron* side, consider Adrian Vermeule's book *Law's Abnegation.*[16] Vermeule starts not with a classical understanding of the Constitution, but with a characterization of modern American society as a whirlwind of technological, economic, and social change. The pace of change outstrips the capacity of our eighteenth-century government institutions, most notably the Congress and the courts, to keep up. Indeed, the rate of change is such that problems emerge requiring action by the government before it is possible to gather enough information to be confident about what the proper response should be. In these circumstances it is inevitable that Congress and the courts have "abnegated" their authority in favor of administrative agencies, which have the capacity and expertise to respond more quickly to emerging social problems. The process, according to Vermeule, should not be resisted but embraced. *Chevron* is not only arguably "the most famous doctrine in all of administrative law,"[17] it should be amplified. Courts should require only "thin rationality" on the part of agencies when they interpret their statutory mandate. The *Chevron* doctrine should apply to agency determinations of the scope of their own authority, as the Court held in its most extravagant extension of the *Chevron* doctrine in 2013.[18] And the *Chevron* doctrine should be extended even to certain constitutional questions, such as whether the requirements of procedural due process have been met.[19]

The conflicting views of Wallison and Vermeule can be said to mark the outer limits of the debate about the *Chevron* doctrine. Jeffrey Pojanowski, in a recent survey of the turmoil in administrative law, calls the former school of thought "administrative skeptics" and the latter "administrative supremacists."[20] Many other commentators and judges have staked out more qualified views, although they tend to lean in either a pro- or an anti-*Chevron* direction.[21]

The reader may be wondering at this point how the *Chevron* doctrine lines up with the deep political divide that currently afflicts our country. In addressing this question, at least in a preliminary way, it is necessary to distinguish between political theory and partisan agendas. The divide over the *Chevron* doctrine clearly lines up with different theories of government. Those who think agencies generally do a better job of setting public policy than Congress or the courts, like Vermeule, tend to be pro-*Chevron*. Those who venerate the original tripartite division of government reflected in the Constitution and dislike the rise of the administrative state, like Wallison, tend to be anti-*Chevron*. This book will have more to say about how the *Chevron* doctrine fits into different theories of government, although I will consider a broader menu of political values than either Wallison or Vermeule does.

In terms of partisan politics, attitudes about the *Chevron* doctrine seem to shift in a discernible way with the political party of the incumbent President.[22] In its early years, the *Chevron* doctrine was thought to favor the deregulation agenda of the Reagan and Bush I Administrations, and was generally opposed by Democrats. The most fervent champion of the *Chevron* doctrine during this period was Justice Antonin Scalia, universally regarded as a conservative. Starting with the Clinton Administration and accelerating in the later years of the Obama Administration, the equation began to shift. Opposition to the *Chevron* doctrine on the part of liberal commentators and judges began noticeably to soften. For example, Elena Kagan, before she was named to the Supreme Court by President Obama, wrote an influential defense of executive initiative in setting policy.[23] Conservative commentators and judges, for their part, became increasingly skeptical about the *Chevron* doctrine. Critical comments about the *Chevron* doctrine by Judges Neil Gorsuch and Brett Kavanaugh seem to have played a role in their nomination to the Supreme Court by President Trump.[24]

The partisan divide over the *Chevron* doctrine reached its peak in the first two years of the Trump Administration. The House of Representatives, then in control of the Republicans, twice passed a statute called the Separation of Powers Restoration Act, which was designed to override the *Chevron* doctrine. The vote both times was almost entirely along party lines, with all Republicans voting in favor and all but a handful of Democrats voting against.[25] The Senate, where the Republicans did not have enough votes to cut off debate, did not take up the measure. In explaining the need to repudiate the *Chevron* doctrine, the House Report said it was inconsistent with the judicial duty, said to be established in *Marbury v. Madison,* to "say what the law is."[26]

Perhaps because the *Chevron* doctrine had become anathema to conservatives, the Trump Justice Department seemed reluctant to ask the courts to apply the doctrine. The reticence of the Administration's lawyers, combined with the hostility of a core group of Justices, had a startling effect: the Supreme Court after 2016 effectively stopped applying the *Chevron* doctrine as a reason to uphold an agency interpretation.[27] The obvious evasion of the doctrine prompted Justice Alito to remark "that the Court, for whatever reasons, is simply ignoring *Chevron,*" which he characterized as "an important, frequently invoked, once celebrated, and now increasingly maligned precedent."[28]

The Court cannot indefinitely continue to dodge the fate of the *Chevron* doctrine. The confusion spawned by the Court's silence must be frustrating to the lower courts, not to mention the lawyers who appear before them and the agencies whose interpretations are challenged in court. A decision by the Court to overrule the *Chevron* doctrine seems unlikely. It would be hard to explain why a doctrine applied by the Court in over a hundred decisions was suddenly discovered to be demonstrably wrong.[29] If the overruling was perceived to be the product of changes in the Court's personnel, this could undermine the Court's legitimacy and make it much harder to elicit obedience to whatever the Court decided to put in its place. And any decision to reject the *Chevron* doctrine during the Biden Administration would undoubtedly be characterized as a partisan effort by Republican-appointed Justices to thwart agencies controlled by a Democratic Administration.

Much more likely is a decision (or series of decisions) adopting new limits on the doctrine, or clarifying it in important respects. The Court has previously imposed limits on the doctrine, most notably in the *Mead* decision in 2001.[30] More recently, the Court substantially rewrote the legal doctrine that applies in a related area, dealing with judicial review of agency interpretations of their regulations.[31] So it is not hard to imagine that the current Court, on which no Justice remains from the Court that decided *Chevron,* may undertake to rewrite the *Chevron* doctrine at some point in the future. The timing and content of any such revision are, as of this writing, unknown. One objective of the book is to suggest what form reasonable modifications of the doctrine might take (see Chapter 13).

Whatever the exact fate of the *Chevron* doctrine, the Court's de facto moratorium on applying the doctrine provides an appropriate occasion to step back and take stock of what can be learned from its thirty-five-year trajectory. The story of the rise and apparent fall of the doctrine is quite remarkable. The more important lessons concern what happened in between. The issues the Supreme Court was forced to confront as the implications of the doctrine were gradually revealed are likely to be presented by any regime that seeks to define the respective spheres of agencies and courts in "saying what the law is." The saga of the *Chevron* doctrine can therefore be regarded as an extended case study in the trade-offs that inevitably arise under any system of administrative government subject to the check of judicial review. The answers the Court developed in resolving these trade-offs—some good, some not so good—provide a cautionary tale for any effort to create a regime of judicial review of agency interpretations of law. In effect, the history of the *Chevron* doctrine reveals important tensions that are inherent in the modern liberal democratic order.

In terms of method, this book is closer in spirit to Vermeule than to Wallison, although I disagree with a number of Vermeule's conclusions. Thus, I agree with Vermeule that the ultimate question "is whether judicial review, at the margin, adds net value to the process of institutional decision-making that begins with agency decision-making."[32] The phenomenon we are considering is the proper division of authority between two decisional bodies that proceed in sequential fashion: first, an agency interprets the statute it administers, then a court reviews the agency interpretation. It makes little sense to have these institutions repeat exactly the same analysis. If they are engaged in the same task from the same perspective, then either the agency should decide the question without any significant judicial review (a position that Vermeule comes close to endorsing) or the question should be decided by the court without regard to the agency view (a position that Wallison endorses). A better approach, I argue, is to try to figure out where agencies have a comparative advantage and where courts have a comparative advantage, and to assign roles to each institution that reflect how each can make a positive "marginal" contribution to the process of saying what the law is.

I also agree with Vermeule that the only way to make an assessment of the comparative advantage of these institutions is by considering how they have performed over time. This not only includes the history reflected in the drafting and ratification of the Constitution, which Wallison emphasizes. It also includes the way the institutions created by the Constitution—and those created by Congress under the authority given to it by the Constitution—have evolved over time. Vermeule associates this approach with Ronald Dworkin's theory of legal integrity, which looks for propositions that satisfy the twin requirements of "fit," in the sense that they account for major institutional practices that have emerged and survived over time, and "justification," meaning that it is possible to identify a general principle that supports these institutional practices.[33] In this book I follow the same general method in considering how the *Chevron* doctrine stands up against important values that should ground the practice of judicial review. Those values have emerged over time and continue to be regarded as central to our system of government. The *Chevron* doctrine has served some of these values well and others poorly. The historical arc of the doctrine has undoubtedly modified our understanding of some of these values. But it has also clarified which ones we should not want to give up.

1

Judicial Review of Agency Interpretation—Four Values

THIS BOOK IS PRIMARILY a work of history about the *Chevron* doctrine—where it came from, how it spread, the fate of attempts to cabin it, and recent arguments that it should be overruled or significantly rewritten. Before plunging into that history, this chapter seeks to describe, in broad outline, four values that are generally relevant in determining what a regime of judicial review of agency interpretations of law should seek to accomplish. These values are grounded in rough generalizations about how courts and agencies compare in terms of their strengths and weaknesses as institutions. The values have been drawn from experience—both before and after the *Chevron* decision itself. In succeeding chapters, as we delve more deeply into the career of the *Chevron* doctrine, we can refine these generalizations. But to anchor the discussion—to provide a baseline for evaluating discrete decisions and events—it will be helpful to start with a brief discussion of the principal values that should be relevant in judging the success or failure of different conceptions of judicial review.

The four values can be briefly described as follows. First, we would like the regime of judicial review to promote rule of law values—the ability of individuals to rely on settled expectations about the law that governs their conduct. Second, we would want the regime to sustain constitutional values, understood broadly to include not just individual constitutional rights but also provisions that structure the relations among the branches of the federal government (separation of powers values) and define the respective authority of the federal government and the states (federalism values). Third, we would want the regime to channel interpretations that entail discretionary policy choices toward the relatively more politically accountable institutions—Congress and, in this context, administrative agencies—rather than having such choices made by courts. Fourth and finally, we would want the regime to create incentives for agencies, over the large run of cases, to make better interpretive choices.

Calibrating Court–Agency Relations

Before turning to the four values, a brief discussion is warranted about the vocabulary courts and commentators use to describe how reviewing courts treat agency interpretations of the statute they administer. The conventional distinction is between a court deciding the question as a matter of "independent judgment" and a court giving "deference" to the agency interpretation. Both terms, however, are used rather loosely to describe multiple postures courts have taken toward agency interpretations. Indeed, some of these postures have been described at times as being a form of "independent judgment" and at other times as a form of "deference"—revealing that these terms are highly ambiguous.

To avoid the ambiguities associated with the two commonly employed terms, the exposition in this chapter will speak of four different characterizations of how a reviewing court might regard an agency interpretation of law. At one end of the scale, the reviewing court might interpret the law "de novo," meaning without attaching any significance to the agency interpretation one way or another. Moving up the scale a bit, the court might give "respectful consideration" to the agency interpretation, meaning the court would attend to the reasons given by the agency for adopting its interpretation, and provide an explanation for either accepting or rejecting the agency view. Going further, a court might give "weight" to an agency interpretation (or subtract "weight" as the case may be), if certain conditions are met that indicate the agency interpretation implicates important values courts generally seek to uphold. Finally, the court might "accept" an agency interpretation, if the court concludes that the agency is clearly the preferred interpreter with respect to a particular question of law.

Each of the last three characterizations—respectful consideration, weight, and acceptance—have at various times been described as forms of "deference." Each of the first three characterizations—de novo review, respectful consideration, and weight—have at various times been regarded as forms of "independent judgment." Given the overlap, one can easily see the need for a more precise vocabulary. When we turn to the history, starting with Chapter 2, it will be necessary to revert to some extent to the conventional (ambiguous) terms, given that these are the terms courts use. Where possible, however, I will attempt to speak of de novo review, respectful consideration, weight, and acceptance, rather than "independent judgment" and "deference."

Rule of Law Values

Because we are considering the interpretation of law, it makes sense that the regime of judicial review should promote what has long been regarded as a central virtue of having human conduct governed by law. The concept of the "rule of law" has multiple meanings.[1] As used in this book, it refers to the good that comes from having a high level of stable expectations about what the law requires. Stability of expectations about the law is good because it makes life more predictable. And predictability is good because it promotes security, makes planning for the future possible, encourages investment, and gives individuals the freedom to pursue their aspirations within the limits established by these stable expectations. Other aspects frequently associated with the rule of law—such as the importance of applying the law equally to all similarly situated persons, the importance of having the official rules of law be the same as the rules actually applied, and the importance of avoiding retroactive changes in the law—can be seen as more particular implications of enforcing settled expectations about the law.[2]

One extremely important set of settled legal expectations is the understanding that American law is defined by a hierarchy of legal authority. At the top sits the Constitution, below that are the many statutes that have been enacted by Congress, and below that are the even more numerous regulations and orders issued by administrative agencies and executive orders issued by the President, not to mention state and local laws and regulations. The Constitution trumps statutes, and statutes trump agency regulations and orders and executive orders of the President (and conflicting state statutes and regulations). These understandings are not set forth in any foundational document. The Constitution's Supremacy Clause speaks of both the Constitution and federal statutes as being the "supreme law of the land" without differentiating between them, and makes no mention of agency regulations and orders or executive orders of the President.[3] The hierarchy of authority is grounded in settled expectations about how our legal order is organized. Fortunately for our purposes, this understanding seems securely settled. Even Adrian Vermeule (whom we encountered briefly in the Introduction and who believes that agencies are generally better at interpreting law than courts are) concedes that "a serious constitutional question would arise if Congress . . . said that agencies, rather than courts, will decide if there is an ambiguity in the law."[4]

It is important to note that rule of law values—stability of expectations about the law—are not the only values we would want society to promote. It is possible to imagine a society that scrupulously observes the rule of law in this sense and yet is fundamentally unjust. The South African regime of apartheid was sometimes characterized this way.[5] Less dramatically, it is even easier to imagine a society that scrupulously observes the rule of law and yet is highly inefficient, or generates large inequalities in wealth, or produces uncontrolled pollution, or suffers from one or more other undesirable features.

That rule of law values can coexist with injustice and other suboptimal conditions means that stability of expectations about the law should give way on occasion to legal change. The question for now is whether judicial review can help strike a proper balance between stability of expectations and accommodating desired change in the law.

Here, a notable difference in the characteristics of agencies and courts becomes relevant. Courts by their very nature are designed to reinforce stability of legal expectations. The primary function of courts is to resolve disputes. The very legitimacy of courts in performing this function is the perception of the parties that the norms courts invoke in resolving these disputes are grounded in existing law.[6] Moreover, courts by institutional design are independent of direct political control. Federal judges enjoy secure compensation and can be removed from office only by impeachment. This high degree of independence is designed to encourage judges to resolve disputes according to settled law rather than according to the preferences of the current President or members of Congress—or of the political party that appointed them.[7]

When it comes to statutory interpretation, which is the staple of administrative law, federal courts nearly always seek to determine the best or the settled meaning of the relevant statute. Which is to say, what other participants in the legal system, as advised by their lawyers, most likely understand to be the law. We can set aside for present purposes whether this means enforcing the ordinary meaning of the text, or interpreting the text in accordance with the legislative intent or purpose. Most judges and lawyers apply a kind of situation sense in shifting from text to purpose or vice versa depending on contextual factors.[8] The common denominator is that courts—as a rule— understand that it is the legislature's job to make policy and the court's job to serve as a faithful agent carrying out the instructions of the legislature. Most judges—certainly the better ones—understand that they have no authority to manipulate the meaning of a statute to achieve some policy objective they regard as desirable.

Courts also rate high on the scale of adhering to settled expectations when it comes to questions determined by extrapolation from precedent. In any area of the law that is largely governed by precedent, the authority of the courts to compel obedience from the parties is the sense that they adhere to decisions that have been authoritatively rendered in the past. Courts will occasionally overrule precedents, and more commonly will narrow them or expand on them. But they almost never disregard a controlling precedent that has been called to their attention.[9] Occasionally the Supreme Court will declare a momentous change in precedent, such as outlawing segregation in public schools or finding a right to same-sex marriage. But usually these decisions, which receive a disproportionate amount of attention, are rendered in the name of a better understanding of the Constitution, and have been anticipated by other evolutions in the law.

Agencies present a much less reassuring picture when it comes to enforcing settled expectations about the law. Some agencies, like the National Labor Relations Board (NLRB), use the dispute resolution function (adjudication) to make policy, which often results in shifts from one administration to another, oscillating between pro-labor and pro-management perspectives.[10] Other agencies that use rulemaking to make policy, such as the Environmental Protection Agency (EPA), can make dramatic turns in direction when one presidential administration is replaced by another. The alternating position of EPA with respect to climate change policy from the Bush II, to the Obama, to the Trump, to the Biden Administration is the most recent example.[11]

As a generalization, one can say that if protecting settled expectations were the only value to be served by judicial review, one should entrust a large measure of interpretive authority to courts rather than agencies. As previously stated, this is not the only relevant value. Nevertheless, the regime of judicial review should draw upon courts to help protect stability of expectations about the law.

One way this can come into play is when consistent agency interpretation has given rise to settled expectations. In these circumstances, rule of law values suggest that the court should give added weight to the agency's view, even if the agency's interpretation diverges from what the court considers to be the best reading of the statute. Another way it can come into play is when agencies change course in a way that is likely to upset expectations that have been created by prior agency action. When this happens, reviewing courts should demand a persuasive explanation from the agency as to why the frustration of expectations is justified in terms of competing policy objectives.[12]

There is another institutional distinction between courts and agencies that is relevant to protecting settled expectations. A central theme of the literature on the rule of law is that changes in the law should ordinarily apply only to future conduct. Making legal change prospective allows those affected by the change to adjust their expectations, and make relevant modifications in their behavior to avoid coming into conflict with the law.[13] Changes in the law that apply to behavior taken in the past are regarded as a paradigmatic example of action contrary to the rule of law, and are commonly regarded as unjust.[14]

The strong preference for making changes in law prospective is relevant to the comparison of courts and agencies in the following sense. Courts nearly always engage in dispute resolution by applying the law to behavior that has already taken place. This means judicial decisions are by their nature retroactive. Indeed, the Supreme Court has ruled that federal courts may not resolve a dispute by offering an interpretation of the law that applies only prospectively.[15] Agencies, in contrast, have a wider array of tools they can use to constrain the behavior of those they regulate. To be sure, most agencies have the power to engage in adjudication, as when they bring enforcement actions or determine eligibility for public benefits. These agency adjudications are analogous to court proceedings in that they typically apply to behavior that has already taken place. In addition, however, most agencies have the power to issue regulations, which always apply prospectively unless Congress has conveyed special authority to the agency to make retroactive rules (which is rare).[16] Agencies can also issue nonbinding statements of policy or interpretations that provide guidance to the public about how they intend to regulate in the future.[17] So agencies, unlike courts, have the power to make changes in the law prospective, which is the way changes should be made if we are concerned about protecting settled expectations.

Putting this together, we have the following implications for how judicial review of agency action should give effect to rule of law values. Courts are in the business of enforcing settled expectations, and are likely to act more consistently to protect settled expectations than agencies. So rule of law values suggest that courts should play close attention to whether agencies are acting in ways that reinforce or upset settled expectations. On the other side of the coin, rule of law values suggest that agencies are the preferred institution for implementing changes in the law relative to courts, given that they have the capacity to make such changes prospective and courts do not. Thus, reviewing courts should look favorably on agencies that make changes by rulemaking or otherwise provide prospective guidance to regulated parties, and more skeptically on agencies that use adjudication to make changes when this may upset reliance interests.[18]

Constitutional Values

As administrative governance grows, it inevitably comes into conflict with values that have been identified as having a constitutional status. Constitutional values can be seen as a species of rule of law values. But they are worth considering separately, given that the ultimate division of authority between courts and agencies in this context is settled. When it comes to interpretation of the Constitution, no court is going to accept what an agency says. The most an agency can expect is respectful consideration and perhaps weight, depending on whether the agency interpretation accords with settled expectations.

This division of authority has not always been clear. *Marbury v. Madison* established that the federal courts would interpret the Constitution de novo, in the sense that they are not obliged to accept the interpretation of the Constitution by Congress. But the Constitution says nothing about whether the federal courts' interpretations of its provisions are binding on nonjudicial actors. After all, the President and the members of Congress, not to mention the principal officers of administrative agencies, are all sworn to uphold the Constitution. From this, an argument can be made that the Constitution contemplates that not just the courts, but all government officers, have equal authority to interpret the Constitution according to their own lights. Indeed, it was not until 1958, when faced with an act of defiance to a district court desegregation decree, that the Supreme Court declared that its interpretations of the Constitution, no less than the document itself, are the "supreme law of the land."[19] Controversy has occasionally bubbled up over whether this is correct. But by convention, it is now generally accepted that the courts, most notably the Supreme Court, have final authority to determine the meaning of the Constitution, and that other governmental actors are duty-bound to accept the decisions of the courts issued in the name of the Constitution.[20] This was made abundantly clear in the wake of the Supreme Court's decision holding that the Constitution requires that same-sex couples have the same right to marry as do mixed-sex couples.[21] Although deeply controversial as a matter of constitutional interpretation (the decision would have dumbfounded the framers of the Fourteenth Amendment), the few state court judges and officials who defied this ruling were either removed from office or suffered disciplinary action.[22]

This does not mean that integrating constitutional values and other policy objectives is always an easy matter. Relatively few constitutional provisions establish fixed rules. Most individual rights, for example, are understood to be general principles that give way if the government can show a "compelling interest" to the contrary.[23] And with respect to structural provisions, the Constitution contains some remarkable gaps.[24] Arguably, courts should share more responsibility for constitutional interpretation with agencies, particularly when the case involves applying the Constitution to different factual circumstances. But it is unlikely that courts will give up their de facto monopoly on constitutional interpretation any time soon.

In considering the role of constitutional values, we can divide the universe into three categories: individual constitutional rights (like freedom of speech), separation of powers provisions (the division of authority among the branches of the federal government), and federalism provisions (the division between federal and state authority). Individual constitutional rights and federalism provisions arise episodically in considering judicial review of agency interpretations of law. When such issues arise, they raise difficult questions about how to integrate agency interpretations of statutes with constitutional values. For example, when an agency action is challenged as violating both the statute under which the agency operates and the Constitution, should the reviewing court consider the statutory challenge first, and the constitutional one second, or the other way around? Another issue involves the role of agencies in determining questions of fact, including general or "legislative" facts, insofar as they bear on constitutional determinations. Should agencies be given a greater role in constitutional fact-finding than in making ultimate judgments of constitutionality? Or should courts take it upon themselves to ascertain the facts that bear on issues of constitutionality?[25]

These are important questions. Nevertheless, much of the recent attention to these issues in the individual rights and federalism contexts has arisen in cases applying the *Chevron* doctrine. It is therefore best to postpone consideration of them until Chapters 8 and 9, after the emergence of that doctrine has been covered.

When we consider separation of powers issues—structural principles derived from the Constitution's division of the federal government into three distinct branches legislative, executive, and judicial—constitutional values have loomed large throughout the history of court–agency relations. In recent separate opinions by Justices Clarence Thomas and Neil Gorsuch, and in conservative commentary, the critical separation of powers question is said to be whether Article III of the Constitution, which establishes the federal judiciary, permits courts to "defer" to legal interpretations reached by agencies.[26] The argument is that the "judicial power" vested in the courts by Article III includes the power "to say what the law is," as *Marbury* put it, and that this power cannot be shared. I put this claim to the side for the moment; in a sense the entire book is devoted to answering it.

Another separation of powers question that looms large concerns how we understand the constitutional role of Congress in our system of government.

Article I of the Constitution says that "all legislative powers herein granted" are given to Congress, and it enumerates in some detail the subjects to which these powers extend. This is augmented by the Necessary and Proper Clause, which gives Congress the power to adopt legislation "carrying into execution" not only its enumerated legislative powers but "all other powers vested by this Constitution in the Government of the United States, or in any Department or Officer thereof." Article I also provides significant detail about how Congress is organized into two houses, the terms of the legislators who hold office in the respective houses, and how they are selected. And it spells out the role of the President in the legislative process, by proposing legislation and exercising the veto, which can be overridden by a two-thirds vote of both houses.[27]

In contrast, Article II, which establishes the offices of the President and the Vice President, creates rather minimal and poorly defined powers. These include vesting the President with "the executive power" (not otherwise defined), the power to appoint the principal officers of the United States (subject to Senate confirmation), and to take care that the laws are "faithfully executed" (which is expressed as a duty rather than a power). The President is given no power, under the Constitution, to create a department or agency, or to confer power on it. The President is explicitly made the "commander in chief" of the armed forces, is instructed to "receive ambassadors," and has the power to "make treaties" (with the concurrence of two-thirds of the Senate), which powers are thought to give the President a degree of autonomous authority in matters of military and foreign affairs.[28] Recent Presidents—Bush II, Obama, Trump, and Biden—have moved aggressively to expand presidential powers and have achieved considerable success at the expense of a divided Congress. But outside the context of foreign and military affairs (and arguably immigration), the conventional understanding is that the President, no less than the many administrative agencies, can exercise only those powers that have been delegated to the executive by Congress pursuant to the Necessary and Proper Clause.

Collectively, the Constitution's expansive provisions dealing with the powers of Congress, especially in contrast to the minimal powers of the President, have always been understood to establish the principle of *legislative supremacy*. What this means is that duly enacted legislation is a higher form of legal authority than any executive order issued by the President or any regulation or order issued by an administrative agency. As previously noted, this is a settled understanding about the American legal system. All agree that if there is a direct and unambiguous conflict between what a statute says and what the President does by executive order or what an agency does by regulation or order, the statute prevails. There is nevertheless a latent ambiguity about the meaning of legislative supremacy. We can distinguish three possible ways of unpacking what it means to say that Congress's legislative power is supreme relative to executive orders or regulations and orders issued by administrative agencies.[29]

One possibility is that legislative supremacy means the Constitution gives Congress the *exclusive power* to set policy in a legally binding fashion. This is the understanding associated with the so-called nondelegation doctrine. The Constitution gives "all legislative powers" to Congress, and therefore, the argument runs, sharing of such power is impermissible. Agencies may be charged with enforcing or implementing the law as established by Congress, but cannot be given the power to make legally binding policy.

A second possibility is that the Constitution gives Congress the exclusive power, if it does not set policy itself, to delegate authority to another institution like the President, the courts, or an agency to set policy in a legally binding fashion. We can call this the *anti-inherency* understanding. Given the allocation of all legislative power to Congress, administrative agencies (and for that matter the President and the courts) have no inherent authority to "make law" that binds the public. They must derive their authority to set policy in a legally binding fashion from some form of enacted law, either a specific provision of the Constitution or, more usually, a statute duly enacted by Congress. Congress, one can say, has exclusive authority to decide who decides.[30]

The third possibility is that the Constitution gives Congress the *last word* in determining legally binding policy. Under this understanding, Congress always has the power to override legally binding policy established by the President or an agency. But if Congress is silent, executive and judicial entities have authority to make legally binding policy in areas where the federal government as a whole is competent to act. In other words, the President and the administrative agencies have inherent authority to act in default of Congress, but must conform to any limitations adopted by Congress that limit this discretion.[31]

Which of these three characterizations of legislative supremacy is correct? The first or exclusive power interpretation has been, for most of our history, what we can call the official understanding. Many Supreme Court opinions, some fairly recent, state flatly that the "legislative power" given to Congress in Article I of the Constitution cannot be delegated.[32] At the same time, the Court has almost never (at least not since 1935) invalidated a statute on the ground that it delegates power to establish legally binding policy to some other entity of government.[33] The established formula is that delegation is permissible as long as the statute lays down an "intelligible principle" for the agency to follow. Under this formula, delegations to agencies to establish "just and reasonable" rates, "fair and equitable" prices, air quality standards that are "requisite" to protect health, and "feasible" work safety standards have all been upheld as constitutionally permissible.[34]

Recently four Justices in separate opinions expressed sympathy with the claim that the "intelligible principle" formula is too lax.[35] So it is conceivable that some tightening in the standards for sustaining delegations of authority to agencies will take place in the future. But what is not conceivable is that the Court will invalidate all delegations of authority to agencies to make "legislative rules" with legally binding effect. These have been upheld since 1911 and are a mainstay of the administrative state.[36] Settled expectations here trump original understandings. The exclusive power interpretation of legislative supremacy has been decisively rejected in practice.

The anti-inherency interpretation has a much stronger claim to being the correct understanding of legislative supremacy. There are, to be sure, relatively few explicit statements of this understanding from the Supreme Court in cases involving a direct clash between Congress and the President. The most famous is Justice Black's opinion for the Court in the *Steel Seizure Case,* which invalidated President Truman's effort to nationalize steel mills threatened by a labor shut down in the midst of the Korean War.[37] Black said flatly that "[t]he President's power, if any, to issue the order must stem from an act of Congress or from the Constitution itself."[38] But the precedential value of this statement was compromised by various concurring opinions, which left the door open to recognizing some inherent but limited presidential power to act in emergencies.[39] Where administrative agencies are concerned and the question involves domestic policy, there are many more statements from the Supreme Court adopting the anti-inherency position.[40]

More impressive than occasional statements by the courts, however, is the consistent practice of both the executive branch and the judiciary over time. Presidents have consistently acknowledged that they have no authority to create new departments or agencies without the authorization of Congress. Agencies have uniformly recognized the need to ground their authority to act in some statutory authority conferred on them by Congress. And courts have repeatedly exercised the power of judicial review to invalidate agency action perceived as going beyond what Congress has authorized, or as transgressing some limitation imposed by statute.[41] If we judge by settled expectations based on actual practice, the anti-inherency position has evolved to become the dominant understanding of the meaning of legislative supremacy.[42]

That said, it must be acknowledged that the third interpretation, limiting Congress to having the last word about setting binding public policy, is arguably emerging as a potential rival. This is not due to any official endorsement by the courts. Instead, it follows from a prolonged period of congressional dysfunction coupled with (and facilitating) aggressive presidential assertions of power. Recent Presidents have claimed authority to create what amount to new agencies by using memorandums of understanding to establish "inter-agency task forces."[43] They have sought to reform immigration statutes and criminal laws by adopting "enforcement guidelines."[44] They have scoured obscure statutes for arguable authority to regulate in novel ways or to spend money on projects not authorized by Congress.[45] Congress's acquiescence in these practices, and the mixed response of the courts, creates momentum for further experiments in executive authority lacking any obvious genesis in legislation. So practice, and hence expectations, is arguably inching toward the third interpretation.

In this book I assume that the anti-inherency conception of legislative supremacy continues to describe the best understanding of our evolved system of separation of powers. I will accordingly evaluate various conceptions of the proper relationship between courts and agencies in resolving questions of law in light of that assumption. The reader is cautioned, however, that the tectonic plates of collective understanding may be shifting in the direction of the last-word understanding, as power continues to shift to the executive branch and drain away from Congress. Should that movement persist, a very different conception of court–agency relations is likely to emerge.

The anti-inherency interpretation of legislative supremacy has important implications for judicial review of agency interpretations of law. Under this view, administrative agencies have no authority to act unless and until they have been delegated such authority by Congress, and their authority to act is limited to whatever powers Congress has in fact granted.[46] Courts, as guardians of the Constitution, should therefore enforce the limitations Congress has placed on the authority of agencies in order to preserve the principle that Congress has the exclusive prerogative to establish agencies and delineate their powers and limits.

Given that courts have final authority to interpret and enforce the Constitution, one might think that the appropriate standard of review in policing these boundaries is de novo review. There are two important considerations that suggest this conclusion needs to be qualified.

First, the administrative state has grown to such enormous dimensions that Congress cannot engage in continual monitoring and adjustment of the scope of agency authority. A certain amount of "policy drift" on the part of agencies is inevitable. For example, when cable television emerged as an alternative to broadcast television, the FCC decided it needed to exercise authority over the new industry. When Congress failed to act in response to repeated requests by the agency to expand its authority, the agency interpreted its existing authority to permit a partial regulation of cable TV. This move was eventually upheld (rightly or wrongly) by the Supreme Court.[47] Here again, settled expectations are relevant. The scope of an agency's authority at any given time is not just a matter of the original meaning of the statutory text but depends also on the evolving practice of the agency and the way that practice has been regarded by Congress and the courts over time. The best source for understanding how the scope of an agency's authority has evolved over time is the agency itself. So reviewing courts should probably give respectful consideration to the agency's view of its own authority, and should probably add or subtract weight to that view depending on whether the agency can show that its conception corresponds to settled expectations.

Second, there will inevitably be disagreement about the extent to which an agency's organic statute grants or limits its authority. A court exercising de novo review might be mistaken about the proper understanding of provisions that seem to limit agency authority. This is another reason to give respectful consideration (and, as appropriate, weight) to the agency's understanding of its authority. Adopting an intermediate standard of review in considering the scope of the agency's authority serves to minimize the risk of error on the part of the reviewing court in determining the limits of an agency's delegated power.

In the chapters that follow, much will be said about the function of courts in enforcing the boundaries of agency authority, including those based on individual constitutional rights and federalism, as well as the separation of powers. Although boundary maintenance has been described here as being rooted in constitutional values, this does not mean that every agency action that exceeds the scope of its delegated authority should be held to be unconstitutional. It is almost never necessary to reach such a judgment.[48] What is necessary—and is required by the anti-inherency understanding of legislative supremacy—is that courts engage in careful review to determine that agencies (and as appropriate the President) have stayed within the boundaries of their authority as established by Congress. The *practice* of careful review by courts in this context is required by the Constitution, even if every exercise of authority by an agency that is *ultra vires* need not be characterized as unconstitutional.[49] It is not necessary to do so, since under our administrative law practice every exercise of authority that is *ultra vires* is for that reason unlawful.

Accountability Values

So far the analysis has pointed toward the importance of courts exercising a large element of autonomous judgment in reviewing agency interpretations of law. When we consider a third set of values—the importance of having discretionary policy decisions made by politically accountable institutions—the balance turns decisively in favor of agencies.

The analysis here appropriately begins by positing that the interpretation in question is one that (a) does not implicate the importance of settled expectations and (b) falls within the boundaries of agency authority derived from considering constitutional values, including the principle of legislative supremacy. In other words, the case presents an unresolved issue that falls within the discretionary authority of the agency. The question then becomes: As between the agency and the reviewing court, which institution has a comparative advantage in resolving such an issue?

When we exclude rule of law and constitutional values, the answer seems clear: matters of discretionary interpretive choice should be resolved by the agency. Such questions commonly present trade-offs between competing values. Do we want safer drugs or faster access to medical innovations? Do we want less pollution or more economic growth? Do we want fewer accidents or more affordable products? Resolving these trade-offs entails decisions that are essentially political. Many would argue that such decisions should be made by the people's elected representatives. This is seemingly what the Constitution contemplates—the document says that all legislative powers are given to Congress. And indeed, this is often how they are resolved: Congress not infrequently enacts statutes that adopt highly precise answers to questions of public policy.

But the Congress and the President (who participates in the legislative process in proposing legislation and exercising the veto) are severely constrained in their capacity to resolve even a fraction of the contested policy issues that arise. This is especially true in today's world, with its rapid rate of technological, economic, and social change.[50] Out of necessity, the Congress and the President, acting through the legislative process, have created administrative agencies to address many of these issues.

So if we want matters of discretionary interpretive choice to be resolved in a way that is responsive to the collective wishes of the people, we are faced with a kind of second-best choice in most circumstances: Should such issues be decided by agencies or courts? Neither institution is directly accountable to the people. Unlike the members of Congress and the President, the heads of agencies and federal judges do not stand for periodic election. Both the heads of agencies and judges are nominated by the President and subject to confirmation by the Senate, which gives each a measure of indirect accountability. But whereas agency heads turn over fairly frequently, usually at a minimum at the end of each four-year presidential term, judges can potentially serve for life.[51] So agency heads are more likely to have received the assent of the current elected representatives of the people as compared to judges, many of whom ascended to the bench decades ago.

As political scientists have elaborated, agencies are also subject to a number of constraints that make them more accountable to elected politicians relative to judges.[52] Most agencies are dependent on Congress for their appropriations, which means the heads of agencies must attend closely to the wishes of appropriations committees. High-level agency personnel also appear periodically before congressional oversight committees, which can expose embarrassing missteps and extract commitments about future action.[53] Under current practice, agency budget requests are also screened by the Office of Management and Budget (OMB), a White House agency, which means the heads of agencies must attend to the wishes of the President.[54] And political appointees of agencies are subject to removal from office by the President, either at will or indirectly through various forms of pressure. Lastly, again as a matter of current practice, agency rules that exceed a certain minimum (e.g., $100 million in annual costs of compliance) are subject to review by another office of OMB, which again gives the White House a measure of control over agency policy choices.[55]

There is nothing comparable in terms of oversight of federal judges. To be sure, federal judges are dependent on Congress for appropriations for their operating expenses. And judges have no inherent authority to enforce their judgments. By statute, the Office of the U.S. Marshall is required to execute all federal judgments, but the statute could be amended if Congress became very unhappy with the performance of the judiciary in certain areas.[56] Congress by law could also strip the courts of jurisdiction to hear particular classes of cases (at least nonconstitutional ones).[57] And as the recent controversy over the predominance of conservative Justices on the Supreme Court reminds us, Congress could "pack" the courts by authorizing more judges appointed by a President of a different political party. Each of these forms of potential constraint on the behavior of judges has remained mostly latent rather than actively exercised. No doubt these constraints help keep federal courts from deviating too sharply from settled expectations about the law. But they do not begin to create the kind of active and ongoing oversight that constrains the action of administrative agencies.[58]

In short, if we want interpretations that involve discretionary interpretive choice to be made by the relatively more accountable decision maker, and the relevant choice is between an agency and a court, the agency wins hands down.[59] Of course, Congress is an even more accountable decision maker than is an agency. So if Congress has made the choice, it must be respected and enforced by the reviewing court. But this is already required by our previous consideration of constitutional values—the boundaries established by Congress must be enforced by courts pursuant to the dominant understanding of legislative supremacy. Adding accountability values to the mix only reinforces this conclusion.

By focusing on accountability we do not disregard a second reason to prefer agencies over courts in resolving discretionary issues of interpretation: the greater expertise of agencies in matters of public policy. A desire to turn policy decisions over to experts has been a theme in the literature on administrative agencies since the progressive movement in the early twentieth century. The progressives and their intellectual heirs wanted to get public policy out of the hands of elected politicians, who were seen as hacks beholden to political machines, and into the hands of persons who were better educated and could be counted on to pursue the public interest in a "disinterested" fashion.[60] This meant transferring authority to administrative agencies, and adopting measures to ensure that their decisions were insulated from influence by elected politicians. Expertise was implicitly regarded as scientific, neutral, and apolitical, and hence as something that had to be shielded from crude political actors. In other words, expertise was seen as incompatible with accountability.

The idea that public policy can be made in a manner that is insulated from ordinary day-to-day politics is naïve in the extreme. Matters of discretionary policy choice inevitably implicate conflicting interests and values, and hence cannot be insulated from politics. The inevitability of politics is reflected, for example, in the efforts of recent Presidents to insert increasingly larger numbers of short-term political appointees in the upper reaches of agency hierarchies.[61] It is also reflected in innovations adopted by Congress, such as requiring the appointment of inspectors general within agencies who must report to Congress, and in the Congressional Review Act, which permits Congress to overturn agency regulations through a fast-track legislative process.[62]

Recognizing that agencies are inevitably political does not mean, however, that agency expertise will be ignored. Public opinion will demand that certain decisions be made by those with the requisite skill and experience to make them correctly—or at least to be more likely to make them correctly than political appointees or courts. Consider in this regard decisions about how to respond to a pandemic, or to determine whether nuclear reactors have been safely designed and operated, or to fix the money supply to provide the proper balance between inflation and employment. The public does not want these sorts of decisions made by White House operatives or by judges with law degrees. And because the public wants expertise, politicians will want these sorts of decisions made by agencies with the requisite degree of expertise. So in structuring judicial review to ensure that discretionary interpretive choices are made by the more politically accountable agencies, the courts will indirectly ensure that decisions which the public thinks should be made by experts *are* made with significant input by experts.

The bottom line is clear: If the agency is not undermining settled expectations and is acting within the scope of its delegated authority, then the decision is one the agency should make, not the court. Thus, whereas courts should give only respectful consideration to agencies with regard to the boundaries of agency authority, as long as the agency acts within the scope of its authority as defined by those boundaries, courts should *accept* the agency's interpretation of the law. This, as we shall see, is the key contribution that the Supreme Court's *Chevron* decision has made to our understanding of the values implicated by judicial review of agency interpretations—and it is one worth preserving.

It has been argued that questions falling within the agency's authority should be characterized not as a matter of legal interpretation, but as something else, like a "policy" determination or a "specification" of the statute under which the agency operates.[63] A better metaphor, as Peter Strauss has argued, is "space."[64] Courts must determine the limits of agency authority, and in so doing determine the space in which the agency has discretion to act. Within that space, the agency can proceed either by "interpretation" of terms of its statutory mandate or by declaring what "policy" it proposes to follow in implementing that mandate, whichever seems more appropriate in context. The focus here is on the division of authority in matters of interpretation, so the discussion will proceed on the assumption that the agency has chosen to characterize its action as an interpretation of the statute it administers.

Better Agency Decisions

A final value to be considered is whether judicial review can be structured in such a way as to improve the quality of agency statutory interpretations. Once again, we are talking about matters of discretionary interpretive choice. As we have seen in the previous section, if the agency is not frustrating settled expectations, and is acting within the boundaries of its statutory authority, the court should generally accept the agency's interpretation of the statute it administers. But perhaps judicial review can be formulated in such a way as to increase the odds that agencies will make good statutory interpretation decisions.

For much of the relevant span of history we will consider, the construct that courts have used to differentiate between "good" and "not so good" agency interpretations has been to ask whether the agency interpretation is "reasonable." Very little, if any, progress has been made in refining what this means. A better way to formulate inquiry is to focus on the process the agency has followed in reaching its interpretation.[65] Two variables are especially important here, both of which are mainstays of contemporary administrative law. One is whether the agency has followed a process that provides a meaningful opportunity for public participation before the interpretation is adopted. The other is whether the agency has offered an explanation for why it chose the interpretation it adopted.

Public participation is important because it allows a variety of objections and alternative interpretations to be raised before the agency settles on its interpretation. If the agency takes these objections to heart, it may modify or even drop its proposed interpretation, and adopt a better one. Public participation also enhances the legitimacy of the agency interpretation, whether or not it is modified in light of objections that are raised.

The requirement of an explanation complements and reinforces the desirability of public participation. The agency should offer reasons for either accepting or rejecting objections to its proposed interpretation, and for adopting the interpretation it selects rather than alternative interpretations.

The reason-giving requirement has been recognized as an aspect of the "arbitrary and capricious" standard of review of the Administrative Procedure Act (APA).[66] It applies to all modes of administrative action, including adjudication, general statements of policy, and interpretive rules.[67] So at least in theory, an explanation is always required whenever an agency adopts a particular interpretation of the statute it administers, without regard to the procedural format in which the interpretation is announced.

The public participation norm will be satisfied when an agency promulgates its interpretation using the notice-and-comment procedures that the APA requires for the issuance of most substantive regulations. But it is highly unlikely that the courts can *compel* agencies to use notice-and-comment when implementing agency policy. This looks too much like mandating that the agency adopt particular procedures, which the Court has said courts have no authority to do.[68]

Even though courts cannot *order* agencies to allow public participation before they adopt an interpretation, there is a way courts can provide an *incentive* for agencies to comply with the public participation norm when they engage in statutory interpretation. The way to do this is to condition the strongest form of deference to agency interpretations—acceptance—on the agency's having promulgated the interpretation after allowing public participation. In effect, the courts would say to agencies: Use public participation (and provide a reasoned explanation) and we will accept your interpretation (provided it is consistent with rule of law and constitutional values); adopt an interpretation in some other format that does not allow public participation, or without offering a reasoned explanation, and we will give your interpretation only respectful consideration and weight as appropriate.[69] Admittedly, it is unlikely that the Supreme Court would adopt such a conditional rule and would stick to it with unfailing consistency. The decisional law on judicial review varies too much from one opinion to another. But it is not inconceivable that the Court could begin to cite the use of public participation as a factor justifying an "extra measure of deference" to an agency interpretation, or words to that effect, and the agencies would get the message.

A secondary benefit of conditioning acceptance of the agency interpretation on public participation returns to the earlier point about the desirability of making changes in the law prospective in order to conform to rule of law values. If acceptance of agency interpretations turns on compliance with public participation, the natural way to comply would be to advance the interpretation in a format such as notice-and-comment rulemaking. Because notice-and-comment rulemaking is nearly always prospective, the interpretation would be prospective as well.

In Sum

We can put the foregoing pieces together to form a composite picture of what a regime of judicial review of agency interpretations of statutes might look like if attention were given to each of the four values considered in this chapter.

The most basic proposition is established by the discussion of constitutional values. The conclusion here is that courts must determine whether the boundaries that limit the authority of an agency have been observed. These boundaries are derived from individual rights, federalism, and separation of powers values reflected in the Constitution, as they have been elaborated over time. We have considered in this chapter only the separation of powers value of legislative supremacy, which tells us that Congress has the exclusive power to create an agency and delineate its powers. In order to protect the assignment of this constitutional prerogative to Congress, courts must determine whether the agency is acting within the scope of its delegated authority. In enforcing the boundaries on agency authority, courts should attend to and give respectful consideration to the agency's view of the proper scope of its own authority (and weight as appropriate). But the final judgment should be the court's.

Once the reviewing court determines that the agency is acting within the scope of its delegated authority, any agency interpretation of the statute it has been charged with administering should be regarded a matter of discretionary interpretive choice, and should be accepted by the reviewing court. The agency, for reasons of political accountability and expertise, is the preferred institution for resolving such issues. Courts should nevertheless condition their willingness to accept the agency's interpretation on a finding that the agency has reached its interpretation in the manner required by the norms of public participation and reason giving. An agency that has failed to follow such a process should be entitled only to respectful consideration of its interpretation.

Rule of law values should be factored into the analysis at both the stage of identifying whether the agency is acting within the scope of its delegated authority and, if so, whether the agency has complied with the twin norms of good process. When an agency can show that its action is consistent with settled expectations, this should be given weight in favor of finding that it has acted within the scope of its authority. If the action is contrary to settled expectations, this should count against a finding that the agency is acting within the scope of its authority. Similar considerations should apply in determining whether the agency has complied with a process that allows for public participation and gives reasons for its interpretive choice. If the agency has followed such a process, the court accepts its interpretation. If not, the court should give the agency view added weight if the interpretation is consistent with settled expectations, and reduced weight if it is not consistent with settled expectations.

2

Before *Chevron*

I<small>N THE YEARS PRECEDING</small> the *Chevron* decision, discussions about the relationship between courts and agencies over who has the authority to "say what the law is" typically distinguished between two modes of review: independent judgment and deference. As we have seen in Chapter 1, these terms are ambiguous. But courts and commentators paid little attention to the ambiguities in this period. In practice, neither independent judgment nor deference accurately described the law. Instead, courts applied a mixed bag of factors in assessing the significance of an agency interpretation of the statute establishing its authority. Courts would often give "weight" or "respect" to such interpretations, especially if the agency interpretation had triggered reliance interests. A handful of decisions from the New Deal era seemed to distinguish between pure questions of law and mixed questions of law and fact, applying independent judgment to the former and deferring to the agency on the latter. One notable decision, *Skidmore v. Swift & Co.,* said courts should follow agency interpretations, even if not legally bound to do so, depending on such factors as the "thoroughness evident in its consideration, the validity of its reasoning, and its consistency with earlier and later pronouncements."[1] Congress intervened on the question when it enacted the Administrative Procedure Act (APA) in 1946, which appeared on its face to require that courts exercise *Marbury*-style de novo review on all questions of law. Finally, on a few occasions Congress expressly directed an agency to resolve the meaning of a statutory term, in which event courts would accept the agency view unless it was arbitrary or capricious.

Standing alone, these diverse factors did not comprise, either individually or collectively, what could be described as a coherent doctrine. No attempt was made to connect the various factors together or explain their relevance in terms of a model of court–agency relations. Still, it would be presumptuous to dismiss these factors as empty rhetoric. Some factors, such as the importance of contemporary and longstanding administrative constructions, have since the early days of the Republic been invoked as reasons for ascribing significance to executive interpretations.[2] Given the durability of the various factors, it is plausible to view them as reflecting deep-seated judicial intuitions about the kinds of considerations that ought to bear on the decision to give weight to agency views. If they did not determine the outcome of cases with logical certainty, neither did any other traditional tool of statutory interpretation. At least the factors turned the attention of courts and litigants— including agency administrators—toward relevant considerations that presumably shaped the judicial response.

Contemporary and Longstanding Interpretations

Going back to the earliest days of the Republic, courts would often give weight to interpretations contemporary with the enactment of the statute in question. They would similarly give weight to interpretations that had been uniformly maintained over time. Aditya Bamzai has provided a comprehensive review of the history of decisions employing these two canons of interpretation.[3] He explains that the "contemporary" and "customary" canons, as he calls them, were not unique to judicial review of agency interpretations. The same canons applied to constitutional interpretation, with the interpretation of that document by Congress being the relevant evidence about contemporary or longstanding understanding. One can also find the canons being used in cases involving treaty interpretation and contact interpretation. In other words, the twin canons were part of the traditional tools of interpretation that courts drew upon in a variety of contexts.

Bamzai offers extensive evidence that the contemporary and longstanding interpretation canons were the primary convention for integrating executive and judicial interpretations of statutes in the years before *Chevron*. The canons operated in both directions. If an agency interpretation was either contemporary with the enactment of the statute, or had been maintained consistently for a significant period of time—or both—it was entitled to extra weight when challenged in court. Conversely, if the agency interpretation was adopted well after the statute was enacted, or had been inconsistently followed by the agency, it was entitled to little or no weight. Indeed, failure to satisfy the canons was sometimes cited as a reason to reject the agency interpretation.[4]

Because contemporary and longstanding agency practice were understood to be canons of interpretation, these conventions were not regarded as being inconsistent with the idea that courts must exercise independent judgment in determining statutory meaning. Courts draw upon all sorts of canons when they interpret statutes.[5] Some canons are generalizations about common linguistic usages, others are designed to highlight particular constitutional values or considerations of public policy. The canons about contemporary and longstanding agency interpretations were simply added to the mix along with other canons. The ultimate judgment about the meaning of the statute was determined by the court after considering the language and purpose of the statute and applying any canons deemed relevant.

To the extent courts offered rationales for the twin canons, two justifications were advanced. First, contemporary and longstanding interpretations were regarded as indicative of congressional intent. Contemporary interpretations were thought to shed light on congressional intent, either because the agency had participated in the drafting process or because such an interpretation was likely to be "evidence of the assumptions—perhaps unspoken by either administrators or Congress—brought to a regulatory problem by all involved in its solution."[6] Longstanding agency interpretations, for their part, were thought to reflect legislative intent insofar as they had survived multiple opportunities for correction by Congress. As one Court put it, where Congress has re-enacted the statute without pertinent change the "failure to revise or repeal the agency's interpretation is persuasive evidence that the interpretation is the one intended by Congress."[7] This rationale was invoked even while occasionally acknowledging that it is "often a shaky business to attribute significance to the inaction of Congress."[8]

A second justification for the twin canons was that they had generated reliance interests. In this respect, the canons reflect what Chapter 1 called rule of law values, which translate into judicial concern with upholding settled expectations about the law. An agency interpretation adopted shortly after the enactment of a statute is likely to generate strong expectations about what the statute means, because the first interpretation will shape how actors comply with the statute. Regulated actors will commonly ask attorneys for advice about the impact of a new statute, and the advice will be strongly influenced by an agency interpretation rendered shortly after its enactment. As one decision put it, the principle of contemporaneous construction is "a wholesome one[] for the establishment and enforcement of justice," not only as between individuals, but also "between the government and those who deal with it, and put faith in the action of its constituted authorities, judicial, executive, and administrative."[9]

The canon that calls for giving weight to longstanding agency interpretations is even more obviously related to protecting settled expectations. This has often been assumed rather than stated explicitly. On occasion, however, the point has been recognized, even with some eloquence:

> [G]overnment is a practical affair intended for practical men. Both officers, law-makers and citizens naturally adjust themselves to any long-continued action of the Executive Department—on the presumption that unauthorized acts would not have been allowed to be so often repeated as to crystalize into a regular practice. That presumption is not reasoning in a circle but the basis of a wise and quieting rule that in determining the meaning of a statute or the existence of a power, weight shall be given to the usage itself—even when the validity of the practice is the subject of investigation.[10]

As Bamzai succinctly puts it, the courts recognized the "utility in not disturbing the expectations of parties who had come to rely on the customary interpretation."[11]

In short, the pre-*Chevron* convention with the longest and most robust pedigree was grounded at least in significant part in rule of law values—the importance of protecting settled expectations about the meaning of the law. This is not to suggest that the canons about contemporary or longstanding executive interpretations were consistently applied, or deeply theorized. Nor did they have the advantage of any exposition in a leading case, such as would have provided general guidance about their application. This gave rise to considerable variability among courts as to how much significance to attribute to the twin canons. But the canons were securely established as traditional tools of statutory interpretation, and were familiar to judges and lawyers alike. They rested on a widely shared intuition that it was important for courts to reinforce settled expectations about the law, which meant that their invocation was uncontroversial.

Mixed Questions of Law and Fact

While the contemporary and longstanding canons had a pedigree that dates to the days of the Marshall Court, if not before, other factors owe their genesis to the New Deal. Two aspects of the New Deal are especially relevant here. The first is that the size and scope of the federal government greatly expanded during the early years of the Roosevelt Administration, as Congress created multiple new agencies staffed with ardent New Dealers. The second is that the attitude of the Supreme Court toward these legislative innovations changed dramatically between Roosevelt's first and second terms. In the first term, the Supreme Court was composed entirely of Justices appointed prior to Roosevelt's election, and the Court invalidated some prominent New Deal programs.[12] In Roosevelt's second term (1936–1940) this changed, as new appointments to the Court created a majority strongly supportive of the New Deal and skeptical about the virtues of judicial review of agency action. This gave rise to some new factors that entered into the body of legal doctrine governing judicial review of agency statutory interpretation.

The first of these new factors seemed to direct courts to defer to agencies on "mixed" questions of law and fact or questions that required the application of law to particular facts. As subsequently rationalized by commentators, the idea was that courts should exercise independent judgment in resolving pure questions of law, but defer to reasonable agency decisions seeking to apply the law in particular factual circumstances. Bamzai argues that this was an extension of the notion, already well established before the New Deal, that courts would decide questions of law independently but defer to agencies on questions of fact.[13] The law–fact distinction, in turn, derived from conventions about the relationship between judges and juries, or between appeals courts and trial courts.[14] Just as juries were given broad discretion to decide mixed questions of law and fact, such as whether a motorist drove "negligently" in causing an accident, the New Deal Justices decided that agencies could resolve "mixed" questions, such as whether someone is an "employee" of a firm.

Although there were some early precursors of the extension of deference to "mixed" questions of law and fact,[15] the case most often cited for this proposition is *National Labor Relations Board v. Hearst Publications, Inc.*[16] The question was whether so-called newsboys who sold newspapers in Los Angeles were eligible to bargain collectively under the provisions of the National Labor Relations Act. Newsboys were actually adult men who sold papers at designated spots in the city. They took an allotment of papers at wholesale prices, sold them at posted retail prices, and took as earnings the difference between retail and wholesale price times the number of paper they sold. The Act protected efforts to bargain collectively by "employees," a term otherwise not meaningfully defined.[17] The newspapers refused to bargain with the newsboys, arguing that they were not employees but independent contractors. The National Labor Relations Board (NLRB) ruled in favor of the newsboys, and the case made its way to the Supreme Court.

In resolving the dispute, the Court began by considering, as a matter of de novo review, whether the statutory word "employee" should be defined in accordance with the common-law meaning of the term—for example, as had been developed in cases in which an employer is held liable for injuries caused by an employee. Relying largely on what it perceived to be the policies of the Act, the Court held that the common-law meaning was inappropriate. The Act was intended to adopt a national program for resolving labor disputes, which required a uniform definition of employee, not one that might vary depending on the common law in each state. Also, the policies of the Act were to prevent industrial unrest and redress inequalities of bargaining power between workers and employers—policies different from those at issue in the typical common-law case. The Court had no doubt that the term should be defined "broadly, in doubtful situations, by underlying economic facts rather than technically and exclusively by previously established legal classifications."[18]

Having rejected the newspapers' argument in favor of a common-law definition, the Court declined to offer an alternative definition. Instead, it concluded that this was a task "assigned primarily to the agency created by Congress to administer the Act." The agency had "[e]veryday experience in the administration of the statute," "familiarity with the circumstances and backgrounds of employment relationships in various industries," and understood "the adaptability of collective bargaining for the peaceful settlement of disputes" between workers and employers.[19] The Court concluded this way:

> Undoubtedly questions of statutory interpretation, especially when arising in the first instance in judicial proceedings, are for the courts to resolve, giving appropriate weight to the judgment of those whose special duty is to administer the questioned statute. But where the question is one of specific application of a broad statutory term in a proceeding in which the agency administering the statute must determine it initially, the reviewing court's function is limited. [T]he Board's determination that specified persons are "employees" under this Act is to be accepted if it has "warrant in the record" and a reasonable basis in law.[20]

And with that, the Court upheld the Board's conclusion that the newsboys were "employees" for collective bargaining purposes.

Hearst has been interpreted as adopting the view that mixed question of law and fact or of application of the law to facts should be resolved by the agency subject to deferential review by the courts. The question whether "employee" should be given a common-law definition was a pure question of law, and was resolved by the Court de novo. The question whether any particular group of workers in any particular industry met the definition of "employee" should be resolved by the agency, created by Congress to administer the Act, under a deferential standard of review.

Another reading of the decision, however, has more far-reaching implications. The de novo review portion of the opinion reached only a negative conclusion: that "employee" should not be defined as having a common-law meaning. The Court never ventured an affirmative definition of the term. An alternative reading of the decision is that the term "employee" was to be determined by the agency, drawing upon the policies of the Act, as applied in different industries. In other words, the Court construed the statute as delegating authority to the agency to give content to the otherwise undefined term, "employee." On this reading, the decision did not hold that *application* of the definition of employee was to be determined by the agency—there was no settled definition to apply. Rather, the agency would decide who was an employee in a case-by-case fashion. Congress had failed to specify who was to define "employee," the agency or the courts. *Hearst* seemed to engage in a kind of comparative analysis of the competence of the agency and the courts to resolve the question, and based on this analysis came down in favor of the agency being the preferred law-interpreter.

Doubts about whether the Court intended to adopt a general doctrine about mixed questions of law and fact in *Hearst* are reinforced by two decisions by the Court several years later. In *Packard Motor Car Co. v. National Labor Relations Board*[21] the question was whether foremen supervising line workers at an auto assembly plant were eligible for collective bargaining as employees. The Board held that foremen were covered by the Act, and designated them as a bargaining unit. Characterizing the issue as a "naked question of law whether the Board is now, in this case, acting within the terms of the statute," the Supreme Court affirmed. Justice Jackson said that it was simply "too obvious to be labored" that "these foremen are employees both in the most technical sense at common law as well as in common acceptance of the term."[22] This has been read as a reversion to complete de novo review in resolving the question about the meaning of "employee." There was no suggestion of a division of functions between court and agency along a pure law / law application line.

Another reading of *Packard,* however, is that the comment about "naked question[s] of law" was directed to the question whether the NRLB was acting within the scope of its delegated authority in holding that foremen were employees. Because foremen are employees under the common law and common meaning of the term, the answer was clearly yes. On this reading, *Packard* and *Hearst* can be readily reconciled. *Packard* holds that the NRLB was clearly acting within the scope of its authority because the *minimal* definition of "employee" includes anyone who would be an employee under the common law or "common acceptance" of the term. *Hearst,* for its part, holds that the NLRB was also acting within the scope of its authority in expanding the definition to go beyond the common-law meaning, because Congress had impliedly delegated authority to the agency to do this, as long as its construction was grounded in an application of the policies of the Act.

A second case decided about the same time, *Social Security Board v. Nierotko,*[23] reinforces this reading of *Packard.* The question was whether the

Social Security Board could define "wages" so as to exclude back-pay awards—
for example, awards to workers whom the NLRB had determined were improperly dismissed for engaging in protected activity. The Court rejected
this interpretation, concluding that "wages" should include awards designed
to provide make-whole relief to workers who have been wrongfully terminated. The Court acknowledged that "the ruling of the governmental agencies charged with the administration of the Social Security Act" was entitled
to respect, and "[t]heir competence and experience in this field command us
to reflect before we decide contrary to their conclusion."[24] Nevertheless it
rejected the Board's interpretation:

> Administrative determinations must have a basis in law and must be
> within granted authority. . . . An agency may not finally decide the limits
> of its statutory power. That is a judicial function. Congress used a well
> understood word—"wages"—to indicate the receipts which were to
> govern taxes and benefits under the Social Security Act. There may be
> borderline payments to employees on which courts would follow admin
> istrative determination as to whether such payments were or not wages
> under the act.
>
> We, conclude, however, that the Board's interpretation of this statute
> to exclude back pay goes beyond the boundaries of administrative rou
> tine and the statutory limits. This is a ruling which excludes from the
> ambit of the Social Security Act payments which we think were included
> by Congress. It is beyond the permissible limits of administrative
> interpretation.[25]

One could not ask for a clearer expression of the boundary enforcement
conception of judicial review of agency statutory interpretations. Whether
the Court correctly drew the boundary is another matter. *Hearst,* even as
qualified by *Packard,* would seem to indicate that the use by Congress of the
undefined term "wages" was a kind of implied delegation to the agency to
fill out the meaning of the term in different contexts.

Gary Lawson has argued that *Hearst* established the pure law / law application distinction, and notwithstanding *Packard* (and *Nierotko*), that the
lower federal courts continued to apply the distinction in the period before
Chevron.[26] There are several problems with this thesis. First, the pure law / law

application distinction virtually disappears from the Supreme Court after *Packard*.[27] It would be odd for the lower courts to continue to employ a distinction that was not at least periodically reaffirmed by the Supreme Court. Second, the many lower-court decisions he cites do not explicitly refer to the distinction. Lawson believes they were in fact following the distinction, but he admits this is based on his characterization of how the courts treated different issues, rather than what they said they were doing.[28] Third, it is plausible, as Bamzai argues, that section 706 of the APA was understood as having overturned *Hearst* and the idea that Congress can impliedly delegate authority to agencies to resolve certain questions of law.

That said, Lawson's research establishes that lower federal courts in the quarter century or so before *Chevron* seemed to exercise de novo review on questions that can be characterized as "abstract, 'ivory tower' legal questions," whereas they were more inclined to defer to agencies with respect to "factbound, inductive" legal questions peculiar to a particular statutory regime.[29] It is possible, as Lawson argues, that these decisions were applying, *sub silentio,* the pure question of law/law application distinction. But an alternative explanation for this pattern is that the courts were engaged in actively determining the boundaries of agency authority as established by Congress. The boundaries are largely set by the "abstract, 'ivory tower'" provisions set forth in the agency's organic act; once the boundaries were ascertained, courts were inclined to accept agency interpretations that fell comfortably within the scope of those boundaries. In other words, the lower courts may have been silently adopting the second reading of *Hearst*—that Congress can impliedly delegate authority to agencies to resolve certain internal or "interstitial" legal issues that fall within the scope of their delegated authority.

Skidmore v. Swift & Co.

Another innovation spawned by the Roosevelt Court came in a decision that would loom large in post-*Chevron* debates about the proper role of agencies and courts in interpreting statutes. *Skidmore v. Swift & Co.*[30] arose under the Fair Labor Standards Act, which, among other things, requires that covered employees be paid time and a half for overtime. The question at issue was whether the time that company firefighters spent on call in the evenings was "working time" that required overtime pay under the Act. Writing for the Court, Justice Jackson acknowledged that Congress had not delegated responsibility to any administrative agency "to determine in the first instance whether particular cases fall within or without the Act."[31] Nevertheless, Jackson noted that the Labor Department was charged with the authority to investigate practices regarding overtime pay, and could bring actions for injunctions to restrain violations of the Act. Pursuant to these functions, the Department's Wage and Hour Administrator had issued an interpretative bulletin that addressed the problem of "waiting time." The Department had filed an *amicus curiae* (friend of the court) brief with the Court outlining how it would apply the standards set forth in that bulletin in the case of the firefighters.

Justice Jackson acknowledged that the views of the Department, as reflected in the bulletin and the brief, were not conclusive or binding on the courts. Still, those views were the product of "more specialized experience and broader investigations and information than is likely to come to a judge in a particular case." Moreover, there were important considerations of uniformity at stake: "Good administration of the Act and good judicial administration alike require that the standards for public enforcement and those for determining private rights shall be at variance only where justified by very good reasons."[32] Jackson sought to reconcile these competing considerations in the following passage that would be often quoted in later years:

> We consider that the rulings, interpretations and opinions of the Administrator under this Act, while not controlling upon the courts by reason of their authority, do constitute a body of experience and informed judgment to which courts and litigants may properly resort for guidance. The weight of such a judgment in a particular case will depend upon the thoroughness evident in its consideration, the validity of its reasoning, its consistency with earlier and later pronouncements, and all those factors which give it power to persuade, if lacking power to control.[33]

With that, the Court sent the case back to the lower court with instructions to reconsider the issue in light of the Department's analysis of the bulletin, as elaborated in the government's brief.

No consensus has developed as to what it means to speak of "*Skidmore* deference."[34] Clearly, the decision presupposes that responsibility for determining the meaning of the law remains with the courts. There was no suggestion that Congress had delegated any authority to the agency to interpret the meaning of "working time." Some maintain that *Skidmore* deference is not really deference at all. To say that the court should follow the agency's interpretation if it is "persuasive" is to say no more than that the court should follow any law review article or *amicus* brief that it finds persuasive. But this ignores *Skidmore*'s invocation of the reliance interest in keeping the administrative interpretation and the judicial interpretation consistent (a version of the importance of protecting settled expectations), and the interest in keeping federal law uniform throughout the Nation. These objectives can be achieved if courts follow the interpretation of an agency with nationwide authority, but not by following a law review article or *amicus* brief (unless the decision is by the Supreme Court).[35]

Others maintain that *Skidmore* establishes a duty of sorts—a duty on the part of courts to give respectful consideration to the administrative interpretation, and weigh it in accordance with the various factors outlined in *Skidmore*. If the court decides to reject the administrative interpretation, the court has a duty to explain why. On this view, it would be reversible error for a court to simply ignore a relevant agency interpretation.

Still others would characterize *Skidmore* as adding to the inventory of "factors" that courts should consider in reviewing an agency interpretation, much in the fashion of the traditional contemporary and longstanding interpretation canons. After all, *Skidmore* explicitly reaffirms the longstanding interpretation canon. The weight given the administrative interpretation is in part a function of "its consistency with earlier and later pronouncements." And there is a strong echo of the concern with protecting settled expectations, such as we find supporting the traditional canons: "Good administration of the Act and good judicial administration alike require that the standards for public enforcement and those for determining private rights shall be at variance only where justified by very good reasons." Yet *Skidmore* also invoked several other factors. One was comparative institutional advantage, which had also appeared in *Hearst*. The Labor Department and its Wage and Hour Division had "more specialized experience and broader investigations and information than is likely to come to a judge in a particular case." Another was the desirability of national uniformity, which also had appeared in *Hearst*. A third and relatively new factor was the emphasis on the "thoroughness" of the agency's consideration of the issue and the "validity of its reasoning." This contains a strong hint that the court should not simply ask whether a reasonable person might adopt the agency interpretation, but should also consider the *process* the agency followed in reaching its interpretation. We will return to the potential advantages of adopting this kind of process review later in the Book.

The Administrative Procedure Act Reaction

Although New Deal gave rise to new ideas about how to think about the relationship between agencies and courts in the interpretation of law, it was perhaps inevitable that a reaction would set in. The American business community was sorely exercised by some of the new agencies, like the NLRB and the Securities and Exchange Commission (SEC). These agencies nevertheless enjoyed the strong support of President Roosevelt and, derivatively, the American voting public. Business leaders, and the elite lawyers who represented them, conceived of a flanking attack on the new agencies.[36] The idea was to adopt a code of administrative procedure that would require agencies to observe procedures closer to those employed by common-law courts, and direct courts to apply more exacting scrutiny to decisions by these agencies when they were challenged in court. More exacting judicial review was seen as beneficial to business interests because, although Roosevelt had secured control of the Supreme Court by 1938, the lower courts were still composed in significant part of judges appointed during the Republican administrations that preceded Roosevelt's election in 1932. And it was the lower-court judges who would review most administrative action.

The strategy went nowhere until Roosevelt's supporters suffered significant losses in the mid-term elections of 1938. This allowed a coalition of northern Republicans and southern Democrats to join forces in enacting the Walter-Logan bill in 1940, which would have adopted just such a code of administrative procedure. Roosevelt, perceiving the measure as an attack on the New

Deal, promptly vetoed the bill. With war clouds gathering, Congress failed to override the veto. Once war came, in late 1941, administrative law reform was sidelined for the duration of the conflict.

The war itself created the conditions for a compromise once hostilities ended. Partly this was due to a sharp reduction in partisan politics during the collective war effort. Roosevelt himself said he had changed from "Dr. New Deal" to "Dr. Win-the-War."[37] Partly it was due to widespread public irritation with government measures adopted during the war, such as wage and price controls and rationing, which, of course, were implemented by administrative agencies. Public sentiment shifted decisively in favor of greater regularity and protection for individual rights in the administrative process.

The compromise that emerged became the Administrative Procedure Act. Although modeled after the Walter-Logan bill and other reform proposals, the precise language was negotiated behind the scenes by key conservatives in Congress and the Justice Department. There were few hearings and little floor debate. Once the text was hammered out behind closed doors, both the House and the Senate passed the legislation by voice vote with no recorded dissent. President Truman, who had succeeded Roosevelt on the latter's death, signed the bill into law on June 11, 1946.

If one goes in search in the legislative history for the intent of Congress behind the APA's provisions that speak to judicial review of questions of law, the result will be frustration. Part of the problem is that the reforms were overwhelmingly focused on agency adjudication. This was understandable, given that adjudication was the dominant mode of administrative action at the time. It was also the tool used by the agencies that were the primary target of the Walter-Logan bill and the conservative proponents of administrative reform—the NLRB and the SEC. So the Act says a great deal about the procedures agencies must follow when they engage in adjudication, and little about rulemaking, which would come to the fore much later. Similarly, the debates that raged during the controversy over the Walter-Logan bill and afterward focused on the standard of review courts should apply in reviewing agency determinations of fact, with relatively little attention given in the debates to the standard of review of questions of law.

Further complicating the quest for evidence of legislative intent, the compromise language hammered out behind the scenes was subject to vigorous spinning both before and after the legislation was passed. The conservative proponents of reform emphasized that the APA would rein in agencies, and result in more exacting judicial review (especially of question of fact). The Justice Department, most prominently through the *Attorney General's Manual on the Administrative Procedure Act,* issued shortly after the Act was passed, insisted that the APA was simply a restatement of existing law, and did not authorize more stringent judicial review.[38] As George Shepherd, who has written the most complete history of the APA, puts it, "each party to the negotiations over the bill attempted to create legislative history—to create a record that would cause future reviewing courts to interpret the new statute in a manner that would favor the party."[39]

The only thing to do in the face of clouded pre- and post-enactment legislative history is to look to the language of the Act. Section 706 begins by stating that a "reviewing court shall decide all relevant questions of law, interpret constitutional and statutory provisions, and determine the meaning or applicability of the terms of an agency action."[40] On its face this seems unequivocally to instruct courts to apply independent judgment on all questions of law. Note too that it applies the same instruction ("decide all relevant questions of law") with respect to both constitutional and statutory provisions. Interpretation of the Constitution ever since *Marbury* has been regarded as something the courts do de novo. By prescribing the same standard of review for statutory provisions, we can again conclude that the APA requires that courts exercise independent judgment in interpreting statutes. It is also relevant that Section 706 prescribes deferential standards for reviewing findings of fact by agencies in adjudications made on the record (to be upheld if there is "substantial evidence" for the finding considering the record as a whole) and for agency policy judgments (to be upheld if not "arbitrary, capricious, an abuse of discretion, or otherwise not in accordance with law").[41] Thus, we know Congress knew how to employ terms of art understood to require a more deferential standard of review when it wanted to; the absence of any such term with respect to questions of law confirms that independent judgment was intended for all such questions. A final point worth noting is that a subsection of Section 706 says that the reviewing court shall set aside agency action "in excess of statutory jurisdiction, authority, or limitations, or short of statutory right."[42] Congress *explicitly* required that reviewing courts determine whether an agency is acting within the scope of its delegated authority.

The APA's directive to courts to "decide all questions of law" was ambiguous, in that it did not foreclose all forms of deference. Clearly, the contemporary and longstanding interpretation canons were not thought to have been called into question by the APA. The twin canons were regarded as part of the package of interpretation tools courts have long employed in interpreting statutes. Unsurprisingly, therefore, citations to the twin canons continued more or less uninterrupted after the enactment of the APA.[43]

The argument probably also extends to *Skidmore*'s "persuasion" factors, insofar as these too are effectively additional canons to be applied by courts as a matter of independent judgment. And as Henry Monaghan famously argued shortly before *Chevron* was decided, there is no conflict between Section 706 and a decision to defer to an agency interpretation if the court concludes, as a matter of independent judgment, that Congress *intended* the court to defer to the agency's interpretation.[44]

What was unclear is whether Section 706 overrules decisions like *Hearst*. As we have seen, *Hearst* can be read either as extending deference to mixed questions of law and fact or, perhaps more plausibly, as sanctioning a kind of implied delegation of authority to agencies to interpret provisions that clearly fall within the scope of their statutory powers. On either reading of the decision, one can devise arguments that Section 706 is either consistent or inconsistent with *Hearst*. The nub of the question is whether *implicit* delegations, either to decide mixed questions of law and fact or to decide interstitial questions within the scope of the agency's authority, are a permissible basis for concluding that Congress has directed the court to accept agency interpretations. The conservative proponents of reform undoubtedly thought that Section 706 overruled *Hearst* and thereby disapproved the idea of implicit delegations. But they did not succeed in making this clear in the text of the statute. The liberal defenders of the New Deal agencies undoubtedly hoped that Section 706 did not overrule *Hearst* and hence perpetuated the idea of implicit delegations. But again, they agreed to statutory language that left this up in the air.

What is more than a little interesting is that, in the aftermath of the APA, neither the courts nor the leading administrative law commentators grappled with the question whether the statute had in fact overruled *Hearst* and the idea of implicit delegations. The attitude of the leading scholars of administrative law is especially telling. Many of these scholars, perhaps most notably Walter Gellhorn of Columbia and Kenneth Culp Davis of Chicago, cut their teeth as staff members of the Attorney General's Committee on Administrative Law, put together in 1940 by the Roosevelt Administration in an effort to *defeat* the movement for administrative law reform.[45] The attitude of these scholars, in writing administrative law treatises and casebooks in the 1950s and 1960s, was essentially to ignore Section 706 insofar as it applies to questions of law. Instead, they highlighted the importance of decisions like *Hearst*.[46] The implicit message was that a statute enacted unanimously by Congress had nothing of significance to say about the court–agency relationship in interpreting statutes, and that students should devote themselves to pondering the ambiguities of *Hearst,* which seemed to endorse at least some significant degree of deference to agencies on questions of law. The result was that multiple generations of lawyers in the postwar era ignored the relevance of the APA in resolving the deference question, and assumed that the proper response in determining the scope of judicial review of questions of law was to look to court decisions on the subject.

Express Delegations

A final element in the mélange of pre-*Chevron* factors emerged in a series of decisions handed down in the decade before *Chevron*. This concerned the relatively rare circumstance in which Congress expressly directs an agency to define the meaning of a statutory term. The leading case, which was to play a role in the *Chevron* opinion, was *Batterton v. Francis*.[47]

Batterton arose under the federal welfare program known as Aid to Families with Dependent Children (AFDC). Originally conceived as a program for single parents, Congress extended the Act on a trial basis in 1961 to include families in which the primary breadwinner was unemployed, called AFDC-UF (the UF being short for "unemployed father"). The trial program allowed each state to determine when the breadwinner would be deemed unemployed. Then in 1968 the program was made permanent, and in an effort to impose some uniformity on eligibility for this benefit Congress provided that participating states should provide assistance when a needy child "has been deprived of parental support or care by reason of the unemployment (as determined in accordance with standards prescribed by the Secretary) of his father."[48] The Secretary (of the then-Department of Health Education and Welfare) issued a regulation that defined unemployment to exclude persons out of work who could not qualify for unemployment insurance compensation under state law. In other words, the regulation largely tracked the policy of the trial program in allowing each state to determine the meaning of "unemployment."

The regulation was challenged on behalf of beneficiaries who were out of work but did not qualify for various reasons for unemployment compensation under state law. When the case reached the Supreme Court, the majority reasoned that the Secretary's regulation was entitled to the strongest measure of deference. The Court wrote:

> Ordinarily, administrative interpretations of statutory terms are given important but not controlling significance. . . . [H]owever, Congress in § 407(a) expressly *delegated* to the Secretary the power to prescribe standards for determining what constitutes "unemployment" for purposes of AFDC-UF eligibility. In a situation of this kind, Congress entrusts to the Secretary, rather than to the courts, the primary responsibility for interpreting the statutory term. In exercising that authority, the Secretary adopts regulations with legislative effect. A reviewing court is not free to set aside those regulations simply because it would have interpreted the statute in a different manner.
>
> The regulation at issue in this case is therefore entitled to more than mere deference or weight. It can be set aside only if the Secretary exceeded his statutory authority or if the regulation is "arbitrary, capricious, an abuse of discretion, or otherwise not in accordance with law." 5 U.S.C. § 706 (2) (A), (C).[49]

The logic here seems unimpeachable. Assuming that Congress can delegate broad policymaking authority to administrative agencies—an assumption regarded as long settled by the time *Batterton* was decided—it would seem that Congress should be able to *expressly* delegate authority to an agency to define a specific term within the statute that confers such authority on the agency. The Court was careful to qualify this proposition by noting that the court should determine whether the Secretary has "exceeded his statutory authority" in adopting the definition (citing the subsection of the APA that instructs courts to determine if an agency has acted "in excess of statu-

tory jurisdiction, authority, or limitations, or short of statutory right"—
Section 706(2)(C)). If the Secretary is acting within the scope of authority
granted, then the administrative definition should be reviewed under the
same standard that applies to agency policy judgments more generally—the
arbitrary, capricious, or abuse of discretion standard of the APA—Section
706(2)(A).

The Court went on to conclude that the Secretary had not exceeded the
scope of his statutory authority by defining "unemployment" to incorporate
state law restrictions on eligibility for unemployment insurance compensation. The Court reasoned that if Congress had intended to restrict the Secretary to adopting a single national definition, it might have said "unemployment (as defined by the Secretary)." Instead, the statute said "unemployment
(as determined in accordance with standards prescribed by the Secretary)."
As the Court observed, "[t]he power to 'determine' unemployment remains
with the States, and we conclude that the power to prescribe 'standards' gives
the Secretary sufficient flexibility to recognize some local options in determining AFDC-UF eligibility."[50]

Batterton was followed in a handful of decisions in the early 1980s arising
under the federal Medicaid program.[51] A somewhat analogous doctrine
emerged in the tax field, where the Court concluded that strong deference
should be given to agency interpretations adopted pursuant to specific delegations of rulemaking authority, but less deference to interpretations adopted
under the Treasury Department's general rulemaking authority.[52]

In Sum

We have seen that the pre-*Chevron* era was characterized by a hodgepodge
of factors that point either for or against giving weight or respect to an agency
statutory interpretation. A few generalizations are nevertheless possible.

First, independent judgment (in the sense of de novo review) was the default rule; deference (however calibrated) required special justification. Each
of the factors canvassed above—the contemporary and longstanding interpretation canons, the *Hearst* doctrine, the *Skidmore* persuasion factors, and
Batterton's rule about express delegations of interpretive authority—
delineated special circumstances in which an agency interpretation would
be regarded as legally significant. Absent one of these circumstances, it was

understood that the court would determine the meaning of the statute de novo. The APA, although generally ignored on this point, seemed to say so explicitly.

Second, there was no uniform understanding about how much weight or respect would be attached to an agency interpretation if one of the discrete factors was applicable. At one end of the scale, the contemporary and long-standing interpretation canons were often applied as a kind of comfort factor—icing on the cake if you will—if the court was otherwise inclined to uphold or reject the agency view.[53] At the other end of the scale, the *Batterton* doctrine required courts to assess agency interpretations under the arbitrary and capricious standard of review reserved for discretionary policy choices. *Hearst*'s effort to assimilate questions of law application to the standard applied to factual findings fell somewhere in between these poles, as did *Skidmore*'s injunction to follow the agency if its reasons were persuasive. Deference was not an all-or-nothing proposition, but existed along a continuum from some to great.

Third, there was no suggestion—none—that a reviewing court should defer to an agency on questions about the scope of the agency's authority. The *Hearst* doctrine, to the extent it applied, was limited to questions of law application or to interstitial issues that fell clearly within the scope of the agency's delegated authority. The *Batterton* doctrine was carefully qualified by the understanding that the agency had to exercise its power to interpret within the scope of its delegated authority, as determined by the court. *Nierotko* emphatically affirmed the point. And of course, the APA in Section 706 was explicit that courts had to set aside agency action that exceeded the scope of its delegated authority.

Fourth, as one would expect from a doctrine that contained a collection of what looked like interpretive canons, courts frequently mixed and matched the factors in particular cases. For example, in *Federal Election Commission v. Democratic Senatorial Campaign Committee*,[54] the Court upheld a Commission interpretation of the campaign finance laws, noting that Congress had delegated broad policymaking authority to the Commission, it had consistently adhered to its interpretation, and the commission in the course of several proceedings had developed "a number of sound arguments" in support of its position.[55] Or, to take another example, in *SEC v. Sloan*,[56] the Securities and Exchange Commission argued that its interpretation was entitled to deference because it was longstanding and consistent and had been cited with approval in a subsequent committee report. The Court rejected these arguments, noting that the interpretation was not supported by a careful analysis of the statutory language, and congressional ratification could not be inferred based on "a few isolated statements in the thousands of pages of legislative documents."[57]

Finally, the idea that courts had to obey Congress when it made an agency the primary interpreter of a statute had gained a toehold, but it was carefully circumscribed. *Hearst* on one reading seemed to say that Congress had impliedly delegated authority to the NLRB to interpret the word "employee," but the opinion invoked this idea only after the Court itself had resolved the large, general questions about how that term should be interpreted, in the exercise of de novo review. *Batterton* also invoked the idea that Congress could deputize the agency as the primary interpreter, but its holding was limited to express delegations of interpretive authority. Such express delegations are rare, and usually appeared in highly complex benefit schemes like AFDC and Medicaid.

Overall, the pre-*Chevron* body of factors did not conform in any obvious way to the four values outlined in Chapter 1. But elements of those values were clearly visible. The rule of law values, understood to mean respect for settled expectations about the law, were directly advanced by the contemporary and longstanding interpretation canons, and also made an appearance in *Skidmore*. The constitutional principle of separation of powers, which Chapter 1 identifies as requiring that courts enforce Congress's decisions about the scope of authority delegated to administrative agencies, was never questioned, and appeared expressly in the APA and in *Nierotko* and *Batterton,* and implicitly in *Hearst* and *Packard.* The understanding that agencies have a comparative advantage in resolving questions of discretionary interpretive choice that fall within the scope of their delegated authority was a central feature of *Hearst,* and made an appearance in *Skidmore.* And the idea that agencies should be given deference only if they engage in a process of reasoned decision making is at least hinted at in *Skidmore.* Thus, fragments of the four values were present, but they were not stitched together in any coherent fashion.

As time marched on, complaints about the unwieldy and manipulative nature of the Court's doctrine began to proliferate. The highly respected appeals court judge Henry Friendly wrote a caustic opinion about two lines of irreconcilable Supreme Court decisions, one requiring independent judgment, the other deference.[58] Congress took note of the confusion, but its primary response was an effort, which nearly succeeded, to amend the APA to reinforce the principle that courts should exercise independent judgment in all cases.[59] Then came the *Chevron* decision.

3

The *Chevron* Decision

W‍E TURN NOW TO THE *Chevron* decision itself. When it was briefed and argued, no one thought *Chevron* presented any question about the court–agency relationship in resolving questions of statutory interpretation. Instead, all understood the case to be about the "bubble concept," a catchy phrase for a particular way of interpreting the term "stationary source" under the Clean Air Act.[1] When the bubble controversy reached the Supreme Court, at first the Justices were closely divided about whether to allow the Environmental Protection Agency (EPA) to adopt the bubble policy. Justice Stevens, who was initially uncertain and drew the assignment to write for the majority, was thus confronted with the need to write a particularly persuasive opinion if he was to hold a majority. His strategy, in addition to writing a long and unusually thorough opinion, was to draft a short section near the beginning of the opinion—including what became a new "two-step" standard of review—that strongly invoked the distinction between law and policy. The bubble controversy, he concluded, was a fight over policy rather than law. Therefore, it was appropriate that it be resolved by the EPA, not a court of law. The strategy succeeded brilliantly. When he circulated his proposed opinion near the end of a very busy Term in June 1984, all participating Justices joined his opinion with no sign of concern about anything Stevens had written, making the decision unanimous.

For present purposes, the most significant thing about Justice Stevens's opinion is that it is largely consistent with the four values implicated by judicial review of questions of law set forth in Chapter 1—at least when one reads the opinion in its entirety. The opening paragraphs, taken out of context, are potentially problematic, and became more so as the Court applied the two-step standard in future cases. But read as a whole, the *Chevron* opinion can be taken as the very model of a correct application of judicial review.

The Bubble Controversy

To understand *Chevron* it is necessary to start with some sense of the controversy over the bubble. Three different programs established by the Clean Air Act require that stationary sources of air pollution, like power plants and smelters, adopt strict technology-based controls on emissions. Each program kicks in when firms either construct "new" stationary sources or "modify" existing stationary sources. Old sources (unmodified existing sources) are subject to much less demanding controls. Yet each of the three programs contains a critical ambiguity about the meaning of "stationary source": it is unclear whether the word "source" refers to each *apparatus* that emits pollution within a plant, like a smokestack, or whether it refers to the *entire plant.*

Under the apparatus definition, if a plant installs a new smokestack, this would be a new source. Hence the new smokestack would have to comply with tough technology-based controls. The plantwide definition, in contrast, in effect puts an imaginary bubble over an entire industrial complex and looks at changes in the amount of pollution coming out of an imaginary hole at the top. Under this bubble definition, if a firm adds a new smokestack, but makes offsetting changes in other parts of the operation such that the net effect is to reduce or hold pollution levels unchanged, the addition of the new smokestack would be neither a new source nor a modification of a source. Hence the change could be ignored for regulatory purposes.

The bubble concept was controversial from the time it was first proposed in the early 1970s. Environmentalists generally opposed the bubble because they saw it as locking in the environmental status quo. Suppose a plant consists of four smokestacks, each of which emits 100 tons of pollution per year, for total emissions of 400 tons. A new smokestack subject to state-of-the-art controls would emit only 25 tons of pollution. Under the bubble concept, the plant could continue to rebuild itself indefinitely, replacing each uncontrolled smokestack with a new uncontrolled smokestack as the old one wore out. Each replacement would result in no net addition of pollution from the plant, and so the tough technology-based standards would never be triggered. After

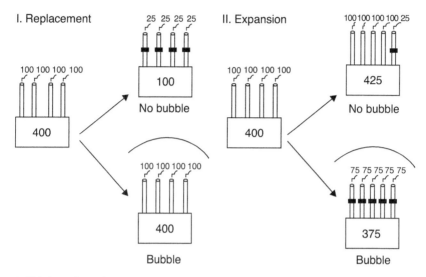

Bubble hypotheticals

a while, the plant would consist of nothing but new smokestacks, and yet it would still be emitting 400 tons of pollution, rather than the 100 tons it would emit if each smokestack had been regulated. The objectives of the new source provisions would be evaded, and no further progress would be made in cleaning up the air, as the accompanying figure illustrates.

Industry representatives and economists countered with a different example. Suppose, as before, a plant with four smokestacks, each emitting 100 tons in an unregulated state. Now suppose the plant wants to expand output by adding a fifth smokestack. Under the narrow single-apparatus definition of source, the new smokestack would be subject to controls, and would emit 25 tons. So the plant would now emit a total of 425 tons. Under the bubble policy, however, the plant could escape technology-based controls if it could somehow hold total emissions from the plant to 400 tons or less. Suppose it could do this relatively cheaply by retrofitting the existing smokestacks with a device that reduces emissions from 100 to 75 tons and by installing the device on all smokestacks. The result would be to reduce total emissions from the plant from 400 (4 × 100) to 375 tons (5 × 75). Application of the bubble in this example could save the plant considerable money *and* would also result in a better outcome for the environment—375 tons of pollution per year versus 425 tons of pollution (again, see the figure).

As with other attempts to resolve policy disputes by hypothetical example, the outcome depends on the assumptions. The case for the single-apparatus definition turns on the assumption that there is a sharp discontinuity between old equipment and new equipment. Old equipment is highly polluting, too costly to retrofit, and will inevitably be replaced by new equipment as it becomes technologically obsolete. Thus, the best policy is to hang tough and insist that technology-based standards apply to each apparatus, because over the long run this will do the most to improve air quality. The case for the bubble concept rests on the assumption that there is a more continuous function between the costs and benefits of retrofitting existing equipment versus installing new equipment. Sometimes retrofitting old equipment might yield more environmental benefits at lower costs than scrapping old equipment and replacing it with new. Thus, the best policy is to give firms general pollution-reduction goals combined with considerable flexibility in determining how to go about meeting those goals.

The D.C. Circuit

The EPA's first encounter with the bubble debate came in connection with the administration of the New Source Performance Standards (NSPS) established by Section 111 of the Clean Air Act of 1970. The NSPS apply to "new sources," which are defined as "any stationary source" whose "construction or modification" begins after a NSPS for that category of sources is published.[2] "Stationary source" is defined in turn as "any building, structure, facility, or installation which emits or may emit any air pollutant."[3] "Modification," for its part, is defined to mean any change in a source "which increases the amount of any air pollutant emitted by such source."[4] The EPA's initial regulations simply repeated the statutory definitions without clarifying whether "source" means each apparatus or an entire plant.[5]

In 1975, after a vigorous lobbying campaign by the nonferrous smelting industry, the EPA endorsed a modest form of the bubble concept under Section 111.[6] The EPA decided that "facility" means a single apparatus, and "source" means either a single apparatus *or* a complex of apparatuses. Consistent with this "dual definition" of stationary source, the EPA amended its regulations to define "source" to mean any "building, structure, facility, or installation" that "contains any one *or combination of*" facilities.[7] This definition thus *rejected* the bubble, which requires that "source" mean the entire plant. The agency nevertheless went on to endorse a qualified form of the bubble in a separate provision of the regulations dealing with the meaning of "modification." Here, the EPA provided that no modification would be deemed to occur when an "existing facility undergoes a physical or operational change" and the owner demonstrates that the "total emission rate of any pollutant has not increased from all facilities within the stationary source."[8]

On rival petitions for review by ASARCO (a firm in the nonferrous smelting industry) and the Sierra Club, a divided D.C. Circuit panel rejected the bubble concept "in toto."[9] The majority opinion was written by Judge J. Skelly Wright, a staunch liberal who was prone to see industry capture of administrative agencies in many of the regulatory controversies that came before him.[10] Wright's opinion portrayed the controversy as one in which the EPA had caved in to industry by adopting a position "contrary to both the language and the basic purpose of the Act."[11]

As to the language of the Act, Judge Wright agreed with the Sierra Club that the "plain meaning" of "source" could not be defined to mean both "facility" and "combination of facilities" (although this was not the feature of the regulation that permitted the bubble—that was the definition of "modification"). With respect to the purposes of the Act, Judge Wright thought the bubble would allow operators to evade their duty to install pollution control systems based on the best available technology, as long as they could devise some way to keep total emissions from an entire plant from increasing. As he vividly put it, "[t]reating whole plants as single sources would grant the operators of existing plants permanent easements against federal new source standards and the worst polluters would get the largest easements."[12] Thus, the bubble was incompatible with the central purpose of Section 111, which Judge Wright said was to enhance air quality. Neither ASARCO nor the EPA petitioned for review by the Supreme Court, so the bubble was dead for purposes of Section 111.

The 1977 Amendments to the Clean Air Act added two additional new source provisions to the Act. These provisions are triggered depending on whether air quality in a particular region is better or worse than required by the National Ambient Air Quality Standards (NAAQS) established under the

1970 Act. New Part C, called Prevention of Significant Deterioration (PSD), is designed to impose limits on the ability of states to allow clean air to deteriorate downward toward the NAAQS level. New Part D, called Plan Requirements for Nonattainment Areas (nonattainment program, or NAP), is designed to prod states to bring dirty air areas into compliance with the NAAQS. Each of these new parts includes, among its statutory requirements, new source review provisions requiring states to adopt technology-based standards for certain new and modified sources. Neither of the new provisions makes any attempt to define "facility" or "source."[13] Nor is there any cross reference in either part to the definition of "stationary source" in Section 111. Both Parts, however, expressly incorporate the definition of "modification" set forth in Section 111.[14]

The 1977 Amendments were enacted after the EPA had adopted the qualified bubble under Section 111, but before that policy had been struck down in *ASARCO*. When the EPA issued regulations implementing the new PSD program,[15] it adopted for that program virtually the same qualified bubble concept keyed to modifications.[16] The agency reasoned that Congress, in adopting the 1977 amendments, had been made aware of the definition of "modification" it had adopted under Section 111. Thus, when Congress directed that "modification" have the same meaning for PSD purposes as under Section 111, Congress implicitly ratified the EPA's qualified bubble under PSD, notwithstanding the D.C. Circuit's subsequent invalidation of this approach under Section 111.[17]

The PSD regulations were challenged in the D.C. Circuit in *Alabama Power Co. v. Costle*,[18] a massive judicial review proceeding that entailed dozens of issues besides the legality of the bubble policy. The panel issued a *per curiam* opinion summarizing its conclusions in June 1979, and issued its final opinion in April 1980. The final opinion was divided up by the three judges who heard the matter, each judge writing a separate section.[19] The challenge to the bubble was assigned to Judge Malcolm Wilkey, one of the court's more conservative and pro-business members.

Although Judge Wilkey concluded that the meaning of "modification" under the PSD program was limited by *ASARCO,* he reasoned that the EPA had broad discretion to define the component terms of the statutory definition of "source" (building, structure, facility, or installation) in different ways in order to advance the purposes of different new source programs.[20] Given this premise, he concluded that the bubble definition was "appropriate" under the PSD program.[21] This was because the PSD program was designed to prevent deterioration of air quality, not enhancement of air quality. Thus, any definition other than the bubble "would be unreasonable and contrary to the expressed purposes of the PSD provisions of the Act."[22] Whereas Judge Wright had implied that the bubble was unlawful in any form under Section 111, the Wilkey opinion seemed to say that the bubble concept was required under the PSD program.

The third leg of the new source review stool was the nonattainment program, also added by the 1977 amendments. In this context, the EPA engaged in a series of flip-flops in an effort to clarify whether the bubble should apply. In a Notice of Proposed Rulemaking issued in response to the June 1979 *per curiam* order in *Alabama Power*,[23] the EPA proposed a qualified bubble definition that could be used by states in full compliance with Part D requirements, while laggard states would have to use the apparatus definition.[24] After the D.C. Circuit's full opinion in *Alabama Power* issued,[25] the EPA determined that the bubble had to be prohibited for all purposes under the Part D program. The court had ruled that the bubble was inappropriate under programs designed to improve air quality, and all agreed that the nonattainment program was designed to improve air quality.[26]

The election of Ronald Reagan as President in 1980 marked a major shift in executive branch policy toward environmental and safety regulation. The philosophy of deregulation, emphasizing the use of markets and market-imitating mechanisms rather than centralized regulatory controls, got its start earlier, as applied to traditional transportation and infrastructural industries like airlines, trucking, railroads, telephones, and utilities.[27] The Reagan Administration extended this philosophy to environmental and safety regulation. Consistent with this new direction in policy, the EPA announced that it would reconsider issues related to the definition of "source" under the nonattainment and PSD new source review programs as part of "a Government-wide reexamination of regulatory burdens and complexities that is now in progress."[28] The upshot was that the agency decided to permit the states, at their election, to adopt an *unqualified* bubble definition of source for both PSD and nonattainment purposes.[29] The change was justified on the ground that allowing the states to choose the bubble definition would give them "much greater flexibility in developing their nonattainment . . . programs."[30]

The new 1981 regulations were challenged in the D.C. Circuit by three environmental groups, led by the Natural Resources Defense Council (NRDC). The case was assigned to a panel composed of Judges Abner Mikva, Ruth Bader Ginsburg, and William Jameson (a visiting senior district judge from Montana). Judges Mikva and Ginsburg were both relatively liberal Carter appointees. Judge Mikva would later resign to serve as White House Counsel to President Clinton, and Judge Ginsburg would be appointed to the Supreme Court by Clinton.

The decision was unanimous to vacate the EPA's regulations as applied to the nonattainment program. Judge Ginsburg's opinion for the court, stripped of details about the statutory and regulatory background, reduced to a syllogism.[31] *Alabama Power* and *ASARCO* "establish as the law of this Circuit a bright line test for determining the propriety of the EPA's resort to a bubble concept."[32] This test provided that the bubble "is mandatory for Clean Air Act programs designed merely to maintain existing air quality," but is inappropriate "in programs enacted to improve the quality of the ambient air."[33] "The nonattainment program's *raison d'être* is to ameliorate the air's quality in nonattainment areas sufficiently to achieve expeditious compliance with the NAAQS."[34] Ergo, the bubble could not lawfully be used under the nonattainment program.

Judge Ginsburg made no attempt to determine whether the bubble concept could be squared with the statutory meaning of "stationary source," and she agreed with the EPA that the legislative history was "at best contradictory."[35] The opinion also gave short shrift to the EPA's judgment that application of the bubble, at least in the context of the nonattainment program, would not interfere with efforts to achieve further improvements in air quality. This was dismissed with the observations that it was inconsistent with the agency's view a year earlier, and the agency had not cited "any study, survey, or support" for its new position.[36] Ordinarily this would be an appropriate judicial response to a change in agency policy.[37] Here, however, the EPA's previous position had been justified largely on the ground that it was required by the D.C. Circuit's decisions in *ASARCO* and *Alabama Power*. The demand for consistency in this context amounted to a demand for conformity with policy judgments previously reached by the D.C. Circuit, not by the agency on its own initiative.

Still, it is ironic that Judge Ginsburg's opinion was the one to be singled out for further review by the Supreme Court. Of the three D.C. Circuit decisions dealing with the bubble controversy, the Ginsburg opinion is the most restrained, in the sense of attempting to resolve the issue through a good faith reading of existing legal authorities (in this case, circuit precedent). In contrast, both Judge Wright's opinion in *ASARCO* and Judge Wilkey's opinion in *Alabama Power* reflected attempts to reach ends consistent with the author's views of appropriate policy. The bubble controversy suggests that D.C. Circuit judges were prone to substitute their own preferences for those of the EPA. But the most flagrant practitioners of this activism were not directly implicated in the case that eventually went before the Supreme Court.

What Happened at the Supreme Court

In tracking the progress of *Chevron* in the Supreme Court there are a number of sources to draw upon. The petitioning papers and merits briefs are available, as is the transcript of oral argument. Justice Blackmun's papers in particular shed significant light on the Court's internal deliberations. For present purposes, the following are the most important points.[38]

First, there is nothing in the papers seeking review by the Supreme Court to suggest that the parties were asking the Court to reconsider basic questions of court–agency relations. The focus was on the practical significance of the bubble concept, the confusion produced by the three D.C. Circuit decisions, and the claim that the D.C. Circuit had overstepped established norms of judicial review. The brief filed by respondent NRDC for the environmental groups provides an important clue to the outcome of the case. The brief declined to defend the approach of the D.C. Circuit, based on that court's perceptions of the dominant purpose behind each new source program. Instead, it argued that the language of the statute and legislative history meant that the term "source" must always mean apparatus, and can never mean plant. The respondents' disavowal of the D.C. Circuit's decisions was a tell-tale sign that the Supreme Court was unlikely to embrace the circuit court's approach.

Second, the Court was severely short-handed. Two Justices (Marshall and Rehnquist) did not participate for medical reasons. Sometime after argument, Justice O'Connor discovered she had a financial interest in one of the industry parties, which required her recusal. Ultimately then, only six justices participated in the decision—a bare quorum. Justice Blackmun's notes reveal that the initial vote at conference (before O'Connor's recusal) was 4–3 to reverse the D.C. Circuit. But each of the four justices in the majority said something to the effect that they were "shaky." For example, Blackmun recorded Justice Stevens as saying he was "not at rest."[39] Chief Justice Burger and Justices Brennan and O'Connor voted to affirm, although Burger seemed to have a weak grasp of the issues. Justice White was the senior justice in the majority; he rarely got to assign opinions and wasted no time in assigning the decision to Stevens. So Stevens faced a daunting task. He could easily lose the Court, or write an opinion that failed to gather five votes and thus might not constitute a binding precedent.[40] Stevens would have to unravel the legal complexities about the bubble concept in a persuasive way, and would have to devise some way of framing the issue that the doubters would find compelling.

Third, with one minor exception, no other Justice sought to influence the content of Justice Stevens's opinion. Shortly after Justice White assigned the opinion to Stevens, Chief Justice Burger asked Justice Brennan if he would prepare a dissent. Brennan equivocated, stating that "we were all somewhat tentative in our votes at Conference" and that he was "hold[ing] out some hope that John [Stevens] will write an opinion that will bring us together."[41] Brennan then wrote Stevens a rather convoluted letter saying he was concerned about an apparent inconsistency in the definition of "source" in two different parts of the EPA regulations. Stevens responded sometime later, saying that he saw no conflict, given that the two provisions addressed different statutory sections. This evidently led to some further communications between the chambers, the result being that Stevens added a short footnote to his draft opinion noting that the second provision was not being addressed.[42] With that face-saving revision, Brennan dropped the idea of writing a dissent. Once Brennan joined, everyone else did too. The Chief Justice, who had voted to affirm at the conference, wrote with typical sangfroid: "With others, I am now persuaded you have the correct answer to this case."

The result was a unanimous opinion, in a matter that had initially produced a confused and closely divided Court. The cascade toward consensus may be explained in part because it was near the end of the Term, and proposed opinions were circulating at a fast pace with everyone anxious to start the summer recess.[43] But it is also likely that the Justices (and their clerks) found Justice Stevens's opinion persuasive, and no one saw anything in it to cause alarm.

Fourth, the copy of Justice Stevens's draft opinion that was reviewed by Justice Blackmun provides some insight as to how the other Justices reacted to his work. In the margin opposite footnote 34, Blackmun wrote "footnotes!" The opinion is more than ordinarily loaded down with footnotes, and the remark may reflect a sense of tedium in having to forge through these complex materials. In the margin opposite the concluding sentence of the section devoted to legislative history, Blackmun wrote a double-underlined "yes." That sentence reads: "We conclude that it was the Court of Appeals, rather than the Congress or any of the decision makers who were authorized by Congress to administer this legislation, that was primarily responsible for the 1980 position taken by the agency."[44] It is possible this may have been the point in reading when Blackmun became fully convinced by Stevens's argument.[45] And on the first page of the opinion, in the top left-hand corner, Blackmun wrote simply: "Whew!" In context, it is safe to say that this was an expression of admiration for Stevens's handiwork, and perhaps also a sense of relief that the opinion handled the complicated issues in a way that absolved Blackmun of any further engagement with the matter.[46] "Whew!" may in fact provide the best insight as to how the Court came to render such an emphatic and unanimous opinion in *Chevron*. Given that he thought he had precarious support, Stevens presumably worked especially hard to produce a persuasive opinion.

Chevron and the Four Values of Review

Chevron is a long opinion, taking up twenty-nine pages in the U.S. Reports, including forty-one footnotes. Although it is probably the most famous and certainly the most cited decision in Administrative Law, it is not surprising that administrative law and legislation casebooks offer a highly abridged version of the opinion. In fact, most renditions of the decision reproduce the opening paragraphs of Part II and three paragraphs near the end of Part VII (under the subheading "Policy"), and either summarize or offer extremely compressed versions of everything in between. This is understandable but unfortunate. If one reads the entire opinion from beginning to end, one discovers a relatively conventional exercise in judicial review. Perhaps more surprising, the opinion can stand as the very model of a decision that reflects the four values set forth in Chapter 1 as critical in a regime of judicial review.

Rule of Law Values

Consider first, rules of law values, which Chapter 1 explicates in terms of protecting settled expectations about the law. Settled expectations can be created by Congress when it legislates. But there is nothing in the body of the *Chevron* opinion to suggest that Justice Stevens found that Congress had created any expectations about how "stationary source" would be defined. He meticulously examined the text of both the original Section 111 provisions dealing with stationary sources, and the NAP and PSD provisions dealing with the same. He probed the legislative history, looking for any evidence that the relevant committees or floor sponsors of the 1977 amendments harbored any thoughts about the meaning of "source." He found no evidence of any legislative direction on this point in either the text or the legislative history. There being no such legislative direction, the action of Congress could not have given rise to legitimate expectations about the law on the part of either the subjects or the beneficiaries of new source regulation by the EPA.

Chevron is often cited as a break with previous tradition regarding the relevance of expectations created by agency action. The opinion makes no mention of the established canons giving extra weight to agency interpretations that are contemporaneous with enactment of the statute, or are longstanding and consistently maintained by the agency.[47] And in a section of the opinion addressing the respondents' argument that the EPA was entitled to no deference because it had changed its position about the meaning of stationary source, Justice Stevens rejected this as a ground for overturning the agency decision. As he wrote in a frequently quoted passage:

> An initial agency interpretation is not instantly carved in stone. On the contrary, the agency, to engage in informed rulemaking, must consider varying interpretations and the wisdom of its policy on a continuing basis.[48]

A fair reading of the opinion's larger discussion of this point, however, suggests that Justice Stevens rejected the relevance of the agency's change in position because *no settled expectation about the definition of source had been established* by the agency. To the contrary, Stevens made clear that the agency had consistently preferred a "flexible" definition of source.[49] Its flip-flop between 1979 and 1980 was caused not by its own inconstancy, but by the insistence of the D.C. Circuit that the statute had to be read "inflexibly to command a plantwide definition for programs designed to maintain clean air and to forbid such a definition for programs designed to improve air quality."[50] The change in agency position was due to the activism of the politically divided D.C. Circuit, not the agency itself. So Stevens was not rejecting the relevance of settled expectations in judicial review of agency interpretations. He was making the point that if there are no settled expectations, the agency should be allowed to explore different interpretations that are otherwise permissible.

Constitutional Values

When we turn to what I called constitutional values in Chapter 1, we also find no reason to fault the *Chevron* decision. No one in the case claimed that the interpretation of "stationary source" implicated individual constitutional rights. So we can put individual rights provisions to one side.

With respect to separation of powers values, the relevant question is whether the EPA, in embracing the bubble interpretation of stationary source, had exceeded the boundaries on its authority established by Congress. The respondents argued vigorously that Congress intended "stationary source" to mean apparatus, and therefore the EPA had exceeded the scope of its delegated authority. Justice Stevens, in the body of the opinion, took this claim very seriously. As previously noted, he carefully canvassed the relevant statutory provisions, and found no "specific definition of the term 'stationary source,'" at least not in the NAP and PSD provisions. There was a definition of "major" stationary source (expressed in terms of tons of emissions), but this did not shed light in any clear fashion on the meaning of "source." Nor was there any discussion of the bubble or the meaning of "source" in the legislative history.

Turning the respondent's specific arguments, Justice Stevens noted that Section 111 did contain a definition of "stationary source," and it was possible that this definition was intended to be applied by the agency in defining the same term under the PSD and NAP programs. The Section 111 definition defined "source," in part, to mean "building," and building "could be read to impose the permit stationary conditions on any individual building that is part of a plant."[51] Stevens then noted that sometimes the meaning of a word in a series is defined in part by associated words in the series (in this case "structure, facility, or installation"), and sometimes a word in a series is understood to have a character of its own not submerged by its association.[52] Stevens implied that either of these conflicting canons of construction could arguably be invoked in parsing the definition in Section 111, leaving the matter in equipoise. Even assuming that the second constructional principle was more relevant, there was also the oddity that the definition of "major source" under the NAP provisions equated source with "facility," which presumably has a broader meaning than building. He concluded: "We are not persuaded that parsing of general terms in the text of the statute will reveal an actual intent of Congress."[53]

This discussion is highly relevant in understanding the role of a reviewing court contemplated by *Chevron*. Justice Stevens did not rest with the absence of any specific definition of "source" under the NAP program. Nor did he resolve the scope of the agency's authority with any casual characterization of the statute as "unclear" or "ambiguous." He carefully reviewed all the relevant language, including that of a related provision (Section 111), and concluded that Congress had no intent with respect to whether "source" means apparatus or plant. He was concerned to determine, through the exercise of de novo review, whether Congress had laid down a boundary that limited the agency's authority, or if, to the contrary, Congress had left the agency with the space to make a discretionary choice between these two meanings.[54]

With respect to federalism values, the *Chevron* opinion made only fleeting references to the fact that the EPA's regulations gave the states a choice between adopting the apparatus definition or the bubble definition of stationary source. The government repeatedly stressed the federalism theme in its brief, noting that the respondents and the D.C. Circuit wanted to put the states in a straitjacket.[55] Was Justice Stevens wrong to ignore this point? Arguably not, if we interpret the federalism boundary to mark a line beyond which beyond which federal authority should not be allowed to intrude, at least not without a clear statement by Congress. The government was arguing that the EPA should be given credit for ceding some additional authority to the states beyond what any conception of federalism as a boundary would require. Stevens may have regarded this as an equitable argument rather than a point that needed to be factored into a determination of the scope of the agency's authority. He may also have believed that federalism boundaries must be fixed by the courts, not by the discretionary actions of agencies.

Accountability Values

Chevron is justly famous for its emphatic affirmation of accountability values. That affirmation occurred at the end of the opinion, once Justice Stevens had established that Congress had no "actual intent" about the meaning of "stationary source." This meant that the meaning of "stationary source" was a discretionary policy choice that fell within a "gap left open by Congress."[56]

Insofar as filling that gap involved a policy choice, Stevens made clear that it should be made by the agency, not the court.[57] This was reflected in his prominent quotation, at both the beginning and the end of his opinion, from *United States v. Shimer,* a relatively obscure decision from the early 1960s. *Shimer* said, "If [the agency's] choice represents a reasonable accommodation of conflicting policies that were committed to the agency's care by the statute, we should not disturb it unless it appears from the statute or its legislative history that the accommodation is not one that Congress would have sanctioned."[58] At the end of his opinion, Stevens also made clear that the reason to defer to agencies on such points was their superior accountability:

> Judges are not experts in the field, and are not part of either political branch of government. . . . In contrast, an agency to which Congress has delegated policymaking responsibilities may, within the limits of that delegation, properly rely upon the incumbent administration's views of wise policy to inform its judgments. While agencies are not directly accountable to the people, the Chief Executive is, and it is entirely appropriate for this political branch of the government to make such policy choices—resolving the competing interests which Congress itself either inadvertently did not resolve, or intentionally left to be resolved by the agency charged with the administration of the statute in light of everyday realities.[59]

This justly famous passage is quoted in all excerpts of the decision. Note carefully, however, that Justice Stevens qualifies the sphere of agency policy choice by noting that Congress must have "delegated policymaking responsibilities" to the agency, and the courts must defer to the agency when it acts "within the limits of that delegation." In other words, there must be a delegation of authority to the agency, and the agency's sphere of superior accountability is limited by the scope of the delegation. Consistent with the discussion of the four values in Chapter 1, the operative realm of the accountability value is subordinate to the need to maintain the boundaries of agency discretion.

Incentives for Better Agency Decisions

The *Chevron* opinion also includes statements that are consistent with ideas sketched in Chapter 1 about how judicial review might improve the quality of agency statutory interpretation decisions. Justice Stevens noted that the bubble definition had been adopted by regulation, and that before it was adopted in 1981, "proposals for a plantwide definition were considered in at least three formal proceedings."[60] After summarizing the earlier proceedings, he noted that the EPA, in the decision under review, observed that the definitional issue was not squarely addressed in either the statute or the legislative history and therefore required a judgment by the agency "as how to best carry out the Act." He then noted that the EPA had offered several reasons for concluding that the plantwide definition was more appropriate. These reasons, Stevens observed, were set forth in a proposed rulemaking in August 1981 that was formally promulgated in October of that year.

This description of the EPA's process establishes that the Court regarded the agency as having provided an opportunity for public participation before it adopted its interpretation that the bubble was permissible.[61] Justice Stevens explicitly recognized that the EPA's determination of the meaning of "stationary source" occurred in a process that included full disclosure of the agency's reasoning to the public, an opportunity for any interested party to comment, and (at least ordinarily) an agency response to any material comments submitted.[62]

The Court's final characterization about the process followed by the EPA in rendering its interpretation is also telling. Justice Stevens concluded that the EPA's interpretation "represents a reasonable accommodation of manifestly competing interests and is entitled to deference: the regulatory scheme is technical and complex, *the agency considered the matter in a detailed and reasoned fashion,* and the decision involves reconciling conflicting policies."[63] Although this is not a complete description of the reasoned decision-making model sketched in Chapter 1, it is consistent with, and it may even be said to presuppose the use of that model.

In short, if one were to take a pair of scissors and cut out the first two paragraphs of Part II of the opinion, one would have an opinion that is almost entirely congruent with the four values of judicial review set forth in Chapter 1. It is likely that this is the way the Justices (and their law clerks) read the opinion, assuming they plowed their way through the entire draft as Justice Blackmun did. Indeed, as we shall see, this is the way the Court as a whole treated the decision in the initial period after it was decided.

The Two Paragraphs

If all but a few pages in the *Chevron* opinion are consistent with the four values traced in Chapter 1, how do we account for the two paragraphs at the beginning of Part II? These are the paragraphs that are quoted in the textbooks and are quoted or paraphrased in thousands of later decisions. They constitute what came to be known as "the *Chevron* doctrine."

The first of these two paragraphs sets forth what came to be called the "two step" approach to judicial review of agency interpretations of law. It is quoted here in its entirety:

When a court reviews an agency's construction of the statute which it administers, it is confronted with two questions. First, always, is the question whether Congress has directly spoken to the precise question at issue. If the intent of Congress is clear, that is the end of the matter; for the court, as well as the agency, must give effect to the unambiguously expressed intent of Congress. If, however, the court determines Congress has not directly addressed the precise question at issue, the court does not simply impose its own construction on the statute, as would be necessary in the absence of an administrative interpretation.

Rather, if the statute is silent or ambiguous with respect to the specific issue, the question for the court is whether the agency's answer is based on a permissible construction of the statute.[64]

There are two principal differences between this paragraph and what Justice Stevens wrote in the balance of the opinion. First, the paragraph speaks in terms of whether Congress spoke directly to the "precise question at issue," whereas the balance of the opinion asks whether Congress left the issue for the agency to determine. This is a subtle but important difference. The "precise question" formulation seems to charge the reviewing court with finding affirmative evidence of a legislative intent in support of a specific interpretation. Finding such evidence will be rare, and therefore the first paragraph seems to require that the agency in nearly all cases will have authority to render a dispositive interpretation. The agency, in other words, is given a very large "space" in which to interpret, subject only to small pockets where Congress has prescribed an answer. In contrast, determining whether Congress left the issue for the agency to decide is more consistent with a boundary maintenance conception of the role of the reviewing court. This would presumably result in a more confined "space" in which Congress has left the agency free to act.

Second, the opening paragraph advances a rule-like conception of the role of the reviewing court, expressed in terms of a sequential inquiry—first step 1, then step 2. This rule-like conception of how a court should proceed when addressing an agency's interpretation undoubtedly accounts for much of *Chevron*'s appeal. Certainly, the description of the review process in terms of two steps seems much more like a concise legal doctrine than the mishmash of factors that prevailed before. That said, if the two-step description was intended to set forth a new standard of review, one would expect to see this standard mirrored in the balance of the opinion. Instead, the remaining pages of the opinion proceed in a much more conventional fashion, carefully seeking to figure out what Congress did and did not decide, and carefully reviewing the course of the EPA's struggle with the issue. The rule-like articulation of the sequencing of the decisional process makes no appearance in the body of the opinion, either as an organizing principle or in terms of the vocabulary used to describe the decisional process.

Also, a close examination of the first paragraph reveals that the two-step sequence is rule-like only in the sense that it prescribes a certain ordering of inquiries. The substance of the inquiries themselves is not rule-like at all. Rather, they describe open-ended standards. The first step is described in terms of whether Congress had a "clear" or "unambiguous" intent. Clear / unclear and unambiguous / ambiguous prescribe very general standards that require an examination of statutory context. The second step is described in terms of whether the agency interpretation is "permissible" or, as stated in the following paragraph, "reasonable." Permissible / impermissible or reasonable / unreasonable are also general standards. What the first paragraph actually seems to mandate, therefore, is a two-part standard, both prongs of which are quite general.

The second paragraph has received less attention in subsequent decisions and commentary. As a matter of jurisprudence, however, it is more potentially radical than the first. Again, it is important to quote the text:

> "The power of an administrative agency to administer a congressionally created. . . . program necessarily requires the formulation of policy and the making of rules to fill any gap left, implicitly or explicitly, by Congress." *Morton v. Ruiz*, 415 U.S. 199, 231 (1974). If Congress has explicitly left a gap for the agency to fill, there is an express delegation of authority to the agency to elucidate a specific provision of the statute by regulation. Such legislative regulations are given controlling weight unless they are arbitrary, capricious, or manifestly contrary to the statute. Sometimes the legislative delegation to an agency on a particular question is implicit rather than explicit. In such a case, a court may not substitute its own construction of a statutory provision for a reasonable interpretation made by the administrator of an agency.[65]

The first three sentences in this paragraph are unproblematic. The quotation from *Morton v. Ruiz* says that agencies must act to fill gaps left in statutes, whether these gaps are left explicitly or implicitly. This is surely correct, although it says nothing about the standard of review courts should apply in reviewing these gap-filling efforts (something that was not at issue in *Ruiz*).[66] The second sentence says that Congress occasionally enacts an express delegation of authority directing an agency to interpret a particular term in a statute, which, as we have seen in Chapter 2, is true but unusual. The third says that in reviewing such an express delegation to interpret, courts have applied the arbitrary-and-capricious standard, which is what the Court held in *Batterton v. Francis.*[67]

The problem comes with the fourth and fifth sentences. The fourth seems to repeat the point from *Ruiz* about implicit gaps, but reframes it in terms of implicit delegations to interpret, a characterization not found in *Ruiz.* Then comes the final sentence, which seems to say that courts should apply the same deferential standard of review to agency interpretations of "implicit" gaps as they apply to explicit delegations of authority to interpret specific terms. Admittedly, the last sentence is not completely clear about this. Saying that courts may not substitute their judgment for a "reasonable" agency interpretation is not quite the same as saying that courts must uphold agency regulations that are not arbitrary and capricious. But most courts and commentators have read the last sentence as directing courts to apply the same highly deferential standard to "implicit" delegations as they apply to explicit delegations.

Particularly when read in connection with the previous paragraph, the notion that the great deference must be given to agency interpretations rendered pursuant to "implicit" delegations can be read as authorizing a revolution in the structure of American government. Taken together, the two paragraphs arguably say that unless Congress has "clearly" or "unambiguously" answered the "precise question" at issue, the agency has been implicitly delegated authority to answer the question at issue, subject only to the most deferential review by the courts. Authority to "say what the law is," by this one sentence, would have been transferred from the judiciary to the executive in almost any case involving ambiguity in a statute establishing an administrative agency.

This revolutionary interpretation of the second paragraph is again hardly supported by the balance of the opinion. The crux of the matter is what is meant by "implicit" authority to fill a gap. If any ambiguity or lack of clarity constitutes an implicit delegation of authority to interpret, this would be revolutionary. Vague statutory provisions are common. Silences about issues that arise concerning issues that perhaps were not anticipated when the statute was adopted are ubiquitous. Inconsistencies and internal tensions abound, especially when statutes have been patched together from different sources. Ordinary ambiguities, in the sense of language having two or more possible meanings, are encountered routinely. All these situations would qualify as implicit delegations of interpretive authority to an agency. The balance of the *Chevron* opinion makes no such assumption. Instead, it proceeds on the understanding that the definition of "stationary source" must be determined by a careful investigation of the relevant text and legislative history of the Clean Air Act, which yields the conclusion that the meaning of this term was left undecided by Congress, requiring that the meaning be determined by the agency.

The second paragraph would prove to have significance beyond the revolutionary idea that any lack of clarity entails a delegation of authority to the agency to interpret. It also contains the seeds of a theory that would provide a legal justification for "the *Chevron* doctrine"—that is, the interpretation of the first two paragraphs taken out of context from the balance of the opinion. The legal justification is that the strong deference seemingly mandated by the first two paragraphs has been directed (if only "implicitly") by Congress. Proponents of this theory (such as Justice Scalia) admitted that any such congressional intent is "fictional."[68] Indeed, it was wholly made up. Congress has on multiple occasions sought to say the opposite—that courts should exercise independent judgment in interpreting agency statutes.[69] And on one occasion—the enactment of the APA in 1946—Congress succeeded in legislating this understanding explicitly.[70] *Chevron*'s greatest weakness as a legal opinion is that it ignores this aspect of the APA. But if we adopt the theory that any ambiguity is an implicit delegation of authority to interpret, then every time Congress enacted an agency statute *after 1946* that contains an ambiguity, it implicitly directed courts to defer to the reasonable agency interpretation of the ambiguity. The second paragraph thus provided a theory for reconciling "the *Chevron* doctrine" with the APA. It also gave rise to the most important attempt to rein in that doctrine, in *United States v. Mead Corp.,* but this gets ahead of our story.

What was the source of the innovations in the opening paragraphs? The first paragraph has no provenance. The idea that judicial review of agency interpretations of law can be reduced to two steps was not advanced in any prior judicial opinion, nor was it set forth in any of the briefs in the case. Similarly, the framing of the initial inquiry in terms of whether Congress spoke to the "precise question" at issue was not foreshadowed in any prior decision or in any of the briefs. The conclusion seems unmistakable that the innovations in the first paragraph came from the creative mind of Justice Stevens alone.[71]

As to the second paragraph, the quotation from *Morton v. Ruiz* appears to have been borrowed from the government's brief.[72] But that brief followed the quotation with a relatively conventional statement of the applicable standard of review: "A reviewing court is not free to overturn the Administrator 'simply because it may prefer another interpretation of the statute' or because 'reasonable men could easily differ as to their construction.'"[73] Justice Stevens was anything but conventional, using the quotation from *Ruiz* as a jumping-off point for the ideas of an implicit delegation of interpretive authority and for the equation of implicit delegations with express delegations.

The question remains why Justice Stevens decided to launch his lengthy opinion with these highly novel paragraphs. This is the ultimate paradox of the *Chevron* decision. The opening paragraphs, which are the font of "the *Chevron* doctrine" and are endlessly quoted or paraphrased in thousands of decisions, do not appear to reflect the standard of review that Justice Stevens actually applied in the decision itself. If courts are always supposed to engage in review using the notions advanced in the opening paragraphs, one would surely expect these ideas to form the foundation for the analysis in the balance of the opinion. Instead, after their appearance in Part II, they effectively disappear.

Although this is necessarily conjectural, Justice Stevens most likely drafted Part II *after* he completed the remainder of the opinion. The best evidence of this is the very lack of integration in the opinion between Part II and the balance of the discussion. If Justice Stevens began by drafting the opening paragraphs, with the two-step decisional sequence and so forth, one would expect him to apply similar concepts in the balance of the opinion. Instead, we find the multiple disconnects previously described.

In addition, we know that Justice Stevens followed a practice of dictating first drafts of his opinions.[74] And the balance of the opinion, after the opening paragraphs, reads like someone proceeding through the steps of the analysis and recording as he went along. Part III describes the history of the Clean Air Act and the features of the Act that led to the adoption of the new source review provisions. Part IV discusses the historical evolution of the 1977

Amendments to the Act. Part V describes the internal legislative history of the 1977 Amendments insofar as it touches on the new source provisions of the NAP and PSD programs. Part VI addresses the EPA's multiple efforts over time to define the meaning of "stationary source." Part VII—the concluding portion of the opinion—considers and rejects the NRDC's specific arguments in opposition to the bubble definition, based on statutory language, legislative history, and policy. One can almost picture Stevens at his desk, patiently pouring through different piles of relevant material, and dictating his conclusions after he completed his review of each pile.

Finally, recall Justice Blackmun's notes about what Justice Stevens said at conference. Stevens is reported as saying he was "not at rest." For a careful and diligent judge like Stevens, the logical thing to do when not at rest would be to unravel the pieces of the puzzle, bit by bit, until the answer became clear. This surmise is reinforced by two memos written by Stevens to Justice Brennan after the conference vote but before Stevens circulated his opinion. The first, dated March 6, 1984, was in response to a memo Brennan had written to Stevens earlier that day. Brennan informed Stevens that he had been assigned to write a dissent in the case, and he asked if Stevens could possibly see his way to resolving the case "in a manner more satisfying than either of the extreme positions offered by the parties." Stevens wrote back saying, "At this point I really am not far enough into the case to give you a definitive answer, but I certainly will do my best to prepare an opinion that will achieve as broad a consensus as possible." The second memo, dated May 23, 1984 reads:

> At long last I have found the time to get back into these cases and to begin work on a draft opinion. Since you wrote to me on March 6, in the hope that you might be able to escape the chore of writing a dissenting opinion if I could see my way clear to accepting your approach to the case, I thought I should let you know that I am now quite firmly persuaded that the Government is correct in arguing that EPA's interpretation of the term "source" is permissible.[75]

These memos confirm that Stevens went from being "not at rest" to being fully convinced that the government was correct, and that this transformation was achieved by working his way through the process of drafting an opinion between March and May. The public evidence of his progress is reflected in Parts III–VII of the opinion, which therefore had to be drafted first.

If this conjecture is correct, why then would Justice Stevens, after drafting the longest portion of the opinion, turn back and draft the short introductory passages that make up Part II? The best explanation for this may be the precarious situation in which Stevens found himself. Recall that only six Justices were still in the case, two of whom had voted to affirm, and the other three (besides himself) had all indicated varying degrees of uncertainty about the right outcome. Stevens had convinced himself about the right outcome, but the written evidence of the steps leading to this confidence took up some twenty pages in the opinion, and required attending to a highly technical set of statutory provisions, a convoluted administrative history, and an esoteric policy debate. What was needed was some *arresting* language that would grab the readers' attention and suggest that the outcome was compelled by first principles.

Reduced to their essence, the first two paragraphs are a strong invocation, albeit expressed in a novel way, of the distinction between law and policy. Courts should concern themselves only with enforcing the law; policy is for politically accountable institutions like legislatures and agencies. The sharp distinction between law and policy resonates strongly with lawyers and judges. Justice Stevens, by raising the distinction early in the opinion (and concluding with it again at the end), was attempting to prime the reader to accept his ultimate conclusion—that the definition of stationary source was a policy question, not a legal one, and hence one in which the view of the administrative agency should be accepted.

In short, Justice Stevens turned to drafting what became Part II in an effort to condense what he had decided following a conventional process of reasoning into a set of precepts sufficiently unconventional to cause readers to sit up and take note. In his own mind, Stevens undoubtedly saw no contradiction between Part II and the balance of the opinion. But by reducing the complexity of his effort to a rule-like framework, and invoking a problematic equation of gaps and implicit delegations to interpret, Stevens inadvertently produced language that could be used by later courts to create something very different—something with which Stevens, for one, was deeply uncomfortable.

In Sum

Justice Stevens's opinion for the unanimous but short-handed Court in *Chevron* was really two opinions in one. The main body of the opinion, which was likely written first, is a careful unraveling of the issue presented by the case, applying the interpretive conventions that prevailed in 1984. This explains why none of the other Justices in the case questioned any aspect of his draft opinion, and why they all rapidly joined it. If we attend closely to this part of the opinion, we can see that it is not inconsistent with the four values of judicial review of agency legal interpretations, as outlined in Chapter 1. Indeed, this part of the opinion can stand as a paradigmatic instantiation of those values.

The introductory part of the opinion's analysis, set forth in Part II, contains some unorthodox expressions characterizing the task of a reviewing court in considering an agency interpretation. It is likely that Justice Stevens drafted this part of the opinion after completing the main body. Having concluded that Congress had expressed no intent about whether "stationary source" means apparatus or plant, he realized that the dispute was about regulatory policy, not law. So he drafted the paragraphs in Part II in an effort to condition the reader to regard the case as a clash about policy that should have been resolved by the agency, not by a court. He also realized that the issue was technical and the body of his opinion was long and somewhat labored. So he made the short summary of the standard of review in Part II a bit snazzy, in an effort to grab the readers' attention. In his own mind, Part II was not intended to change the law of judicial review. If that had been his design, he surely would have followed the precepts set forth in Part II in the balance of the opinion. He did not do this. But that is not the way this part of the opinion would be read by others.

4

The Rise of the *Chevron* Doctrine

W E HAVE SEEN THAT a close reading of the *Chevron* opinion suggests that the two paragraphs in Part II, which were destined to be enshrined as "the *Chevron* doctrine," were not intended to displace the approach to agency interpretations of questions of law as it had developed up to 1984. What then explains the transformation of the *Chevron* decision, from just another case applying principles of administrative law, into "the *Chevron* doctrine"— a transformative precedent that would become the flashpoint of intense controversy?

An Inauspicious Beginning

The initial reception of *Chevron* in the Supreme Court gave every impression that the decision was regarded as a normal precedent, no different from most other cases resolved by the Court. In the year following the release of the decision, the Court decided nineteen cases—an unusually high number—presenting some kind of question about whether the Court should give weight to an agency interpretation of a statute. *Chevron* made an appearance in only one of these cases; otherwise it was ignored.[1] In the only decision to cite *Chevron* that year, *Chemical Manufacturers Association v. Natural Resources Defense Council*,[2] Justice White invoked *Chevron* for the proposition that the view of the agency charged with administering a statute "is entitled to considerable deference," unless, "[o]f course," he added, "Congress has clearly expressed an intent contrary to that of the agency," in which case the Court's duty "is to enforce the will of Congress."[3] This borrowed the notion from *Chevron* that Congress must have a "clear intent" to preclude giving def-

erence to the administering agency. But there was no mention of other pro-
vocative elements of Justice Stevens's opinion in *Chevron,* such as the two-
step approach, the inquiry into whether Congress had addressed the "precise
question" at issue, the idea of an implicit delegation of interpretive authority,
or the superior accountability of the agency based on presidential oversight.
The dissenting opinion of Justice Marshall, which Justice Stevens joined, had
no quarrel with the majority's statement of the standard of review, but argued that the statute contained limiting language the agency had ignored.[4]

Chevron gradually began to appear with more frequency in succeeding
terms. But it took more than six years before it was referenced in over half of
the cases in any given term presenting an issue about accepting or rejecting
an agency interpretation of its statute.[5] Most citations to the decision in the
early years were to uncontroversial propositions, perhaps most commonly
that reviewing courts "must give effect to the unambiguously expressed intent of Congress."[6] And even when it was cited in support of upholding an
agency interpretation, the supporting reasons often seemed to reflect the traditional pre-*Chevron* factors rather than the two-step approach or the theory
of implicit delegation of interpretive authority found in Part II of the *Chevron*
opinion. For example, in *Commodity Futures Trading Commission v. Schor,*[7]
the Court accepted the Commission's interpretation that it had authority to
entertain common-law counterclaims filed by commodity traders against
their clients. The Court concluded that this interpretation was entitled to
"considerable weight," noting that it was a "long-held position" of the Commission, that it had been adopted contemporaneously with the statute, that
it was "eminently reasonable," and that it was "well within the scope of its
delegated authority," citing in support of these factors—*Chevron.* Nor is there
any reason to believe, in these early years, that invocation of *Chevron,* in the
small number of cases when it was invoked, made any difference in whether
the Court accepted or rejected the agency interpretation.[8]

Not until 1986—some two years after the *Chevron* decision was handed
down—did the Court in any case actually apply the two-step framework
based on Part II of the *Chevron* opinion as a standard of review. *Young v.
Community Nutrition Institute*[9] presented what was essentially a procedural
question—whether the Food and Drug Administration was required in all
cases to adopt regulations setting "tolerance levels" for potentially harmful
substances added to foodstuffs, or whether the agency could establish more

informal "action levels" in particular circumstances indicating what level would not trigger an enforcement action. Reversing a D.C. Circuit decision holding that tolerance levels were required in all cases, the Court upheld the FDA practice.[10] The case was argued at the tail end of the term, and both the majority and dissenting opinions were relatively brief. Writing for the majority, Justice O'Connor quoted the two-step paragraph from *Chevron* as the applicable standard of review.[11] She concluded that the relevant sentence in the Food and Drug Act was ambiguous as to whether tolerance levels were mandatory in all cases, and that the FDA's interpretation that it could use action levels in addition to tolerance levels was reasonable. For good measure, she noted that the FDA's interpretation in this respect was "longstanding."[12] The sole dissent was authored by none other than Justice Stevens, who found the agency's practice inconsistent with the statutory language.

Community Nutrition was not regarded as an especially noteworthy decision, and there was only a modest movement in the Supreme Court toward applying the two-step approach in reviewing agency statutory interpretations in the ensuing years. Not until 1990 did the two-step approach appear in more than half of Supreme Court cases presenting a claim for deference to an administrative interpretation.[13] The weight given to agency interpretations remained as eclectic as it had been in the pre-*Chevron* era.

The Court's relative indifference to *Chevron*'s two-step approach in the years following the decision is reinforced by looking more closely at the behavior of Justice Stevens. Surely, if some significant change in the relevant standard of review was intended by *Chevron*, one would expect this to be reflected in the decisions of its author. Yet there is no evidence that Justice Stevens regarded *Chevron* as setting down a new standard of review that would point toward greater acceptance of agency interpretations. To the contrary, as revealed by his dissenting votes in *Chemical Manufacturers* and *Community Nutrition*, he was quite willing to reject particular agency interpretations of their own statute. And both before and after *Chevron* was decided, Justice Stevens authored opinions that analyzed agency interpretations using the traditional factors approach that pre-dated *Chevron* rather than the two-step framework.[14]

The conclusion is inescapable that the Supreme Court, at least in the initial years after *Chevron* was decided, did not view the decision as having established some novel approach to reviewing administrative legal determinations. Based on its initial trajectory as a precedent in the Supreme Court, *Chevron* seemed destined to obscurity.

The D.C. Circuit

The response to *Chevron* was very different in the courts of appeals—or, more accurately, in the D.C. Circuit, the lower court that hears a disproportionate number of challenges to agency decisions. The role of the D.C. Circuit in creating "the *Chevron* doctrine" has been advanced by others,[15] and is broadly consistent with much of the data about *Chevron*'s rise from obscurity.

According to Gary Lawson, the most prominent proponent of D.C. Circuit origins, the pivotal decision was *General Motors Corp. v. Ruckelshaus*.[16] At issue was a provision of the Clean Air Act authorizing the EPA to order the recall of motor vehicles that fail to comply with EPA-established tailpipe emissions standards. The statute said the EPA could require the recall of any nonconforming vehicles "in actual use throughout their useful life (as determined under section 7521(d) of this title)."[17] Section 7521(d), in turn, defined "useful life," for purposes of setting emissions standards, as five years or 50,000 miles. Evidently it was the practice, under early recall orders, for auto companies voluntarily to extend the recall to all cars of an affected model run, without regard to whether individual cars were beyond their statutory "useful life."[18] But when the EPA ordered a recall of certain 1975 Cadillacs, General Motors balked, and the company argued that five years or 50,000 miles was the outer limit of the EPA's recall authority. The EPA responded by issuing an interpretive rule that construed the Act to mean that a recall could be ordered for any vehicle still in actual use, without regard to its age or mileage.

When General Motors challenged the EPA's interpretation in the D.C. Circuit, a divided three-judge panel agreed with the auto company's position, largely on the ground that it was compelled by the plain meaning of the statute.[19] But the full court ordered that the matter be reconsidered by all active judges in the circuit—that is, by en banc review. In a decision released in September 1984, barely three months after *Chevron* was decided, the en banc court reversed the panel and upheld the EPA's interpretation.[20] Writing for the majority, Judge Patricia Wald wrote that "[t]he Supreme Court has recently outlined our proper task in reviewing an administrative construction of a statute that the agency administers."[21] She proceeded to provide a close paraphrase of the two-step standard of review set forth in Part II of the opinion in *Chevron,* effectively interpreting it as a new standard of review for questions of statutory interpretation.[22] Concluding that the statute was sufficiently ambiguous to trigger deference under the two-step approach, Judge Wald upheld the EPA's view about its recall authority as reasonable. Underscoring that this was a change in the relevant law, the dissenting judges pointed out that the EPA interpretation did not stack up well under the factors traditionally considered in assessing agency interpretations. The interpretation was neither contemporary nor longstanding, nor did it implicate agency expertise; to the contrary, it involved "an interpretation of the law based on the language, legislative history and policy of the Clean Air Act" as to which "no factual data need be analyzed or commented on."[23]

The interpretation of *Chevron* in the *General Motors* case was immediately reinforced in another decision authored by Judge Wald, *Rettig v. Pension Benefit Guaranty Corp.*[24] Issued less than a week after *General Motors, Rettig* provided an even more elaborate summary of the two-step idea, again treating it as having established a new standard of review for assessing agency interpretations of law.[25] *General Motors* and *Rettig,* according to Lawson, are "the source of the *Chevron* doctrine"—that is, the source of the approach to agency interpretations that treats the paragraphs of Part II of *Chevron* as establishing a new and general standard of review.[26]

In hindsight, it is startling to think of Judge Wald as the "true author" of the *Chevron* doctrine. Appointed to the bench by President Carter, she was generally regarded as a thoughtful liberal, sympathetic to expansive consumer protection and environmental regulation, and skeptical of jurisprudential innovations associated with conservative jurists like then-judge Scalia. The *Chevron* doctrine, once it got going, was likewise regarded for some time as a "conservative" doctrine, given its association with the Reagan Administration's deregulation efforts and strenuous advocacy of the doctrine by Justice Scalia.[27]

The explanation may be that Judge Wald, in writing for the court in the *General Motors* case, found herself in a dilemma somewhat analogous to that of Justice Stevens in *Chevron.* The panel opinion, which had invalidated the EPA interpretation of its recall authority, seemed to be supported by the most plausible reading of the statute. Moreover, the panel opinion was written by Judge Bazelon, an old-line liberal who had been joined by another seasoned judge of more conservative views. In order to reverse the panel decision, and uphold the EPA's interpretation, Judge Wald needed some device that would prevent a coalition of liberal and conservative judges from rallying behind the panel decision. The two-step framework, which had recently appeared in Part II of *Chevron* and which carried the imprimatur of the Supreme Court, could be portrayed as a directive to jettison the traditional deference doctrine and allow the court to endorse what seemed like a sensible, if legally dubious, interpretation by the EPA. Judge Wald's opinion in *Rettig,* which circulated at almost the same time, softened the possible implication that courts would now routinely defer to agency interpretations. This was because Judge Wald, after endorsing the two-step approach in *Rettig,* went on to hold that the agency interpretation in that case (by the Pension Benefit Guarantee Corporation) was unreasonable.[28]

In short, the two-step approach was seized upon by Judge Wald as a device to justify a sensible, if legally questionable, EPA interpretation in *General Motors,* but was interpreted in *Rettig* as preserving a significant degree of discretion for courts to overturn decisions regarded as less sensible. If this is indeed where the seeds of "the *Chevron* doctrine" were planted, it suggests that a large part of its appeal was that it *enhanced* the discretion of judges to accept or reject particular agency interpretations based on the nebulous requirements of "clarity" and "reasonableness"—free from the encrustations of the traditional doctrine.

Whatever Judge Wald's objectives in September 1984, the two-step approach did not immediately sweep the D.C. Circuit, let alone other courts of appeals. Yet to borrow a metaphor from Lawson, the seeds began to germinate.[29] The D.C. Circuit increasingly turned to the two-step framework, even though many circuit judges seemed oblivious to the change at first, and many decisions were rendered—including one by Judge Wald—that seemed to revert to the pre-*Chevron* approach.[30] Rather than attempt to follow the ups and downs of *Chevron* in the D.C. Circuit in detail, we can trace the "germination" of the *Chevron* doctrine in broad outline by attending to citations to the decision in the D.C. Circuit in the years immediately following its debut.[31]

The D.C. Circuit handed down 23 decisions citing to *Chevron* in the first year after the decision was announced. This grew to 40 in the second year,

and 64 in the third year after the decision was announced.[32] This is a dispro-
portionately large percentage of *Chevron* citations relative to other courts of
appeals.[33] Given the increasing rates of citation, it is unsurprising that by the
end of the second year, the two-step approach was being referred to as established doctrine in the Circuit. One finds statements from this period describing *Chevron* as the "now familiar framework," the "familiar two-step
framework," the "familiar dictates," or the standard that applies "as always"
in reviewing agency interpretations.[34]

Interestingly, there is no evidence during these early years that *Chevron*
was associated with partisan affiliation.[35] The judge who cited *Chevron* most
frequently during these years was Judge Wald, who first invoked the *Chevron*
doctrine in the en banc decision in *General Motors*. She cited *Chevron* in 13
opinions in the first two years, easily outdistancing the top Republican appointee, Judge Kenneth Starr, who cited the case in 8 opinions. Indeed, Democratic appointees out-cited *Chevron* relative to Republican appointees 38 to
21 in the first two years, and out-cited Republicans 62 to 53 over all three
years.[36]

There are some interesting variations in citation patterns among the judges
in these early years, but they appear to have more to do with age and open-
ness to legal change than with politics. Thus, Judge Spottswood Robinson,
the most senior Democratic appointee, made relatively little use of *Chevron*,
citing it only once the first two years. He tended to stick to the traditional
factors, and even after *Chevron* became established he referred to it mostly
in string citations. Similarly, Judge Mikva never showed much affinity for
Chevron. Judges Wald and Harry Edwards, in contrast, who were younger
and arguably more open to change, made greater use of *Chevron*. On the Republican side, Judge Starr, who was the youngest judge on the circuit, was
the most frequent user of *Chevron*. In contrast, Judge Robert Bork, who was
more senior, made little reference to *Chevron* until the third year after it came
down (he cited it in only two opinions the first two years). Interestingly, Judge
Antonin Scalia, who was to become identified as *Chevron*'s champion after
he was named to the Supreme Court, cited *Chevron* in only three opinions
during the four years he sat on the D.C. Circuit.[37]

In the third year of *Chevron*'s existence, the picture in the circuit began to
change slightly, although this may be due to the fact that the Republican appointees, with their increasing numbers, were getting more of the opinion-
writing assignments in major regulatory decisions. Republican appointees

in 1986–87 used *Chevron* slightly more than Democratic appointees (32 to 25 citations in majority opinions). Judge Starr became the leading user of *Chevron* that year (11 citations), slightly eclipsing Judge Wald (9 citations). Judge Bork discovered *Chevron* (8 citations), as did Judge Laurence Silberman (6 citations). So there is some evidence that *Chevron* was becoming more of a Republican-favored doctrine, but it is at most suggestive on this point.[38]

It is important to add that there is little evidence, from these first years, that *Chevron* caused the judges of the D.C. Circuit to accept more agency interpretations. In terms of cases citing *Chevron* in which there was a clear disposition affirming or reversing the agency, affirmances barely outnumbered reversals (64 to 52). If we look only at those cases that expressly frame the inquiry in terms of *Chevron*'s two-step formula, the ratio of affirmances to reversals improves slightly (30 to 20).[39] Of course, all this could be due to selection effects: judges are more likely to invoke a presumably deference-promoting framework when they have decided to affirm (and need to justify this result) than when they have decided to reverse. Still, the D.C. Circuit judges took virtually no time at all to learn how to reverse agency interpretations at step 1 or step 2 of the *Chevron* framework.[40] As noted in the Introduction, there is scant evidence that *Chevron* has increased the rate at which judges accept agency interpretations.

Whatever its impact on agency win rates in the D.C. Circuit, there is telling evidence that the two-step doctrine was regarded by the judges of that court as a significant jurisprudential development. No less than four of the active judges on the D.C. Circuit in those years took to the law reviews to expound, positively or negatively, on the significance of the *Chevron* doctrine.[41] The judges saw that something important was happening, and they sought to comprehend it. Meanwhile, the Supreme Court, with the exception of the little-noticed decision in *Community Nutrition*, behaved as if nothing had changed at all.

Cardozo-Fonseca

Antonin Scalia's short stint on the D.C. Circuit came to an end in the summer of 1986, when he was nominated by President Reagan and unanimously confirmed by the Senate as an Associate Justice of the Supreme Court. In his first year on the Court, Justice Scalia wasted no time in loudly proclaiming

his support for the D.C. Circuit's "*Chevron* doctrine." His intervention occurred in a decision called *Immigration and Naturalization Service v. Cardozo-
Fonseca,* which was argued the first week Scalia sat on the high court bench.[42]

Cardozo-Fonseca* presented a question of statutory interpretation under the
immigration laws. One section of the relevant act gave the Attorney General
discretion to grant asylum to aliens based on a "well-founded fear of persecution" if they were returned to their country of origin. Another section required the Attorney General to withhold deportation of aliens if they could
show it was "more likely than not" that they would be persecuted if returned
to their country of origin. The government argued that, for practical purposes, the two provisions required an identical showing by the alien. Justice
Stevens, writing for the majority, concluded that the plain language of the
statute set forth different standards: asylum contained a subjective element
("fear") but did not require a showing that persecution was more likely than
not; withholding of deportation was objective and required evidence of probability. He reinforced the analysis of the statutory language with a lengthy
discussion of the legislative history. Then, at the end of the opinion, he turned
to the government's argument that its interpretation was entitled to "substantial deference." He observed in a footnote that the government, in support of
this claim, placed "heavy reliance on the principle of deference as described
in *Chevron.*"[43]

What followed was Justice Stevens's understanding of why deference to the
government's interpretation was not required. Under the two-step framework, the straightforward answer would be that the statute had a "clear"
meaning, and so the Court should stop at step 1. But that is not what Stevens
wrote.

Justice Stevens began by noting that the question whether Congress intended the two standards to be identical "is a pure question of statutory
construction for the courts to decide."[44] Standing alone, this might be a reference to step 1, a reading reinforced by his immediately quoting from the
discussion of step 1 in *Chevron.* But he continued:

> The narrow legal question whether the two standards are the same is,
> of course, quite different from the question of interpretation that arises
> in each case in which the agency is required to apply either or both stan-
> dards to a particular set of facts. There is obviously some ambiguity

in a term like "well-founded fear" which can only be given concrete meaning through a process of case-by-case adjudication. . . . But our task today is much narrower, and is well within the province of the Judiciary. We do not attempt to set forth a detailed description of how the "well-founded fear" test should be applied. Instead, we merely hold that the Immigration Judge and the BIA [Bureau of Immigration Affairs] were incorrect in holding that the two standards are identical.[45]

This passage was an obvious invocation of the doctrine of *NLRB v. Hearst Publications, Inc.,*[46] considered in Chapter 2. *Hearst* is commonly interpreted as having adopted a distinction between pure questions of law and questions of law application. By drawing the same distinction, Stevens seemed to be saying that *Chevron* was essentially an updated version of *Hearst.* That Stevens would seek to cabin his *Chevron* opinion in this manner confirms that he had no design to change the pre-*Chevron* body of factors used by courts in reviewing agency interpretations of questions of law.

Justice Scalia wrote an opinion concurring in the judgment. He agreed that the "plain meaning" of the statute required that the two standards be different. He objected to Justice Stevens's lengthy discussion of legislative history, in one of the first of his many separate opinions in which he condemned the practice of invoking legislative history to interpret the meaning of a statute. He then went on to say he was "far more troubled" by the Court's "superfluous discussion" of *Chevron,* which he asserted contained "erroneous" views and "badly misinterprets" the decision. He upbraided Stevens for engaging in an "unjustifiable" discussion of "an extremely important and frequently cited opinion, not only in this Court but in the Courts of Appeals"—thus putting his fellow Justices on notice that *Chevron* had taken on something of a life of its own in the lower courts.[47]

As to why Justice Stevens's interpretation of *Chevron* was wrong, Justice Scalia first objected to what he perceived to be the suggestion that courts should enforce their interpretation of a statute using "traditional tools of statutory interpretation," without regard to whether they found the meaning "clear" or "unambiguous." This, he said, "would make deference a doctrine of desperation, authorizing courts to defer only if they would otherwise be unable to construe the enactment at issue. This is not an interpretation but an evisceration of *Chevron.*"[48] He also objected to what he perceived to be the equation of *Chevron* with the distinction between pure questions of law and questions of law application. This, he said, was contradicted by *Chevron* itself, because it deferred to the EPA's "abstract interpretation of the phrase 'stationary source'"—a pure question of law.[49]

Finally, the junior Justice chastised Justice Stevens for his "eagerness to re-fashion important principles of administrative law in a case in which such questions are completely unnecessary to the decision and have not been fully briefed by the parties."[50] This was highly ironic, given that the *Chevron* doc-trine, the "important principle of administrative law" that Justice Scalia sought to preserve, was itself less than three years old and had been "estab-lished" (if at all) in a decision in which the possibility of changing the ap-proach to reviewing agency interpretations of law had not been briefed by the parties.

The cause of Justice Scalia's sharp concern is not entirely clear. The law re-view article he would write in 1989 approved of *Chevron* for adopting a "rule that is easier to follow and thus easier to predict."[51] He also wrote that it "more accurately reflects the reality of government," which requires "needed flexi-bility, and appropriate political participation, in the administrative process."[52] Thus, he pronounced that "*Chevron* is unquestionably better than what pre-ceded it."[53] These comments would account for his general support for the *Chevron* doctrine, but they hardly explain the intensity of his advocacy for it when he first joined the Court. Perhaps Scalia was genuinely upset that Jus-tice Stevens's discussion pulled the rug out from under the D.C. Circuit's interpretation of *Chevron,* which had already become settled law in the cir-cuit. Evidently it did not occur to him that the D.C. Circuit's interpretation might have been wrong.

Whatever the source of his concerns, Justice Scalia's opinion adopted a rather brash tone for a newly minted Associate Justice disagreeing with a more senior Justice's interpretation of his own opinion. No other Justice joined Scalia's concurrence, perhaps because of its dismissive attitude toward Justice Stevens's opinion. Perhaps for the same reason, Stevens made no re-sponse to Scalia's specific accusations, other than to reproduce the entirety of Part II of *Chevron* in a footnote.[54] However understandable, Stevens's si-lence may have had fateful consequences for the future development of the *Chevron* doctrine.

Cardozo-Fonseca, although far from the last word from the Supreme Court on the meaning of *Chevron,* at least provides some insight into the origins of the *Chevron* doctrine. Justice Stevens made clear that he regarded his *Chevron* opinion as essentially a restatement of existing law. This remained his position for all his remaining years on the Court.[55] Justice Scalia, for his part, made clear that he regarded *Chevron* as marking a fundamental transformation in the law. Scalia also effectively announced that he intended to fight for adoption of this view by the Court. Stevens, by failing to respond to Scalia's specific accusations, arguably signaled that he did not intend to fight for his view of the decision. Although four other Justices joined Stevens in *Cardozo-Fonseca,* his characterization of *Chevron* as a restatement of *Hearst* could plausibly be characterized as dictum. The dispositive holding was that the BIA's views were not entitled to deference, which would follow from either Stevens's or Scalia's position.

Whatever his motivation, Justice Scalia was clearly eager for a showdown on the significance of *Chevron.* He decided that just such an opportunity had arrived in a case argued early in the next term, *National Labor Relations Board v. United Food & Commercial Workers Union.*[56] The case involved a technical issue under the labor laws, specifically, whether a decision by the General Counsel of the NLRB to settle a case over the objection of the complaining party was subject to judicial review. In a unanimous decision authored by Justice Brennan, the Court held that such "prosecutorial" settlements are not reviewable. The bulk of the opinion was devoted to dissecting statutory detail and legislative history. At one point, however, Brennan inserted a paragraph about the relevant standard of review for an agency interpretation of law. The paragraph was obviously designed to say nothing definitive about the disagreement between Justice Stevens and Justice Scalia in *Cardozo-Fonseca.* The relevant standard was said to be the one prescribed in *Cardozo-Fonseca,* but Justice Brennan also quoted *Chevron* to the effect that if the statute is silent or ambiguous, the question is whether the agency interpretation is permissible. For good measure, he also referenced prior decisions reviewing NLRB decisions that emphasized the importance of the contemporary and longstanding canons.[57]

Justice Scalia seized on the inclusion of the inconclusive paragraph as an opportunity to declare victory in the dispute over the meaning of *Chevron.*

In a concurring opinion, he crowed: "I join the Court's opinion, and write separately only to note that our decision demonstrates the continuing and unchanged vitality of the test for judicial review of agency determinations of law set forth in *Chevron*."[58] In support of this claim, he argued that the question presented had to be classified as a pure question of law, and the Court's quotations from *Chevron* meant that the *Chevron* standard necessarily applies to pure questions of law, not just matters of law application. Thus, he claimed, the "dicta" in *Cardozo-Fonseca* had been repudiated by Justice Brennan's opinion,[59] ignoring Brennan's statements that the standard of review was the one "prescribed in *INS v. Cardozo-Fonseca*" and that "[o]n a pure question of statutory construction, our first job is to try to determine congressional intent, using 'traditional tools of statutory construction.'"[60]

United Food Workers was a poor choice for engaging in a decisive battle over the significance of *Chevron*. Justice Brenan's unanimous opinion, other than the ambiguous paragraph about the standard of review, was basically an exercise in de novo review. Little or nothing was made of the NLRB's position on the question to be decided. That question—whether the General Counsel's decision to settle was subject to judicial review—concerned the scope of judicial authority, and thus under later clarifying decisions was a matter for judicial determination without regard to the agency's opinion on the matter.[61] Lastly, there were only eight active Justices on the Court, because Justice Powell had resigned over the summer, and his designated successor, Robert Bork, had gone down to defeat in the Senate shortly before *United Food Workers* was decided. Under the circumstances, it is unclear why three Justices—Chief Justice Rehnquist and Justices White and O'Connor—chose to join the Scalia concurrence. Perhaps it was a show of solidarity in the wake of the Senate's rough handling of Scalia's former colleague on the D.C. Circuit. In any event, Brennan ignored the Scalia concurrence. And Justice Stevens joined Brennan's opinion without comment.

As a matter of precedent, *United Food Workers* settled nothing about *Chevron*. The only thing one could perhaps say was that the Court was evenly split (4–4) on the correct metric for considering agency interpretations of law—*Cardozo-Fonseca* or the *Chevron* doctrine. Nevertheless, for some inexplicable reason, a small boomlet in the lower courts that had broken out in favor of *Cardozo-Fonseca* quickly ended. As Lawson has written: "Through a process that we can observe but do not purport to explain, the 4-4 split in

United Food was almost universally taken by the lower courts as a vindication of Justice Scalia's position in his concurrence, that *Chevron* would extend deference to agency determinations involving pure legal questions."[62] Perhaps the critical factor was Justice Stevens's reluctance to engage Scalia in a battle of concurring opinions. As the author of *Chevron,* his views would carry obvious weight. But he preferred to avoid a personal clash over the issue. Stevens never changed his view that *Chevron* did not apply to pure questions of law. As late as 2009 he reiterated his adherence to the views set forth in *Cardozo-Fonseca.*[63] But Stevens's diffidence was no match for the aggressive advocacy of Scalia.

The Court never resolved the question broached in *Cardozo-Fonseca* and *United Food Workers.* Over time, *Cardozo-Fonseca* faded from view and the *Chevron* doctrine surged to the fore. Other questions about the rationale and scope of the *Chevron* doctrine would draw the Court's attention. But the idea that courts should always resolve pure questions of law de novo, by some unstated consensus, quietly disappeared.

The Gradual Triumph of the *Chevron* Doctrine

What followed the dust-up in *Cardozo-Fonseca* and Justice Scalia's self-proclaimed victory in *United Food Workers* was a strange process in which the two-step standard of review set forth in Part II of the *Chevron* decision gradually spread, without being unequivocally endorsed by a majority opinion of the Supreme Court as the required approach to reviewing agency interpretations of law. It became an accepted part of the legal lore of court–agency relations, and grew in dominance over time, but it never succeeded in completely displacing earlier notions about how to calibrate the appropriate response to agency interpretations of law. One could say the *Chevron* doctrine, at least at this stage in its career, had become yet another canon of interpretation used by courts in resolving disputed questions of law.[64] Like other canons, it came in handy when circumstances warranted, but its use was optional.

We see evidence of the *Chevron* doctrine's growing acceptance in decisions authored by different Justices. By 1992 most of the Justices had authored at least one decision that employed the two-step standard as a framing device for reviewing an agency interpretation. Justice Kennedy, soon after he joined the Court, used the two-step standard in 1988.[65] Similarly, one can find decisions by Justice O'Connor (1986), Justice Marshall (1989), Justice Blackmun (1990), Justice Scalia (1990) and Chief Justice Rehnquist (1991) employing the two-step device.[66] By 1992 Justice White could write, as a preface to invoking the two-step standard, "Our principles for evaluating agency interpretations of congressional statutes are by now well settled."[67]

Two holdouts were Justices Brennan and Stevens. After the unfortunate experience with his "compromise" paragraph in *United Food Workers,* Brennan never used the two-step framework as a way of resolving a challenge to an agency interpretation. Indeed, we find him in one decision quoting the proposition that no deference is owed to an agency on a "pure question of statutory construction."[68] Brennan would soon retire; Stevens remained on the Court for many more years. Stevens would not infrequently refer to the *Chevron* decision, but usually to say it was inapplicable.[69] On one occasion he paraphrased the two-step approach, but said it supported giving "some degree of deference to the Secretary's reasonable interpretation."[70] That, of course, was not what the critical paragraph in *Chevron* said; it said the agency interpretation must be *accepted* if the statute is unclear and the agency interpretation is reasonable.

As a majority of the Justices wrote at least one opinion for the Court using the *Chevron* doctrine as a device for reviewing an agency interpretation, lower-court judges became increasingly confident that it was appropriate to do so. We have already seen how the D.C. Circuit quickly embraced the two-step idea shortly after *Chevron* was decided. After a brief pause in the wake of the *Cardozo-Fonseca* episode, reliance on the *Chevron* two-step in that court resumed its steady march upward. Although other circuits confront agency interpretations less often than the D.C. Circuit, the use of the *Chevron* doctrine to tackle such issues eventually diffused throughout the other circuits as well.[71]

How did the *Chevron* doctrine, which was thought to be about the permissibility of the bubble concept when it was decided in 1984, come to be regarded as announcing a new relationship between courts and agencies? The primary explanation has to be the embrace of the doctrine in the lower courts, particularly the D.C. Circuit. Lower-court judges were drawn to the *Chevron* doctrine because it is refreshingly simple in contrast to the complex matrix of factors that prevailed in the pre-*Chevron* era.[72] Lower-court judges have heavy caseloads, and will often find it difficult to untangle complex regula-tory statutes and agency decisions implementing them. If a lower-court judge sees nothing particularly disturbing about an agency action, and the chal-lenge can be characterized as raising a question of statutory interpretation, the *Chevron* doctrine offers a quick exit ramp. As long as the statute can be characterized as either clearly supporting the agency, or as ambiguous but being resolved by the agency in a reasonable way—case closed. If the chal-lenger can convince the judge that something is amiss, the statute can be in-terpreted as either clearly foreclosing the agency position, or (more rarely) the agency interpretation can be condemned as unreasonable. Either way, the case can be resolved with minimal research, and without any need to weigh multiple factors as had to be done under the pre-*Chevron* regime.

The attraction of simplicity does not apply, at least not to the same degree, at the level of the Supreme Court. The Justices now hear argument in only about seventy-five cases a year, and have almost complete discretion about what cases they will decide. Each Justice is authorized to hire four law clerks, who prepare research memos and preliminary drafts of opinions. And the Court is collectively backstopped by a first-rate law library and the resources of the Library of Congress. Getting to the bottom of the occasional regulatory case is not an insuperable burden for the Supreme Court.

If the lower courts had come up with the *Chevron* doctrine on their own, one can easily imagine the Supreme Court rejecting this as an excessively re-ductive approach to the problem of monitoring agency interpretations of law. But Judge Wald and her compatriots on the D.C. Circuit did not come up with the *Chevron* doctrine on their own. They simply adopted the lan-guage found in two paragraphs from a recent decision by a unanimous Su-preme Court. It would be difficult, to say the least, for the Court to say: "But wait, don't take literally what we said in those paragraphs! Read the whole opinion." The difficulty was compounded when a majority of Justices, in in-dividual decisions in the late 1980s and early 1990s, adopted the *Chevron* doctrine in a handful of their own opinions. If the Justices occasionally used the *Chevron* doctrine, what could be wrong with lower-court judges using the doctrine?

No doubt there were other contributing factors at work that also help ex-plain the emergence of the *Chevron* doctrine. The advocacy of the executive branch probably played a role. The *Chevron* doctrine was regarded as a godsend by executive branch lawyers charged with writing briefs defending agency interpretations of law. Not only did the two-step standard provide an effective organizing principle for busy brief-writers, the opinion seemed to say that deference was the default rule in any case where Congress has not spoken to the precise issue in controversy. Because this describes (or can be made to seem to describe) virtually every case, *Chevron* seemed to say that the government should nearly always win. *Chevron* may have meant little to the Justices when it was decided, and it may have taken time for courts other than the D.C. Circuit to accept it as orthodoxy. But it was quickly adopted as a kind of mantra by lawyers in the Justice Department, who pushed relentlessly to capitalize on the perceived advantages the decision presented.[73]

It turns out the Justice Department lawyers were deluded. Accurately considered, the *Chevron* doctrine is a decisional framework that reduces to two nebulous standards: clarity and reasonableness. This (over)simplifies the relevant values at stake, but it does not necessarily translate into more government victories. What it translates into is reduced decisional costs for judges and more judicial discretion. This should have been increasingly evident to government lawyers over time, but it took some time for the reality to sink in.

Enthusiasm for the *Chevron* doctrine among government lawyers is one thing; acceptance by courts is another. But here it is plausible to suppose that the Justice Department's role as the ultimate institutional litigant is relevant. The Department urged that the two-step framework should serve as the relevant standard of review at nearly every turn, and the Department appeared in court much more frequently in agency-review cases than any other litigant. By highlighting the *Chevron* doctrine in nearly every brief they filed involving a challenge to an agency legal interpretation, the government no doubt contributed to the sense that the doctrine was the legitimate framework for assessing such agency interpretations.[74]

A third factor is the role of Justice Scalia. It is unlikely that his sharp remarks in *Cardozo-Fonseca* and *United Food Workers* persuaded any of his fellow Justices that his interpretation of *Chevron* was correct. These short concurring opinions were largely polemical exercises, not fully reasoned arguments in support of the *Chevron* doctrine. Nor is it likely that the law review article on *Chevron* that he published in 1989 overcame any doubters—assuming they read it. His influence at this time was mostly negative. The message of the concurring opinions was that any Justice who ventured forth with a conception of the appropriate judicial role other than the *Chevron* doctrine would be subjected to a sharp rebuke by Justice Scalia. Justice Souter would incur such treatment when he sought to develop a sounder conceptual foundation for the *Chevron* doctrine in 2001, and Justice Thomas would incur such a treatment when he extended the logical implications of the doctrine in a way Scalia did not like in 2005.[75] In the early 1990s, no Justice was sufficiently invested in the fight over the role of the *Chevron* doctrine to want to incur this kind of critique. So, for want of any pushback from the Court, the *Chevron* doctrine became a settled feature of the law of judicial review.

Back to the Four Values

It is appropriate to offer a preliminary assessment of how well the *Chevron* doctrine, once it became institutionalized, comports with the four values associated with judicial review of administrative legal interpretation sketched in Chapter 1. We have seen that the pre-*Chevron* factors at least contained glimmers of insight about the relevance of the four values, and that Justice Stevens's opinion in *Chevron,* when considered in its entirety, is largely consistent with those values. The *Chevron* doctrine, based on two paragraphs in the *Chevron* opinion taken out of context, was largely a regression.

With respect to rule of law values, understood to mean promoting stability of legal expectations, the problem with the two-step formula is that it provides no obvious way to consider or enforce such values. Step 1 appears to direct the court to engage in de novo review to determine whether the statute has a "clear" meaning. The consistency of the agency interpretation seems irrelevant to such an inquiry. Step 2, which asks if the agency interpretation is reasonable, could conceivably be used to ask if the agency interpretation reinforces or upsets settled expectations. But the dominant understanding of step 2 has been to ask if the agency interpretation is reasonable in light of judicial interpretational norms.[76] As a result, assessing the agency interpretation against settled expectations effectively drops out under the *Chevron* formula. It of course persists, because this is an important value long recognized by courts (see Chapter 7). But its persistence occurs largely in the form of random, ad hoc consideration extraneous to the *Chevron* doctrine.

With respect to constitutional values, most prominently the separation of powers principle of legislative supremacy, step 1 of the *Chevron* doctrine correctly charges reviewing courts to enforce clear or unambiguous congressional directives. But the scope of an agency's delegated authority is often implicit in a series of legislative enactments over time or becomes apparent only when considered in light of established conventions about the role of different agencies or the functions of the federal government as opposed to state and local governments. These contextual understandings are ones that courts are particularly well suited to discern, but it is misleading to say they are "clear" or "unambiguous." Taken literally, the *Chevron* doctrine seems to say that unless Congress has the foresight to spell out the scope of an agency's authority in unambiguous language, the agency can exploit any gap, silence, or ambiguity in its organic act to expand or contract the scope of its authority in any way that passes muster as a permissible interpretation.[77] The principle of legislative supremacy would inevitably devolve from the anti-inherency understanding to the last-word conception.

At the very least, one might think, the *Chevron* doctrine would advance the idea that when a question of interpretation is really a matter of discretionary policy choice, the agency interpretation should prevail. Justice Stevens made plain in the concluding paragraphs of his opinion that this was his understanding. The *Chevron* doctrine, however, is a compound of two highly indeterminate standards (see Chapter 5). Given these indeterminacies, the *Chevron* doctrine, in practice, does little to constrain judicial willfulness. If a court dislikes an agency interpretation that entails a policy choice, it can declare that the statute "clearly" requires a different choice, or, more unusually, that the agency's interpretation is "unreasonable." Worse, because the two-step formula is highly streamlined compared to the eclectic doctrine and elaborate investigations of legislative history that proceeded it, the *Chevron* doctrine actually reduces the cost of judicial willfulness, inevitably increasing its incidence.

In terms of providing incentives for agencies to make better interpretations, the *Chevron* doctrine also comes up short. The key here is the ambiguity about what it means for an agency interpretation to be reasonable. The Supreme Court could have interpreted this to mean reasonable as a matter of the decisional process followed by the agency, but it has not done so, at least not on any consistent basis. In other contexts the Court seems comfortable with the understanding that the Administrative Procedure Act requires reasoned decision making when an agency makes a policy decision, whether it be through rulemaking or adjudication. But it has failed to condition acceptance of agency interpretations of statutes by requiring agency compliance with such a process. In particular, the Court has applied the *Chevron* doctrine to interpretations announced in adjudications when there has been no opportunity for public participation before the interpretation is rendered, and even when the agency has given no explanation for its interpretation.[78]

In Sum

The *Chevron* story reveals a remarkable course of legal evolution in which a decision regarded by the Supreme Court as business-as-usual was interpreted by one of the courts of appeals as effecting a fundamental change in the law—and then the Supreme Court gradually acquiesced in this understanding. The history of the *Chevron* doctrine reveals that legal change does not always proceed from the top down, but sometimes occurs from the bottom (or perhaps in this case the middle) up. The most plausible explanation for this curious path of the law is that the *Chevron* doctrine reduced the decisional costs for lower-court judges, especially the D.C. Circuit, by replacing a relatively elaborate and unwieldy doctrine with a more streamlined one. Because the Supreme Court hears many fewer administrative appeals, it was much less affected by the high costs of dissecting complicated administrative decisions. Given that the Court was less burdened by the pre-*Chevron* status quo, it is perhaps not surprising that its embrace of the doctrine took the form of an acquiescence in the reading of the D.C. Circuit, rather than any explicit affirmance of the view championed by Justice Scalia that the *Chevron* doctrine had displaced all competing forms of judicial review of questions of law. The Supreme Court came to *use* the *Chevron* doctrine, much as it uses various canons of interpretation. But the Court did not, at least in the initial decade and a half after *Chevron* was decided, offer an express justification of it. This, as we shall see, meant that the Court left itself room for revisions in the doctrine down the road. But that possibility would not be realized until more time had passed.

5

The Indeterminacies
of the *Chevron* Doctrine

ONCE THE *CHEVRON* doctrine came to be regarded as the leading formula for calibrating the relationship between courts and agencies in matters of statutory interpretation, the Supreme Court paid little attention to its inner workings—just how steps 1 and 2 should operate. This was not unusual. In many areas where the Supreme Court establishes a standard for lower courts to follow, the Court does little to clarify ambiguities that emerge about what exactly the standard means. A non-exhaustive list would include the various tests for determining when federal law preempts state law, the standard for determining whether the requirements of procedural due process have been met, and the test for determining when a regulation is so burdensome that it should be considered a taking of property.[1]

Why this phenomenon should repeat itself in multiple areas of law is not clear. The Court has an obligation to provide guidance to lower courts, which must decide many more cases governed by these standards than the Court itself. One would think the Court, having produced a general standard, would have a duty to provide needed clarification. Perhaps the explanation lies in the Court's perception that petitions for review seeking clarification of such standards are merely quarreling with the way the standard was applied in a particular case—a common reason for denying review. Or perhaps the Court does not want to tie its own hands too much, which might constrain it from reaching what it considers the right result in future cases.

In the case of the *Chevron* doctrine, the failure of the Court to clarify the meaning of step 1 and step 2 may also be a product of ambivalent attitudes among the Justices toward the *Chevron* doctrine more generally. Sometimes the doctrine has been described in opinions as "well settled"; sometimes it has been completely ignored. Sometimes it has been treated like a canon of interpretation to be used at the discretion of the opinion writer; sometimes it has been regarded as a binding rule of law.[2] A Court that is ambivalent about a legal doctrine is unlikely to invest significant effort in clarifying it.

The exact reasons for the Court's indifference to the mechanics of the *Chevron* doctrine are necessarily a matter of speculation. What is not a matter of speculation is that the two parts of the *Chevron* doctrine—step 1 and step 2—were both highly indeterminate. Law professors and judges writing in academic journals were well aware of this, and bewailed the resulting uncertainty and opportunities for judicial manipulation. But the Court, throughout the reign of the *Chevron* doctrine, has done nothing to resolve these uncertainties.

Step 1: What *Chevron* Said

In considering the indeterminacies of step 1, it is best to begin by reviewing what Justice Stevens wrote, in the fateful paragraphs of Part II of his opinion for the Court in *Chevron* that became the foundation of the *Chevron* doctrine. These paragraphs became the "text" that lower courts referred to in assessing agency interpretations—almost as if the paragraphs were some kind of statute. The words were quoted endlessly—and, of course, selectively. Here are the key sentences bearing on the inquiry at step 1:

> "First, always, is the question whether Congress has directly spoken to the precise question at issue."
>
> "If the intent of Congress is clear, that is the end of the matter, for the court, as well as the agency, must give effect to the unambiguously expressed intent of Congress."
>
> "The judiciary is the final authority on issues of statutory construction and must reject administrative constructions which are contrary to clear congressional intent."
>
> "If a court, employing traditional tools of statutory construction, ascertains that Congress had an intention on the precise question at issue, that intention is the law and must be given effect."

"If . . . a court determines that Congress has not directly addressed the precise question at issue, the court does not simply impose its own construction on the statute."

"[I]f the statute is silent or ambiguous with respect to the specific issue, the question for the court is whether the agency's answer is based on a permissible construction of the statute."[3]

The first thing to note about these sentences is that they invoke two different ideas about what the court should look for in the relevant statutory materials—precision and clarity. Although these often overlap, they are not the same thing. One can imagine a statute that addresses the precise question at issue, but does so in a fashion that is not clear. For example, the National Bank Act of 1864 gives a federal bank regulator exclusive power to exercise "visitorial" authority over national banks, but does not clarify what that outdated and unfamiliar term means.[4] Conversely, one can imagine a statute that does not address the precise question but contains a general principle that renders the answer clear. Title VII of the Civil Rights Act contains not a word about discrimination based on sexual orientation, but a divided Supreme Court has concluded that the statute's prohibition on sex discrimination logically compels the conclusion that discrimination based on sexual orientation is also prohibited.[5] The sentences in *Chevron* that describe step 1 seemed to equate precision and clarity, but the question whether to accept or reject an agency interpretation may depend on which of these two concepts is emphasized.

It is also uncertain whether the court at step 1 is to confine its inquiry to the text of the statute being interpreted, or whether it can also look for answers in other provisions of the statute or in legislative history. There is a hint of the primacy of the relevant text in stating that the question is whether "Congress has directly spoken" to the precise question at issue. Congress speaks authoritatively through the statutes it enacts. But on balance Justice Stevens refers more frequently to congressional "intent," which was the conventional characterization of the interpretive enterprise at the time he wrote. And the search for legislative intent was associated with the use of legislative history. Indeed, Stevens considered the legislative history in detail in the body of his opinion.[6] Once Justice Scalia provoked an intramural dispute in the Court over text versus intent, it seemed for a time that much turned on whether step 1 was limited to textual exegesis or permitted courts to engage in a more wide-ranging investigation of legislative intent or purpose.

The *Chevron* opinion also said nothing about what is included in the reference to the "traditional tools of statutory construction." Unsurprisingly, disputes arose as to what is and is not properly included in this category. Whether substantive canons of interpretation should be included in the toolbox, such as the canon that courts should interpret statutes to avoid serious constitutional questions (Chapter 8), is but one example of the uncertainly about what should be included in the step 1 exercise.

How Clear Is Clear?

In recent years, it has become common to observe that the *Chevron* doctrine does not explain what it means for a statute to be "clear."[7] At a minimum, to say that the meaning of a statute is "clear" is to claim more certainty about it being correct than is associated with asserting that the meaning is merely more-likely-than-not correct.[8] In an ordinary civil case, with no agency in the picture, a court must give the statute the meaning that it concludes is more-likely-than-not correct. If there are two possible meanings, and one is 51% likely to be correct, and another 49% likely to be correct, the court is required to adopt the 51%-likely meaning.[9] When we add the requirement that the court can enforce a meaning only if it is "clear," we are necessarily requiring that the court's certainty about the correctness of the meaning be higher than 51%. But how much higher must the court's confidence level rise beyond 51% in order to characterize the meaning as "clear?" Must the degree of certainty rise to 60%? 75%? 90%? The *Chevron* doctrine does not specify any particular confidence level in numeric terms. In this respect, it is like legal doctrine more generally. Courts do not translate standards like "beyond a reasonable doubt" or "clear and convincing evidence" into numeric probabilities. And one does not expect them to translate what it means for an interpretation of a statute to be "clear" into such a numeric probability either.

The indeterminacy of the "clarity" requirement at step 1 has generated significant criticism of the *Chevron* doctrine. Justice Brett Kavanaugh, when he was a judge on the D.C. Circuit, authored a critique in the *Harvard Law*

Review of the use of the concept of clarity at step 1.[10] With his elevation to the Supreme Court, this critique obviously deserves attention. Kavanaugh made two principal points. First, there is no common understanding among judges about how much more certain they must be about a statute's meaning, beyond more-likely-than-not, before they can find that the meaning is clear. This makes the application of the *Chevron* doctrine highly unpredictable, depending on what individual judges implicitly imagine the relevant certainty requirement to be in any given case. Second, because there is no settled understanding about what clear means, the *Chevron* doctrine makes it "harder for judges to ensure that they are separating their policy views from what the law requires of them."[11] In other words, step 1 is vulnerable to result-oriented decisions by judges, the exact opposite of what the *Chevron* doctrine was supposed to accomplish.

These criticisms are well taken, but Ryan Doerfler has offered responses to both points.[12] Regarding the absence of any uniform understanding of what "clear" means, Doerfler notes that it would not make sense to impose any uniform metric of clarity, because the degree of certainty about the correct answer to any problem should vary with the size of the stakes involved. If the stakes are very high—for example, if the question is whether the FDA has jurisdiction over tobacco products or if subsidies are available to persons through health insurance exchanges established by the federal government— it makes sense to devote a great deal of effort to getting the answer right.[13] In contrast, if the stakes are not that high—if the issue involves, say, how to calculate registration fees for interstate motor carriers under the Intermodal Surface Transportation Efficiency Act—then a lesser degree of effort is warranted in determining the correct answer.[14]

Doerfler is surely correct that the degree of effort put into interpreting an instruction should vary with the stakes in getting the answer right or wrong. But this does not tell us *which* interpreter, in a two-stage consideration of the same issue, should be the one that puts in the effort. In Doerfler's homey example about a student interpreting a teacher's instruction to attend a class, there is only one interpreter (the student), and the degree of effort should vary with the stakes (missing an optional review session or flunking the course).[15] But when a court reviews an agency interpretation, it is not clear which institution should put in greater or lesser interpretive effort, depending on the stakes. In the case of the FDA's jurisdiction over tobacco, the agency put in a very large amount of effort in considering whether it had jurisdiction over tobacco.[16] In the case of subsidies on federally created exchanges, the agency failed to perceive the issue at all.[17] Should this matter in terms of the degree of certainty the court should have before it rules for or against the agency? Perhaps it should, but the Court put a great amount of effort in considering the correct interpretation in both the tobacco and the Affordable Care Act cases.

To Kavanaugh's point that the indeterminacy of clarity invites willful judging, Doerfler's response is that this is true of any standard of review. He admits that some standards of legal certainty may make it easier to disguise willful or motivated decisions "without serious reputational harm."[18] Characterizing the issue as having a "clear" or "unclear" answer may be a prime example of a standard that is especially susceptible to judicial manipulation without reputational costs. Perhaps asking whether the agency is operating within the boundaries of its authority (as I argue in later chapters) would do better in this regard. At the very least, such an inquiry would require courts to engage in a more detailed examination of the statute and its settled understanding, which might result in greater self-discipline relative to declaring that the statute is or is not "clear." Be that as it may, the *Chevron* doctrine's clarity standard has done little to reduce judicial willfulness in matters in which judges take an interest in the outcome.

The Precise Question at Issue

The original formulation of step 1 also requires courts to ask whether Congress has spoken to the "precise question at issue." This language, more than the injunction to enforce "clear" congressional intent, seems to point toward a very robust measure of deference to agency interpretations. The search for legislative direction regarding the "precise question" implies a quest for targeted evidence directly on point, either in the text or (consistent with the interpretational norms of 1984) the legislative history. Because it will be rare for an agency to ignore a legislative instruction on the "precise question at issue," deference to the agency would seemingly be required in almost every case that makes it to court. Certainly, any issue that has not been addressed by Congress (a "silence") or that is not covered by the relevant statutory language (a "gap") would be fair game for agency lawmaking. Provisions that are general or vague would also seem to fall within the ambit of agency discretion, since they are difficult to characterize as speaking "precisely" to the question. So too provisions that are ambiguous in the classical sense of having multiple possible meanings.

In contrast to the requirement of clarity, the directive to courts to look for an answer to the precise question at issue seems much less prone to manipulation by courts. This is not because the meaning of "precision" is precise. In the abstract, precision, like clarity, is a matter of degree.[19] Rather, it is because cases that arise on judicial review come with "questions presented" by the person or entity challenging the agency. In most cases this will be the same as the "precise question" that step 1 directs the court to scour the legislative materials in search of an answer. Thus, in most cases, given the way the parties frame the issues for decision by the court, it will be difficult to avoid deferring to an agency by claiming that some general statutory provision provides an answer to the "precise question at issue."

How, then, can courts escape the implication that deference is required as long as Congress left no direct evidence on the precise question presented? The answer would seem to be that they have selectively ignored the language in Part II of the *Chevron* opinion framing the inquiry in these terms. A survey of Supreme Court decisions applying the two-step *Chevron* doctrine indicates that less than half include the language about the "precise question at issue," with omissions increasing over time.[20]

The pattern is especially striking in the opinions of Justice Scalia. It appears that during his last decade on the Court he never included the precise question formulation in his summary of the *Chevron* doctrine. Instead he increasingly paraphrased the doctrine in terms of clarity (or ambiguity) and reasonableness. A representative statement was: "*Chevron* directs courts to accept an agency's reasonable resolution of an ambiguity in a statute that the agency administers."[21] When Justice Stevens, in a dissent, questioned why Scalia had omitted the precise-question formulation in an opinion applying the *Chevron* doctrine, he responded: "[S]urely, if Congress has directly spoken to an issue then any agency interpretation contradicting what Congress has said would be unreasonable."[22] Increasingly, Scalia seemed to recast the *Chevron* doctrine as consisting of nothing more than step 2—asking whether the agency interpretation is "reasonable." Indeed, Scalia went so far as to assert that "'step 1' has never been an essential part of *Chevron* analysis."[23] This would effectively return the deference doctrine to its pre-*Chevron* formulation—asserting that courts should defer to reasonable agency interpretations—which would allow courts to exercise something like independent judgment in resolving questions of law.

There is an important reason to reject Justice Scalia's latter-day conversion to the position that the *Chevron* doctrine has only one step—to wit, asking whether the agency interpretation is "reasonable."[24] Step 1 establishes whether or not the agency has *discretion* to adopt different possible interpretations of the statute. If a court decides at step 1 that the statute has a clear meaning, then the agency has no discretion to adopt a different meaning. Conversely, if the court decides the case at step 2, the court implicitly finds that the statute has more than one permissible interpretation, and thus that the agency retains the discretion to change its mind—within the limits of what is reasonable—in the future.[25] If the two steps were collapsed into one, asking simply whether the agency interpretation is "reasonable," this would obscure the question—important to the agency and to future reviewing courts—whether the agency has the discretionary authority to modify its interpretation down the road. Keeping the two steps distinct thus provides important information that collapsing the inquiry into one step would not.[26]

It is not possible to show that Justices other than Scalia have had any strategic objective in mind when they have either included or omitted the precise question formulation from their opinions applying the *Chevron* doctrine. There are many reasons for variability in opinion writing, including accidents like which law clerk is assigned to prepare the initial draft of the opinion. But the inconsistent use of the precise-question formulation clearly magnifies the uncertainty about the *Chevron* doctrine, and undermines its potential utility as a rubric for bringing some consistency to the judicial treatment of agency interpretations of law.

Text or Intent?

Justice Scalia's ascension to the Court in 1986 was not only a primary cause of the Court's gradual acceptance of the *Chevron* doctrine, it also marked the beginning of a highly visible struggle within the Court over the proper approach to statutory interpretation more generally. Justice Scalia pronounced himself a "textualist," and denounced the rival form of interpretation as "intentionalism." Textualism was said to be grounded in the objective meaning of the statute as it would be understood by an ordinary reader. Intentionalism was characterized as resting on the subjective expectations of the legislature, with skepticism about whether it is possible to depict any body of individuals with divergent views as having a collective "intent." Scalia advanced his preferred method in scores of separate concurring and dissenting opinions as well in a series of speeches delivered at law schools.[27] He was eventually joined in these views by Justice Thomas, and to a degree by Justice Kennedy. Scalia achieved significant success in this campaign. To some extent this was due to his persuasive advocacy, supported by Judge Frank Easterbrook on the Seventh Circuit and for a time by the Justice Department.[28] But his success was also due to sheer stubbornness. Scalia made it plain that he would refuse to join any portion of a majority opinion that relied on legislative history—which he regarded as the key tool of intentionalism. When Thomas adopted the same position, this meant that any Justice who relied on legislative history in a majority opinion would lose two votes for at least a portion of the opinion. Presumably to avoid this, the other Justices greatly reduced their use of legislative history.[29]

The rise of textualism had an effect on the characterization of step 1 of the *Chevron* doctrine. It meant that summaries of the required inquiry increasingly dropped the references to the "intent" of Congress. In some cases it produced a reformulation of step 1 in terms of the "plain meaning" or the "text" of the statute.[30] According to a survey of decisions by Linda Jellum, references to legislative intent effectively disappeared from step 1 in Supreme Court cases for a time.[31]

Whether the reformulation of step 1 in terms of the language of textualism resulted in a change in the willingness of courts to move on to step 2, and hence to give more deference to agencies, is uncertain.[32] Justice Scalia argued that the intentionalist method, with its recourse to legislative history, produced "agency-liberating ambiguity" and thus created a greater tendency to consider agency interpretations at step 2. In contrast, he portrayed textualism as generating more conclusive outcomes, and hence less need to defer to agency interpretations.[33] But there is reason to think that the opposite is more likely true. Although the use of intentionalism and its associated reliance on legislative history was subject to abuse, there is evidence that it was used more often to reduce ambiguity than to create it.[34] In contrast, textualism, deprived of any reliance on issue-specific data contained in legislative history, was forced to make greater use of dictionary definitions, inferences drawn from statutory structure and from other statutes, and canons of interpretation. Interpreting statutes using these more general but supposedly more objective interpretative sources tends to require an exercise in creative ingenuity on the part of judges.[35] In the hands of modest judges this would likely result in more acknowledgment of ambiguity at step 1. In the hands of self-assured judges, it arguably produced results at greater variance with the objectives of enacting legislature—and fewer candid admissions of uncertainty.

As the debate sparked by Justice Scalia's aggressive advocacy of textualism unfolded, the practical difference between textualism and its foil (whose proponents tended to prefer "purposive" interpretation rather than "intentionalism") narrowed. The advocates of purposive interpretation generally conceded that only the text is the law, and that any attribution of purpose to the legislature must be consistent with the text.[36] The textualists, for their part, conceded that the words of the statute must be interpreted in "context."[37] Understanding the context, in turn, requires attributing a purpose to the language—either the one that the legislature was thought to have, or the one an ordinary reader could attribute to the legislature as having had.[38] So in the end, both sides ultimately agreed—at least in their more reflective writings—that interpreting a statute requires attributing a purpose to the language of the statute. The only remaining point of disagreement was whether legislative history should be consulted in an effort to determine the purpose. There are overlapping reasons to question the routine use of legislative history. Doerfler's point that the degree of effort to be put into interpreting a text depends on the stakes is directly relevant here. The payoff from examining legislative history is often modest or nil, and the effort it takes to do a survey of legislative history—at least when done honestly—is often very large. By the time of Scalia's death in 2016 the use of legislative history by the Supreme Court—in *Chevron* cases as well as elsewhere—was greatly reduced relative to its profligate use in the 1970s and 1980s. But it has not disappeared.

What Is in the Toolkit?

The phrase "traditional tools of statutory construction," which appeared in a footnote, was destined to become one of the most widely quoted phrases from the *Chevron* opinion. Justice Stevens made no attempt to spell out what was included among the "traditional tools," and this would later become the subject of controversy.

Consideration of legislative history was the most obvious point of disagreement. The avowed textualists could not deny that legislative history had become a standard tool; they asserted that it was an illegitimate tool, and worked to gather support for throwing it out of the toolbox. Nevertheless, it came in handy on occasion. Justice O'Connor made extensive—and generally persuasive—reference to legislative history in her opinion holding at step 1 that the Food and Drug Administration had "clearly" been denied authority to regulate tobacco products.[39] Justices Scalia and Thomas joined the opinion without comment.

It was also uncertain whether or to what extent various canons of interpretation are included in the toolkit. The so-called linguistic canons, such as the idea that a general word in a list should be interpreted as having the same range of application as more specific words in the list,[40] were accepted as proper tools for determining whether the statute has a clear meaning at step 1. But substantive canons—such as the presumption against interpreting statutes to apply retroactively, the canon preferring interpretations that avoid serious constitutional questions (considered in Chapter 8), and the presumption against preemption of state laws (considered in Chapter 9)—were problematic. The *Chevron* doctrine is grounded in the proposition that when statutory interpretation implicates discretionary policy choice, the agency is the one to do the interpreting, not the court. If a court invokes substantive canons at step 1, this will necessarily impose a constraint on the range of policies the agency can reach. Perhaps this is justifiable, but the Court has never ventured to offer a justification.[41]

Most courts seem to assume that the traditional canons giving weight to contemporary and longstanding agency interpretations (discussed in Chapter 2) are not part of the "traditional tools" used to discern the clear meaning of a statute. This is may seem odd, given that the contemporary and longstanding canons (which would have to be classified as substantive canons) are among the ones that are the most "traditional" and most directly related to whether to accept an agency interpretation. But it is not obvious that they are relevant to whether the statute has a clear meaning or whether it addresses the precise question at issue. The twin canons would seem to be more relevant to asking whether the agency interpretation is "reasonable" at step 2, and on a few occasions the Court has invoked them in this context (see Chapter 7). But the *Chevron* doctrine's principal cheerleader—Justice Scalia—thought that *Chevron* had abolished these canons, and his insistence on this matter presumably discouraged consideration of these canons at step 2 also.

Is This the Right Question?

Perhaps the most far-reaching question about step 1 was its rationale for making a court's perception of the clarity and / or precision of the statute the gateway to giving deference to agency interpretations. Justice Stevens's language was read by Justice Scalia and other proponents of the *Chevron* doctrine as saying that if Congress leaves a gap or ambiguity in a statute the agency administers, this should be regarded as an implicit delegation making the agency the preferred interpreter.[42] The suggestion was reinforced by the concluding paragraphs of the *Chevron* opinion, which seemed to sanction a very broad conception of congressional delegation, including delegations based on a failure of Congress even to consider the question at issue or based on a decision of rival factions in Congress to "take their chances with the scheme devised by the agency."[43] The Court, in an opinion by Justice Scalia, would later make explicit the theory that ambiguity constitutes an implicit delegation.[44]

Grounding deference in a theory of implicit delegation based on ambiguity—which even *Chevron* proponents concede is a fiction[45]—creates a very large puzzle. If the duty of courts is always to enforce the instructions of Congress, why isn't the central question at step 1 whether Congress *actually* delegated interpretational authority to the agency? The *Chevron* opinion was correct that the principle of legislative supremacy means courts should "reject administrative constructions which are contrary to clear congressional intent." But doesn't the same principle mean that courts should at least try to discern and enforce Congress's *actual* intent with respect to who is to be the interpreter if the statute requires interpretation? The presumption of universal agency authority to interpret any ambiguity or gap was contrary to the established understanding before *Chevron* was decided. As we have seen (Chapter 2), the pre-*Chevron* view was that courts are presumed to be the primary interpreter unless some affirmative evidence—based perhaps on the breadth of the statutory language or the technical nature of the subject matter—points to a legislative design to make the agency the preferred interpreter.

Step 2: What *Chevron* Said

In considering the indeterminacies of step 2, it is again appropriate to begin by reviewing what Justice Stevens said in the portion of *Chevron* that became the basis for the *Chevron* doctrine:

> "[I]f the statute is silent or ambiguous with respect to the specific issue, the question for the court is whether the agency's answer is based on a permissible construction of the statute."
>
> "The court need not conclude that the agency construction was the only one it permissibly could have adopted to uphold the construction, or even the reading the court would have reached if the question initially had arisen in a judicial proceeding."
>
> "Sometimes the legislative delegation to an agency on a particular question is implicit rather than explicit. In such a case, a court may not substitute its own construction for a reasonable interpretation made by the administrator of an agency."
>
> "[Once it was determined] that Congress did not actually have an intent regarding [the bubble policy] . . . the question before [the court] was . . . whether the Administrator's view that it is appropriate in the context of this particular program is a reasonable one."[46]

Again, note that these passages draw upon two different words—"permissible" and "reasonable"—to describe the quality an agency interpretation must have before it must be accepted by a reviewing court. At least potentially, these words differ in connotation. "Reasonable," which is the way most courts have rendered the characterization of step 2, is a word of protean meaning, as we shall see. Conceivably it could mean that the agency interpretation is one that a reasonable interpreter would not adopt, which would allow the court to substitute its judgment for the agency in nearly all cases. "Permissible" seems more clearly to suggest that the agency interpretation is "acceptable," in the sense that one can imagine an interpreter who is more than minimally competent adopting such an interpretation. That this was the intended meaning of the inquiry at step 2 was reinforced by the statement (in a footnote) that the interpretation need not be the one that the court itself would adopt. This signals that "reasonable" and "permissible" in this context mean that the reviewing court should give the agency significant leeway to adopt interpretations that deviate from what the court regards as "the best" reading of the statute.

Subsequent courts seemed to use the words "reasonable" and "permissible" interchangeably. In this book I will generally refer to the basic requirement of step 2 to be that the agency interpretation must be "reasonable," with the understanding that this implies that it is "permissible." Still, these terms conceal considerable indeterminacy about what exactly the reviewing court is to demand in order to find that an agency interpretation passes muster at step 2.

The Indeterminacy of "Reasonableness"

Invoking reasonableness as a condition of deferring to agency interpretations was hardly an innovation. Decisions from the New Deal era had deferred to "reasonable" agency interpretations of statutes.[47] And in the run up to the *Chevron* decision, the Court often spoke of courts deferring to "reasonable agency interpretations" of the statutes they administer.[48] The *Chevron* doctrine, once it was adopted by the D.C. Circuit and migrated back to the Supreme Court, simply codified the reasonableness requirement as part of a more streamlined, all-purpose doctrine, without any explanation of what "reasonableness" means in this context.

In broad outline, reasonableness in the context of judicial review of agency interpretations could mean one of three things. It could mean that the court finds the agency's interpretation to be reasonable as an exercise in the norms of statutory interpretation applied by courts. Alternatively, it could mean that the court finds that the agency's interpretation reflects a policy that the court finds reasonable. Finally, it could mean that the agency has engaged in a process of reasoned decision making in reaching its interpretation, as that norm has been developed in cases applying the "arbitrary, capricious, or abuse of discretion" standard of review under the Administrative Procedure Act.[49]

The first understanding of "reasonable"—that it means reasonable as a matter of interpretation—may or may not make sense as part of the *Chevron* doctrine, depending on how broadly one interprets the role of the court at step 1. If one interprets step 1 narrowly, as asking whether the *text* of the statute addresses the precise question at issue, then it might make sense to interpret step 2 as a more general inquiry into whether the agency's interpretation is one that a reasonable interpreter might adopt in light of broader considerations of statutory structure, purpose, or legislative history. Step 1 on this understanding would command a narrow "clause bound" interpretation that would readily translate into agency discretion; step 2 would then require the court to engage in a more wide-ranging consideration of context to see if the agency's interpretation is within the bounds of reason.

Contrariwise, if one interprets step 1 broadly, as enjoining courts to utilize all "traditional tools" of statutory construction to determine if the statute has a clearly preferred meaning, then it would make little sense for the court to ask at step 2 whether the agency's interpretation is reasonable as a matter of judicial norms of interpretation. After all, if the court has undertaken a wide-ranging interpretive exercise, and has concluded that one interpretation is superior to all others, this would seem to be the only "reasonable" interpretation the agency could adopt. This line of thought suggests an inverse relationship between the scope of step 1 and the scope of step 2. The broader the judicial inquiry at step 1, the narrower the room for finding the agency interpretation unreasonable if it diverges from the conclusion reached by the court. In the limit, if courts interpret very broadly at step 1, step 2 becomes an irrelevant appendage.

In theory, one can imagine a regime in which courts exercise great self-restraint by cabining their exercise of interpretation at step 1 to review of the text and whether it addresses the precise question at issue, then considering broader considerations of statutory context and purpose at step 2. In practice, this seems unrealistic.[50] Once courts are told to engage in de novo review at step 1, and to do so armed with all the "traditional tools" of statutory interpretation (as instructed by *Chevron*), it is inevitable that step 1 will expand into a full-scale judicial exposition of the court's understanding of the statute's best meaning. Once this happens, as inevitably it did, step 2 becomes in nearly all cases effectively otiose.

The Supreme Court's decisions applying the *Chevron* doctrine confirm the essential irrelevance of step 2. Over the large run of cases, the Supreme Court has adopted a broad conception of the interpretive exercise at step 1. Thus, as one would predict, the Court has only rarely invalidated an agency interpretation under step 2. It never did so before 1999, and it has disapproved agency interpretations at step 2 in only three cases over the full span of thirty-five years.[51] These are outliers. The big picture, at least at the Supreme Court level, is that all the action has been at step 1. In functional terms, the *Chevron* doctrine, at least in the Supreme Court, operates as a form of de novo review that stops at step 1.

The second possible reading of "reasonable" at step 2—that the court finds the agency interpretation reasonable as a matter of policy—is subject to a different and more decisive objection. *Chevron*'s signal contribution to our understanding of the court–agency relationship is that if a question of interpretation is ultimately a matter of discretionary policy choice, the agency is the preferred interpreter. The agency is more politically accountable to the elected branches than is the court. And the agency will nearly always have more expertise in understanding both the phenomenon being regulated and how the statute and associated regulations work in practice. That being the case, it is incongruous for a court to superintend the agency's policy choice by asking whether it is "reasonable." During the 1970s, the D.C. Circuit occasionally claimed that it was in a "partnership" with agencies in determining appropriate regulatory policy, and because the court had the last word, it was effectively the senior partner.[52] *Chevron* revealed the fallacy in this reasoning. It follows that interpreting "reasonable" at step 2 to mean reasonable as a matter of policy contradicts the very premises on which the *Chevron* doctrine is built.

The third understanding of "reasonable" under step 2 is that it simply incorporates the "arbitrary and capricious" standard of review in the APA.[53] There is a basis for this in the *Chevron* opinion, which observed, following

Batterton v. Francis, that the standard of review for agency interpretations adopted under an explicit delegation of interpretive authority is the arbitrary-and-capricious standard.[54] The opinion, in the next sentence, seemed to equate implicit delegations with explicit delegations, suggesting that the same standard of review would apply to implicit delegations.[55] Subsequent decisions, in restating the Court's understanding of the *Chevron* doctrine, have also seemingly equated step 2's reasonableness requirement with the arbitrary-and-capricious standard of the APA.[56]

Several commentators, starting with a classic article by Ron Levin in 1997, have pointed out that if unreasonable means arbitrary and capricious, then step 2 simply replicates the APA standard, and the two should be deemed to be identical.[57] One of two things follow. Either step 2 should be dropped, leaving it up to the parties (in addition to alleging that the interpretation is wrong) to decide whether to challenge the agency interpretation as arbitrary and capricious. Or, step 2 should be explicitly deemed to incorporate the APA standard, making it a general requirement for upholding any agency statutory interpretation that it not be arbitrary and capricious.[58]

Unfortunately, arbitrary-and-capricious review under the APA also has its share of ambiguities. Here, it is useful to adopt a distinction advanced by Gary Lawson between asking whether the outcome (i.e., the policy) adopted by the agency is arbitrary and capricious, and asking whether the process followed by the agency in developing the interpretation is arbitrary and capricious.[59] If a court asks whether the *outcome* is arbitrary and capricious, it commits the same mistake condemned by the core insight of *Chevron*—namely, that the agency is the preferred institution for resolving contested issues of policy. Process review, in contrast, asks whether the agency has engaged in a process of reasoned decision making in reaching the outcome. If conducted in good faith, process review should be compatible with a variety of outcomes and thus does not carry the implication that the reviewing court is a kind of censor with the power to veto policies with which it disagrees. I will argue in Chapter 12 that the tenets of process review should be required as a condition of accepting any agency interpretation adopted within the scope of its delegated authority.

A brief glance at the three decisions in which the Supreme Court has rejected agency interpretations at step 2 confirms that the Court has not developed any clear conception about what "reasonable" means in this context.

All three cases, not coincidentally, were authored by Justice Scalia, the Court's most enthusiastic proponent of the *Chevron* doctrine but also one of its less deferential Justices.[60]

The first invocation of step 2 to invalidate an agency interpretation occurred in *AT&T Corp. v. Iowa Utilities Board*.[61] This was a wide-ranging review of the FCC's implementation of the Telecommunications Act of 1996, which sought to stimulate competition in local landline telephone markets. Justice Scalia's opinion for the Court upheld every aspect of the Commission's regulation, with one exception. The Act required that incumbent local carriers lease elements of their network to competitors if these elements are "necessary" to the successful provision of competitive service and the inability to access such elements would "impair" the ability of the newcomer to offer the service. The FCC, eager to make competition a reality, interpreted this standard very broadly, effectively allowing competitors to lease an incumbent's facilities if any other option would be more expensive. Scalia held that this feature of the Commission's regulation was unreasonable. The rationale was a blend of statutory interpretation—he thought "necessary" and "impair" suggest a more demanding showing than higher cost—combined with a vaguely articulated disagreement with the Commission's policy as being too generous to competitors at the expense of incumbents. Presumably the Court chose to ground its restrictive interpretation under step 2, rather than step 1, because it would be implausible to hold that "necessary" and "impair" are either precise or clear.[62]

The second step 2 decision, *Utility Air Regulatory Group v. EPA*,[63] is considered more fully in Chapter 10. In that decision step 2 was used to hold that the agency's interpretation of "air pollutant" exceeded the scope of its delegated authority. The agency's interpretation that greenhouse gas emissions can trigger PSD permitting requirements "would bring about an enormous and transformative expansion in the EPA's regulatory authority without clear congressional authorization."[64] Presumably Justice Scalia chose to rely on step 2 because a ruling at step 1 would run straight up against the Court's holding in *Massachusetts v. EPA*[65] that greenhouse gases *are* "air pollutants" under the Act.

The third and most recent step 2 decision, *Michigan v. EPA*,[66] concerned a provision of the Clean Air Act instructing the EPA to adopt additional regulations of coal-burning power plants if "necessary and appropriate" to reduce toxic air pollutants. The Court, again speaking through Justice Scalia, held that it was unreasonable to construe this language to preclude any consideration of costs in deciding to issue such regulations. The agency argued that costs would be considered in adopting permits for each plant, but Scalia said it was unreasonable to interpret "necessary and appropriate" as precluding costs in deciding whether to regulate at all. As in *Iowa Utilities,* the Court presumably used step 2, rather than step 1, to impose its preferred interpretation of the statute because it would be implausible to claim that "necessary and appropriate" has a precise or clear meaning.

In short, the Court's handful of invalidations of agency interpretations under step 2 of *Chevron* seem to rest primarily on an unstated understanding that unreasonable means unreasonable as a matter of statutory interpretation, with a strong undercurrent that unreasonable means unreasonable *as a matter of policy.* Distressingly, two of the three decisions (*Iowa Utilities* and *Michigan*) appear to be driven by a desire on the part of the Court majority to override discretionary agency interpretations with which it simply disagreed. None of the three decisions offers any explicit guidance about the general meaning of reasonable in this context.

A recent survey of court of appeals decisions invalidating agency interpretations at step 2 confirms that confusion reigns on this subject.[67] The survey suggests that the appeals court decisions fall into three categories: (i) unreasonable as a matter of interpretation, taking into account the structure of the statute as a whole and related statutes; (ii) unreasonable in light of the general purposes of the statute (presumably equivalent to unreasonable as a matter of policy); and (iii) unreasonable in the sense of being developed in an arbitrary and capricious process. Based on the struggles of the lower courts, step 2 of the *Chevron* doctrine is badly in need of clarification—which the Court has never provided.

In Sum

The *Chevron* doctrine, once it got going, required courts to determine at step 1 whether Congress provided an answer to the question of statutory interpretation at issue. This became the principal focus of most decisions applying the *Chevron* doctrine. Unfortunately, the language used by Justice Stevens in describing the inquiry at step 1 turned out to be highly indeterminate on several dimensions.

Justice Stevens described the inquiry in terms of whether Congress had supplied a "clear" or "unambiguous" answer. But it became apparent over time that "clear" refers to an unspecified level of certainty that varies from judge to judge and case to case. He also said that the question was whether Congress had spoken directly to the "precise question at issue." But this formulation proved to be inapt in some cases, and was often dropped in later decisions. Step 1 was originally formulated in terms of congressional "intent." But the Court was soon embroiled in an internal dispute over textualism versus intentionalism, which resulted in step 1 being reformulated, at least in some cases, in terms of the text of the statute, with uncertain effects on the degree of deference given to agencies. And Justice Stevens made reference to courts determining whether Congress had provided an answer using "traditional tools of statutory construction." It soon became obvious that there was no consensus about what is exactly included in the toolkit.

Step 2, which asks whether the agency interpretation is reasonable, is also ambiguous, and could mean one of three things: reasonable as a matter of conventional interpretational norms, reasonable as a matter of policy, or reasonable as a matter of the process followed in reaching the interpretation. This ambiguity, like the many indeterminacies of step 1, has never been resolved by the Court.

None of this is to cast blame on Justice Stevens. He was not writing a statute when he drafted the early paragraphs of the *Chevron* opinion that became the foundation of the *Chevron* doctrine. He was writing a preamble to a fairly conventional exercise in reviewing a statutory interpretation adopted by an agency. But when others found it to be in their interest to elevate those paragraphs into a "doctrine," they necessarily endorsed a doctrine filled with indeterminacy. The net result, quite arguably, was to enhance, rather than constrain, the discretion of courts in accepting or rejecting agency views about the law.

6

The Domain of the *Chevron* Doctrine

IF THE SUPREME COURT did nothing to clarify the many indeterminacies of the *Chevron* doctrine—its internal plumbing—the same cannot be said about its sphere of application—the range of issues over which it would apply. To be sure, in the early years after *Chevron* was decided the Court paid virtually no attention to the circumstances that would require courts to apply the *Chevron* doctrine as opposed to some other deference doctrine, or to give no consideration to the agency interpretation at all. The early trajectory of the doctrine was generally in the direction of expansion, but the Court offered no justification for this. By the end of the 1990s, however, issues about when the new doctrine should or should not apply had proliferated. Perhaps most critically, the Court had reaffirmed that the *Skidmore* standard of review should continue to apply in certain circumstances, which made it imperative to clarify when courts should apply *Skidmore* and when they should apply *Chevron*. This in turn required the Court to clarify the underlying principles of the *Chevron* doctrine.

The crux of the matter was what the Court meant in Part II of the *Chevron* opinion when it referred to an "implicit" delegation from Congress to make an agency rather than the court the primary interpreter of a statute. Justice Scalia, in his 1989 law review article, noted insightfully that pre-*Chevron* law had determined on a statute-by-statute basis whether Congress intended such an implicit delegation.[1] *Chevron,* he concluded, had replaced this with an across-the-board presumption, to the effect that whenever Congress leaves an ambiguity in a statute that is administered by an agency, this should always be regarded as an implicit delegation to make the agency the primary interpreter.[2] This theory, if correct, would logically mean that the *Chevron* doctrine had swept away *Skidmore,* the contemporaneous and longstanding canons of interpretation, and the distinction between pure questions of law and questions of law application. Being ruthlessly logical, at least in this matter, Scalia was prepared to accept all these implications. But when a majority of the Court reaffirmed the use of the *Skidmore* standard in certain situations, the Court could not—at least not logically—adhere to the idea that any ambiguity is an implicit delegation. The Court had to identify some other or additional triggering condition for applying the *Chevron* doctrine.

A secondary issue, without regard to whether ambiguity or something else was the condition for identifying an implicit delegation, was what kind of agency action would qualify as an interpretation eligible for *Chevron* deference. *Chevron* itself involved an agency regulation adopted using notice-and-comment procedures, and everyone agreed that this kind of agency action was sufficient to trigger the *Chevron* doctrine. But questions began proliferating about whether *Chevron*-style deference should apply to interpretations adopted in agency adjudications, or in even more informal agency action, such as an opinion letter from agency official.

Both issues—what constitutes an implicit delegation for *Chevron* purposes and what kinds of agency action are sufficient to qualify as an exercise of implicit power—would ultimately be addressed by the Court in its 2001 decision in *United States v. Mead Corp.*[3] The Court in *Mead* seemingly agreed that an across-the-board presumption, rather than a case-by-case determination, was required for identifying the domain of the *Chevron* doctrine. The presumption it identified, which garnered eight votes, was the existence of an agency interpretation adopted in the exercise of a certain type of delegated power—the power to take action having "the force of law." But this resolution was heavily qualified by equivocations, which papered over an internal disagreement among key members of the majority. As a consequence, the *Mead* doctrine (as Justice Scalia called it in his dissent), like much else associated with the *Chevron* doctrine, proved to be unstable.

The Period of Expansion

Chevron involved an interpretation of the Clean Air Act issued by the EPA in a regulation adopted using a version of notice-and-comment procedures. The only clue offered in Part II of Justice Stevens's opinion as to why the two-step doctrine was appropriate in this context was passing reference to the fact that the EPA had been "entrusted to administer" the Clean Air Act.[4] Which, of course, is true: the EPA had been given extensive authority to fill out the provisions of the Act with regulations and to bring enforcement actions against persons alleged to be in violation of the statute or the agency's implementing regulations. But the *Chevron* opinion offered no guidance as to which of these features of the EPA's administrative authority was a necessary or sufficient condition for identifying the EPA as the "administering" agency. Many years would pass before the Court offered any guidance on this point.[5]

In the ensuing years, the *Chevron* doctrine spread to a variety of agencies exercising a variety of administrative powers. In a sense this was not surprising: The much-quoted paragraphs in Part II of the *Chevron* opinion were written in general terms, not in terms limited to rulemaking by the EPA under the Clean Air Act. Where there was a pre-existing body of precedent that employed a different formula than the two-step standard, there was inevitably resistance to the *Chevron* doctrine. But given the factors responsible for the rise of the *Chevron* doctrine mentioned in Chapter 4—the general embrace of the two-step approach by lower courts, the Justice Department's persistent advocacy, and Justice Scalia's fervent support—the *Chevron* doctrine slowly prevailed in these situations.

One potential stopping point concerned whether the *Chevron* doctrine should apply to pockets of law where a different deference doctrine was seemingly securely established. Labor law and tax law both fit this description. Judicial review of decisions by the National Labor Relations Board (NLRB) had a rich tradition before *Chevron*, including notable precedents like *NLRB v. Hearst Publishing Co.* and *Packard Motor Co. v. NLRB*, discussed in Chapter 2. Up through the early 1990s the Supreme Court continued to apply this pre-*Chevron* precedent in reviewing legal determinations by the NLRB. Then, without any explicit analysis of the proper standard of review, the Court began switching to the *Chevron* doctrine.[6] Lower courts eventually followed suit.

Tax law followed a similar pattern. Before *Chevron*, courts tended to treat tax interpretations under precedents specific to tax law. The Supreme Court continued to follow this approach up until the early 1990s, then began shifting to the *Chevron* doctrine.[7] Again there was no explicit analysis supporting this change. Uncertainty about the proper standard of review persisted in the lower courts until 2011, when the Court, in a unanimous decision by Chief Justice Roberts, emphatically endorsed the use of the *Chevron* doctrine for reviewing all types tax regulations. In so ruling, the Court overruled the leading pre-*Chevron* decision applying traditional pre-*Chevron* factors, and disapproved pre-*Chevron* decisions distinguishing between interpretations based on specific grants of rulemaking authority and a general "housekeeping" grant.[8]

Another potential fault line concerned the procedural format in which agency interpretations are rendered. The *Chevron* decision itself involved an interpretation contained in a regulation, which meant that a variety of affected persons had an opportunity to comment on the proposed interpretation before it was adopted. This also ensured that, if the interpretation were adopted, it would apply prospectively. Other procedural formats—namely, formal and informal adjudication—do not offer the same opportunity for public participation or the same assurance of prospective application. Nevertheless, the Court in a number of decisions applied the *Chevron* doctrine to interpretations advanced in adjudications, without giving any consideration to the possible reasons for distinguishing adjudication from rulemaking.[9] The propriety of this extension was seemingly sealed in 1999 when the Court explicitly ruled that the *Chevron* doctrine applies to interpretations adopted in individual deportation proceedings by the Bureau of Immigration Appeals.[10] In a twist of fate, the Court cited *Cardozo-Fonseca* as having established that *Chevron* deference applies to interpretations rendered "through a process of case-by-case adjudication."[11] As we have seen, Justice Stevens had sought in *Cardozo-Fonseca* to *limit Chevron* to cases of law application, typically through adjudication.

Yet another expansive development was the Court's willingness to disregard congressional signals that a more searching review was required. In considering the application of the *Chevron* doctrine to the meaning of tariff statutes, the Court brushed aside a statute that had long been construed to mean that the reviewing court should if necessary conduct a trial de novo if it could not "determine the correct decision" based on the evidence presented.[12] The Court insisted that determining the facts de novo did not mean the court should interpret the law de novo: "Deference can be given to the regulations [of the Customs Service] without impairing the authority of the court to make factual determinations, and to apply those determinations to the law, de novo." The Court acknowledged that Congress, if it wanted to, could instruct a court to review questions of law de novo. But it seemingly required Congress to enact a statute containing a clear statement to this effect before the Court would be convinced to turn off the *Chevron* doctrine.[13]

Notwithstanding the general expansion of the *Chevron* doctrine in the 1990s, the Supreme Court adopted two important limitations on the doctrine, both drawing upon pre-*Chevron* law. In *Adams Fruit Co. v. Barrett,*[14] the question was whether a federal statute (the Agricultural Workers' Protection Act, or AWPA), which created a private right of action for farm workers injured by unsafe motor vehicles, preempted a state statute that made worker compensation remedies the exclusive remedy for workers injured on the job. The Department of Labor had issued a regulation affirming that exclusive state worker compensation statutes were not preempted. The employer argued that this regulation was entitled to deference under the *Chevron* doctrine.

In a unanimous opinion by Justice Marshall, the Court held that *Chevron* did not apply because the statute "established the Judiciary and not the Department of Labor as the adjudicator of private rights of action under the statute." Marshall explained:

> A precondition to deference under *Chevron* is a congressional delegation of administrative authority. . . . No such delegation regarding AWPA's enforcement provisions is evident in the statute. Rather, Congress established an enforcement regime independent of the Executive and provided aggrieved farmworkers with direct recourse to federal court when their rights under the statute are violated. Under the circumstances, it would be inappropriate to consult executive interpretations of [the statute] to resolve ambiguities surrounding the scope of AWPA's judicially enforceable remedy.[15]

Adams Fruit was important for two reasons. First, it established that an agency is "entrusted to administer" a statute only when it has been given decisional authority under a statute. A statute giving *courts* decisional authority is not subject to the type of deference outlined in *Chevron*. Second, the decision reaffirmed that courts should determine de novo whether the required delegation of authority has been made. Quoting pre-*Chevron* caselaw, the Court said that "[a]lthough agency determinations within the scope of delegated authority are entitled to deference, it is fundamental 'that an agency may not bootstrap itself into an area in which it has no jurisdiction.'"[16]

A second limitation on the *Chevron* doctrine, again incorporating pre-*Chevron* law, was that courts should not give *Chevron* deference to "post-hoc rationalizations" of agency counsel. In *Bowen v. Georgetown University Hospital*,[17] the Court considered whether a particular Medicare statute authorized the issuance of retroactive regulations. The government argued that it was entitled to *Chevron* deference for its view that this was permissible, but the Court held that the *Chevron* doctrine was inapplicable because the interpretation had been first advanced by government counsel in the course of defending the validity of the retroactive rule. Again quoting from pre-*Chevron* caselaw, the Court stated that

> we have declined to give deference to an agency counsel's interpretation of a statute where the agency itself has articulated no position on the question, on the ground that "Congress has delegated to the administrative official and not to appellate counsel the responsibility for elaborating and enforcing statutory commands." . . . Deference to what appears to be nothing more than an agency's convenient litigating position would be entirely inappropriate.[18]

For good measure, the Court noted that the interpretation in question was inconsistent with the way the agency had interpreted the statute in the past.

As the 1990s wound down, it became increasingly obvious that the ever-expanding *Chevron* doctrine was spawning a large number of questions about what sorts of statutes are covered by the doctrine, what types of agency interpretations are entitled to the deference described by the doctrine, and when courts should decide questions of interpretation on their own authority. Many of these questions had generated conflicts in the circuits or had been specifically reserved by the Supreme Court. An article I co-authored with Kristin Hickman enumerated fourteen unresolved questions about "*Chevron*'s domain."[19] The Court was undoubtedly aware of the proliferating disagreement in the lower courts about the scope of the doctrine. But the development that forced its hand was its own precedent that reaffirmed the existence of two different deference doctrines: *Chevron* and *Skidmore*. Either the one would have to swallow the other, or the Court would have to develop an explanation for when each should apply.

Skidmore Reemerges

Skidmore v. Swift & Co.,[20] discussed in Chapter 2, was not initially regarded as setting forth a separate deference doctrine. Instead it was generally referenced as part of the larger body of decisions giving weight or respect to agency interpretations of law, as appropriate.[21] This began to change in 1976. The question in *General Electric Co. v. Gilbert*[22] was whether a corporate disability benefit plan that excluded disability due to pregnancy was a form of sex discrimination prohibited by Title VII of the Civil Rights Act of 1964. The Court had recently ruled that a similar exclusion required by state law did not violate the Equal Protection Clause.[23] The Equal Employment Opportunity Commission (EEOC), which has certain enforcement responsibilities under Title VII of the Civil Rights Act of 1964 but does not have legislative rulemaking authority under that statute, had issued an enforcement guideline saying that pregnancy-based exclusions violate Title VII. The plaintiffs in *Gilbert* filed a class action challenging General Electric's exclusion of pregnancy as a violation of Title VII. The plaintiffs naturally argued that the EEOC guideline was entitled to "great deference" in interpreting how the mandate of equal treatment should be interpreted in this context.

Speaking through then-Justice Rehnquist, the Court refused to follow the EEOC guideline. Rehnquist noted that Congress did not give the EEOC authority to issue legislative regulations when it enacted Title VII. This meant "that courts properly may accord less weight to such guidelines than to administrative regulations which Congress has declared shall have the force of law."[24] The proper standard, he held, was the one set forth in *Skidmore,* which had involved an agency that had enforcement responsibilities but did not have authority to resolve claims. Rehnquist observed that the pregnancy benefit guideline had not been adopted contemporaneous with the enactment of Title VII and was inconsistent with advisory opinions the agency had given in the 1960s. These factors, Rehnquist observed, detracted from the persuasiveness of the guideline. "In short, while we do not wholly discount the weight to be given the 1972 guideline, it does not receive high marks when judged by the standards enunciated in *Skidmore*."[25] The Court accordingly concluded that the exclusion of pregnancy-related conditions from a general disability plan did not violate Title VII. (Congress would soon overrule the decision.)[26]

We have seen that Justice Scalia, in his 1989 law review article, had assumed that the *Chevron* doctrine had wiped out *Skidmore* and other pre-*Chevron* doctrines, including traditional factors like the longstanding interpretation canon.[27] This assumption was tested by the Court in 1991. The fateful decision again involved the EEOC.

The issue this time was whether Title VII's prohibition on employment discrimination applies to U.S. firms that employ U.S. nationals in locations outside the territorial limits of the United States. Speaking again for the Court, now-Chief Justice Rehnquist held in *EEOC v. Arabian American Oil Co. (Aramco)*[28] that the antidiscrimination statute did not apply in these circumstances. The main part of the analysis turned on a strong version of the canon of interpretation that statutes are presumed not to apply extraterritorially. The EEOC again argued for deference to its view that Title VII should apply in the particular circumstances presented (U.S. employer and U.S. employee). Rehnquist said that "the proper deference to be afforded the EEOC's guidelines," as had been held in *Gilbert,* was the standard set forth in *Skidmore*. As in *Gilbert,* Rehnquist characterized the EEOC's position as neither contemporaneous nor consistent, and thus "its persuasive value is limited when judged by the standards set forth in *Skidmore*."[29] The Court accordingly ruled for the firm. (This decision too would eventually be overruled by Congress.)[30]

Justice Scalia concurred in the outcome but dissented from the portion of Chief Justice Rehnquist's opinion reaffirming that the proper standard of review of EEOC guidelines was *Skidmore*. The correct standard of review, Scalia insisted, was that prescribed in *Chevron*. He wrote: "In an era when our treatment of agency positions is governed by *Chevron,* the 'legislative rules vs. other action' dichotomy of *Gilbert* is an anachronism."[31] Implicit in his concurring opinion was the supposition that the *Chevron* doctrine was the sole standard for determining what weight to give agency interpretations of statutes, and that *Chevron* had wiped out all other conceptions of the court–agency relationship, including *Skidmore*. As often happened in his applications of the *Chevron* doctrine, however, Scalia concluded that the

EEOC's interpretation was not "reasonable in light of the principles of construction courts normally employ."[32] So he would reject the agency's interpretation at step 2. No other Justice joined Scalia's opinion.[33]

The Court persisted in seemingly differentiating between "*Chevron* deference" and some lesser form of "deference" in a variety of opinions throughout the balance of the 1990s. For example, it concluded that an internal agency guideline that had not been "subject to the rigors of the Administrative Procedures Act, including public notice and comment," was entitled only to "some deference."[34] Similarly, it remarked that interpretive rules and enforcement guidelines are "not entitled to the same deference as norms that derive from the exercise of the Secretary's delegated lawmaking powers."[35] But it did not explain why interpretations that are clothed with "the force of law" were to be reviewed under the *Chevron* doctrine while other interpretations were entitled only to "some deference."

A more considered effort to resolve this question was inevitable. What was needed was a "meta-rule" that would indicate when the issue should be reviewed under the *Chevron* doctrine, when under *Skidmore,* and when it should be decided de novo. Because *Chevron* had already commandeered step 1 and step 2, the author and Kristin Hickman in the aforementioned article dubbed this threshold inquiry "*Chevron* step zero," and this locution caught on.[36]

Christensen v. Harris County

The issue came to a head in *Christensen v. Harris County,*[37] decided in 2000. Although *Christensen* is generally regarded as a skirmish that took place before the main battle, which occurred in *United States v. Mead Corp.* a year later, it is worth our attention because it revealed the fault lines among the Justices more clearly than can be discerned in *Mead.*

By 2000 the Court had experienced a significant turnover in personnel. Justices Brennan, Marshall, White, and Blackmun were gone. They had been replaced by two Bush I appointees—Justices Clarence Thomas and David Souter—and two Clinton appointees—Justices Ruth Bader Ginsburg and Stephen Breyer. The addition of Breyer was particularly significant in terms of the mix of attitudes on the Court toward the *Chevron* doctrine. Before Breyer's arrival, Justice Scalia was the only member of the Court who had a sig-

THE DOMAIN OF THE *CHEVRON* DOCTRINE

nificant background in administrative law. He had taught the subject at Virginia and Chicago law schools and had served in a variety of administrative posts before his appointment to the D.C. Circuit, which specializes in administrative cases. As previously noted, he wrote a law review article in 1989 praising the *Chevron* doctrine and interpreting it as a new and universal standard for review of agency interpretations of law.

Breyer was now a second Justice with a strong background in administrative law, having taught the subject at Harvard for many years before being appointed to the First Circuit and then the Supreme Court. In 1986, while serving on the court of appeals, Breyer had written a law review article sharply critical of the D.C. Circuit's recent embrace of "the *Chevron* doctrine."[38] The gist of his criticism was that this interpretation of the *Chevron* decision was overly simplistic. He wrote:

> [T]here are too many different types of circumstances, including different statutes, different kinds of application, different substantive regulatory or administrative problems, and different postures in which cases arrive, to allow "proper" judicial attitudes about questions of law to be reduced to any single simple verbal formula. Legal questions dealing with agencies come in an almost infinite variety of sizes, shapes and hues. To read *Chevron* as laying down a blanket rule, applicable to all agency interpretations of law, such as "always defer to the agency when the statute is silent," would be seriously overbroad, counterproductive and sometimes senseless.[39]

In effect, Breyer thought courts should continue to determine in a case-by-case fashion whether Congress had "implicitly delegated" primary interpretive authority to an agency. He predicted that "[d]espite its attractive simplicity," the emerging *Chevron* doctrine "seems unlikely in the long run[] to replace the complex approach. . . ." As we have seen in Chapter 4, its "attractive simplicity" was precisely what caused the *Chevron* doctrine to proliferate, especially in the lower courts.

Christensen arose under the Fair Labor Standards Act (FLSA), the same statute at issue in *Skidmore*. Amendments to the statute in the years since *Skidmore* provided that the Act applied to state and local government employees. In an effort to reduce the potential fiscal burden this imposed, the Act provided that government employees could be offered compensatory time off with pay ("comp time") in lieu of being paid time and a half for overtime, provided employees agreed to such a practice. The issue that arose in Harris County, Texas, was whether deputy sheriffs could be ordered to take comp time when they did not want to. Neither the statute, nor the agreement with the deputy sheriffs, specifically addressed this issue. When Harris County wrote the Administrator of the Wage and Hour Division of the Labor Department asking if it could adopt such a practice, the response was that the office interpreted the FLSA to mean that mandatory comp time was permissible only if this was included in the agreement with employees. Harris County then sued, arguing that the Administrator's interpretation was contrary to the statute.

When the matter reached the Supreme Court, Justice Thomas drew the assignment to write for the majority. Attending closely to the details of the FLSA amendments, he concluded that the statute contained language that prohibited state and local governments from *denying* an employee's request for comp time (if an agreement was in place), but did not restrict an employer from *requiring* that an employee take comp time. Thomas also rejected the Labor Department's argument that its interpretation was entitled to deference under the *Chevron* doctrine. As he wrote:

> Here . . . we confront an interpretation contained in an opinion letter, not one arrived at, for example, in a formal adjudication or notice-and-comment rulemaking. Interpretations such as those in opinion letters— like interpretations contained in policy statements, agency manuals, and enforcement guidelines, all of which lack the force of law—do not warrant *Chevron*-style deference. . . . Instead, interpretations contained in formats such as opinion letters are "entitled to respect" under our decision in *Skidmore v. Swift & Co.*, but only to the extent that those interpretations have the "power to persuade." As explained above, we find unpersuasive the agency's interpretation of the statute at issue in this case.[40]

This was a reasonably straightforward extrapolation from what the Court had said in *Aramco* and follow-on cases in declining to give *Chevron* deference to agency action that lacks the "force of law."

Predictably, Justice Scalia concurred in the judgment but declined to join the portion of the opinion discussing the relevant standard of review. As in

Aramco, he argued that there was only one deference doctrine—the *Chevron* doctrine. *Skidmore* was an "anachronism" and should be relegated to the dustbin of history. He contended that a court should apply *Chevron* whenever it finds that the administering agency has rendered an "authoritative" interpretation of a statute that contains a gap or ambiguity. An opinion letter signed by the Administrator of the Wage and Hour Division, by itself, might not be sufficiently authoritative. But the view expressed in the opinion letter had been endorsed in an *amicus* brief filed in the Supreme Court and co-signed by the Secretary of Labor. This was not a "post hoc rationalization" advanced in litigation, but a high-level validation of the view that had been taken by the agency before litigation commenced. As in his *Aramco* concurrence, Scalia nevertheless agreed that the Labor Department interpretation should be rejected under the *Chevron* standard, because "the Secretary's position does not seem to me a reasonable interpretation of the statute."[41]

Justice Breyer also entered the fray with a dissenting opinion, joined by Justice Ginsburg. *Skidmore,* he wrote, had very much survived *Chevron* and was not an "anachronism."[42] In this respect, "*Chevron* made no relevant change. It simply focused on an additional, separate reason for deferring to certain agency determinations, namely, that Congress had delegated to the agency the legal authority to make those determinations." Whether such a delegation has been made, he implied, requires an all-things-considered examination of the particular context. *Skidmore* rather than *Chevron* should continue to apply "where one has doubt that Congress actually intended to delegate interpretive authority to the agency (an 'ambiguity' that *Chevron* does not presumptively leave to agency resolution)." As to whether such a delegation should be found in the present case, Justice Breyer thought that Justice Scalia "may well be right" that the position set forth in the opinion letter and brief was enough to warrant deference under *Chevron.* In any event, whether the applicable standard was *Skidmore* or *Chevron,* the Labor Department position should have prevailed.

Justice Stevens filed another dissenting opinion, focusing on the merits. He concluded that a state or local government could compel employees to take comp time only if this possibility had been included in the agreement with employees. In a footnote near the end of his opinion, he wrote: "I fully agree with Justice Breyer's comments on *Chevron.*"[43] This confirms, if further confirmation is needed, that Stevens did not regard his opinion in *Chevron* as

having established an exclusive standard of review for assessing agency interpretations of law.

United States v. Mead Corporation

The three-way split over the proper scope of the *Chevron* doctrine in *Christensen* evidently persuaded the Court that better guidance was required about
the content of step zero. The vehicle the Court chose for offering this guidance, *United States v. Mead Corp.*,[44] was arguably an unfortunate choice.
Mead involved an unusual administrative process called tariff classification
rulings. These rulings do not correspond to any of the more familiar modes
of administrative action, such as legislative rules, interpretative rules, opinion
letters, adjudications, and so forth. They are letter rulings issued by the Customs Service in response to a request by an importer for advice as to what
tariff applies to a proposed importation of goods. The statute and implementing regulations specify that these rulings are "binding on all Customs
Service personnel."[45] But they are not binding on anyone outside the agency,
including the importer, who is free to challenge the tariff in court after im-
porting. Nor are they treated as precedents for any other importation of
goods. Typically, no public notice or opportunity to comment is provided before tariff classification rulings are issued, nor is the importer entitled to a
hearing beyond the request for a ruling and the responsive letter. Tariff classification rulings are extremely numerous; forty-six different Customs Service offices issue over ten thousand classifications every year. In effect, they
are a safe harbor pass given to an importer for purposes of a single importation of goods.

Given the oddball nature of tariff classification rulings, it was hard to see
how the Court's decision about whether the *Chevron* doctrine would apply
to an interpretation reflected in such a ruling would generalize to other, more
typical mode of administrative action. Perhaps the Court agreed to hear the
case simply because it was the next one to come along presenting an issue
about the scope of the *Chevron* doctrine. The Court may also have been
attracted by the fact that the issue had no discernible political valence. *Christensen* had carried echoes of earlier debates over whether the Tenth Amendment shields states from federal regulation of state employees, and the lineup

of the Justices was congruent with the lineup in those debates.[46] No Justice would give two hoots, as a policy matter, about whether the Mead Corporation's day-planners were properly classified as "diaries" for tariff purposes.

Chief Justice Rehnquist's decision to assign Justice Souter to write the opinion for the Court is also somewhat curious. Souter was a scholarly and somewhat reclusive figure whose primary background was as a state court judge in New Hampshire. He had little familiarity with administrative law, and had taken no position in previous debates about the scope of the *Chevron* doctrine. Yet this may have been a plus in Rehnquist's mind: Souter could serve as a neutral arbiter who might bring together the competing factions on the Court over the scope of the *Chevron* doctrine. Still, Souter's lack of background in administrative law posed risks, in that his approach to the case might fail to resonate with administrative law conventions.

Justice Souter drafted a lengthy opinion that, all in all, was a commendable effort to synthesize the jurisprudence as it had developed up to that time about the rationale and limits of the *Chevron* doctrine. At the end of the day, his effort commanded eight votes, including all the Justices who had joined Justice Thomas and all who had joined Justice Breyer in *Christensen.* In that sense, the effort was a success.

Justice Souter's opinion reaffirmed or settled a number of contested questions. It reaffirmed that federal administrative law includes two deference doctrines, the one articulated in *Chevron* and the one expressed in *Skidmore.* It reaffirmed that the ultimate touchstone for determining the proper standard of review is the intent of Congress, and that courts must decide de novo which standard applies. It reaffirmed the proposition set forth in *Aramco* and *Christensen* that *Chevron* applies only to agency interpretations that have the "force of law." It even seemed to endorse the two-part exegesis of that notion advanced in the article written by the author and Kristin Hickman (which appeared before *Mead* was decided and was quoted by the Court in a footnote), stating: "We hold that administrative implementation of a particular statutory interpretation qualifies for *Chevron* deference when it appears that Congress delegated authority to the agency generally to make rules carrying the force of law, and that the agency interpretation claiming deference was promulgated in the exercise of that authority."[47] In other words, *Mead* held that *Chevron* is subject to a step-zero inquiry, that this inquiry looks to congressional intent, and the critical signpost of congressional intent is whether the agency has been given and has exercised delegated authority to interpret in a procedural format that carries the force of law.

Perhaps in order to garner the support of Justice Breyer, the majority opinion was nevertheless hedged with qualifications. Breyer, if we can take his 1986 law review article and his dissent in *Christensen* as guides to his thinking, agreed that Congress can implicitly delegate authority to an agency to interpret statutory gaps and ambiguities. But he did not believe that the signal of such legislative intent could be reduced to whether Congress has conferred particular procedural powers on the agency, such as the power to engage in rulemaking or adjudication. Rather, he thought a more holistic or contextual inquiry was necessary to establish the requisite intent. The effort to accommodate Breyer's views may explain why Justice Souter was unable to reaffirm in a straightforward manner the relatively bright-line rule set forth by Justice Thomas in *Christensen*: legislative rules and formal adjudication create *Chevron*-eligible interpretations; anything else—"policy statements, agency manuals, and enforcement guidelines"—does not.[48] Thus, we find sentences in *Mead* such as the following: "Delegation of such authority may be shown in a variety of ways, as by the agency's power to engage in adjudication or notice-and-comment rulemaking, or by some other indication of a comparable congressional intent."[49] Or: "It is fair to assume generally that Congress contemplates administrative action with the effect of law when it provides for a relatively formal administrative procedure tending to foster the fairness and deliberation that should underlie a pronouncement of such force."[50] Or: "That said, and as significant as notice-and-comment is in pointing to *Chevron* authority, the want of such procedure here does not decide the case, for we have sometimes found reasons for *Chevron* deference, even when no such administrative formality was required, and none was afforded."[51]

Justice Scalia, in dissent, had a field day lampooning these equivocations, stating that the "utterly flabbiness of the Court's criterion" would produce "protracted confusion."[52] Scalia had a point. As events would soon reveal, Justice Breyer was unwilling to surrender his views about the need for an all-things-considered inquiry to determine whether there has been an implicit delegation of interpretive authority to an agency. Justice Souter's effort to patch together a near-unanimous decision by injecting ambiguity into the opinion failed to produce a lasting consensus, and left as its legacy primarily ambiguity.

Given that Justice Souter equivocated about whether notice-and-comment rulemaking and formal adjudication exhaust the conditions for applying the *Chevron* doctrine, he was required to explain why the grant of authority to the Customs Service to issue tariff classification rulings did not qualify for *Chevron* deference. His strategy here, in some of the murkier passages in the opinion, was to cast doubt on whether such rulings could fairly be characterized as "law" at all. He had been given litttle guidance by the briefs as to what it means for agency action to have the "force of law." For ordinary administrative law purposes, it is generally good enough to say that agency action has the force of law when it binds actors outside the agency. Justice Souter evidently wanted to probe more deeply about what constitutes "law," yet he did not have the material at hand to do so in more than a suggestive fashion. He ultimately concluded that tariff classification rulings are not sufficiently lawlike to qualify as a type of agency action that has the force of law. The key factors were that the rulings were a day ticket having no precedential value for other imports, and could be issued, potentially in contradictory terms, by forty-six different regional offices.[53] In other words, Congress had not authorized the agency to adopt rules or precedents that generalize to more than a single case and it had not authorized the agency to prescribe legal norms that apply uniformly throughout its jurisdiction.[54]

A deeper problem with "the *Mead* doctrine" is that there is no necessary correlation between agency procedures and whether the agency acts with the force of law. Justice Scalia pointed out that the Administrative Procedure Act contains some large exceptions to the use of notice-and-comment procedures in issuing legislative regulations, yet the resulting rules are understood to have the force of law.[55] Even more problematically, the APA's requirements for formal adjudication are designed to ensure accurate fact-finding by agencies. A legislative requirement to use formal adjudication procedures may or may not signify anything about whether Congress expects an agency to function as a law-interpreter.[56] Justice Souter had no response to these points. His opinion was grounded in an extrapolation from precedent, and Supreme Court precedent from *Adams Fruit* forward had focused on congressional assignment of certain procedures as a signpost of whether it was proper to apply the *Chevron* doctrine. As will be argued in Chapter 12, procedures are important insofar as they allow for public participation and encourage agency deliberation about the proper interpretation of law. There are hints of this perspective in the Souter opinion.[57] But the elevation of particular procedural formats, however qualified, as the determining factor in whether the *Chevron* doctrine applies, arguably failed to provide a sound connection between *Chevron* review and legislative intent to make the agency the primary interpreter.

Justice Scalia penned a lengthy and harsh dissent, which no other Justice joined. Although he scored some points, as previously indicated, much of the dissent was wide of the mark. He claimed that the majority opinion represented an "avulsive change in judicial review of federal administrative action."[58] But this characterization was accurate only if one accepts that *Chevron* had rendered *Skidmore* an anachronism, and that the two-step standard of review applies to every "authoritative" interpretation by an agency of a statute it administers. These were propositions that Scalia advocated—but always in solo opinions that no other Justice had joined. Justice Souter's opinion was a conscientious attempt to restate what the Court had previously held. The only "avulsive change" in view would have been a Court opinion embracing Scalia's idiosyncratic position, not one rejecting it.

It was clear that Justice Scalia was primarily exercised by the perpetuation of *Skidmore* as an alternative to *Chevron*. Scalia viewed *Skidmore* as a mushy standard—one he sarcastically characterized as "that test most beloved by a court unwilling to be held to rules (and most feared by litigants who want to know what to expect): the ol' 'totality of the circumstances' test."[59] But whereas the *Chevron* doctrine has fewer moving parts than the *Skidmore* doctrine, it is hardly any less a standard than *Skidmore*. The *Chevron* doctrine, as we have seen, is composed of two very general standards—clarity and reasonableness. In the hands of willful judges, it imposes little constraint in overturning agency decisions they dislike, and because it has fewer moving parts, it arguably makes it easier to be willful. In any event, the other eight Justices were all committed to the perpetuation of *Skidmore* in some circumstances, and so these fulminations fell on deaf ears.

Justice Souter, like a patient schoolmaster addressing a turbulent child, summed up the disagreement as follows: "Justice Scalia's first priority over the years has been to limit and simplify. The Court's choice has been to tailor deference to variety." With that, the Court remanded the case to the Federal Circuit to assess the Custom Service's interpretation under the *Skidmore* standard.

Post-*Mead* Confusion

It soon became clear that *Mead* had only papered over the division of views about *Chevron* evident in *Christensen*. Less than a year after *Mead,* Justice Breyer was assigned to write a majority opinion in a low-visibility Social Security case, *Barnhart v. Walton.*[60] After *Mead,* one would have thought that *Chevron* clearly supplied the appropriate standard of review. The agency, "[a]cting pursuant to statutory rulemaking authority," had promulgated the challenged interpretation in a regulation using notice-and-comment procedures.[61] And indeed, for the better part of the opinion, Justice Breyer framed the analysis in terms of a conventional version of the *Chevron* doctrine. The question, first, was whether the statute was silent or ambiguous; if the answer was affirmative, then the second question was whether the agency interpretation was permissible. Breyer concluded that deference was appropriate because the statute "[did] not unambiguously forbid the regulation" and "the Agency's construction is 'permissible.'" End of case—or so one would have thought after *Mead.*

Instead, Justice Breyer continued on. He noted that the agency's interpretation was "longstanding," citing various informal rulings and agency manuals dating back more than thirty years, and citing pre-*Chevron* authority that courts "will normally accord particular deference to an agency interpretation of 'longstanding' duration."[62] He also noted that Congress had frequently amended or reenacted the relevant provisions of the statute without change, suggesting congressional ratification. These sorts of considerations are not wrong, and as we will see in Chapter 7, they are not that unusual, even in the post-*Chevron* era. But Breyer did not explain their relevance to the *Chevron* doctrine.

In response to the respondent's argument that the regulation was only recently enacted, "perhaps in response to this litigation," Justice Breyer said this was irrelevant, citing other cases applying the *Chevron* doctrine in similar circumstances. This claim, however, opened to door for Justice Breyer to explain why, in his view, deference would be required under *Chevron* even if the only evidence of the agency's interpretation had been the informal rulings and agency manuals that preceded the issuance of the regulation. He wrote:

> If this Court's opinion in *Christensen v. Harris County* suggested an absolute rule to the contrary [i.e., that informal guidance and agency manuals do not qualify for deference under *Chevron*], our later opinion in *United States v. Mead Corp.* denied the suggestion. . . . Indeed, *Mead* pointed to instances in which the Court applied *Chevron* deference to agency interpretations that did not emerge out of notice-and-comment rulemaking. It indicated that whether a court should give such deference depends in significant part upon the interpretive method used and the nature of the question at issue. And it discussed at length why *Chevron* did not require deference in the circumstances there present—a discussion that would have been superfluous had the presence or absence of notice-and-comment rulemaking been dispositive.[63]

Breyer was correct that *Mead* did not limit the *Chevron* doctrine to interpretations rendered through notice-and-comment rulemaking. But it does not follow that *Mead* contemplated that interpretations rendered in informal guidance documents and agency manuals could qualify for *Chevron* treatment. *Mead* said that interpretations must have the *force of law* to qualify for *Chevron* review, and informal guidance and agency manuals do not have the force of law because they are not legally binding on persons outside the agency.[64]

Justice Breyer then wrapped up the discussion with the following remarkable sentence:

> In this case, the interstitial nature of the legal question, the related expertise of the Agency, the importance of the question to administration of the statute, the complexity of that administration, and the careful consideration the Agency has given the question over a long period of time all indicate that *Chevron* provides the appropriate legal lens through which to view the legality of the Agency interpretation here at issue. See *United States v. Mead Corp., supra.*[65]

Breyer seemed to be saying that step zero as recognized in *Mead* consists of an all-things-considered evaluation of the propriety of deferring to an agency interpretation—not unlike the conception of judicial review of agency legal interpretations he had argued for in his 1986 law review article.

Neither Justice Souter nor any of the other seven Justices who joined his opinion in *Mead* bothered to respond to this reading of *Mead*. That task fell to none other than Justice Scalia. He condemned the notion that "long-standing" agency interpretations are entitled to particular deference, insisting once again that this was an "anachronism" after *Chevron*.[66] Turning to the question whether the agency's interpretive guidelines and agency manuals could qualify for *Chevron* deference, Scalia said "I think the Court should state why these interpretations were authoritative enough (or whatever-else-enough *Mead* requires) to qualify for deference. I of course agree that more than notice-and-comment rulemaking qualifies, but that concession alone does not validate [the informal agency interpretations here]."[67]

About the only thing one can say with confidence about *Barnhart v. Walton* is that Justices Breyer and Scalia were the only Members of the Court sufficiently invested in the dispute over the foundation of the *Chevron* doctrine to carry the fight to another day. All other Justices had no appetite for reopening the schism temporarily obscured—for all of one year—by the ambiguities of *Mead*.

In the wake of *Walton*'s reconstruction of *Mead*, confusion reigned in the lower courts. Some read *Mead* as having adopted Justice Thomas's opinion in *Christensen*, with the result that only legislative rules and binding adjudications—agency actions having the force of law—are eligible for deference under the *Chevron* doctrine. Others read *Mead*, following Justice Breyer's revisionist opinion in *Walton*, as having adopted an all-things-considered test for determining whether the *Chevron* doctrine applies. Still others read the two decisions as having abandoned the two-step approach of *Chevron* altogether in favor of a multifactor analysis similar to the one that had prevailed before *Chevron*.[68]

The Supreme Court, in a manner similar to the way it responded to the dispute between Justices Stevens and Scalia in 1986–87 over whether *Chevron* should apply to pure questions of law, never clarified which reading of *Mead* was correct. Gradually, decisions began accumulating at the Court in which *Mead* was implicitly understood as having adopted the view of Justice Thomas in *Christensen*.[69] Interpretations adopted through notice-and-comment rule-making or rendered in a binding adjudication were treated as presumptively having the force of law, and hence as being eligible for the *Chevron* doctrine.[70] Interpretations advanced in interpretive rules, internal guidance documents, proposed rules, and other formats conventionally understood as not having the force of law were assumed to be entitled only to *Skidmore* deference.[71]

The outliers were Justices Breyer and Scalia. Justice Breyer's vision of an all-things-considered version of *Mead* continued to pop up in decisions in which he was assigned to write for the Court. For example, in *Long Island Care at Home Ltd. v. Coke*,[72] Justice Breyer described "the *Mead* doctrine" this way:

> Where an agency rule sets forth important individual rights and du-ties, where the agency focuses fully and directly upon the issue, where the agency uses full notice-and-comment procedures to promulgate a rule, where the resulting rule falls within the statutory grant of au-thority, and where the rule itself is reasonable, then a court ordinarily assumes that Congress intended it to defer to the agency's determina-tion. *See Mead*.[73]

This seemed to take the "all things considered" approach to identifying the conditions for applying the *Chevron* doctrine to a new extreme. The factors listed by Breyer included the nature of the delegation from Congress, the pro-cedural format adopted by the agency, and even the "reasonableness" of the agency view. At times Breyer seemed to equate "apply the *Chevron* doctrine" with "accept the agency view," with every conceivable relevant consideration open for examination before reaching such a conclusion.

For his part, Justice Scalia persisted in his lonely campaign to oust *Skid-more* and make *Chevron* the universal standard for reviewing agency inter-pretations. To this end he continued his assaults on *Mead* in separate opinions in multiple decisions, none of which gathered the support of any other Justice.[74] His quixotic crusade ended only when he suddenly found himself in a position to write a majority opinion that again expanded the *Chevron* doctrine—*City of Arlington v. FCC*,[75] which held that agencies are entitled to *Chevron* deference when they determine the scope of their own authority (see

Chapter 11). The small price he had to pay in order to secure five votes in *Arlington* was to stop carping about *Mead*.[76]

Mead and the Four Values

It is worth pausing to consider whether *Mead*'s reconstruction of the *Chevron* doctrine moved the law closer to the four values discussed in Chapter 1. The verdict here is mixed.

In terms of rule of law values and the importance of protecting settled expectations, the reaffirmation of *Skidmore* as the default standard of review when the conditions are not met for applying the *Chevron* doctrine was a plus. The primary tools for reinforcing settled expectations—the contemporary and longstanding canons—clearly have a significant role under the *Skidmore* doctrine. As we have seen, they were the only factors cited by Chief Justice Rehnquist in his EEOC decisions for concluding that the Commission's guidance documents were unpersuasive. So, by reining in the *Chevron* doctrine, and filling the vacated space with *Skidmore,* the Court modestly increased the range of cases in which settled expectations can be considered.

Constitutional values, which establish a series of boundary-maintenance limits on enforcing agency interpretations of law, present a more equivocal picture. In a little-noticed footnote in *Mead,* Justice Souter observed that the *Chevron* doctrine only applies if "the agency's exercise of authority is constitutional and does not exceed its jurisdiction," citing in support the relevant provisions of the APA.[77] But this was not the focus of the decision. More obviously, by grounding the *Chevron* doctrine in implicit congressional intent, *Mead* reaffirmed the principle of legislative supremacy, in the form of the anti-inherency understanding of that idea (Chapter 1). Congress must delegate specified authority to an agency before the court will accept its interpretation of a statute. And when Congress delegates power to an agency to act with the force of law, it cannot be gainsaid that Congress has conferred a significant power on the agency that distinguishes it from the kind of inherent powers any executive officer, including the President, can exercise.

The central problem with the *Mead* doctrine, which did not emerge clearly until later, is that it did not question the proposition that, once step zero has been satisfied, any ambiguity in the relevant statute constitutes an implicit delegation of interpretive authority to the agency to act as the primary interpreter.[78] But the prerequisites for satisfying step zero—the power to adopt legislative regulations and to resolve adjudications (the paradigmatic delegations of authority to act with the force of law)—do not begin to exhaust all the limits on an agency's authority that may have been imposed by Congress. Often, regulatory statutes will contain *general* grants of rulemaking authority and *general* provisions authorizing agencies to adjudicate broad classes of disputes. It is implausible that Congress would understand the conferral of what are essentially general procedural powers to mean that agencies have primary authority to interpret all gaps, silences, and ambiguities in the substantive legislative provisions delineating the agency's powers and their limits. *Mead* did not perceive this problem, because the sequence of Supreme Court decisions starting with *Adams Fruit* and culminating in *Christensen* characterized the potentially relevant limit on the *Chevron* doctrine in terms of the delegation of particular types of procedural powers. In this respect, *Mead* further obscured the importance of judicial review in delineating the space within which Congress has determined that the agency—rather than Congress itself—is to serve as the policymaking body.

Mead was also a mixed bag in terms of moving toward an understanding of the importance of public participation and reason-giving in providing incentives for improved agency interpretation. As the *Mead* doctrine came to be implemented in practice, it operates as a kind of procedural review. The *Chevron* doctrine applies only to interpretations adopted pursuant to certain kinds of procedure—namely, notice-and-comment rulemaking and adjudication. Procedural review is arguably closer to process review than is substantive review, and some lower courts and commentators read *Mead* as conditioning *Chevron* deference on the use of procedures that would ensure at least some public participation and deliberation by the agency.[79] But *Mead* nowhere spelled out the desirability of providing advance notice and an opportunity for public comment on proposed agency interpretations. And its emphatic affirmation that the *Chevron* doctrine applies to interpretations announced in adjudications—an affirmation driven by precedent rather than by any consideration of whether adjudication provides opportunities for advance notice and public comment equivalent to rulemaking—arguably impeded further development of the idea that an opportunity for public participation should be an important qualification on acceptance of agency interpretations.

In Sum

The relentless expansion of the *Chevron* doctrine was not checked until the Supreme Court had to find some way to accommodate the competing standard associated with *Skidmore v. Swift & Co.* The solution, most authoritatively pronounced in *United States v. Mead Corp.*, was to require courts to determine at "step zero" whether the preconditions for *Chevron* deference are met. In keeping with the understanding that *Chevron*-style deference must be grounded in implicit congressional intent, *Mead* ruled that the *Chevron* doctrine applies only when Congress confers certain powers on an agency that can be taken as a sign of such an intent. The Court further ruled that the critical indicator of such an intent is a delegation to the agency to act with "the force of law." The Court identified the paradigmatic cases of interpretations having the force of law as those adopted pursuant to a delegated power to issue legislative rules using notice-and-comment procedures and those promulgated in a delegated power to render adjudications. *Mead* left enough wiggle room that other circumstances might also qualify, and Justice Breyer, in post-*Mead* cases, sought to exploit the wiggle room by urging an all-things-considered conception of step zero. This created considerable confusion in the lower courts, but the Supreme Court, without resolving the intramural dispute, seemed by its behavior to treat the *Chevron* doctrine as limited to interpretations adopted through notice-and-comment rulemaking or in adjudication. In practice, therefore, the *Chevron* doctrine has been confined to agency interpretations adopted using particular procedures.

One consequence of the *Mead* reformation of the *Chevron* doctrine, which stimulated Justice Scalia's ire, is that the doctrine lost much of its appealing simplicity. Questions of statutory interpretation that arise in reviewing agency action can no longer be resolved by ticking off step 1 and step 2. To be sure, if the interpretation is advanced in notice-and-comment rulemaking or adjudication, the step-zero inquiry can be resolved in one sentence with a citation to *Mead.* But in more unusual situations, the need to decide which deference doctrine to apply can add a new layer of complexity and new grounds for litigation that did not exist in the early years of the *Chevron* doctrine.

After *Mead,* the *Chevron* doctrine was trimmed back. The trimming did not yield large benefits, because the Court perpetuated the notion that any ambiguity in a statute means the agency has been implicitly delegated power to serve as the statute's primary interpreter. But the trimming came with significant costs, in that the simplicity of the *Chevron* two-step approach was now compromised. Some of the complexity, such as leaving open the possibility that interpretations contained in informal adjudication might qualify for *Chevron* treatment, was an unforced error. But even a perfectly executed revision along the lines outlined by the Court would have necessarily resulted in reduced enthusiasm for the doctrine.

7

Rule of Law Values

Rᴜʟᴇ ᴏꜰ ʟᴀᴡ ᴠᴀʟᴜᴇꜱ, in the form of protecting settled expectations about the law, have not disappeared in the post-*Chevron* world. The *Chevron* doctrine, a streamlined two-step approach to review of agency interpretations of law, eliminated any obvious place for courts to consider the relevance of these values. But they continued to bubble to the surface, demonstrating their continuing relevance to the judicial mind. Which strongly indicates that a sensible deference doctrine must give explicit recognition, in an appropriate form, to the importance of such values.

The Persistence of the Traditional Canons

We have seen in Chapter 2 that the twin canons that dominated pre-*Chevron* jurisprudence—the contemporary and longstanding canons—were a device for giving weight to settled expectations about the law created by agency interpretations. We have also seen in Chapter 6 that many commentators, including most prominently Justice Scalia, assumed these canons had been banished by the *Chevron* doctrine. Indeed, there is no obvious place for the twin canons under the two-step approach. If we view the twin canons as a way to measure the degree to which settled expectations have developed around the agency interpretation, neither step 1 nor step 2 directs the reviewing court to consider this value explicitly.

Nevertheless, courts continue to find the duration of an agency interpretation relevant. William Eskridge and co-authors have found a measurable difference in the Supreme Court's willingness to accept agency interpretations that are longstanding and consistently maintained (73.2% upheld) relative to "evolving" agency interpretations (60.5% upheld). They report that the difference is statistically significant.[1] The persistence of the traditional canons (whether explicitly acknowledged or not) is unsurprising given Aditya Bamzai's study, discussed in Chapter 2, documenting the extensive historical pedigree of the contemporaneous and longstanding canons.

Another recent study, by Anita Krishnakumar, confirms the continuing use of the longstanding interpretation canon after the emergence of the *Chevron* doctrine.[2] Krishnakumar examined every Supreme Court decision between 1976 and 2013 in which there was some reference to the duration of an agency interpretation under review. She also looked at a large number of court of appeals decisions during the same time period. She concluded that the courts continue to regard the duration of an agency interpretation as significant. Her study allows us to drill down further by looking at how the Supreme Court in particular handles agency interpretations of significant duration in the post-*Chevron* era.

We can take as our starting point the Supreme Court's 1986 decision in *Community Nutrition,* which, as discussed in Chapter 4, is the first decision by the Court to apply the two-step formula as a standard of review. Between *Community Nutrition* and the cutoff date of Krishnakumar's study (2013), the Court decided twenty-one cases in which some reference was made to the significant duration of the agency interpretation under review. Of these decisions, the ratio of decisions upholding the agency interpretation to those rejecting it (fifteen to six) is about two-to-one. By itself, this does not tell us very much, because two-to-one is roughly the same ratio of affirmances to reversals of agency decisions overall.[3] There is also the problem of selection effects: Justices writing an opinion upholding an agency interpretation may be more inclined to cite its longevity as part of the mix of considerations supporting an affirmance, and less inclined to do so when justifying a decision to overturn an agency interpretation. But it is doubtful that selection effects explain everything. In some of the cases the longevity of an interpretation is mentioned only in a concurring or dissenting opinion. So we can be sure that longevity was drawn to the attention of the Justices in all twenty-one cases, without regard to whether it was cited as a supporting reason by the controlling opinion. At the very least, one can say that longevity is positively correlated with a majority vote to uphold the agency interpretation.

Looking more closely at the decisions, we find that longevity is invoked as a relevant consideration in *Skidmore* cases (as one would expect) but also in cases that apply the *Chevron* doctrine (as one would perhaps not expect). Of the fifteen cases that uphold a longstanding agency interpretation, eight applied the *Chevron* doctrine, three applied the *Skidmore* standard, and four applied either a hybrid standard or no apparent standard at all. Most of the *Chevron* decisions citing the longstanding nature of the agency interpretation do so in support of its being "reasonable." The same is true of the *Skidmore* decisions. The decisions that apply a hybrid standard or no standard generally uphold the agency interpretation as being legally correct, which obviates the need to specify the relevant standard. Turning to the six decisions that reject an agency interpretation, only one (*Aramco*) discusses the relevant standard—*Skidmore;* and as we have seen in Chapter 6, the Court discounted the agency interpretation in that case because it was neither contemporaneous nor longstanding. The other decisions reject the agency interpretation as a matter of de novo review, and do not discuss the relevant standard for determining whether deference is appropriate.

We also find a fairly wide spectrum of Justices citing the longstanding interpretation canon. The Justices who allude to the canon in majority or controlling opinions that apply the *Chevron* doctrine include O'Connor, Stevens, Breyer, Ginsburg, and surprisingly, Scalia.[4] Kennedy, Breyer, and Ginsburg also allude to the canon in majority or controlling opinions applying the *Skidmore* standard.

Often the longstanding nature of an agency interpretation is cited as a "comfort factor" that reinforces the Court's conclusion based on an analysis of the statutory language and history. The most striking instance, perhaps, is a case in which Justice Scalia upheld the agency interpretation but failed to note the standard of review (perhaps because precedent indicated it should be *Skidmore,* which he repeatedly condemned as an "anachronism"). Justice Ginsburg filed a short concurring opinion, offering what she described as a "fortifying observation: That today's decision accords with the longstanding view of the Equal Employment Opportunity Commission (EEOC), the federal agency that administers Title VII."[5] Occasionally the longstanding nature of the interpretation is cited as supporting an inference that Congress, by reenacting the relevant language, has acquiesced in this interpretation.[6]

And on rare occasions we find statements recognizing that the extra weight given to longstanding agency interpretations protects settled expectations about the requirements of the law. Thus, Justice Brennan, in supplying critical support to a plurality opinion by Justice Kennedy in a trademark case, observed: "We do not lightly overturn administrative practices as longstanding as the ones challenged in this action. This is particularly true where, as here, an immense domestic retail industry has developed in reliance on that consistent interpretation."[7] It is mildly puzzling why there are not more such statements in the post-*Chevron* cases, which continue to make reference to the canon. Perhaps it is because the *Chevron* doctrine supposedly rendered such a consideration irrelevant. Or perhaps it is because the connection between longstanding interpretations and settled expectations is intuitively obvious.

Chevron and Conflicting Judicial Precedent

Another prominent intersection between the *Chevron* doctrine and rule of law values concerns the relationship between prior judicial precedent and agency interpretations for which *Chevron* deference is claimed. If the judicial precedent in question applied the *Chevron* doctrine, there should be little difficulty in integrating judicial and agency understandings. A judicial precedent that resolved the matter at step 1 would represent a finding by the court that the statute has a clear or unambiguous meaning. Such a ruling by a court, under shared assumptions of American law, would be binding on the agency and cannot be revised by the agency in the future. In contrast, a judicial precedent rendered at step 2 would represent a finding by the court that the statute is unclear or ambiguous. Implicit in such a ruling is the understanding that the statute has more than one possible interpretation (it is, after all, unclear). Thus, if the agency later changes its mind, the question for the court would be whether the new interpretation is reasonable, whether or not the prior judicial decision found the first interpretation to be either reasonable or unreasonable. If the new interpretation is deemed to be reasonable, it should be upheld under a step 2 analysis.

The problem of integrating agency interpretations and judicial precedent arises when the relevant judicial precedent either predates the *Chevron* doctrine or has been rendered by a court that (for whatever reason) fails to follow the two-step *Chevron* doctrine. To simplify, assume that the judicial precedent dates from before 1984, when *Chevron* was decided, and thus was rendered at a time when it was generally assumed that courts would exercise independent judgment (however defined) in reviewing agency interpretations of statutes. Assume further that the agency decides, sometime after 1984, that the statute should be given a different meaning than the one adopted by the court in the pre-1984 era. Finally, assume that the agency successfully establishes that the statute is ambiguous and that its interpretation is reasonable. How should the reviewing court respond in such a situation? Should it follow the pre-*Chevron* judicial precedent, or should it allow the agency, under the *Chevron* doctrine, effectively to "overrule" the old judicial precedent?

A court faced with a clash between (pre-*Chevron*) judicial precedent and (post-*Chevron*) agency interpretation is forced to decide between two competing principles. The principle that favors the judicial precedent is called *stare decisis*—stand by what is decided. Courts as a rule faithfully follow their own precedents. Overruling is rare and requires a special justification, such as an intervening change in the legal landscape that fatally undermines the soundness of the precedent. *Stare decisis* is vital to preserving the legitimacy of courts as an institution for resolving disputes.[8] Courts must be seen as neutral dispute-resolvers, applying settled principles of law in an objective fashion. This means respecting and applying the rules that have been laid down in the past, including by past decisions of the court.[9]

If judicial legitimacy were the only value at stake, perhaps courts could be selective in deciding whether or not to follow a judicial precedent. For example, they could decline to follow a precedent that in hindsight seem unfair, or they could ignore a precedent when neither party can show that it has relied upon it. Assuming that courts could accurately differentiate among precedents along these lines (which is doubtful), the parties might continue to regard the judiciary as a legitimate institution for resolving disputes.

But *stare decisis* performs a broader function. It powerfully reinforces the understanding that the nation is governed by the rule of law, in the sense of respecting settled expectations about the law. If the judiciary, as the institution that applies the law in individual cases, consistently adheres to what has been decided in the past, this greatly enhances the perception that the law which governs individuals and institutions (including the government) does so in a predictable manner. As discussed in Chapter 1, predictability about the law is a source of individual security, allows people to plan for the future, encourages investment, and promotes individual autonomy. In addition, adhering to precedent channels demands for legal change to institutions like legislatures and administrative agencies, which are relatively more accountable to the people and have the capacity to make legal change prospective, which allows individuals to make adjustments before the change takes effect.[10] So *stare decisis* is important not only in preserving judicial legitimacy in resolving disputes, it has profound implications for how everyone in society—whether or not they have a dispute to resolve—regards the legal system, and in particular whether they see it as respecting rule of law values.

The competing principle that favors administrative interpretation is the desirability of channeling issues of discretionary policy choice to administrative agencies. If the question is one that falls under step 2 of the *Chevron* framework—or, using a slightly different formulation, if the court determines that it falls within the space that Congress has delegated to the agency to decide—it should be resolved by the relatively more accountable and expert interpreter. Again as discussed in Chapter 1, agencies are more politically accountable than courts, given the extensive oversight of agencies by both Congress and the President. And all agree that agencies are more likely to have extensive experience with implementing the statutory regime and to have relevant scientific and technical expertise among their staff. An offsetting consideration is that agencies are more likely to be biased in favor of their own policy preferences in applying the law in particular cases.[11] But this concern arises primarily (although not exclusively) when agencies engage in adjudication.

When faced with a direct tradeoff between the principle of *stare decisis* and the principle that questions of discretionary interpretive choice should be made by agencies, one might predict that courts would come down on the side of *stare decisis*. This is because *stare decisis* is critical to the court's legitimacy as a dispute-resolution institution, and is of vital importance more generally to preservation of the rule of law. In contrast, enforcing older judicial interpretations that are suboptimal from the perspective of comparative institutional advantage is likely to be regarded by courts as imposing only localized harm (in the form of an outcome in a particular controversy that is more likely to be incorrect). And the courts can always rationalize that the suboptimal outcome can be corrected by Congress—even if the constrained capacity of Congress to legislate makes this increasingly unlikely.

We have some data with which to test this prediction, in the form of six Supreme Court decisions that have addressed a conflict between pre-*Chevron* (or non-*Chevron*) precedent and an agency's claim for deference under the *Chevron* doctrine. This is admittedly a small number, but the results are highly suggestive. Of the six decisions, five enforced judicial precedent at the expense of an agency interpretation. The sixth ruled in favor of the agency interpretation, but at the expense of a precedent of the Ninth Circuit, not one of the Supreme Court's own prior decisions. And the author of this particular decision has recently announced that he now believes it should be reconsidered.[12]

It is worth taking a brief look at the six decisions to gain a sense of the types of conflicts that have emerged, and why the Court has generally gravitated to enforcing judicial precedent rather than post-*Chevron* agency views.

The first decision in the series, *Maislin Industries, U.S. Inc. v. Primary Steel, Inc.*[13] involved a conflict between older precedents requiring strict adherence to tariff filings in the railroad and motor carrier industries and a policy statement by the Interstate Commerce Commission (ICC) announcing that it would be an "unreasonable practice" to enforce tariff filings in certain circumstances. What had changed in the interim was a major change in the legal landscape—the substantial deregulation of the motor carrier industry in 1980.[14] This led to widespread negotiations between carriers and shippers of contract rates lower than published tariff rates. The practice of negotiating rates was encouraged in various ways by the ICC, including its adoption of a relaxed approach to enforcing tariff filing requirements. Consequently, many carriers became careless about filing tariffs reflecting the lower rates they had negotiated with particular shippers. As long as such carriers remained in business, reputational constraints presumably kept them from attempting to collect the higher tariff rate: no one would give repeat business to a carrier that engaged in bait-and-switch tactics by negotiating a lower rate and then charging a higher one. But when carriers declared bankruptcy, their trustees often sought to recoup the difference between the filed rate and the negotiated rate as a way of augmenting the assets of the bankrupt's estate. Shippers

complained loudly about this, and the ICC responded with its policy statement declaring an attempt to collect the higher rate in these circumstances
an unreasonable practice, and hence unlawful.

When the validity of the ICC's policy statement was challenged in the Supreme Court, it emphatically rejected the agency's interpretation of the Motor
Carrier Act, in a 7–2 decision authored by Justice Brennan. He wrote in part:

> For a century, this Court has held that the Act, as it corporates the filed
> rate doctrine, forbids as discriminatory the secret negotiation and col-
> lection of rates lower than the filed rate. . . . Once we have determined a
> statute's clear meaning, we adhere to that determination under the doc-
> trine of *stare decisis,* and we judge an agency's later interpretation of
> the statute against our prior determination of the statute's meaning. . . .
> "Congress must be presumed to have been fully cognizant of this in-
> terpretation of the statutory scheme . . . [and] Congress did not see fit
> to change it when Congress carefully reexamined this area of the law
> in 1980."[15]

Justice Stevens, dissenting, argued that the 1980 deregulation produced a
fundamental change in the industry that rendered the older precedents obsolete. Given that negotiated rates had largely superseded filed tariff rates,
forcing an unsuspecting shipper to pay the higher tariff rate when the carrier went bankrupt violated legitimate commercial expectations. He would
have deferred to the ICC's policy statement under *Chevron.* The Court was
kept busy with follow-on cases seeking to mitigate the effects of *Maislin* until
Congress came to the rescue by largely overriding it in the Negotiated Rates
Act of 1993.[16]

The second and third decisions in the series essentially followed *Maislin.*
Lechmere, Inc. v. National Labor Relations Board[17] arose under the National
Labor Relations Act. The issue was whether the Act permits labor organizers
to trespass on an employer's property (such as a parking lot) in an attempt
to convince workers to unionize. The Court followed one of its own precedents from 1956, which it interpreted as allowing nonemployee organizers
to trespass only when there is no other feasible way to contact workers,
and overturned a recent NLRB decision adopting a balancing test in these
circumstances.[18]

Neal v. United States[19] involved an effort by the U.S. Sentencing Commission to mitigate the harsh consequences of a Supreme Court interpretation of how the federal drug laws apply to distributors of LSD. Pure LSD is very potent, and is sold in very small quantities dissolved on an inert substance like blotter paper. The Court nevertheless held that the weight of the blotter paper should be added to the LSD for purposes of determining whether the threshold for a mandatory minimum sentence has been met. The decision was controversial, and the Sentencing Commission sought to mitigate its perceived inequities by adopting a guideline stating that the weight of the carrier medium used in distributing LSD should be presumed to be 0.4 milligrams per dose. The Court refused to follow this interpretation. Although it admitted that its earlier decision had resulted "in significant disparity of punishment meted out to LSD offenders relative to other narcotics traffickers," any adjustment in the statute would have to come from Congress, not the Sentencing Commission.[20]

With the decision in *Neal,* it appeared that the conflict between judicial precedent and agency interpretation was settled—in favor of judicial precedent. Then the Court did an abrupt about-face in *National Cable & Telecommunications Association v. Brand X Internet Services.*[21] At issue was whether cable television systems that offer internet access as part of their package of services should be classified as telecommunication service providers or information service providers. The former are regulated as common carriers (as are traditional telephone companies); the latter are regulated much more lightly. The Federal Communications Commission (FCC) concluded that cable companies offering internet service should be regulated as information service providers. When the Commission's order was reviewed by the Ninth Circuit, the court of appeals overturned it, on the ground that prior circuit precedent (decided before the FCC had weighed in on the issue) classified cable internet service as telecommunications service. The Supreme Court, in an opinion by Justice Thomas, reversed, holding that the court of appeals should have applied the *Chevron* doctrine rather than relying on circuit precedent, and that under the two-step *Chevron* standard the statutory definition of telecommunications service was ambiguous and the FCC's determination that cable internet service did not qualify was reasonable.

Justice Thomas was able to conclude that the *Chevron* doctrine governed, rather than circuit precedent, by switching the vantage point for considering the matter from *stare decisis* to the *Chevron* doctrine. When the conflict is viewed from the perspective of the two-step doctrine, it follows that if the statute is ambiguous, a reasonable agency interpretation trumps judicial precedent. Thomas wrote:

> A court's prior judicial construction of a statute trumps an agency construction otherwise entitled to *Chevron* deference only if the prior court decision holds that its construction follows from the unambiguous terms of the statute and thus leaves no room for agency discretion. . . . [A]llowing a judicial precedent to foreclose an agency from interpreting an ambiguous statute, as the Court of Appeals assumed it could, would allow a court's interpretation to override an agency's. *Chevron*'s premise is that it is for agencies, not courts, to fill statutory gaps. The better rule is to hold judicial interpretations contained in precedents to the same demanding *Chevron* step one standard that applies if the court is reviewing the agency's construction on a blank slate: Only a judicial precedent holding that the statute unambiguously forecloses the agency's interpretation, and therefore contains no gap for the agency to fill, displaces a conflicting agency construction.[22]

Implicit in this resolution of the conflict is that the reviewing court must re-analyze pre-*Chevron* judicial precedent (or, as in the case before it, non-*Chevron* judicial precedent) and classify it as resting on either step 1 or step 2 reasoning. The Ninth Circuit precedent that was said to preclude the agency interpretation was found to rest on what the Ninth Circuit regarded as the better reading of the statute, not a conclusion that the statute was unambiguous. So it was grounded in step 2 reasoning and did not qualify as a precedent that would foreclose the *Chevron* doctrine.

In contrast, Thomas characterized each of the Court's three decisions holding that *stare decisis* trumps the agency's interpretation—*Maislin, Lechmere,* and *Neal*—as resting on precedent holding that the statute in question was *unambiguous* and hence as grounded in step 1 reasoning. This was a doubtful reading of those cases. A better reading of the trilogy is that the Court in each of the three previous decisions thought, not that the *statute* was unambiguous, but that the Court's previous interpretation had *made the statute unambiguous.* The key sentence from *Maislin* (repeated in *Lechmere* and *Neal*) was: "*Once* we have determined a statute's clear meaning, we ad-

here to *that determination* under the doctrine of *stare decisis,* and we judge
an agency's later interpretation of the statute *against our prior determination*
of the statute's meaning."[23] One might say that the metaphysic of *Maislin,
Lechmere,* and *Neal* is that the Court's prior interpretation enters into and
qualifies the meaning of the statute; the interpretation is in effect incorporated into the meaning of the statute, making it "clear." In the constitutional
law context, some commentators (following James Madison) have described
this as "liquidating" the meaning of the text.[24]

Justice Thomas's approach to resolving the conflict between judicial precedent and *Chevron*—the *Brand X* doctrine—required courts faced with such
a conflict to re-examine the allegedly conflicting precedent and classify it *as
if* it had been decided at step 1 or step 2 of the *Chevron* doctrine. The idea
that courts should engage in such a re-examination and classification of past
decisions is open to serious objections on grounds of practicality and judicial economy. The process of case-by-case classification would be fraught with
difficulties, given that the precedent court by definition did not apply the two-
step *Chevron* doctrine. The task of re-examination would have to be undertaken largely by the lower courts, which would undoubtedly lead to conflicts
among the circuits about the proper classification of key precedents. The proposed exercise would generate a type of "litigation over litigation," which is
generally thought to provide a poor return on investment in both private and
public litigation resources.[25]

Justice Scalia filed a vigorous dissent, most of which was a rehash of his
arguments against the *Mead* doctrine, which he somehow blamed for giving
rise to the *Brand X* doctrine. He characterized *Brand X* as creating "another
breathtaking novelty: judicial decisions subject to reversal by executive officers." He thought this was "not only bizarre" but "probably unconstitutional."[26] This was an odd argument for Scalia to make, given that Justice
Thomas's opinion was a straightforward explication of how to resolve the conflict between judicial precedent and agency interpretation from the perspective of the *Chevron* doctrine, which Scalia otherwise sought to champion at
every turn. *Brand X* rested, not on *Mead,* but on an analysis that ruthlessly
followed the logic of the *Chevron* doctrine and effectively ignored the competing values associated with *stare decisis.*

More telling perhaps was a short concurring opinion filed by Justice Stevens, who said in effect that he would go along with *Chevron* trumping a
precedent of the court of appeals, but that this would not "necessarily be

applicable to a decision by this Court that would presumably remove any pre-existing ambiguity."[27] This was a clear reference to the incorporation theory of *Maislin, Lechmere,* and *Neal.* Stevens did not explain why Supreme Court precedents are incorporated into the meaning of statute whereas court of appeals' precedents are not. From the perspective of a Supreme Court Justice, a precedent of the lower courts is not entitled to *stare decisis.* But from the perspective of the lower court that rendered the precedent, it is. Given that the vast majority of regulatory matters are resolved by the lower courts, the conflict between judicial precedent and agency interpretation should be resolved the same way at all levels of the judicial hierarchy.[28]

The next decision in the sequence is *United States v. Home Concrete & Supply, LLC,*[29] in which the Court reverted to the incorporation theory of *Maislin* and rejected the *Brand X* approach. At issue was the meaning of a provision of the Internal Revenue Code that extends the statute of limitations for the government to assess a tax deficiency from three to six years if the taxpayer "omits from gross income" an amount greater than 25% of the gross income reported in a tax return. In *Colony, Inc. v. Commissioner,*[30] decided in 1958, the Court held that the exception did not apply when a taxpayer inflates the basis of property that is sold, with the result that gross income is understated by more than 25%. Overstating basis, the Court ruled, was different from omitting from gross income. *Colony* was decided under the 1939 Tax Code. In 2010 the Treasury Department issued a regulation providing that, under the current 1954 Tax Code, an "overstatement of unrecovered cost or other basis constitutes an omission from gross income."[31] It argued for *Chevron* deference for this interpretation, invoking *Brand X.*

Home Concrete appeared to be an ideal case for applying the *Brand X* theory to a Supreme Court precedent. The language of the 1939 Code and of the 1954 Code was virtually identical. The precedent in question, *Colony,* had said that the language was "not unambiguous." This would appear to be exactly the kind of statement that would support a finding that the precedent Court in 1958 would have decided the matter at step 2 of *Chevron,* if it could only foresee the future. But Justice Breyer, speaking for the Court, would have none of it. "In our view," he wrote in a section of the opinion joined by five Justices, "*Colony* has already interpreted the statute, and there is no longer any different construction that is consistent with *Colony* and available for adoption by the agency."[32]

As to why the theory of *Chevron* and hence of *Brand X* did not support deference to the new regulation, Justice Breyer spoke only for a plurality. His answer consisted of yet another version of his understanding of the *Mead* doctrine. Under the Breyer version of *Mead* (see Chapter 6), the court must engage in an all-things-considered examination of the statute to determine whether Congress has left a gap in the statute that it implicitly intends the agency to fill. Here Breyer invoked considerations such Congress's enactment of the identical language in the 1954 Code, after the IRS had made known its preference for treating inflated basis the same as omitting gross income. Re-enactment of the language of the 1939 Code thus could not be taken as a signal to courts to accept the gap-filling views of the IRS. Breyer concluded that "[t]here is no reason to believe that the linguistic ambiguity noted by *Colony* reflects a post-*Chevron* conclusion that Congress had delegated gap-filling power to the agency." "And there being no gap to fill, the Government's gap-filling regulation cannot change *Colony*'s interpretation of the statute."[33]

Justice Scalia joined all of Justice Breyer's opinion except its effort to distinguish *Brand X*. Here, he acknowledged that it would be "reasonable" for the Court to overrule *Colony* as contrary to the *Chevron* doctrine. But, he immediately added, he would not take that course—"[b]ecause of justifiable taxpayer reliance." Scalia went on to provide an astute appraisal of the unworkability of the *Brand X* approach to resolving a conflict between older judicial precedent and subsequent agency interpretation. Before *Brand X* and indeed before *Chevron,* courts had no idea that a finding of ambiguity would transfer primary interpretive authority to the agency:

For many of those earlier cases, therefore, it will be incredibly difficult to determine whether the decision purported to be giving meaning to an ambiguous, or rather an unambiguous, statute. . . . Before then it did not really matter whether the Court was resolving an ambiguity or setting forth the statute's clear meaning. The opinion might (or might not) advert to the point in the course of its analysis, but either way the Court's interpretation of the statute would be the law.[34]

Rather than overruling *Colony,* Justice Scalia concluded that *Brand X* should be overruled. What should replace it, in his view, was evidently the theory that pre-*Chevron* judicial interpretations of a statute are incorporated into the meaning of the statute. "I join the judgment announced by the Court because it is indisputable that *Colony* resolved the construction of the statutory language at issue here, and that construction must therefore control."[35] The justification for this, beside the unworkability of *Brand X*, was the imperative "to sustain the justifiable reliance of taxpayers."[36] For all his enthusiasm about the change wrought by the *Chevron* doctrine, Justice Scalia fully appreciated the importance of *stare decisis* in protecting settled expectations about the law.

There is nothing in the Court's post–*Home Concrete* decisions to suggest that a return to *Brand X* may be in the offing. In our sixth and final example, *Epic Systems Corp. v. Lewis*,[37] the Court was presented with the question whether an employer may require employees to arbitrate disputes over pay and overtime and thereby forbid them from joining class actions contesting these issues. Writing for a 5–4 majority, Justice Gorsuch relied on a series of Supreme Court precedents broadly interpreting the Federal Arbitration Act as permitting agreements to compel arbitration in lieu of class actions. He refused to give *Chevron* deference to a recent decision by the NLRB interpreting federal labor laws as precluding such agreements. Although there was no direct conflict between a Supreme Court precedent and the NLRB's interpretation, the general thrust of the decision is consistent with the Court's solicitude for its own precedent and its disparagement of the idea of bowing to the contrary views of an agency by applying the logic of the *Chevron* doctrine.

What are we to make of this somewhat tortuous odyssey by the Court in seeking to reconcile pre-*Chevron* judicial precedent with the *Chevron* doctrine? Justice Scalia in *Home Concrete* condemned the *Brand X* doctrine as an "exile to the Land of Uncertainty."[38] Although this was hyperbolic, he was clearly correct that the re-examination and classification exercise contemplated by *Brand X* is unworkable. The bigger point is that, with the exception of *Brand X*, the Court has consistently enforced pre-*Chevron* (or non-*Chevron*) precedent at the expense of the *Chevron* doctrine. This is a testament to the importance of *stare decisis* to the legal system, and, more generally, to the centrality of rule of law values and the protection of settled expectations. It tells us that, without regard to the workability of *Brand X*, a regime of judicial review based on an unadulterated application of the two-step doctrine—and *Brand X* is perhaps the premier example of an unadulterated application of that doctrine—must be qualified by competing values.

The Requirement of Fair Warning

A third manifestation of the continued importance of rule of law values is the emergence in recent years of a refusal to accept agency interpretations that fail to give "fair warning" of a change in law likely to upset reliance interests. This theme first emerged in 2012 in a decision by the Supreme Court refusing to accept an agency interpretation of its own regulations. The second shoe dropped in 2016 when the Court held that the *Chevron* doctrine cannot be applied when the agency fails to provide an adequate explanation for a sudden change in position. Both decisions arose under the Fair Labor Standards Act (FLSA), which requires employers to pay time and a half for work in excess of forty hours per week.

The first decision, *Christopher v. Smithkline Beecham Corp.*,[39] involved something generally called *Auer* deference. A word of explanation about this. The *Chevron* doctrine, strictly speaking, involves judicial review of agency interpretations of *statutes* that they administer. Well before *Chevron* was decided, a similar doctrine emerged with respect to judicial review of agency interpretations of their own *regulations*. In 1945, in a decision involving the proper interpretation of World War II price control regulations, the Court offhandedly stated that the agency's interpretation of its own regulations is entitled to "controlling weight unless it is plainly erroneous or inconsistent with the regulation."[40] This formulation is, if anything, even more deferential than the *Chevron* doctrine. Courts must reject agency interpretations if they are "plainly erroneous or inconsistent with the regulation"—something close to *Chevron*'s step 1. Otherwise, an agency's interpretation of its regulation is entitled to "controlling weight"—arguably even more deference than an agency gets under *Chevron*'s step 2, which requires that the agency interpretation be upheld if it is "reasonable." The sentence from the 1945 decision was reaffirmed in later decisions, most prominently in *Auer v. Robbins*,[41] decided in 1997, where Justice Scalia added that the "controlling weight" standard applies even if the agency interpretation is advanced for the first time in a government *amicus curiae* brief filed in the very case where the application of the regulation is challenged.

Auer deference, like the *Chevron* doctrine, became controversial with conservative legal commentators and then judges, especially during the years of the Obama Administration.[42] Even Justice Scalia, shortly before his death, repudiated the *Auer* doctrine.[43] In 2019, in a decision called *Kisor v. Wilkie*,[44] the Court substantially rewrote the *Auer* doctrine, preserving the doctrine in name while changing its substance.

The *Auer* decision that is of special interest, *Christopher v. Smithkline Beecham,* occurred in the run-up to the reconstruction of the doctrine in 2019. Smithkline Beecham is a major pharmaceutical company. Like other companies in the industry, Smithkline employs "detailers" whose job is to call on doctors in an effort to inform them about the company's products and persuade them to prescribe those products for their patients. Detailers function in a manner analogous to the proverbial traveling salesmen, in that they circulate in a designated territory, without punching a time clock or under other significant supervision, and are paid in significant part by incentive pay keyed to the number of prescription drugs sold in their territory. The industry employs in total some 90,000 persons as detailers.

The FLSA, as enacted in 1938, contains an exception for persons employed "in the capacity of outside salesman (as such terms are defined and delimited from time to time by regulations of the Secretary [of Labor])."[45] This was obviously an express delegation of interpretational authority to the agency, such as the Court considered in *Batterton v. Francis* (discussed in Chapter 2). The Secretary adopted regulations under this authority, but they had not been changed in any material way since the 1940s. The regulations did not advert to the occupation of detailer, which did not emerge in a significant way until the 1950s. The agency issued an opinion letter in 1945, tentatively concluding that "medical detailists" would be exempt from the overtime requirement, but under a different provision of the Act for administrative employees. After that, for over seventy years no interpretive ruling or advice was offered by the agency as to whether detailers would qualify under either the exemption for outside salesmen or for administrative employees. Throughout this time the industry did not offer to pay, and active detailers evidently did not seek, time and half for hours spent on the road in excess of forty per week.

The litigation in *Christopher* arose when two former detailers of Smithkline filed suit seeking back pay and liquidated damages for the failure to pay them overtime during the time they had been employed by the company. When the case reached the Ninth Circuit, the Department of Labor filed an *amicus* brief in support of the former employees, stating that it interpreted the regulation for outside salesmen to mean that detailers were not covered by the exemption because they did not personally consummate sales of the company's products. The Ninth Circuit rejected this interpretation. On further review by the Supreme Court, the Department filed another *amicus* brief in support of the employees, but changed its theory—now taking the position that they were not covered by the exemption because there was no transfer of title by the company at the time when the detailers met with doctors. The Department claimed that this interpretation, advanced in an *amicus* brief signed by the Secretary and the Solicitor General, was entitled to *Auer* deference.

In a majority opinion for five Justices written by Justice Alito, the Court refused to recognize *Auer* deference in these circumstances. The switch in reasoning by the government in its *amicus* briefs was one factor. But the stronger ground for refusing to apply *Auer* was that the government's interpretation threatened to "impose potentially massive liability on respondent for conduct that occurred well before that interpretation was announced."[46] Citing a string of lower-court decisions and dicta in some of its own cases, the Court held that the lack of "fair warning" to the industry about the Department's interpretation meant that it was unreasonable. Alito concluded, "It is one thing to expect regulated parties to conform their conduct to an agency's interpretations once the agency announces them; it is quite another to require regulated parties to divine the agency's interpretations in advance or else be held liable when the agency announces its interpretation for the first time an in enforcement proceeding and demands deference."[47]

Christopher represents a dramatic affirmation of the proposition that courts play an important role in protecting settled expectations about the law. Significantly, the settled expectations it enforced in *Christopher* were created entirely by practice—seventy years of industry practice in assuming detailers were exempt from the FLSA combined with deafening silence by the agency. It is conceivable that the entire industry was in violation of the statute for this period without the agency noticing. But the "more plausible hypothesis" was that the agency did not think the industry practice was unlawful and the industry had relied on this unspoken understanding.[48] *Christopher* also represents a powerful affirmation of the proposition that changes in the law, if made by an agency, should be made in a format that provides fair notice in advance so the regulated community can make appropriate adjustments before incurring liability. The dissent by Justice Breyer did not disagree with these propositions.

The Court substantially rewrote the *Auer* doctrine in 2019, turning it into a multifactor balancing test. In so doing, it incorporated settled expectations into the decisional framework:

> [A] court may not defer to a new interpretation, whether or not introduced in litigation, that creates 'unfair surprise' to regulated parties. That disruption of expectations may occur when an agency substitutes one view of a rule for another. We have therefore only rarely given *Auer* deference to an agency construction "conflict[ing] with a prior" one. Or the upending of reliance may happen without such an interpretive change. This Court, for example, recently refused to defer to an interpretation that would have imposed retroactive liability on parties for longstanding conduct that the agency had never before addressed. See *Christopher*, 567 U.S. at 155–56. Here too the lack of "fair warning" outweighed the reasons to apply *Auer*.[49]

Thus, rule of law values, in the form of giving added weight (or subtracting weight) to agency interpretations depending on whether they comport with settled expectations, was expressly incorporated into the doctrine that governs judicial review of agency interpretations of their own regulations. Note that the incorporation includes the understanding both that the duration of the agency interpretation matters and that abrupt changes in agency policy that can upset reliance interests should, if possible, be made prospectively.

Four years after *Christopher*, the Court extended to the *Chevron* doctrine the exception for interpretations that do not provide fair notice. This time the issue involved a statutory amendment to the FLSA adopted in 1961 for "any salesman, partsman, or mechanic" at an automobile dealership who is "primarily engaged in selling or servicing automobiles."[50] As amended, the statute expressly exempts persons employed at auto dealerships who sell cars or repair cars, but says nothing about persons employed to sell car repair services. The question in *Encino Motorcars, LLC v. Navarro,*[51] was whether the exception covered "service representatives" whose job is essentially to sell repair services at a dealership. Over time the Labor Department accumulated an unenviable record in interpreting whether the statutory exception applied to service representatives. In 1970 the Department adopted an interpretive regulation saying the service representatives were not exempt. This interpretation was rejected by several courts. In 1978 the Department issued an opinion letter agreeing with the courts that service representatives were exempt. This was confirmed in a Field Operations Handbook in 1987. In 2008 the Department issued a notice of proposed rulemaking, in which it proposed to revise its regulations to make the exemption of service representatives permanent, and inviting comments. When it got around to issuing a final rule, in 2011, the Department changed its position and reverted once again to its original 1970 position that service representatives were not exempt. Due to "an inadvertent mistake in drafting," however, the provision regarding service representatives was omitted from the final regulation.[52]

The Supreme Court was not impressed. Although the Department sought *Chevron* deference for its latest interpretation, Justice Kennedy reasoned that the *Chevron* doctrine did not apply because the 2011 regulation was "procedurally defective."[53] By this he did not mean that the Department had failed to follow notice-and-comment procedures, or even that it had failed to publish the relevant provision in the final regulation. What he meant was that the Department had failed to supply a "reasoned explanation" for its last-minute change in position. The Court noted that automobile dealers had relied since 1978 on the understanding that service representatives are exempt, and they had "negotiated and structured their compensation plans against this background understanding." Dealerships that had not compensated their service representatives "in accordance with the Department's new views could also face substantial FSLA liability."[54]

The Court concluded:

In light of the serious reliance interests at stake, the Department's conclusory statements do not suffice to explain its decision. This lack of reasoned explication for a regulation that is inconsistent with the Department's longstanding earlier position results in a rule that cannot carry the force of law. It follows that this regulation does not receive *Chevron* deference in the interpretation of the relevant statute.[55]

The Court was unanimous on this point.[56]

In Sum

The foregoing should convince the reader that rule of law values remain very much alive even under a regime of deference—the *Chevron* doctrine—that makes no apparent provision for such values. We see this in the persistent invocation by courts of the importance of the contemporaneous and long-standing interpretation canons, in the strong judicial preference for adhering to *stare decisis* at the expense of agency interpretations, and in the refusal to defer to agency interpretations that upset important reliance interests.

There are three important takeaways in terms of how a better deference doctrine might be formulated. First, that doctrine should attempt to integrate reliance interests created by contemporary or longstanding agency interpretations into the deference regime, rather than treating such reliance interests as a kind of random or ad hoc element of uncertain weight or significance. Second, previous judicial precedent that has settled the meaning of the law should be enforced as a matter of *stare decisis,* even if the question is properly characterized as a matter that, if it arose today as an original matter, should be decided by the agency. Third, acceptance of agency interpretations that change the meaning of the law, or that upset reliance interests created by longstanding agency acquiescence in a particular practice, should be conditioned on requiring a persuasive explanation by the agency of the need for the change and should be implemented in a manner that is prospective rather than retroactive. Chapter 13 will undertake the task of suggesting how these propositions might be incorporated into a reformulated deference doctrine.

Justice Gorsuch may have been guilty of overstatement in a recent opinion accompanying a denial of certiorari, but he had a point:

> [T[hese days it sometimes seems agencies change their statutory interpretations almost as often as elections change administrations. How, in all this, can ordinary citizens be expected to keep up—required not only

to conform their conduct to the fairest reading of the law they might expect from a neutral judge, but forced to guess whether the statute will be declared ambiguous; to guess again whether the agency's initial interpretation of the law will be declared "reasonable"; and to guess *again* whether a later and opposing agency interpretation will *also* be held reasonable? And why should courts, charged with the independent and neutral interpretation of the laws Congress has enacted, defer to such bureaucratic pirouetting?[57]

8

Constitutional Avoidance

JUDICIAL REVIEW OF QUESTIONS of law performs an important function in preserving boundaries of agency authority—something that is grounded in principles of constitutional law. These boundaries come in three major categories: individual constitutional rights, federalism, and separation of powers. Courts, by contemporary understanding, have the final say on questions of constitutional law, so enforcement of these boundaries is of central importance in calibrating the proper judicial role in reviewing agency interpretations of law.

This chapter and Chapters 9–11 take up the question of boundary enforcement in the era of the *Chevron* doctrine. The four chapters correspond loosely to the division between individual rights, federalism, and separation of powers. More accurately described, they concern the general question of boundary enforcement when there is both a question of statutory interpretation resolved by an agency and a constitutional principle in the picture. This chapter addresses the question of how to integrate the *Chevron* doctrine with canons of interpretation designed to protect constitutional values, most prominently canons that instruct courts to interpret statutes so as to avoid constitutional questions. Chapter 9 addresses the question of preemption of state law, where the question of statutory interpretation implicates the constitutional principle of federalism. Chapters 10 and 11 concern boundary enforcement when the question is whether the agency has complied with limits on its authority established by Congress—boundaries that must be enforced under the separation of powers principle of legislative supremacy.

In general, whether courts perceive that constitutional boundaries are implicated by an agency interpretation depends in significant part on how

sharply the relevant constitutional principle is delineated. Individual constitutional rights, such as the First Amendment right of freedom of speech or
the Fourth Amendment right against unreasonable searches and seizures,
tend to be sharply delineated. This does not mean they are easy to resolve. It
means only that they are perceived as being distinct from questions of statutory interpretation. Courts have developed a variety of interpretational canons
that are designed to protect these sorts of constitutional rights. Questions
have inevitably arisen about how these constitutionally influenced canons
should be integrated with the *Chevron* doctrine.

The most prominent of these constitutionally influenced canons is the
canon of constitutional avoidance. At least in its modern incarnation, this
says that if a statute is fairly susceptible to two interpretations, one of which
raises a *serious but unresolved question* of constitutionality and the other does
not, the court should adopt the interpretation that avoids the need to address
the constitutional question. Other canons of interpretation can be seen as more
particularized versions of constitutional avoidance. The rule of lenity (requiring
that ambiguities be resolved in favor of the accused), the presumption against
retroactivity, and canons requiring a clear statement by Congress before
intruding upon traditional state functions can all be seen as instructions to
interpret legislation in a way that avoids trenching upon particular constitutional principles, such as due process and federalism.[1] Still other canons,
such as the presumption against extraterritorial application and various
canons favoring Native American tribes, have a kind of quasi-constitutional
foundation grounded in notions of political sovereignty.[2]

The most general question presented by these constitutionally influenced
canons is whether courts should enforce such canons before considering the
agency interpretation—thereby limiting the discretion of the agency to adopt
a contrary interpretation—or whether courts should allow agencies to develop
their own preferred interpretation of the statute free of such constraints, intervening only if the court is convinced the resulting interpretation intrudes
impermissibly on constitutional principles. In practice, this is a question of
sequencing: Should the reviewing court consider the agency interpretation
first, under the *Chevron* doctrine or some other principle of judicial review,
and turn to the constitutional question only if the agency interpretation is
permissible as a matter of statutory interpretation, or should the court go

directly to the constitutional question—or a constitutionally based canon—without considering the agency interpretation? The Court has given inconsistent answers to this sequencing question.

A second question posed by some of these constitutionally influenced canons concerns how they should apply under so-called hybrid statutes that can apply in different types of proceedings. The rule of lenity, in particular, traditionally applies only in cases in which the government seeks to impose a criminal sanction on a defendant. But many modern regulatory statutes contain provisions that can be enforced in either civil or criminal proceedings. Should an agency that satisfies the *Mead* conditions for securing *Chevron* deference to its interpretation in the civil context (Chapter 6) be able to determine the meaning of the statute for purposes of criminal prosecutions, without regard to the doctrine of lenity? Or should the fact that the provision can potentially apply in a criminal proceeding mean that the doctrine of lenity should constrain the agency in its interpretation of the statute, even for purposes of civil liability? Here the Court has also spoken inconsistently, but a consensus of sorts seems to have emerged to the effect that the constitutionally influenced canon should be applied in both contexts.

In this chapter I argue that the emerging answer reached with respect to the rule of lenity and its application to hybrid statutes offers a clue as to how the question of sequencing should be resolved more generally. When a constitutionally grounded canon—such as the rule of lenity or the presumption against retroactivity—is well settled, it should constrain the authority of the agency to interpret otherwise. In effect, the discretionary space in which the agency is allowed to develop its own interpretation should be limited by the canon. This is a more specific application of rule of law values and the role of courts in protecting settled understandings about the law. In contrast, when the constitutional question potentially implicated by the case is unsettled, as is generally the case when the canon of constitutional avoidance is invoked, the opposite approach is preferable: the agency interpretation should be considered first, free of any doubts about constitutionality the court may harbor. The agency may decide on its own to adopt an interpretation that eliminates the constitutional question, or it may offer reasons that bear importantly on consideration of the constitutional question. If the agency adopts an interpretation of the statute that does not eliminate the constitutional question, the court should then face the constitutional music and decide, up or down, whether the interpretation is constitutional.

The Baseline Principle: Judicial Supremacy in Constitutional Interpretation

We begin by underscoring the baseline principle that the Supreme Court has the final word about the meaning of the Constitution if the issue is properly presented in a case before it. This emerges most clearly when the constitutional question is not complicated by questions of statutory interpretation. For example, when federal courts review challenges to state law under the federal Constitution, they will accept the interpretation of state law adopted by the state courts, but will generally decide the federal constitutional question without giving any deference to the views of the state actors involved. Similarly, when federal agencies adopt a policy that is not perceived as turning on a question of statutory interpretation, and the action is challenged as violating the federal Constitution, courts will resolve the constitutional question without giving any deference to the agency.

Consider, by way of illustration, the enforcement action of the Federal Communications Commission (FCC) against a radio station for broadcasting a comic monologue laced with profanity (George Carlin's "seven dirty words").[3] Although a statute was implicated, the Court had little trouble finding that the FCC's policy was consistent with its statutory mandate, which prohibited broadcasting "obscene, indecent, or profane" speech.[4] The principal point of contention was whether the decision violated the First Amendment's guarantee of freedom of speech. The Justices resolved the constitutional question according to their own lights, balancing the relevant considerations as they thought appropriate. A majority held that the enforcement action was permissible, largely because of the prospect that impressionable young children would be listening. The dissenters disagreed, and would limit restrictions on the content of broadcasting to material that is obscene. Although a concurring opinion made brief reference to the importance of respecting the judgment of the FCC,[5] the tenor of the opinions was overwhelmingly that of de novo review by the Justices. The views of the

Commission were invoked only for the factual predicate—the likely presence of children in the audience—supporting the adoption of the policy.

Another illustration, also involving the FCC, is *Metro Broadcasting, Inc. v. Federal Communications Commission*.[6] At issue were certain policies adopted by the FCC designed to increase ownership of broadcast stations by members of minority groups. The rationale for these policies was that increased minority ownership would produce greater diversity in the content of the programming offered to the public by broadcasters. The policies were challenged by nonminority applicants, on the ground that they violated the equal protection mandate reflected in the Fifth Amendment. On the "complex" empirical question of whether more minority ownership would actually produce more diversity in broadcast programming, the majority said that "great weight" should be given to the "experience of the Commission."[7] In contrast, the majority affirmed that it would "not 'defer' to the judgment of Congress and the Commission on a constitutional question."[8] The relevant constitutional standard, it concluded, was whether the policy served an important governmental objective and was substantially related to achievement of that objective. The dissenters insisted that strict scrutiny should apply, a position that prevailed when *Metro Broadcasting* was overruled a few years later.[9]

In general, we can see that the Constitution establishes certain boundaries that limit the exercise of authority by the government. These boundaries apply to administrative agencies no less than to legislatures and other government actors. By convention, courts exercise de novo review in determining what the Constitution requires. The role of the agency in such cases is effectively that of an expert witness. Ideally, perhaps, courts should give respectful consideration to the agency's views on the matter and give it weight insofar the agency has special knowledge of relevant facts. But it would cut too strongly against the grain of established institutional roles to expect courts to defer in any strong sense to the agency's view about the Constitution.

The Question of Sequencing

When agency action is challenged as violating both the statute under which it operates and the Constitution, the matter becomes more complicated. In the post-*Chevron* world, the court may be required to defer to the agency's interpretation of the statute. But the established convention of judicial supremacy in matters of constitutional interpretation requires that the court resolve the constitutional question de novo. A central problem with this division of authority concerns the proper sequencing of inquiries. Should a reviewing court consider the matter of statutory interpretation first, applying the *Chevron* doctrine (or whatever measure of deference to the agency interpretation is appropriate), and then consider whether the interpretation violates the Constitution? Or should courts consider the constitutional question first, and interpret the statute in such a way that avoids any possibility of constitutional infirmity, without regard to what the agency thinks the statute means? The Court in the *Chevron* era has issued prominent decisions associated with both approaches.

The approach that considers the *Chevron* doctrine first was adopted in *Rust v. Sullivan*.[10] Title X of the Public Health Act authorizes the appropriation of funds to support family-planning services. One section of the Act prohibits the use of such funds "in programs where abortion is a method of family planning."[11] This was originally interpreted by the Department of Health and Human Services to mean that programs providing abortions are ineligible for funding. In 1988 the Department adopted a more restrictive regulation, banning funding for any program that provides information to women about the identity of abortion providers. This so-called gag rule was challenged as violating both the statute and the First Amendment's guarantee of freedom of speech.[12]

The Court, in an opinion by Chief Justice Rehnquist, first considered whether the 1988 regulation was a permissible interpretation of the statute under the *Chevron* doctrine. He concluded that the prohibition on funding abortion as a method of family planning was ambiguous and that the agency rule was reasonable, given the concern with preventing evasion of the legislative policy against subsidizing abortions. Only after upholding the agency interpretation under *Chevron* did Rehnquist turn to the question whether the gag rule was an unconstitutional restriction on speech by health professionals. He admitted that the constitutional arguments were not "without some force," but concluded this did not warrant adopting a different interpretation in order to avoid a "serious question of constitutional law."[13] Given that three Justices in dissent thought the regulation was unconstitutional and a fourth thought the matter was close enough that the Court should have overturned the regulation in order to avoid deciding the constitutional question, it seems implausible that the regulation did not at least implicate a "serious constitutional question." Nevertheless, Rehnquist concluded that the rule was constitutionally permissible under precedents allowing the government to subsidize some kinds of speech but not others.

Another case in which the Court considered the question of statutory interpretation before turning to the Constitution was *Verizon Communications, Inc. v. FCC*.[14] The Telecommunications Act of 1996 required incumbent local telephone companies to lease certain of their facilities to firms seeking to enter their market, and provided that they were to be reimbursed for the "cost" of doing so. The FCC interpreted "cost" to mean "forward-looking" cost (essentially the replacement cost of these facilities) rather than "historical" cost (what the local carrier had actually paid for them in the past less depreciation). The Commission's interpretation was challenged by incumbent carriers, who argued that cost, as a matter of plain meaning, had to mean historical cost. They also argued that interpreting cost to mean forward-looking rather than historical costs would constitute a taking of their property without just compensation, in violation of the Takings Clause of the Fifth Amendment.

In a long and scholarly opinion by Justice Souter, the Court considered the statutory question first, and concluded that "cost" had sometimes been defined to mean historical costs and at other time had been defined as replacement costs. The term was thus sufficiently ambiguous to require further interpretation. The Court also concluded that the FCC's interpretation of cost as forward-looking cost was reasonable in light of the objective of Congress to stimulate competition in local telephone markets. Turning to the constitutional question, the Court found ample precedent in older cases involving constitutional challenges to restrictions on public utility and railroad rates to support the use of forward-looking costs in determining the permissible limits on rates when they have been challenged as confiscatory.

By contrast, in *Edward J. DeBartolo Corp. v. Florida Gulf Coast Building & Construction Trades Council*,[15] the Court held that the canon favoring avoidance of serious constitutional questions took precedence over the *Chevron* doctrine. At issue was a union's distribution of handbills designed to convince consumers not to patronize a shopping mall where one of the stores had hired a contractor that was in a dispute with the union. The object of the handbills was clearly to put pressure on the shopping mall owner to convince the store and its contractor to settle with the union. The National Labor Relations Act generally condemns secondary boycotts as an unfair labor practice, but includes a proviso that this does not "prohibit publicity, other than picketing" to inform consumers about the existence of a labor dispute.[16] The NLRB held that, notwithstanding the proviso, the distribution of handbills in question was a prohibited secondary boycott. The Supreme Court, on review, reversed.

The opinion for the Court, by Justice White, quickly dispatched the *Chevron* doctrine, ruling instead that the statute should be construed in such a way as to avoid a substantial constitutional question under the First Amendment. He noted that the information on the handbills was truthful, their distribution was peaceful, and no picketing was involved. "Had the union been leafletting the public generally," he wrote, "there is little doubt that legislative proscription of such leaflets would pose a substantial issue of validity under the First Amendment."[17] Ergo, the Board's ruling raised a substantial constitutional question. The statutory proviso, authorizing "publicity, other than picketing," would seem to provide ample basis for reversing the agency interpretation as contrary to the plain language of the statute.[18] Yet Justice White delved at length into the legislative history, to see if it contained evidence that Congress had harbored an intent to proscribe leafletting as well as picketing designed to stimulate a secondary boycott. Unsurprisingly, he found none.

The Court extended the sequencing associated with *DeBartolo* to a question of constitutional federalism in *Solid Waste Agencies of Northern Cook County v. U.S. Army Corps of Engineers (SWANCC)*.[19] At issue was whether the Army Corps of Engineers, which administers the wetland permitting program under the Clean Water Act, had authority to require a permit to fill an abandoned gravel pit in Illinois that was frequented by migratory birds. Congress, in a classic exercise in ambiguity, provided in the Act that federal permitting authority extends to "the navigable waters," which were defined in turn to mean "the waters of the United States, including the territorial seas."[20] The evident purpose of the definition was to define "navigable waters" more broadly than the traditional understanding—navigable traditionally meaning capable of floating a boat. But the definition of "navigable waters" to mean "the waters of the United States" left the question of how much broader completely obscure.

In its first confrontation with the puzzle of what "waters" are included beyond those that are navigable, the Court applied the *Chevron* doctrine and upheld a regulation of the Army Corps that extended its authority to wetlands that are adjacent to navigable waters.[21] No issue of federalism was identified as being implicated by this interpretation. Subsequently, when the Rehnquist Court tightened protections for states' rights after 1992, the Court announced a new and somewhat stricter understanding of the scope of federal power under the Commerce Clause and other enumerated powers in the Constitution.[22] Meanwhile, the Army Corps had revised its interpretation of "waters of the United States" to include isolated ponds that have no connection to navigable waters but are frequented by migratory birds. The abandoned gravel pit in Illinois had no hydraulic connection with navigable waters as conventionally defined, but some 121 species of migratory birds had been spotted using the waters as a rest stop during their travels.

The Court, in a 5–4 decision authored by Chief Justice Rehnquist, thought this was going too far. The migratory bird rule, he reasoned, raised a serious question as to whether it exceeded the scope of Congress's power under the Commerce Clause. Quoting *DeBartolo* (but not *Rust*), Rehnquist wrote that "where an otherwise acceptable construction of a statute would raise serious constitutional problems, the Court will construe the statute to avoid such problems unless the construction is plainly contrary to the intent of Congress."[23] He added that "[t]his concern is heightened where the . . . interpretation alters the federal-state framework by permitting federal encroachment upon a traditional state power." Thus, the Court "would not extend *Chevron* deference here."[24]

If the Court hoped that its decision in *SWANCC* would force Congress or the Army Corps to clarify the scope of the federal authority over wetlands it was sorely disappointed. Congress could not agree on appropriate amendatory language. The Army Corps could not agree on a new regulation. When the issue returned to the Court for a third time, in *Rapanos v. United States*,[25] it turned out that the Court could not agree either. Justice Scalia wrote a plurality opinion that offered an interpretation of the word "waters," following Webster's New International Dictionary (second edition), to mean "relatively permanent, standing or flowing bodies of water."[26] Any interpretation of the Army Corps beyond this was impermissible. It was unclear whether this interpretation—which had not been advanced by any party in the case—was based on the doctrine of constitutional avoidance, step 1 of *Chevron*, or was just a clever way to resolve the controversy. In any event, there was no pretense of deference to the Army Corp's understanding of the scope of its authority. Justice Kennedy concurred only in the judgment. He would define the agency's authority in terms of whether the wetland in question has a significant nexus with navigable waters.[27] Justice Stevens, writing for four dissenters, would defer to the Army Corp's regulations, still unmodified after *SWANCC*, under the *Chevron* doctrine.[28] Chief Justice Roberts joined Scalia's plurality opinion, but in a separate opinion chastised the Army for failing to revise its regulations in a way that would garner the support of a majority of the Court.[29]

Which Version of Avoidance?

Rust / Verizon and *DeBartolo / SWANCC* correspond to two different versions of the avoidance doctrine identified by commentators.[30] Under the "classical" canon of avoidance, if two interpretations of a statute are possible, one of which is constitutional and the other unconstitutional, a court should adopt the constitutional interpretation. *Rust* and *Verizon* are examples of this approach because the Court concluded that the agency's interpretations were constitutional, and hence there was no reason to avoid them. *DeBartolo* and *SWANCC* reflect what has been called the "modern" version of avoidance. This says that if two interpretations of a statute are possible, and one raises a serious constitutional question while the other does not, a court should pick the interpretation that does not require it to resolve a potentially difficult constitutional question.[31]

Commentators have been generally critical of the modern version of the avoidance doctrine as reflected in *DeBartolo* and *SWANCC*. In theory, the modern doctrine reflects a form of judicial modesty: It allows Congress to take a second look at the issue, and if Congress disagrees with the court's avoidance interpretation, it can override this interpretation with clarifying legislation that forces the court to face up to the constitutional question.

Avoidance of the constitutional question thus allows a second branch of government to weigh in on the issue before it is ultimately resolved. The critics, however, point out that modern avoidance creates a "penumbra" around constitutional rights, in which the court effectively rewrites the statute without having to engage in a serious analysis of either the Constitution or the statute.[32] They add that although in theory Congress can intervene and force the courts to reconsider the issue, in practice this almost never happens. Instead, the avoidance precedent often takes on a life of its own, and by operation of *stare decisis* becomes an enlarged realm of judicial policymaking, assumed to have a constitutional status although never justified in terms of a correct understanding of the Constitution.[33]

When we add an agency interpretation to the picture, and consider the matter in terms of the proper sequencing of inquiries by a reviewing court, we can identify some additional reasons for questioning the modern version of the avoidance doctrine. Under the *DeBartolo* and *SWANCC* sequencing, once the court decides that the modern avoidance canon is implicated, the court proceeds to decide the issue on its own authority without any consideration of the agency interpretation. This has two undesirable consequences.

First, the *DeBartolo/SWANCC* approach eliminates the possibility that the constitutional question can be avoided by overturning the agency interpretation as a matter of ordinary (nonconstitutional) judicial review. In *DeBartolo*, for example, the Court could have decided that the NLRB interpretation conflicted with the statute, which permits publicity but prohibits picketing, and left it at that. Or in *Rust*, the Court could have decided (if the vote had gone the other way) that the agency's gag rule was an unreasonable stretch of the statutory language prohibiting the funding of facilities "where abortion is a *method* of family planning." In *SWANCC* the constitutional question could have been avoided (if the Court had adopted the view subsequently advanced by Justice Scalia in *Rapanos*) by concluding that the meaning of "waters" is limited to relatively permanent, standing or flowing bodies of water. In general, if the statutory issue is considered first, and the court concludes that the agency interpretation is impermissible, the court has engaged in a version of constitutional avoidance—the court has adopted a permissible interpretation that is constitutional, and has avoided one that may not be. *Rust* and *Verizon* thus got the sequencing right purely in the interest of avoiding unnecessary constitutional decisions (whatever one may think of the outcomes in those cases).[34] And by requiring that the court confront the statutory issue first, the *Rust/Verizon* sequencing requires the court to proceed in a more disciplined fashion, using traditional tools of statutory interpretation rather than invoking a vague "penumbra" based on constitutional concerns.

Second, the *DeBartolo/SWANCC* sequencing eliminates any possibility of considering the executive's view of the constitutional question.[35] To be sure, under the contemporary understanding of the division of powers under the Constitution, it is unrealistic to expect courts to defer in any strong sense to the executive's interpretation of the Constitution. But it is not beyond the realm of possibility that a doctrine can be developed that at least requires courts to address the executive understanding, and explain why it is wrong, if that is what the court concludes. By adopting the *Rust/Verizon* sequencing—putting the *Chevron* doctrine (or whatever replaces it) first, and constitutional consideration second—the courts would necessarily have to engage with the agency's reasoning for adopting its interpretation. That reasoning might not address the constitutional question: Agencies have historically been reluctant to consider whether the powers delegated to them by Congress might transgress constitutional limits. But this is changing, and the use of the avoidance canon would be enriched if the courts had to weigh the agency's reasoning in support of the constitutionality of its interpretation, before they tackle that issue on their own.[36]

The Rule of Lenity and the Problem of Hybrid Statutes

The canon of constitutional avoidance is not the only interpretive canon grounded in constitutional concerns. Other, more specific canons can also be seen as instructions to interpret unclear or ambiguous statutes in order to avoid possible unconstitutionality. The rule of lenity, which has a provenance far more venerable than the *Chevron* doctrine,[37] says that ambiguities in criminal statutes should be interpreted in favor of the accused. This has been said to rest on two constitutional concerns: the need to give persons fair notice of what conduct makes them vulnerable to criminal prosecution, and the importance of having the legislature, rather than prosecutors or courts, decide when it is appropriate to subject persons to criminal punishment.[38]

The concern with fair notice is associated with due process; the desirability of having the legislature determine what conduct is criminal rests on the anti-inherency version of the separation of powers principle of legislative supremacy.

For the most part, the rule of lenity has been unaffected by the rise of the *Chevron* doctrine. This is largely because the Court has never suggested that *Chevron* applies in criminal cases.[39] The doctrinal explanation for this, which hearkens back to *Adams Fruit* (Chapter 6), is that the criminal law is administered by the courts, not by federal prosecutors. Justice Scalia spelled this out in an influential concurring opinion in *Crandon v. United States*.[40] *Mead* points to the same conclusion: There has been no delegation to prosecutors to apply criminal statutes in a manner that has the force of law. There is, to be sure, a certain lack of reality to the proposition that prosecutors simply bring criminal charges and courts do the deciding. The vast majority of criminal cases these days are resolved by plea bargaining conducted by prosecutors. This has given rise to academic arguments that the policies underlying the *Chevron* doctrine should extend to criminal laws.[41] But the Court has been impervious to such notions, stating without elaboration that "we have never held that that the Government's reading of a criminal statute is entitled to any deference."[42]

The *Chevron* doctrine nevertheless enters the picture when, as in not uncommon, a statute is subject to both civil and criminal penalties. It is settled that a statute subject to such a hybrid enforcement regime can have only one meaning.[43] This in part reflects the assumption, which we saw at work in Justice Souter's *Mead* opinion, that "law" by its very nature must have a uniform meaning whenever it applies.[44] A statute that means one thing when enforced against A, and something different when enforced against B, "would render every statute a chameleon, its meaning subject to change depending on the presence or absence of constitutional concerns in each individual case."[45] A statute that has a different meaning depending on its mode of enforcement would also create distorted incentives for enforcement agents, who might choose how to enforce the statute based on which meaning would apply, rather than considering other factors that typically inform such a decision.

Given the shared assumption that a hybrid statute can have only one meaning, the tension between applying the *Chevron* doctrine and the rule of lenity becomes acute. If *Chevron* applies (based on the possibility of civil enforcement), the agency is likely to adopt a broad meaning of the statute, giving the agency more authority to implement its policies. If the rule of lenity applies (based on the possibility of criminal enforcement), the statute is likely to be given a narrower meaning, restricting its scope of application and confining the agency's discretion.

The Court, alas, has provided conflicting statements about how to resolve this tension. In *United States v. Thompson / Center Arms Co.*,[46] the Court applied the rule of lenity in reviewing a civil enforcement action under the tax code, on the ground that the provision in question was also subject to criminal penalties. Yet in *Babbitt v. Sweet Home Chapter of Communities for a Great Oregon*,[47] the Court distinguished *Thompson / Center Arms* and declined to apply the rule of lenity in reviewing a regulation interpreting a section of the Endangered Species Act that was subject to both civil and criminal enforcement. Subsequent decisions have appeared to endorse *Thompson / Center Arms* without disapproving *Sweet Home Chapter*.[48] Recent court of appeals opinions, including a thoughtful concurring opinion by Judge Sutton of the Sixth Circuit, have endorsed *Thompson / Center Arms* as the better view.[49] But the question remains unresolved.

The issue could conceivably be determined by the proper sequencing of inquiries, as suggested above with respect to the canon of constitutional avoidance. However, in the context of a canon of interpretation like the rule of lenity, this would require the court to review the agency interpretation *twice*. First the reviewing court would apply the *Chevron* doctrine (or whatever succeeds it) without applying the rule of lenity, and then the court would review the agency interpretation with the rule of lenity factored in to see if this requires a different result. This solution seems awkward if not a little silly.

A better approach is to apply the rule of lenity in determining the space available to the agency to develop its own discretionary interpretation of the statute as part of the initial determination of what is now step 1. The justification for this would be that the rule of lenity, although not technically a rule of constitutional law, is a canon of interpretation grounded in constitutional principles of due process and separation of powers. It is also a highly settled canon of interpretation. Thus, given the important role of courts both in enforcing settled expectations about the law and in enforcing principles of constitutional law, the rule of lenity should enter into the determination of how much freedom the agency has to interpret.

In contrast, the modern canon of constitutional avoidance is brought to bear when the reviewing court perceives that the constitutional boundary is by definition *unsettled*. In such a case, applying the canon of avoidance to foreclose the agency's ability to interpret the statute has all the problems commentators have identified with modern avoidance (e.g., creating constitutional penumbras). It also eliminates a possible avenue of constitutional avoidance and cuts off any consideration of the agency's view of the constitutional question as discussed above. When the limits of constitutional law are unsettled, the reviewing court should apply the sequencing solution—considering the agency interpretation as a matter of statutory interpretation first, and then asking whether the agency's interpretation is constitutional.

In Sum

When cases arise that present both statutory interpretation and constitutional questions, sorting out the respective authority of agencies and courts is especially difficult. Under the *Chevron* doctrine (or whatever replaces it), the authority to say what the law is on statutory questions is divided between the agency and the court. Under established conventions about judicial authority to interpret the Constitution the court retains exclusive (or near-exclusive) authority to decide constitutional questions. This makes it critical to identify the presence of a constitutional question if there is one.

The approach suggested in this chapter would have reviewing courts approach the question differently depending on whether the constitutional principle at issue is settled or unsettled. If the constitutional principle is settled—either as a matter of constitutional law or in the form of a canon of interpretation (like the rule of lenity) that has constitutional roots—courts should enforce that principle in establishing the space the agency has to exercise discretionary authority to interpret. If the constitutional principle is unsettled, courts should hear the agency out before turning—if necessary—to resolving the unsettled constitutional question.

Some federalism questions, most prominently those that involve preemption of state law, and many separation of powers questions, most prominently those that implicate the principle of legislative supremacy, do not present sharply delineated questions of constitutional law. Rather, the constitutional dimension of the issue is largely subsumed in what is commonly characterized as a question of statutory interpretation. The difficulty of adjusting the *Chevron* doctrine to account for these often overlooked constitutional boundaries will take up the Chapters 9–11.

9

The Preemption Puzzle

ANOTHER PROMINENT LIMIT on agency authority is established by principles of federalism, which delineate—in a fashion that has shifted over time—the boundary between the authority of the federal government and that of the states. Chapter 8 noted one manifestation of this contested boundary line, in the efforts of Congress, the U.S. Army Corps of Engineers, and the Supreme Court, to determine the limits on federal authority over the preservation of wetlands unconnected to navigable waters. Another and much more frequently litigated category of cases implicating federalism concerns preemption of state law. The Court sometimes speaks of preemption as simply a matter of statutory interpretation.[1] But it also affirms that preemption has a constitutional foundation—the Supremacy Clause—which says that the laws enacted by Congress are the supreme law of land, notwithstanding anything in state law to the contrary.[2] Accurately considered, preemption is based on a combination of constitutional and statutory interpretation. Whatever its legal foundation, preemption clearly plays a major role in fixing the boundary between federal and state authority. Preemption means that federal law displaces state law. A determination of preemption acts like an erasure of state law, leaving federal law the sole source of legal authority. A judgment of preemption thus expands the sphere of federal authority, and diminishes that of the states.[3]

The Supreme Court tells us there are four categories of preemption.[4] One is express preemption. This occurs when Congress, as part of a statutory regime, adopts a provision expressly stating that certain types of state laws are preempted—that is, may no longer be enforced. A second is conflict preemption. This occurs when federal law and state law are mutually incompatible, as where federal law says X and state law says not-X. A third category, which is sometimes presented as a subset of the second, is variously called obstacle or frustration preemption. This occurs when federal law says X and state law says Y, and a court determines that X requires displacing Y in order to fully effectuate the purposes or functions of X. The fourth is called field preemption. This occurs when Congress adopts a regulatory scheme that governs a particular field in such a comprehensive fashion that it is fair to conclude that the federal scheme should be exclusive.

One cross-cutting issue, which has become a matter of controversy, is whether courts should apply a "presumption against preemption" in resolving preemption controversies in all or some subset of the foregoing categories.[5] Justice Scalia, in particular, argued that the presumption should not apply in construing express preemption clauses; other Justices have disagreed.[6] The presumption is another example of a substantive canon of interpretation, and if it applies, presumably it qualifies as one of the "traditional tools" that courts are instructed to apply at step 1 of the *Chevron* doctrine. The case that first articulated the presumption said it should apply when Congress has "legislated . . . in a field which the States have traditionally occupied."[7] Perhaps this is the key to understanding the proper scope of the presumption. In fields largely reserved to the state and local governments, such as domestic relations and land use controls, the presumption makes sense. In fields largely occupied by the federal government, such as the conduct of foreign or military affairs or the regulation of foreign and interstate trade, the presumption does not make sense.[8]

Most preemption questions are resolved by courts, applying the judge-made categories of preemption listed above. But administrative agencies are increasingly drawn into preemption controversies as well. One possibility, which is rare but not unheard of, is that Congress has expressly delegated authority to an agency to preempt (or de-preempt) state law.[9] Another, which is more common, is that administrative action having the force of law, such as a legislative regulation, will be deemed to have the effect of preempting state law.[10] Most commonly, an administrative agency will offer its opinion, perhaps in a regulatory preamble or in an *amicus curiae* brief, that federal law, including administrative action having the force of law, should be regarded as preempting state law.[11]

Each of these forms of administrative involvement presents different issues. The discussion here will focus on the category of cases in which an agency has in some fashion offered its opinion about whether federal law does or does not preempt state law.[12] The underlying question in these cases is whether, or to what extent, the court should defer to the legal judgment of the agency, and in particular whether it should apply the *Chevron* doctrine in reviewing the agency's legal conclusion. Because a determination of pre-emption implicates both statutory interpretation and constitutional federalism concerns, which are difficult if not impossible untangle, the Court has struggled to calibrate the proper role of the *Chevron* doctrine in this context. One strategy, which we see most clearly in cases arising under the National Bank Act, has been to insist on rigid distinction between the "question of statutory interpretation" (where *Chevron* applies) and the "question of preemption" (where it does not). Another strategy, which emerged in cases involving the preemption of state tort law, has been to reject the *Chevron* doctrine in favor of an intermediate standard of review (like *Skidmore*) that gives "some weight" to the agency view about preemption, but does not regard the agency's judgment as conclusive. A third strategy, which has prevailed after 2016, has been to avoid saying anything about the possible relevance of the *Chevron* doctrine to preemption controversies, one way or another.

The National Bank Cases

The Court's first explicit comment on the relationship between the *Chevron* doctrine and preemption occurred in *Smiley v. Citibank (South Dakota), N.A.*[13] The Court had previously construed the National Bank Act of 1864 to mean that federally chartered banks can lend money to credit card customers living in other states, and the law of the state where the bank is chartered determines the permissible rate of interest that can be charged to these out-of-state cardholders.[14] Although this was not the Court's intent, the decision created a kind of race to the bottom in which major banks were able to establish credit card subsidiaries in states with high or nonexistent usury limits on interest charges, and then charge these high rates to cardholders nationwide.

The issue that arose in *Smiley* was whether late fees charged by such credit card subsidies are encompassed within the term "interest." After a class action was filed in a California state court contending that the law of the residence of the cardholder should apply in determining whether late fees are "unconscionable," the Office of the Comptroller of the Currency (OCC), which administers the National Bank Act, scrambled to issue a regulation providing that "interest" for purposes of the Act includes charges like late fees. Under this interpretation, the law of the state where the credit card subsidiary is chartered determines the validity of the late fees. Citibank (South Dakota) then argued successfully in the California courts that the regulation preempted the contrary law of California.

In a unanimous opinion written by Justice Scalia, the Supreme Court affirmed. His opinion sharply bifurcated the question of interpretation of the National Bank Act and the question of preemption. The question of statutory interpretation was governed by the *Chevron* doctrine. Scalia found that the meaning of "interest" was ambiguous and the OCC's interpretation of that term to include late fees was reasonable. Various counterarguments, such as the fact that the interpretation was neither contemporary with enactment of the Bank Act nor longstanding, and that it was adopted in an effort to affect the outcome of litigation, were rejected.[15] In a single paragraph Scalia then rejected the petitioner's argument that no deference should apply because the regulation preempted state law and the Court had repeatedly said that ambiguous statutes should be interpreted with a presumption against preemption. Scalia wrote:

> This argument confuses the question of the substantive (as opposed to preemptive) *meaning* of a statute with the question of *whether* a statute is pre-emptive. We may assume (without deciding) that the latter question must always be decided de novo by the courts. That is not the question at issue here; there is no doubt that § 85 pre-empts state law.[16]

In support of the settled nature of the preemption question, he cited the 1978 decision of the Court holding that the usury laws of the chartering state control in establishing the allowable rate of interest and thus effectively preempt the laws of any other states where consumers may have obtained credit from the bank.[17]

The sharp distinction in *Smiley* between the statutory interpretation question, resolved under the *Chevron* doctrine, and the preemption question, resolved as a matter of judicial precedent, had the effect of avoiding any need on the part of the Court to consider the federalism implications of allowing national banks to wipe out limits on bank charges by manipulating the state of incorporation of bank subsidiaries. The law of the state with the least restrictive (or even nonexistent) controls would determine the interest rates and late fees that would apply nationwide. Note that in terms of sequencing, *Smiley* followed the path of *Rust v. Sullivan* (Chapter 8): First apply the *Chevron* doctrine to the challenged agency interpretation, then consider whether that interpretation is preemptive. *Smiley* also suggested, without deciding, that the preemption issue should be resolved, like constitutional questions more generally, de novo.[18]

Soon the Court followed up with other preemption cases under the National Bank Act that also implicated interpretations by the OCC. Of particular interest is *Watters v. Wachovia Bank, N.A.*[19] The Act immunizes national banks from state "visitorial" regulation, and authorizes them to engage in mortgage lending. As amended, it also enables national banks to create operating subsidiaries that perform banking functions. But the Act does not explicitly exempt operating subsidiaries from state visitorial regulation. The OCC issued a regulation indicating that state laws apply to operating subsidiaries to the same extent as they apply to national banks, which meant that an operating subsidiary engaged in originating mortgages is immune from state visitorial regulation. Wachovia, which had no banking operations in Michigan, created an operating subsidiary under Michigan law to originate mortgages in Michigan. Wachovia then claimed that Michigan laws regulating mortgage originators were preempted by the OCC regulation.

Writing for a majority, Justice Ginsburg concluded that it was unnecessary to consider the preemptive effect of the OCC regulation. She reasoned that the combination of the statutory provision immunizing national banks from state visitorial authority and the statutory provision authorizing the creation of operating subsidiaries logically produced the same result.[20]

Justice Stevens filed a lengthy dissent, joined (rather unusually) by Chief Justice Roberts and Justice Scalia. Stevens concluded that the statutory provisions relied upon by the majority merely authorized the creation of operating subsidiaries but did not address the question whether such a subsidiary was immune from state regulation. Thus, the only possible source of preemption was the OCC regulation. After expressing doubt that the OCC intended its regulation to have a preemptive effect, he wrote:

Even if the OCC did intend its regulation to pre-empt the state laws at issue here, it would still not merit *Chevron* deference. No case from this Court has ever applied such a deferential standard to an agency decision that could so easily disrupt the federal-state balance. To be sure, expert agency opinions as to which state laws conflict with a federal statute may be entitled to "some weight," especially when "the subject matter is technical" and "the relevant history and background are complex and extensive." But "[u]nlike Congress, administrative agencies are clearly not designed to represent the interests of States, yet with relative ease they can promulgate comprehensive and detailed regulations that have broad pre-emption ramifications for state law." For that reason, when an agency purports to decide the scope of federal pre-emption, a healthy respect for state sovereignty calls for something less than *Chevron* deference.[21]

Here we see an express articulation of the understanding that the scope of preemption implicates not just statutory interpretation but also the balance of authority between the federal government and the states—a matter of constitutional federalism. We also see an express articulation of the view that federal courts have superior ability to strike the balance in a manner consistent with settled understandings, since "administrative agencies are clearly not designed to represent the interests of States." Agency views should be given respectful consideration ("some weight") on questions that implicate their expertise, but they are not entitled to the strong deference associated with the *Chevron* doctrine.

Even if the Court had upheld Michigan's regulation of Wachovia's mortgage-originating subsidiary, it would have come too late. Within six months of the decision, Wachovia had to be hastily merged into Wells Fargo Bank to prevent its collapse due to its large portfolio of defaulting mortgages.

Two years later it had become clear that reckless mortgage-lending practices had triggered a worldwide economic crisis. When the New York Attorney General sought to subpoena information from national banks as part of an investigation into possible discriminatory lending practices, the Comptroller of the Currency and a banking trade organization sought an injunction barring enforcement of the subpoenas. The ground for the requested injunction was that the investigation was preempted by a regulation of the OCC defining the scope of the visitorial power.

In *Cuomo v. Clearing House Association*,[22] Justice Scalia, writing for himself and the four more-liberal Justices, held that the OCC regulation adopted an unreasonable definition of the visitorial power. He acknowledged that the *Chevron* doctrine applies to an interpretation by a federal agency—here, the OCC—of a statute that it administers. He also acknowledged that the term "visitorial powers" was ambiguous. But then, proceeding to examine in detail the "scope" of the ambiguity, he engaged in a detailed examination of the historical understanding of the term. In what amounted to de novo review, Scalia concluded that "visitation" refers to a supervisor inspecting the books or records of an institution, but does not include judicial actions to enforce generally applicable state laws. The OCC's regulation interpreting visitation to include judicial enforcement of state laws thus impermissibly preempted a large swathe of state law. Although he did not expressly apply the presumption against preemption in interpreting the Act, he cautioned that "the incursion that the Comptroller's regulation makes upon traditional state powers" should not be "minimized."[23]

Justice Thomas, writing for the remaining four conservatives, would have applied an orthodox understanding of the *Chevron* doctrine.[24] The Act itself preempted state exercise of visitorial power over national banks. The term "visitorial power" is ambiguous. The OCC regulation interpreting that term was reasonable. To the extent that the OCC regulation conflicted with prior Supreme Court opinions, the *Brand X* doctrine meant that the agency interpretation should supersede the understanding in those opinions (this was the largest number of votes ever for the *Brand X* theory as applied to Supreme Court precedent; see Chapter 7). There was no reason to worry about the balance of authority between the federal government and the states, because national banks had coexisted with state banks ever since the National Bank Act was passed in 1864.

In effect, both the majority and the minority opinions in *Cuomo* reverted to the bifurcated approach of *Smiley*. Justice Scalia implicitly treated the question as a matter of preemption, and engaged in de novo review to determine whether the agency's interpretation trenched impermissibly on traditional state police powers. Justice Thomas treated the question as a matter of statutory interpretation, to be reviewed under the *Chevron* doctrine, and presumed that preemption followed automatically based on the National Bank Act's conferral of exclusive visitorial powers on the OCC. Neither opinion showed any interest in Justice Stevens's more nuanced approach in *Watters,* in which the agency view was given "some weight" on variables as to which its expertise was relevant, while leaving the ultimate judgment to the Court.

The Products Liability Cases

At roughly the same time as the Court was considering preemption under the National Bank Act, it was also struggling with cases about whether federal law preempts state-law tort suits based on injuries allegedly caused by defective products. The possibility of federal preemption of such lawsuits gained salience with *Cipollone v. Liggett Group, Inc.,*[25] which held that a suit against tobacco companies based on failure-to-warn theories was partially preempted by the Cigarette Labeling Act. It was given further impetus by *Geier v. American Honda Motor Co.,*[26] which held that a design defect claim based on the failure to install air bags in 1997 Honda Accords was preempted by a federal regulation giving manufacturers the option of installing air bags or automatic seat belts for that model year. In both cases, the Court itself determined that the federal law was preemptive, although *Geier* cited the views of the federal agency (as communicated through the government's brief) as deserving "some weight" in reaching the judgment.[27]

In *Medtronic, Inc. v. Lohr,*[28] the Court moved a step further toward giving at least a degree of deference to administrative judgments about preemption. The decision held that tort suits against medical device manufacturers are not preempted by the Medical Device Amendments of 1976, insofar as the lawsuit concerned devices exempt from FDA pre-market approval. Although the Amendments included an express preemption clause prohibiting states from adopting any "requirement" different from those of federal law, the majority relied on the presumption against preemption in holding this did not apply to the common-law claims at issue.[29] It also said the result was "substantially informed" by regulations promulgated by the FDA, which interpreted the preemption clause to mean that only specific state requirements inconsistent with federal requirements would be preempted.[30] Given that the statute expressly delegated authority to the FDA to exempt state requirements from preemption, the Court said these views were entitled to "substantial weight."[31]

During the Bush II Administration, pharmaceutical and medical device manufacturers found a more receptive audience for their efforts to enlist administrative agencies in promoting preemption of products liability suits. The FDA, in particular, embarked on a policy of adding statements to regulations indicating that it regarded compliance with the regulations as preempting state tort suits.[32] The strategy seemed to bear fruit in *Riegel v. Medtronic, Inc.*,[33] where the Court distinguished *Medtronic v. Lohr* and held that medical devices that have gone through pre-market approval *are* protected from tort suits by the medical devices preemption clause. Justice Scalia took note of the FDA's changed position on preemption, but ultimately declined to give it any weight, because he concluded that the statute itself compelled preemption.[34]

The FDA's campaign for "preemption by preamble" came to a crashing halt in *Wyeth v. Levine*.[35] The case involved a large judgment against the pharmaceutical company Wyeth for failing adequately to warn health professionals about the dangers of administering a certain drug using an "IV-push" rather than an "IV-drip." Since drugs, as opposed to medical devices, are not favored with an express preemption clause, the argument boiled down to whether the FDA's approval of Wyeth's warnings impliedly conflicted with, and therefore preempted, any tort judgment based on the failure to provide more emphatic warnings. In support of preemption, Wyeth cited a passage in the preamble to a regulation governing the content of prescription drug labels in which the FDA stated that approved label warnings should be regarded as "both a 'floor' and a 'ceiling'" and that any contrary requirement based on state law should be preempted.[36]

Justice Stevens, writing for the majority, rejected preemption, finding it significant that, at least with respect to drugs, state tort actions and FDA regulation had long coexisted. Turning to the FDA's preamble, Stevens acknowledged that previous cases (like *Geier* and *Lohr*) had given "some weight" to the agency's views about preemption. But the weight was based on the agency's "explanation of how state law affects the regulatory scheme"; in no case had the Court "deferred to an agency's *conclusion* that state law is preempted."[37] In this respect he reasoned that unless an agency has been delegated express authority to preempt state law, its judgment about preemption is entitled only to *Skidmore* deference, based on its "thoroughness, consistency, and persuasiveness."[38] Under this standard, the agency was entitled to little deference, because the position taken in the preamble was inconsistent with its "longstanding position" that FDA approval did not preempt state tort law.

Especially noteworthy with regard to the weight to be given to the FDA's preamble was Justice Stevens's conclusion that the agency failed to comply with the norms of reasoned decision making. In the notice of proposed rulemaking the FDA had stated that the proposed rule about labeling did not "contain policies that have federalism implications or that preempt state law."[39] Then, "[i]n 2006, the agency finalized the rule and, without offering States or other interested parties notice or an opportunity for comment, articulated a sweeping position on the FDCA's pre-emptive effect in the regulatory preamble."[40] This patent failure to adhere to established norms about notice-and-comment rendered the FDA view "inherently suspect."[41]

Justice Stevens's *Wyeth* opinion, like his dissent in *Watters v. Wachovia,* seemed to point toward a compromise position on the proper standard of review of agency judgments about preemption—neither the *Chevron* doctrine nor de novo review, but something in between, like *Skidmore,* combined with a healthy dose of process review.

To date, however, there is little sign that the Court as a whole is committed to this kind of intermediate standard of review. The Court has continued to struggle with questions involving the preemptive effect of federal regulation on tort liability. The general direction of the decisions, notwithstanding *Wyeth,* has been toward preemption.[42] In reaching these judgments the Court has generally reverted to something like de novo review. The *Chevron* doctrine has quietly disappeared, but no competing standard, such as *Skidmore,* has been clearly embraced as an alternative.[43]

Toward a Better Approach to Agency Views About Preemption

As the foregoing surveys suggest, preemption controversies, under any category, entail a complex decisional process. Express preemption clauses are often ambiguous, and present difficult issues of interpretation. Conflict preemption (in the sense of genuine mutual exclusivity) is rare, and what is labeled "conflict" often turns out, more realistically, to be a judgment about the permissible degree of frustration of the purposes of federal law.

More fully considered, we find that virtually any determination of preemption entails something like the following steps: (1) An interpretation of federal law, including an assessment of its purposes and functions; (2) a characterization of state law, including an assessment of its purposes and functions; (3) a determination of whether the state law operates in an area that has been regarded as a traditional state function; (4) an assessment of the degree of tension between the federal law, its purposes and functions, the state law, and its purposes and functions; and (5) a judgment about whether the degree of tension between federal and state law is sufficiently great that it warrants displacing state law, giving due regard to whether the state law falls within an area of traditional state functions. This last and crucial step entails a judgment that implicates constitutional values, because it determines the respective authority of—the boundary between—the federal government and the states under our system of divided political sovereignty.[44]

Administrative agencies may well have valuable insights to contribute to this complex decisional process, as in determining the purposes and functions of federal law (step 1) and determining the degree of tension between federal and state law (step 4). But it seems unlikely that agencies have superior institutional capacity relative to courts in characterizing existing state law (step 2), determining whether the state law operates in an area regarded as a traditional state function (step 3), or making the final determination whether the degree of tension warrants displacing state law (step 5). Agencies fall short relative to courts on these dimensions in part because agencies are specialists, with intensive knowledge about one area of federal law, whereas federal courts are generalists, exposed to a wide range of law, including both federal and state law. But agencies also fall short because they are charged by federal law with carrying out a particular mission, and they are likely to give exaggerated weight to that mission and correspondingly insufficient weight to the purposes and functions of state law that may complicate their ability to carry out the mission.

More fundamentally, the determination whether state law operates in an area that is a traditional state function entails a sensitivity to settled expectations—which, as we have seen, is a variable as to which courts generally have a superior advantage relative to agencies. And the final judgment about whether the degree of tension warrants the displacement of state law implicates constitutional values—namely, federalism values—which by consensus have been assigned to courts rather than agencies.

In general, we can see that federalism, most prominently but not exclusively preemption, constitutes another boundary that constrains the authority of administrative agencies. Fixing the federalism boundary entails a complex decisional process and a delicate exercise in judgment. Courts should elicit and give respectful attention to the view of administrative agencies on the variables in which agencies are most likely to have valuable input. But the courts should determine on their own authority exactly where the boundary lies.

Preemption controversies constitute a significant portion of the Supreme Court's docket from year to year. That the Court has failed to agree on a way to factor the *Chevron* doctrine into preemption stands as a significant indictment of the doctrine. The *Chevron* doctrine won significant support from federal judges because of its appealing simplicity relative to the multifactor approach that proceeded it. But it is evidently too simple to serve as an all-purpose device for integrating agency interpretations into every judicial task that requires the interpretation of federal law. Certainly, it is too simple to deploy in resolving the complex calculus presented by preemption questions.

In Sum

Preemption decisions entail an assessment of statutory meaning and purpose, but also an assessment of the degree of tension between federal and state law and an understanding of the existing division of authority between the federal government and the states in any particular area of law. Consequently, preemption decisions nearly always require courts not just to interpret federal law but also to engage in a subtle consideration of the evolving balance of governmental authority under our federalism. Statutory interpretation is intermixed with judgments grounded in an appreciation of constitutional boundaries, which in turn are largely a function of settled expectations. Determining how agency interpretations of law and agency judgments about the impact of state law on a federal statutory scheme should be factored into preemption decisions is no easy matter.

We have seen how the Court, in a series of decisions arising under the National Bank Act, sought to bifurcate the question of interpretation and the question of preemption into separate inquires. Insofar as the *Chevron* doctrine was assumed to govern the question of interpretation, this resulted in wide swings in the outcome, sometimes erasing state authority and something vindicating it, depending on whether the Court accepted or rejected the views of the OCC. In contrast, cases that consider the preemptive effect of federal law on state tort law have tended to gravitate toward an intermediate standard, one that gives "some weight" to agency views on certain issues, while reserving the ultimate judgment about preemption for the courts. This means that some standard other than the *Chevron* doctrine is appropriate in assessing agency legal interpretations that bear on preemption.

It is interesting, and indeed ironic, that the Justice who was most willing to break from the influence of the *Chevron* doctrine in this context was Justice Stevens. His dissenting opinion in *Watters v. Wachovia Bank* (joined by Chief Justice Roberts and Justice Scalia) offered the most insightful analysis of why the *Chevron* framework does not work in resolving controversies about the preemptive effect of the National Bank Act. And his opinion for the Court in *Wyeth v. Levine* offered a similar model for factoring agency interpretations into questions about the preemption of state tort law. His departure from the Court has made this kind of nuanced analysis much harder to advance.

10

The Principle of Legislative Supremacy

We turn to boundaries on agency authority associated with separation of powers principles, which are ubiquitous. In theory, every time a question arises about whether the power to say what the law is belongs to an agency or a federal court, we have a separation of powers question—namely, a question about the division of authority between Article II agencies and Article III courts. Another question, which is the primary focus of the present chapter, is whether the power to say what the law is belongs to an agency or the legislature, a question about the division of authority between Article II agencies and the institution created by Article I of the Constitution, the U.S. Congress.

Two Separation of Powers Principles

Before turning to the issues raised by the principle of legislative supremacy, a brief word is warranted about the separation of powers principle that has been invoked most often by the contemporary opponents of the *Chevron* doctrine, including Justices Thomas and Gorsuch, which can be called the principle of *judicial* supremacy.[1] The idea here is that Article III of the Constitution, which confers the "judicial power" on federal courts, includes plenary authority to determine the meaning of the law in all cases that come before them. This in turn, the argument runs, means that federal judges have an unflagging duty in every case "to say what the law is," and it is therefore impermissible to "defer" to the legal interpretations of agencies, which are part of the Executive Branch.[2]

No one should quarrel with the proposition that judges are duty-bound to interpret the law in a fair and impartial fashion in the cases that come before them. This duty, as Philip Hamburger has demonstrated, is part of the judicial office, and was recognized well before the Constitution and Article III were adopted.[3] Indeed, if judges fail to interpret and enforce the law in a fair and impartial fashion, we are in big trouble, because this is a central pillar of the rule of law and what it means to live in a society governed by law. But this judicial duty applies when judges perform their central task, which is to decide concrete disputes that come before them for resolution. Those who claim that the *Chevron* doctrine violates Article III repeatedly quote the line from *Marbury v. Madison* that "it is the province and duty of the judicial department to say what the law is."[4] They nearly always omit the next sentence, which explains why this is so: "Those who apply the rule to particular cases, must of necessity expound and interpret the rule."[5] *Marbury*, in other words, establishes that judges have an *independent duty* to interpret the law in cases they are charged with deciding. The decision does not establish that other branches of government, including Congress, the President, and all executive branch and independent agencies, do not also have a "province and duty" to interpret and apply the law as they best understand it. Nor does it establish that courts, in the exercise of their independent duty, may not in appropriate cases conclude that the legal understanding of other constitutional actors is worthy of respectful consideration, weight, or even acceptance. After all, *Marbury* also cautioned that "[q]uestions, in their nature political, or which are, by the constitution and laws, submitted to the executive, can never be made by this court."[6] With respect to such "political questions," *Marbury* itself established that *acceptance* of the executive interpretation is mandatory.

The argument that Article III or *Marbury* establishes judicial supremacy in matters of legal interpretation is also inconsistent with history.[7] For a significant period of time after *Marbury*, it was sharply contested whether judicial understandings of the law are binding on other government actors when they are not a party to a particular case or controversy but are mere readers of judicial opinions.[8] The proposition that government officials are duty-bound to accept judicial interpretations of the Constitution solidified only after the decision in *Cooper v. Aaron* in 1958.[9] With respect to statutory interpretations, at least insofar as federal officers are concerned, it solidified earlier, probably by the time of the decision in *Crowell v. Benson* in 1932.[10] This understanding is also arguably embodied in the APA, with its broad recognition of a right to judicial review for persons adversely affected by agency action.[11] It has become a central postulate about how our tripartite system of government operates.[12] The point is that the premise of judicial supremacy in matters of law interpretation cannot be ascribed to any original understanding of Article III. Like much else, it is the product of a gradual evolution over time, in which the implicit requirements of a workable constitutional order were tested and became settled.

The argument that Article III courts have some kind of exclusive power to interpret the law is also unworkable. The power to interpret the law is shared by all government officials—indeed, by all citizens. Every government officer is required to interpret the law all the time, without the benefit of any guidance from an Article III court. Agency officials, in particular, probably interpret the statute they are charged with administering dozens of times for each time an issue ends up in court. In a society that purports to be governed by law, these officials are also duty-bound to interpret the law in a fair and impartial manner. It is imperative that they do so, and they cannot run to court for an advisory opinion every time a question arises that requires legal interpretation.

Once the permissible bounds of the judicial power referenced by Article III are understood to be established by convention or evolving consensus, not by original meaning, then the argument that Article III courts can never "defer" to agency interpretations collapses. "Deference" is a big tent that includes a number of practices, most of them quite sensible. As we have seen in Chapter 2, courts have given weight or respectful consideration to agency interpretations in various contexts since the beginning of the Republic. Many of these practices, like the contemporary and longstanding canons and the notion articulated in *Skidmore* that courts should give respectful consideration to agency interpretations informed by extensive experience, are unquestionably devices that help courts come to the best understanding of the meaning of the law. The question of concern is whether the *Chevron* doctrine, in its orthodox formulation, is also such a practice. This cannot be answered by referencing the original understanding of Article III or by quoting *Marbury v. Madison*, but must be determined by other arguments, many of which are also grounded in the Constitution, including other provisions of separation of powers.

If the invocation of the judicial power created by Article III does not resolve the constitutionality of the *Chevron* doctrine, another separation of
powers principle, the principle of legislative supremacy, has distinct and profound implications for that doctrine. As discussed in Chapter 1, agencies
cannot act in ways that transgress the scope of their authority as delegated
to them by Congress. This follows from the shared premise, grounded in
separation of powers, that administrative agencies have no inherent authority
to act.[13] Only Congress, acting through the legislative process, has the power
to create agencies and delineate their powers.[14] Courts, as guardians of the
Constitution, must therefore enforce the limitations Congress has placed on
the authority of agencies in order to preserve the principle that Congress
has the exclusive prerogative to establish agencies and delineate their powers
and limits.

From the Progressive Era up through the enactment of the APA in 1946,
and for nearly four decades thereafter, the established device for monitoring
an agency's compliance with the scope of its delegated authority was through
judicial review of final agency action. When Congress created a federal agency
and gave it delegated powers, Congress would also provide for judicial review
of the agency's decisions on behalf of persons aggrieved by final agency action. If the aggrieved person claimed that the agency was exceeding the
scope of its delegated power, the reviewing court would interpret the scope
of the agency's delegated authority de novo, and if it agreed that the agency
had exceeded its authority, it would set aside the agency action as unlawful.[15]
Except in unusual cases, the reviewing court would make no reference to the
separation of powers premise underlying this mode of review—the need to
protect the superior power of Congress to create an agency and delimit the
scope of its delegated powers. There was no need to elevate the issue to constitutional status, because it was sufficient to invalidate the agency action as
contrary to the statute creating its delegated powers. The constitutional
principle remained in the background, because Congress routinely provided
for judicial review, implicitly recognizing that such review was the most re-
alistic device available for ensuring that its intentions about the scope of
power it had delegated to an agency would be respected.[16]

The two-step *Chevron* doctrine, once it became entrenched, made it more
difficult for reviewing courts to enforce the boundaries of agency authority
as established by Congress. This is because the *Chevron* doctrine treats all

legal interpretations by an administering agency the same: It draws no distinction between statutory provisions that limit agency authority and those that confer discretionary power. Once the *Chevron* doctrine became the dominant formula for reviewing agency legal interpretations, there were only three ways for reviewing courts to enforce limits on the scope of agency authority: ignore the *Chevron* doctrine and determine de novo whether the agency is acting within the scope of its authority; decide at step 1 that the agency has transgressed a "clear" or "unambiguous" limitation on its authority; or hold at step 2 that the agency interpretation is "unreasonable" because it exceeds the scope of its authority. None of these options, as we shall see, is particularly satisfactory, which reveals a central weakness of the *Chevron* doctrine.

Enforcing Boundaries of Authority by Ignoring or Rejecting *Chevron*

Courts have occasionally enforced the boundaries of agency authority by simply ignoring the *Chevron* doctrine and engaging in de novo review of the agency's authority. A good example, from the early days of the *Chevron* doctrine, is *Dole v. United Steelworkers of America*.[17] Congress enacted the Paperwork Reduction Act in 1980 in response to widespread complaints that individuals and small businesses were "being buried under demands for paperwork" by federal agencies.[18] In order to eliminate unnecessary or unduly burdensome paperwork requests, the Act required agencies to submit new "information collection requests" to the Office of Management and Budget (OMB), which was given authority to disapprove requests deemed excessive. In the case that reached the Court, the Occupational Safety and Health Administration (OSHA) had issued a major regulation designed to limit the exposure of workers to hazardous chemicals in the workplace.[19] Rather than attempt to regulate the exposure to hazardous chemicals directly, OSHA adopted a policy requiring employers to provide information to their workers about the presence of such chemicals. The regulation, among other things, required employers to affix warning labels to containers of dangerous chemicals and to make material safety data sheets about those chemicals available for inspection by workers.

The OMB required OSHA to submit its hazard communication regulation for review under the Paperwork Reduction Act. The Act contains a broad definition of "information collection requests,"[20] which the OMB interpreted to include not only requests to submit information to an agency, but also policies adopted by agencies requiring the disclosure of information to third parties such as workers or consumers, in order to achieve some regulatory objective. Pursuant to its review of the OSHA regulation, the OMB disapproved several provisions of the hazardous communications regulation as excessive. The Steelworkers Union sued, arguing that the OMB had no authority to amend the regulation in this fashion.

The issue obviously implicated the scope of the OMB's authority under the Act. Did Congress give the OMB authority to regulate only requests for information to be submitted to agencies or made available for agency inspection? Or did it also give the OMB authority to override information disclosure policies adopted by agencies as part of a mission-specific regulatory strategy? The former view cast the OMB in the role of ensuring that agencies achieve their various tasks with as little paperwork burden on the public as possible. The latter view cast the OMB, in addition, in the role of a kind of uber-regulator of information disclosure policies. This second conception involved a much more direct clash between the OMB and other agencies regarding which entity has ultimate authority over the use of information disclosure to achieve regulatory goals—an obvious boundary question.

In a 7–2 decision authored by Justice Brenan, the Court held that the Paperwork Reduction Act did not give the OMB authority to review information disclosure requirements directed at third parties. The opinion was a classic exercise in statutory interpretation that could have been written if the *Chevron* doctrine did not exist. The Court examined the language of the statute, canons of statutory interpretation, the structure of the Act, and congressional statements of purpose included in the Act, and concluded that the best interpretation of the Act was that it was limited to information collection requests for the use of an agency. Brennan's opinion was persuasive, and attracted broad support, including the votes of Justices Stevens and Scalia.

The dissent, authored by Justice White and joined by Chief Justice Rehnquist, would have upheld the OMB's view of its authority under the *Chevron* doctrine. Noting ambiguities in the statutory definitions of "information collection request" and "collection of information," and that Congress had not directly spoken to the question whether the OMB could review information disclosure to third parties, White argued that the OMB's interpretation was reasonable, even if it was not the only possible interpretation of the statute.[21] He also observed, as Justice Brennan did not, that the union challenging the OMB's action had argued that the *Chevron* doctrine should not apply because the OMB's interpretation implicated "the scope of its jurisdiction under the Act."[22] White rejected this contention, on the ground that the Court had previously applied *Chevron* in cases that arguably affected an agency's jurisdiction.

Dole v. Steelworkers should have served as a warning about the capacity of the *Chevron* doctrine to enforce limitations on the scope of agency authority. A traditional exercise in statutory interpretation looking for the best understanding of the statute readily identified the type of information requests the OMB was expected to review. An orthodox application of the *Chevron* doctrine allowed the agency to expand its authority into a new sphere of regulation. The decision gathered little attention, however, perhaps because it did not divide the Justices along ideological lines.

A more recent decision that rejected the application of the *Chevron* doctrine—and attracted a huge amount of attention—is *King v. Burwell*.[23] The Affordable Care Act (known colloquially as Obamacare) was adopted on partisan lines in 2010 and became effective in 2014.[24] Shortly after it went into effect, opponents of the Act discovered an obscure definitional provision, in the part of the Act authorizing tax credits designed to make health insurance more affordable for persons who purchase policies on exchanges established by the Act. The definitional provision spoke of such credits being available in health insurance exchanges "established by a State."[25] Other provisions of the Act directed states to establish such exchanges, but provided that if they did not do so an exchange would be established by the federal government. It turned out that a majority of states—thirty-four by the time the Court rendered its decision—chose to let the federal government establish the exchange. The plaintiffs in *King* argued that the "plain language" of the definitional provision meant that tax credits were not available in states where the exchange was established by the federal government, because these were not exchanges "established by a State." Had they prevailed, it is likely that the Affordable Care Act would have been severely destabilized, and because opponents of the Act were then in control of Congress, it is unlikely that Congress would have acted to fix what was fairly obviously a drafting glitch.

In a 6–3 decision authored by Chief Justice Roberts, the Court rejected the plaintiffs' argument and upheld an IRS regulation that made tax credits available on both state and federally created exchanges.[26] One might have thought that the way to rescue the Affordable Care Act was to declare the expression "established by a State" a so-called scrivener's error, created by the haste with which the 900-page bill was patched together in the final days when the Democrats controlled both houses of Congress. Instead, Roberts held that the phrase "established by a State" was "ambiguous" when read in context of the whole Act and its avowed purposes. One might also have thought, given the *Chevron* doctrine, that the Court would therefore have accepted the IRS interpretation as a reasonable construction of an ambiguous statute. This is in fact the way the Fourth Circuit, in the decision under review, had proceeded.[27]

The Chief Justice, however, ruled that *King* was an "extraordinary" case in which ambiguity should not be assumed to reflect an implicit delegation by Congress to the agency to interpret the Act. He wrote:

> The tax credits are among the Act's key reforms, involving billions of dollars in spending each year and affecting the price of health insurance for millions of people. Whether those credits are available on Federal Exchanges is thus a question of deep "economic and political significance" that is central to this statutory scheme; had Congress wished to assign that question to an agency, it surely would have done so expressly. It is especially unlikely that Congress would have delegated this decision to the *IRS*, which has no expertise in crafting health policy of this sort. This is not a case for the IRS.[28]

There has been much speculation about whether *King v. Burwell* should be read as creating a "major questions" exception to the *Chevron* doctrine.[29] It is not obvious when such an exception would apply, or whether it could be implemented by the courts in a predictable manner (how major is major?). A more straightforward interpretation is that Roberts was engaging in boundary maintenance. Given his exposition of what he called "Congress's plan" as reflected in the Act, the agencies implementing the Act (including the IRS) had been given no discretion to interpret the Act to disallow tax credits on federally created exchanges.[30] Just as *Dole v. Steelworkers* rejected the idea that the ambiguities in the Paperwork Reduction Act could be exploited by the OMB to expand its authority in a way not contemplated by Congress, *King v. Burwell* rejected the idea that the "ambiguity" in the Affordable Care Act (more accurately considered, a drafting error) could be exploited by a future administration to undo a critical reform enacted by Congress.[31] Both decisions ultimately rest on the understanding that it is the courts' duty to enforce the boundaries of permissible agency authority in the exercise of de novo review.

Enforcing Boundaries of Authority at Step 1

A more common strategy for enforcing limits on agency authority in the *Chevron* era has been through aggressive efforts to find "clarity" about the scope of agency authority under step 1. An early and instructive example is *MCI Telecommunications Corp. v. American Telephone & Telegraph Co.*[32] The Communications Act of 1934 created the FCC and gave it authority to regulate long-distance telephone service. In so doing, Congress borrowed from the Interstate Commerce Act the requirement that all regulated carriers must file tariffs reflecting their charges and services and must faithfully comply with those tariffs. In 1934 the AT&T system had a virtual monopoly on long-distance service, and the filed tariff doctrine was regarded as an essential element in facilitating the efforts of the FCC to prevent discrimination and the charging of excessive rates by the near-monopolist. Beginning in the 1970s, however, MCI and other upstart carriers managed to gain a foothold in the long-distance market, and were competing against AT&T. The Commission soon came to the conclusion that competition among long-distance providers was a superior way to prevent discrimination and unreasonable rates. In a series of Reports and Orders starting in 1980, the Commission gradually relaxed the tariff-filing requirements for "nondominant" carriers (i.e., for carriers other than AT&T), culminating in an order that made tariff filing by such carriers voluntary. AT&T, which was put at a competitive disadvantage by the new policy (because preparing and filing tariffs is a cost only it had to bear) sued, arguing that the Act mandated that all regulated carriers must file tariffs.

The legal issue was essentially a reprise of the one the Court considered in the context of the motor carrier industry in *Maislin Industries* (discussed in Chapter 7)—namely, did the FCC have the authority essentially to deregulate the industry it was charged with regulating? This time, however, the case arose under the Communications Act rather than the Interstate Commerce Act. Although the tariff-filing provisions of the Communications Act were borrowed from the Commerce Act, the Communications Act did not have a legacy of Supreme Court precedents interpreting the Act as requiring strict compliance with filed tariffs. So the Court majority, in an opinion by Justice Scalia, approached the issue under the *Chevron* doctrine.

The result was the same—the FCC's deregulation effort was held to be beyond the scope of its delegated authority. But why was this "clear," as required by step 1 of the *Chevron* doctrine? The Commission cited in support of its de-tariffing orders a provision of the Act that allowed it, "in its discretion and for good cause shown," to "modify any requirement made by or under the authority" of the tariff filing provisions.[33] The critical legal question, according to Justice Scalia, was the meaning of the word "modify." He proceeded to survey a variety of dictionaries and concluded that, at least as of 1934 when the Act was adopted, the word "modify" was understood to mean to make a minor change in something. An alternative definition, that "modify" can mean to make a basic or important change, was not introduced until later, most notably in Webster's Third New International Dictionary first published in 1961. He concluded that the de-tariffing order was a major, rather than minor, change, and thus exceeded the scope of authority given the Commission to "modify any requirement" related to tariff filing. Justice Stevens, in dissent, countered with his own survey of dictionaries, and concluded that the Commission's policy was consistent with a definition existent in 1934 ("to limit or reduce in extent or degree") because the Commission had eliminated tariff filing only for nondominant carriers.[34]

MCI v. AT&T is famous for its battle of warring dictionaries, and illustrates how the rise of textualism as the preferred mode of statutory interpretation, assiduously promoted by Justice Scalia, transformed the inquiry that courts engage in when applying step 1 of the *Chevron* doctrine.[35] But the claim that the word "modify" had a clear meaning in 1934 that resolved the case was unpersuasive. Even under the dictionaries cited by Scalia, to modify is a matter of degree, and the question was whether making tariff filing voluntary for what was then 40% of the market was a "minor" or "major" change, which required a more extensive consideration of context in which the authority to modify tariff-filing requirements appeared. Fortunately, Justice Scalia moved on from dictionaries to provide the needed contextual understanding.

This understanding emerged in a dispute between Justice Scalia and Justice Stevens over the nature of the authority that Congress had delegated to the FCC. Scalia understood the delegation to be to establish and enforce a regulatory regime in which tariff-filing was the central regulatory instrument. The tariff-filing requirement was "the heart of the common-carrier section of the Communications Act," and much of the rest of the Act was premised on this requirement.[36] He concluded that "[w]hat we have here, in reality, is a fundamental revision of the statute, changing it from a scheme of rate regulation in long-distance common-carrier communications to a scheme of rate regulation only where effective competition does not exist. That may be a good idea, but it was not the idea Congress enacted into law in 1934."[37]

Justice Stevens understood the scope of the delegation in broader purposive terms, as an instruction to regulate in such a way as to "ensure that carriers do not charge unreasonable or discriminatory rates."[38] Tariff-filing may have been an appropriate tool to achieve these ends in 1934, when AT&T had a de facto monopoly on long-distance service. But competition, unforeseen when the Act was passed, had recently emerged. And the Commission had made a "considered judgment that tariff filing is altogether unnecessary in the case of competitive carriers."[39] Justice Scalia responded that "we (and the FCC) are bound, not only by the ultimate purposes Congress has selected, but by the means it has deemed appropriate, and prescribed, for the pursuit of those purposes."[40]

Justice Scalia had the better of the argument here, at least if we accept the anti-inherency conception of legislative supremacy (Chapter 1). If Congress directs an agency to achieve goal X using regulatory tool Y, it is not within the scope of the agency's delegated authority to announce that it will continue to pursue goal X, but will drop tool Y and instead use tool Z never authorized by Congress. Justice Stevens's conception of the scope of agency

authority as defined solely by goal X was a step down the road to the last-
word conception of legislative supremacy (Chapter 1), in the sense that the
agency would be free to abandon regulatory tools prescribed by statute
unless Congress intervenes and says it cannot.

Congress responded to *MCI v. AT&T* two years later in the Telecommunications Act of 1996, by empowering the FCC to effectively abolish the tariff-
filing requirements for all long-distance carriers.[41] In this context at least,
enforcing the anti-inherency conception of legislative supremacy forced the
issue back to Congress to resolve, which is how the principle of legislative supremacy indicates it should be resolved.

Another notable example of the Court straining to enforce limits on agency
authority under step 1 occurred in *FDA v. Brown & Williamson Tobacco
Corp.*[42] The issue was whether the Food and Drug Administration (FDA) had
authority to regulate tobacco products as conventionally marketed—i.e.,
without any claim of health effects—as a combination drug and drug-delivery
device under the Food and Drug Act. A closely divided Court overturned a
major regulatory initiative of the Clinton Administration, holding that the
FDA had "no jurisdiction" over tobacco products. Both the majority opinion
by Justice O'Connor and the dissent by Justice Breyer framed the issue in
terms of step 1 of the *Chevron* doctrine.

Under a textualist version of step 1, Justice Breyer had the better of the
argument. The Act contains broad definitions of "drug" and "device" that
confer authority on the FDA to regulate "articles (other than food) intended
to affect the structure or any function of the body."[43] The only possible issue
as to whether tobacco products fit the general statutory definition was whether
tobacco manufacturers had the requisite "intent" to affect the structure or
function of the body. The FDA found such an intent existed, given that the
effects of tobacco, including the addictive nature of nicotine, had been well
known for many years. Regulation of tobacco also coincided with the general purpose of the Act, which was to protect the health and safety of the
public. To this end, the FDA had mustered massive evidence showing the del-
eterious effects of smoking on human health. The fact that the FDA had
consistently disclaimed any "jurisdiction" over tobacco products until it
abruptly changed its mind in 1996 was of no consequence, according to
Breyer, because *Chevron* itself said that "[a]n initial agency interpretation is
not instantly carved in stone."[44] If we take the two-step approach of the

Chevron doctrine literally, and implement it in textualist terms, the Act arguably *required* the FDA to assert authority over tobacco, once the requisite intent of manufacturers became incontrovertible.

The majority, to the contrary, concluded that "Congress has *clearly* precluded the FDA from asserting jurisdiction to regulate tobacco products," and on this basis overturned the FDA regulation under step 1.[45] Justice O'Connor advanced two arguments in support of this conclusion.

The first argument was that regulation of tobacco under the Act would be self-defeating, because the agency would be forced by various provisions of the Act to ban all tobacco products as "unsafe." Such a prohibition would arguably be more harmful to public health than leaving tobacco unregulated, since it would likely lead to a black market in homemade or contraband cigarettes, which could pose greater dangers than legally marketed ones. The argument required the Court to offer its opinion about multiple provisions of the Act that the agency had yet to consider. Justice Breyer countered, more persuasively, that the Act contained enough discretionary qualifications that the FDA could take the possibility of a black market emerging into account in formulating a proper response to regulating cigarettes as a "drug delivery device."[46]

Justice O'Connor's second argument was more powerful. She pointed out that from 1938, when the current version of the Act was passed, until 1996, FDA officials had repeatedly testified before Congress that the agency had no statutory authority to regulate tobacco. Congress had responded by enacting six separate statutes, none of which were to be administered by the FDA, that addressed the proper regulation of tobacco. Some of these statutes prohibited certain types of advertising of tobacco products, some mandated warning labels on packages of cigarettes, some required restricting the sale of tobacco products to minors. Congress had also on several occasions considered and rejected bills that would have granted the FDA jurisdiction over tobacco products. She concluded that "[u]nder these circumstances, it is clear that Congress' tobacco-specific legislation has effectively ratified the FDA's previous position that it lacks jurisdiction to regulate tobacco."[47] This was in part an invocation of the canon that the meaning of a statute can be altered by the implications of later statutes. More generally, it represented an especially vivid illustration of the proposition that consistent agency action can create settled expectations that help define the proper scope of an agency's authority.

Justice Breyer's primary response to the majority's recitation of the long-standing position of the FDA and the many legislative actions establishing alternative forms of regulation of tobacco was to note—correctly—that Congress had never specifically addressed the "precise question" whether the FDA had authority to regulate tobacco. He argued that the legislative record was therefore ambiguous in this respect, and the FDA's recent about-face and assertion of jurisdiction was entitled to deference. The majority's answer was that this characterization of the legislative history lacked "common sense." And indeed, near the end of his dissenting opinion, Breyer seemed to admit that even if his interpretation of the Act and later statutes "gets the words right, it lacks a sense of their 'music.'"[48]

Justice O'Connor concluded her opinion with an interesting reflection on the possible limits of the *Chevron* doctrine. That doctrine, she noted, rests "on the theory that a statute's ambiguity constitutes an implicit delegation from Congress to the agency to fill in the statutory gaps."[49] She continued: "In extraordinary cases, however, there may be reason to hesitate before concluding that Congress intended such an implicit delegation."[50] The question of the FDA's jurisdiction over tobacco was such an extraordinary case. She implied, without quite explicitly stating, that when cases present important questions about the scope of an agency's authority, Congress most likely intends that courts will exercise some form of independent judgment in resolving the question. Which, of course, is what the Court had done. Notwithstanding the majority's claim that Congress had "clearly" answered the "precise question" about the FDA's jurisdiction as required by *Chevron* step 1, these claims were implausible. O'Connor's painstaking analysis, taking up some thirty-six pages in the official reports, established that it was more likely than not that Congress never intended to give the FDA authority to regulate tobacco. But it was a stretch to say this was "clear," and it was not true that Congress had addressed the "precise question" of the FDA's authority over tobacco. The passage in *Brown & Williamson* about congressional intent in "extraordinary" cases would later give rise to the "major questions" exception to the *Chevron* doctrine in *King v. Burwell*, discussed above.[51]

Tobacco regulation took a number of twists and turns in the wake of *Brown & Williamson*. When a large number of state attorneys general sued the major tobacco companies to recover expenses the states had incurred for treatment of tobacco-related illnesses, a massive settlement was eventually reached that resulted in new restrictions on the marketing of tobacco—and large financial payments to state treasuries.[52] Finally, in 2009, Congress enacted the Family Smoking Prevention and Tobacco Control Act,[53] which gave the FDA the regulatory authority denied by the Supreme Court. One can bemoan the number of additional smoking-related deaths plausibly caused by the nine-year delay. On the other hand, the express conferral of authority by Congress means that the FDA's regulation of tobacco products is now secure and cannot be reversed by future changes in political control of the executive branch.

The Court reached a very different result in another case that raised an "extraordinary" question about the scope of agency authority toward the tail end of the George W. Bush Administration. The question was whether the EPA has authority under the Clean Air Act to regulate greenhouse gas emissions thought to contribute to climate change. Most of the Court's attention in *Massachusetts v. EPA*[54] was focused on whether state governments had standing to challenge the EPA's denial of their request to institute a rule-making proceeding to regulate motor vehicle emissions in the interest of reducing the accumulation of greenhouse gases, mainly carbon dioxide, in the atmosphere. Although climate change is the ultimate "generalized grievance" affecting everyone in the world, a sharply divided Court held that Massachusetts had standing based on its allegation that climate change was causing sea levels to rise, eroding shoreline that the state owned.

With respect to the merits, the issue of the EPA's authority to regulate greenhouse gases seemed to parallel in many respects the question of the FDA's jurisdiction over tobacco products. The Clean Air Act contains a very broad definition of "air pollutant," which would seem to cover any chemical found in the air, including carbon dioxide and other greenhouse gases, not to mention oxygen and water vapor.[55] This was analogous to the Food and Drug Act's very broad definitions of "drugs" and "medical devices." If one takes the definition of "air pollutant" literally, and plugs it into various discrete authorizations of regulation of air pollution, then virtually every provision of the Clean Air Act becomes a mandate to regulate climate change.

The Bush EPA did not like this result for a number of reasons, perhaps most prominently because none of the discrete regulatory provisions of the Act had been designed with a ubiquitous and global phenomenon like CO_2 emissions in mind. Taking its cue from *Brown & Williamson,* the agency argued that Congress had implicitly withheld regulatory authority over greenhouse gas emissions. The problem of climate change was virtually unknown when the basic regulatory structure of the Clean Air Act was established. Under the major regulatory provisions that became law in 1970, the central objective was reducing conventional pollutants like sulfur dioxide and particulate matter that hover near the ground and have an immediate impact on human health and welfare. Congress first reflected an awareness of climate change in 1978, when it enacted a statute directing the President to establish a program to study the issue.[56] This was augmented in 1987 by another statute directing the EPA to develop a coordinated national strategy for dealing with climate change and instructing the State Department to work on diplomatic solutions to combat global warming.[57] In 1990, by which time the threat of climate change was well known, Congress substantially amended the Clean Air Act.[58] In so doing, it adopted new regulatory programs addressing transboundary acid rain and global depletion of the ozone layer of the atmosphere. But it rejected proposals to enact a regulatory program for dealing with domestic sources of greenhouse gases, opting instead for several discrete provisions directing further study and funding of research about the problem. One of these provisions expressly disclaimed that it conferred any authority on the EPA to regulate emissions of carbon dioxide.[59] With respect to the specific proposal of the states to regulate emissions of greenhouse gases by motor vehicles, the EPA noted that the only way to do this would be to require vehicles to burn less fuel—something that the Department of Transportation was given authority to regulate under the Corporate Average Fuel Economy (CAFE) program.[60] The EPA reasoned that this litany of congressional actions, none of which conferred regulatory authority on the EPA, represented, as in *Brown & Williamson,* an implied limitation on the scope of its regulatory authority over greenhouse gas emissions by motor vehicles.[61]

Writing for a 5–4 majority, Justice Stevens rejected the EPA's disavowal of authority. In a unusual move for Stevens, his primary argument in support of EPA authority was purely textualist. The definition of "air pollutant," he said, was unambiguous and gave the EPA sweeping authority over any and all chemicals discharged into the ambient air. In effect, Stevens adopted the argument for expansive regulatory authority based on a broad definitional provision that Justice Breyer had advanced in dissent in *Brown & Williamson.* Although Stevens professed to apply a highly deferential standard of review, and twice cited *Chevron* in his opinion, he virtually handcuffed the agency by holding that the only grounds the agency could advance for declining to engage in rulemaking on the subject were those found in the particular statute conferring regulatory authority. Thus, the EPA could decline to set greenhouse gas emissions standards for vehicles only if it found that such gases do not contribute to air pollution reasonably anticipated "to endanger public health or welfare."[62] The Administration's stated preference to postpone regulation under the existing Act in order to develop a comprehensive legislative and / or diplomatic solution was deemed legally irrelevant.

Chief Justice Roberts and Justice Scalia wrote tag-team dissents, joined by all members of the conservative block other than Justice Kennedy (whose vote with the liberals explained the different outcome from the tobacco case, where Kennedy voted with the conservatives). Roberts addressed standing; Scalia, the merits. Scalia did not attempt to write an opinion along the lines of Justice O'Connor's effort in *Brown & Williamson,* relying on the EPA's historical and contextual rationale for abjuring regulatory authority over greenhouse gases. Instead he argued rather lamely that the statute's definition of "air pollutant" was different from its reference to "air pollution," and that the latter term was ambiguous, requiring deference to the EPA under *Chevron.*[63] He was rather more effective in maintaining that an agency like the EPA can invoke a variety of reasonable grounds to postpone regulating a novel problem, and should not be limited to factors specifically mentioned in a statutory grant of authority.[64]

Massachusetts v. EPA represents a remarkable decision in which the Court did not act to check an agency that was attempting to abdicate part of its traditional sphere of regulatory authority—as in *MCI v. AT&T.* Nor did the Court act to block the agency from seeking to expand its scope of authority— as in *Dole v. Steelworkers* and *Brown & Williamson.* Instead, the Court sought to force the agency to begin regulating a problem it had not previously regulated and which Congress had not signaled in any authoritative fashion it intended the agency to regulate. Whatever else one thinks of the decision, it was not a form of boundary maintenance but instead a form of judicially imposed boundary expansion.

The majority in *Massachusetts* was probably moved by increasing frustration with the failure of the Bush Administration to push for legislation dealing with climate change.[65] But the strategy of expanding agency authority to tackle the problem—or perhaps to inject so much disruption into the statutory scheme that Congress would be forced to act—did not work either. The Obama Administration early in its tenure proposed a bill creating a general cap-and-trade system for reducing greenhouse gases. It passed the House but failed in the Senate.[66] Conceivably the outcome would have been different if the Court had held that the EPA had no authority to regulate greenhouse gases. At least it is plausible that the Court's decision holding that the EPA could deal with the problem under its existing authority gave cover to Senators to oppose the bill. In the wake of the legislative setback, the Obama Administration turned to a number of initiatives designed to tackle the problem of climate change under existing EPA authority. Some of the more prominent ones were repudiated by the Trump Administration before they could be implemented. Others revealed more starkly than *Massachusetts* the incompatibility of regulating greenhouse gases under statutory provisions designed to control conventional air pollutants.

Enforcing Boundaries of Authority at Step 2

The third way for reviewing courts to enforce limits on agency authority in the *Chevron* era has been to hold at step 2 that the agency interpretation is "unreasonable" because it exceeds the scope of its authority. *Utility Air Regulatory Group v. Environmental Protection Agency,* where the Court returned to the scope of the EPA's authority over greenhouse gases, is the most prominent example.[67] Reviewing a regulation by the Obama EPA that was designed to use the Prevention of Significant Deterioration (PSD) provisions of the Clean Air Act to reduce greenhouse gas emissions from major stationary sources of air pollution, a narrow majority cut back significantly on the rationale of *Massachusetts*. The PSD provisions require the use of technology-based controls on any stationary source that emits more than 250 tons of "any air pollutant" per year. The phrase "air pollutant" had, of course, been interpreted by *Massachusetts* to include greenhouse gases. The EPA therefore reasoned that controls were required for stationary sources that emit greenhouse gases. The agency nevertheless recognized that this would produce an unworkable situation, because a very large number of stationary sources emit more than 250 tons of carbon dioxide in any given year. The EPA accordingly decided that the PSD regime would be triggered only for sources that emit more than 100,000 tons of greenhouse gases per year. In other words, in order to make the PSD system usable as a system for controlling greenhouses gases, the EPA effectively crossed out the statutory tonnage figure enacted by Congress and substituted a new and much higher figure of its own devising.

In an opinion for the Court cobbled together with different coalitions of Justices, Justice Scalia overturned the rule in part. The most significant ruling was that *Massachusetts* had held only that the term "air pollutant" *may* include greenhouse gases, but did not establish that it *must* include greenhouse gases for all purposes.[68] He pointed out that EPA, by "longstanding constructions," had limited the term in various contexts to mean only the subset of pollutants actually regulated under a particular provision.[69] Thus, it would be within the authority of the EPA to interpret "air pollutant" to mean only conventional pollutants for PSD purposes—or at least to interpret the term to exclude greenhouse gases for purposes of establishing the 250-ton threshold. Without explicitly discussing whether the term "air pollutant" was ambiguous as applied in different sections of the Act, Scalia went on to rule that it would be "unreasonable" to interpret the term as including greenhouse gases for purposes of establishing the 250-ton threshold. This would produce "the single largest expansion [in] the scope of the [Act] in its history," and a surge in regulatory permitting requests that would have "calamitous consequences" for both industry and the EPA.[70]

Thus, in contrast to *MCI v. AT&T* and *Brown & Williamson*, both of which used step 1 to police the boundaries of agency authority, *Utility Air* did the policing under step 2.[71] The majority held that the EPA's interpretation of "air pollutant" for purposes of the PSD program was unreasonable. The most important reason was that the EPA's interpretation

> would bring about an enormous and transformative expansion in EPA's regulatory authority without clear congressional authorization. . . . .[I]n EPA's assertion of that authority, we confront a singular situation: an agency laying claim to extravagant statutory power over the national economy while at the same time strenuously asserting that the authority claimed would render the statute "unrecognizable to the Congress that designed it." Since, as we hold above, the statute does not compel EPA's

interpretation, it would be patently unreasonable—not to say outra-
geous—for EPA to insist on seizing expansive power that it admits the
statute is not designed to grant.[72]

In effect, Justice Scalia came around to the analysis he should have advanced
in his dissent in *Massachusetts*. The definition of "air pollutant" cannot include greenhouse gases, at least not for all purposes, because individual provisions of the Act that reference this term simply do not make sense as applied
to greenhouse gases. Justice Scalia did not have the votes to overrule, as opposed to reinterpret, *Massachusetts*. Indeed, in order to get five votes he had
to hold, somewhat inconsistently, that stationary sources that meet the 250-
ton requirement based on conventional pollutants may be required to adopt
technology designed to reduce the emission of greenhouse gases.

Unsurprisingly, Justice Scalia also held that the EPA could not fix the incompatibility problem by rewriting the statute to eliminate the statutory
threshold for regulation of 250 tons and substitute in its place 100,000 tons.
This, the Justice wrote, would "deal a severe blow to the Constitution's separation of powers."[73] Agencies have authority, under the *Chevron* doctrine, to
interpret gaps and ambiguities that arise in the course of implementing a
statute. But this "does not include a power to revise clear statutory terms that
turn out not to work in practice."[74]

Writing in dissent, Justice Breyer would have allowed the EPA to engage
in just such a rewriting. He argued that if the majority was willing to rewrite
"any air pollutant" to mean "any air pollutant except greenhouse gases," the
EPA should be allowed to rewrite "250 tons" to mean "250 tons except 100,000
tons in the case of greenhouse gases."[75] The difference, of course, was that
"any air pollutant" had been held to have an unambiguous meaning in a prior
decision of the Court (*Massachusetts*), which was subject to revision by the
Court as further cases arose revealing the need to qualify this conclusion. In
contrast, the statutory term "250 tons" cannot under any stretch of imagina-
tion be interpreted to mean "100,000 tons." Breyer's opinion was an extension, albeit in extreme form, of the argument set forth by the dissents in
MCI v. AT&T and *Brown & Williamson*, namely, that an agency can jettison
settled interpretations of a statute in the name of realizing its general purposes
under changed conditions. Here, however, he pushed the argument beyond
settled interpretations to include the revision of incontrovertible texts. This

was moving perilously close to the "last word" conception of legislative supremacy.[76]

In Sum

The foregoing discussion, limited to five decisions, represents only a fraction of the cases in which the Court has confronted the need to enforce limits on agency authority under the *Chevron* doctrine. They do not provide a basis for a more complete assessment of how that doctrine might be reformulated to address the boundary limitation question more forthrightly and effectively, a task taken up in the next chapter. A few preliminary takeaways are nevertheless possible.

The primary conclusion is that neither the formulation of step 1 in terms of "clarity" nor step 2 in terms of "reasonableness" is adequate to allow courts to enforce boundary limitations. Step 1 seems to direct courts to look for "clear" statutory language that addresses the "precise question" at issue. But the word games featured in *MCI v. AT&T* did not provide a persuasive basis for limiting the authority of the FCC to deregulate the long-distance telephone market. And the plain-meaning version of textualism, as deployed by Justice Breyer in dissent in *Brown & Williamson* and by Justice Stevens in *Massachusetts,* reveals that textualism can be used just as easily to blow up limits on agency authority as to enforce them. Justice Scalia's suggestion in *Utility Air* that boundaries can be enforced under the "reasonableness" inquiry of step 2 exploits the ambiguity about what reasonableness means, but provides little guidance about what kinds of factors should be used in considering whether an agency is acting "unreasonably" because it has slipped the bounds of its delegated authority.

Another lesson would seem to be that there is no escape from considering history in delineating the scope of agency authority. The history of the original enactment is, of course, of primary relevance here. But the history of the statute's evolution also matters, as vividly illustrated by *Brown & Williamson.* Determining boundaries is significantly about ascertaining settled expectations about what sorts of issues an agency is expected to regulate. A related lesson is that the whole act must be considered, not just preliminary definitional provisions. Justice Brennan explored the all relevant provisions of the

Paperwork Reduction Act in *Dole v. Steelworkers,* to persuasive effect. Justice Scalia did a good job of explicating the boundaries of agency authority in light of the whole act in both *MCI v. AT&T* and *Utility Air.* Justice Stevens egregiously ignored this element in *Massachusetts.*

A more disturbing takeaway is that we see how judicial enforcement of statutory boundaries is critically dependent on the assumption that Congress remains actively engaged in monitoring and revising the scope of agency authority.[77] Both *MCI v. AT&T* and *Brown & Williamson* were decided at a time when Congress could respond (if slowly) by amending the statute to revise the agency mandate in response to the issue highlighted by the litigation. But the challenge of climate change has defied an effective legislative response, both before and after *Massachusetts.* This creates tremendous pressure to rewrite the scope of agency authority, in search of a solution that Congress seems unwilling to provide. In the extreme, it can lead to a demand to allow the agency to rewrite the statute, as Justice Breyer advocated in dissent in *Utility Air.* This book is written on the premise that courts should continue to enforce the anti-inherency conception of legislative supremacy. But whether that understanding endures is ultimately up to Congress, not the judiciary.

Discerning the Boundaries of Agency
Authority to Interpret

CHAPTERS 8, 9, AND 10 considered three types of boundaries that limit an agency's authority to interpret statutes, grounded in different constitutional values: individual constitutional rights, federalism, and separation of powers. In each case, there is the potential for a clash between agency interpretations of the statutes they administer and the principle that courts have the last word in giving effect to the requirements of the Constitution.

Where the constitutional principle is sharply delineated—as will be the case with respect to individual rights and discrete federalism and separation of powers challenges—courts should not have great difficulty in identifying the presence of a constitutional limit on agency authority. The party opposing the agency interpretation will identify the possibility that the agency view violates the Constitution. Once alerted to the relevance of the Constitution, the court will be on notice that it must resolve that aspect of the controversy on its own authority. Issues of sequencing may arise as to which should be considered first: statutory or constitutional interpretation. But otherwise, the distinction between statutory and constitutional questions should be readily discernable.

Where more general principles of federalism are involved, as in preemption cases, identifying the constitutional dimension is more difficult. To some extent this depends on whether the parties identify the question as one of preemption or one of statutory interpretation. But even when the issue is clearly framed as one of preemption, the answer will be significantly affected by the interpretation of the federal statute said to give rise to preemption. If an agency has weighed in on the question of interpretation or preemption, courts must decide how much weight to give the agency on different dimensions on the problem. The agency will plausibly have a comparative advantage on some dimensions, such as in finding the relevant facts and explaining the rationale behind the federal regulation. These are important questions, and the degree of deference the court owes to the agency in these matters remains unresolved. But at least the court should be aware that it has final authority on the ultimate question of preemption.

With respect to the separation of powers principle of legislative supremacy, the matter is different. Here the constitutional principle of legislative supremacy is potentially implicated in every act of statutory interpretation, and the clash between agency interpretations of the law and enforcing the relevant constitutional principle is pervasive, inescapable, and often overlooked. Yet if one accepts the principle of legislative supremacy—and the construction of that principle to mean that agencies have no inherent authority to exercise regulatory authority unless it has been delegated to them by Congress—then it is imperative that courts enforce any and all limits on agency authority that Congress has prescribed by statute. The constitutional principle compels a *practice* by courts of making and enforcing their best judgment of as to the scope of an agency's delegated powers, even if courts do not (and need not) invoke the Constitution directly in making these determinations. Moreover, there is no easy out in terms of labeling certain statutory provisions "jurisdictional" and others "nonjurisdictional." *Every* legislated restriction on agency authority must be enforced by the courts, or else we will have slipped into an understanding of legislative supremacy that gives agencies (or the President) authority to make law on their own authority, subject to possible override by Congress.

Mississippi Power & Light: A Preliminary Skirmish

The relationship between agency and court interpretations of the limits on agency authority arose early in the history of the *Chevron* doctrine, in a case called *Mississippi Power & Light Co. v. Mississippi ex rel. Moore.*[1] In response to court decisions in the 1920s and 30s offering conflicting views about the respective roles of the federal government and the states over sales of electric power, the Federal Power Act was amended in 1935 to clarify the division of authority. The amended Act drew a bright line distinction between interstate and wholesale sales of electricity and local retail power markets.[2] A federal agency (today the Federal Energy Regulatory Commission or FERC) was given exclusive authority over interstate and wholesale sales of electricity; the states were assured of exclusive authority over retail sales of electricity to consumers.

Mississippi Power involved an agreement among power companies in several southern states to pool their resources to construct and pay for a nuclear power plant. As seemed to happen more often than not, the plant ended up costing many times more than originally projected. FERC interpreted the arrangement as a wholesale power pool and allocated the high construction costs among the individual power companies. The Mississippi Public Service Commission (MPSC) then announced that it would consider whether it was prudent for Mississippi Power & Light Co. (MP&L) to purchase its share of the expensive power for resale to retail customers in Mississippi. The Court, in an opinion by Justice Stevens, concluded that the issue of MP&L's prudence in participating in the pool could have been, but was not, raised in the proceeding before FERC, and that the FERC order allocating the costs among the participating power companies preempted any authority of the MPSC to consider the prudence of MP&L's purchase of its participation share as a matter of state law. The Stevens opinion was an exercise in de novo review; there was no mention of deference to FERC, under the *Chevron* doctrine or otherwise.

Justice Scalia, who was then engaged in the opening round of his campaign to establish the *Chevron* doctrine in the Supreme Court (Chapter 4), filed a concurring opinion. He said the "critical issue" was whether FERC had "jurisdiction" to consider the prudence issue.[3] And he said this should be decided under the *Chevron* doctrine, which required upholding FERC's assertion of jurisdiction, because it was reasonable.

Justice Brennan filed a dissenting opinion, joined by Justices Marshall and Blackmun. He agreed with the majority that the MPSC could not revisit the allocation of wholesale costs among the utilities as approved by FERC. But he argued that the MPSC had authority to consider whether it was prudent for MP&L to purchase that power for resale to retail customers, if a cheaper source of power was available. Brennan then went after Justice Scalia's suggestion that the *Chevron* doctrine should be applied in answering the jurisdictional question. He wrote in part:

> Agencies do not "administer" statutes confining the scope of their jurisdiction, and such statutes are not "entrusted" to agencies. . . . [P]olicies in

favor of limiting the agency's jurisdiction . . . have not been entrusted to the agency [and may conflict] with the agency's institutional interests in expanding its own power. . . . [F]or similar reasons, agencies can claim no special expertise in interpreting a statute confining its jurisdiction. Finally, we cannot presume that Congress implicitly intended an agency to fill "gaps" in a statute confining the agency's jurisdiction, since by its nature such a statute manifests an unwillingness to give the agency the freedom to define the scope of its own power. . . . It is thus not surprising that this Court has never deferred to an agency's interpretation of a statute to confine the scope of its jurisdiction.[4]

Brennan added that the Federal Power Act was written not only to define the jurisdiction of FERC, but also to protect the "authority of the states." "Congress could not have intended courts," he wrote, "to defer to one agency's interpretation of the jurisdictional division where the policies in conflict have been committed to the care of different regulators."[5] For good measure, he added that FERC's interpretations of the prudence question had not been consistent and were not contemporaneous with the 1935 amendment to the Federal Power Act.[6]

Justice Scalia made two arguments in response to this attack. First, he suggested that there is no meaningful distinction between limits on agency jurisdiction and other questions about whether an agency has exceeded the limits of its authority. As he put it: "[T]here is no discernible line between an agency's exceeding its authority and an agency's exceeding authorized application of its authority. To exceed authorized application is to exceed authority. Virtually any administrative action can be characterized as either one or the other, depending upon how generally one wishes to describe the 'authority.'"[7] Second, he argued that the Court had deferred to agency interpretations of their own jurisdiction, citing several pre-*Chevron* decisions and one decision that cited *Chevron* but did not apply the two-step standard. He did not explain how, if the distinction between the scope of authority and exercise of authority was meaningless, he was able to identify these decisions as implicating the scope of agency authority. Nor did he explain how he was able, in his opening statement, to identify the critical issue as whether FERC had "jurisdiction" to determine the prudence of a wholesale power pooling agreement.

The debate between Justices Brennan and Scalia was important in two respects. First, it defined the relevant question as whether there should be an "exception" to the *Chevron* doctrine for questions about agency "jurisdiction." Lower courts and commentators would debate this issue for years, most siding with Brennan, but some agreeing with Scalia that no such distinction can be meaningfully drawn.[8] Second, as happened with respect to other intramural debates with Justice Scalia over the proper interpretation of the *Chevron* doctrine, the Court for many years shied away from any effort to resolve the issue. The Court gradually came to accept the view that the *Chevron* doctrine is a rule of law, but it was not sufficiently invested in that rule to engage in prolonged conflict with its most emphatic proponent over the proper scope of the doctrine.

City of Arlington v. FCC

Twenty-five years would pass before the Court, faced squarely with a circuit conflict on the issue, finally agreed to decide whether the *Chevron* doctrine applies to questions about an agency's "jurisdiction." The fateful decision was *City of Arlington v. FCC*.[9] The underlying question concerned a provision of the Telecommunications Act of 1996 that requires local land-use agencies to process applications to construct or expand wireless transmission towers "within a reasonable period of time."[10] The statute provided that wireless companies that believe requests are not being processed within a reasonable time should seek relief in a "court of competent jurisdiction."[11] There was not a word in the legislation about FCC implementation or enforcement of the reasonable-time mandate. After initially disclaiming authority to interpret the provision, the FCC changed its mind and issued a declaratory order interpreting "reasonable time" presumptively to mean no more than 90 days in the case of an expansion or 150 days in the case of new construction of a wireless tower. The Fifth Circuit, in reviewing a challenge to the declaratory order by several local governments, recognized that the case presented a question about whether the FCC had "jurisdiction" to interpret the reasonable-time provision.[12] Following earlier circuit precedent, it held that *Chevron* applies to jurisdictional questions, and it deferred to the FCC's interpretation that it had jurisdiction. It also applied *Chevron* on the merits and upheld the FCC's time limits as a permissible interpretation of "reasonable period of time."

The Court granted review, but limited its consideration to the question whether "a court should apply *Chevron* to review an agency's interpretation of its own jurisdiction."[13] It declined to review either the question whether the FCC did in fact have jurisdiction over the reasonable-time requirement or whether the Fifth Circuit had properly applied *Chevron* in deferring to the FCC's construction of the reasonable-time provision on the assumption that it had jurisdiction. In other words, the Court agreed to decide the abstract question whether courts should apply *Chevron* to agencies' interpretations of their own authority, and nothing else.[14] Five Justices joined in an opinion by Justice Scalia that answered the abstract question in the affirmative. Justice Breyer concurred in the judgment. Chief Justice Roberts, joined by Justices Kennedy and Alito, dissented.

The primary thrust of Justice Scalia's opinion followed the arguments set forth in his concurring opinion in *Mississippi Power & Light,* twenty-five years earlier. He argued that there is no principled distinction between agency statutory interpretations that are "jurisdictional" and those that are not. Taking rhetorical pugnacity to a new level, he heaped scorn on the jurisdictional–nonjurisdictional distinction, calling it "a mirage," an "empty distraction," a "bogeyman," "specious," and caricaturing the opposing view as urging a distinction between "big, important" decisions and "humdrum, run-of-the mill stuff."[15] As before, he cited numerous Supreme Court decisions in which "jurisdictional" questions about agency authority had been resolved by applying or citing *Chevron.* Again, he did not acknowledge the irony that somehow he could identify these cases as posing jurisdictional questions, even while professing that the distinction was meaningless. Nor did he note that nearly all these decisions were precedents in which the jurisdictional–nonjurisdictional distinction had not been discussed.

The clinching argument for the majority, however, was that recognizing an exception for jurisdictional questions would fatally undermine the *Chevron* doctrine. Admit an exception for jurisdictional questions, the argument went, and litigants and lower courts would manipulate the exception to recapture for courts the authority that *Chevron* had ceded to agencies. As Justice Scalia wrote:

Make no mistake—the ultimate target here is *Chevron* itself. Savvy challengers of agency action would play the "jurisdictional" card in every case. Some judges would be deceived by the specious, but scary-sounding "jurisdictional"-"nonjurisdictional" line; others tempted by the prospect of making public policy by prescribing the meaning of ambiguous statutory commands. The effect would be to transfer any number of interpretative decisions—archetypical *Chevron* questions, about how best to construe an ambiguous term in light of competing policy interests— from the agencies that administer the statutes to the federal courts.[16]

This passage is revealing about the motivation behind Justice Scalia's rather fanatical advocacy of the *Chevron* doctrine during his years on the Court. In his mind, the *Chevron* doctrine was of critical importance because it put a brake on lower courts willfully substituting their judgment for that of agencies on matters of policy. Scalia never acknowledged that *Chevron*'s dual standards of "clarity" and "reasonableness" can hardly be said to deter such willful behavior. If anything, the *Chevron* doctrine reduced the costs of overturning agency policy decisions relative to the preferred device of the pre-*Chevron* era, which was to engage in an extensive (and often manipulative) analysis of legislative history. Justice Scalia's own behavior over the years, which reveals a strong proclivity to overturn agency interpretations with which he disagreed using the *Chevron* doctrine, confirms the point.[17]

Aside from the charge that the "jurisdictional–nonjurisdictional" line would be endlessly manipulated to undermine the *Chevron* doctrine, Justice Scalia's arguments were not terribly persuasive. Perhaps most notably, he failed to address the relevance of the Administrative Procedure Act. The APA specifically instructs reviewing courts to decide "all relevant questions of law."[18] This provision can be reconciled with deference to agency interpretations of law under a theory of delegated interpretational authority. When Congress instructs an agency to determine the meaning of a statutory term (like "employee"), the courts should defer to the agency's interpretation because Congress has delegated interpretive authority to the agency. The court decides the "question of law," in the exercise independent judgment, by determining that Congress intended that the agency resolve the question.[19] However, the APA also enjoins reviewing courts to "hold unlawful and set aside agency action, findings, and conclusions found to be . . . *in excess of statutory jurisdiction, authority, or limitations, or short of statutory right.*"[20] This command cannot be reconciled with deference to the agency interpretation, because the very question at issue is whether such a delegation does or does not exist. The text of the APA therefore seems plainly to require that courts exercise independent judgment about whether the agency is acting "in excess of statutory jurisdiction." Ordinarily a master at statutory exegesis, Scalia made no effort to square his extension of *Chevron* to questions of agency jurisdiction with the text of the APA.

Justice Scalia also acknowledged that, insofar as the authority of courts is concerned, there is a "very real distinction" between jurisdictional and nonjurisdictional questions.[21] Courts quite commonly inquire whether they have jurisdiction over a matter, and only if the answer is affirmative do they proceed to decide the merits. Scalia nevertheless insisted that the ease with which courts apply the distinction to their own decision making does not carry over to their review of agency decision making. The explanation he gave was that decisions made by a court outside its jurisdiction are *ultra vires* and hence can be attacked in later enforcement actions, whereas erroneous decisions by a court within its jurisdiction cannot be collaterally attacked. In contrast, he insisted, every agency decision contrary to law is *ultra vires*.[22] This may be, but the proffered distinction does not explain why the jurisdictional–nonjurisdictional line is conceptually meaningful and capable of judicial determination in the one context but not in the other. If courts can apply the jurisdiction–nonjurisdiction distinction in considering judicial authority, they should be capable of applying the same distinction in deciding what standard of review to apply to an agency interpretation of law.

Justice Scalia also dismissed out of hand the idea that discerning the limits of the FCC's authority had anything to do with federalism. The only thing at issue was a federal statute, he said, and the question was whether its ambiguity should be resolved by a federal agency or a federal court. That, he insisted, was simply a separation of powers question, not a question of federalism. To which there are two responses. First, since when are separation of powers questions of little consequence, especially the principle of legislative supremacy and its corollary that agencies have no authority to act unless it is delegated to them by Congress? Second, the statute in question quite clearly *did* involve a federalism question. The underlying dispute involved the exercise of local land-use authority, which is unquestionably a matter of traditional state and local authority. Congress had partially preempted such authority by requiring that applications for wireless transmission towers had to be resolved in a "reasonable period of time." But the FCC's interpretation turned a general standard to be given meaning by courts on a case-by-case basis into a presumption that local zoning boards must abide by specific deadlines established by a federal agency. This expanded the scope of federal preemption, which necessarily contracted state and local land-use authority. Justice Scalia made no mention of the fact that the Court has consistently rejected the application of *Chevron* to preemption questions, precisely because those questions have a pronounced effect on the balance of authority between the federal government and the states (Chapter 9).

Finally, Justice Scalia had little to say in response to the central theme of the Chief Justice's dissent—namely, that deferring to agency interpretations of their own authority undermines the role of the courts in ensuring that agencies act within the boundaries laid down by Congress. Scalia did not deny that this was an important function of judicial review. The solution to the "fox-in-the-henhouse syndrome," according to Scalia, was for courts to strictly enforce statutory limits that are clear or unambiguous. What this means, of course, is that agency power will be limited only when Congress has legislated unambiguously to limit it. In other words, it is up to Congress to draft better statutes if the principle of legislative supremacy is to be preserved. With many challenges to unilateral assertions of power by the Obama Administration on the horizon when *City of Arlington* was decided, one wonders if this blank check for executive authority partially explains why Justices Ginsburg, Sotomayor, and Kagan signed on to the Scalia opinion.

Justice Breyer filed a discursive opinion concurring in part and concurring in the judgment, which must be a puzzle to observers not familiar with his previously expressed views about *Chevron*. Justice Breyer agreed that the jurisdictional–nonjurisdictional line could not be consistently maintained in a meaningful fashion. But he insisted that ambiguity is not enough to infer a delegation of authority to an agency to exercise primary interpretational authority. Instead, he quoted from his opinion in *Barnhart v. Walton* for the proposition that a variety of contextual factors are relevant in determining whether *Chevron* should apply. Justice Breyer ultimately concurred in the judgment on the ground that he believed the FCC had determined correctly

that it had authority to interpret the meaning of the phrase "reasonable period of time"—which, of course, was a question the Court had declined to
review.[23]

Chief Justice Roberts's dissent, joined by Justices Kennedy and Alito, deserves to enter the annals as a classic statement of the principles of administrative law. His disagreement with the majority was "fundamental." As he
summed up in his opening paragraph:

> A court should not defer to an agency until the court decides, on its own,
> that the agency is entitled to deference. Courts defer to an agency's in-
> terpretation of law when and because Congress has conferred on the
> agency interpretative authority over the question at issue. An agency
> cannot exercise interpretative authority until it has it; the question
> whether an agency enjoys that authority must be decided by a court,
> without deference to the agency.[24]

The Chief Justice sought to deflect Justice Scalia's debunking of the
jurisdictional–nonjurisdictional line by admitting that "jurisdiction" is a
word of many meanings and that the "parties, amici, and the court below
often use the term 'jurisdiction' imprecisely."[25] The correct way to frame the
inquiry, according to Roberts, was whether "Congress has granted the agency
interpretive authority over the statutory ambiguity at issue."[26] Moreover, this
question must be addressed in terms of the specific provision before the court.
If Congress has delegated authority to the agency to implement or enforce a
provision with the force of law, and the agency has done so, then *Chevron*
applies in assessing the agency's interpretation. But if Congress has not delegated authority to the agency over the provision in question, or the agency
has not exercised this authority in rendering its interpretation, then *Chevron*
should not apply.

By way of illustration, the Chief Justice pointed out that many statutes
"parcel out authority to multiple agencies."[27] Clearly, courts must determine
de novo which agency (if any) has been delegated authority to administer the
provision in question. He conceded that "[a] general delegation to the agency
to administer a statute will often suffice to satisfy the court that Congress has
delegated interpretative authority over the ambiguity at issue." But, he added,
"if Congress has exempted particular provisions from that authority, that ex-

emption must be respected, and the determination whether Congress has done so is for the courts alone."[28]

With respect to Justice Scalia's fears of judicial manipulation of the inquiry into the scope of agency authority, and of potential judicial intrusion into the policymaking sphere of the agencies, the Chief Justice responded that larger considerations of constitutional structure were at stake. The judiciary is obligated not only to confine itself to its proper role, but also "to ensure that the other branches do so as well." The Court could not abdicate its basic task of fixing the "boundaries of delegated authority." "Our duty to police the boundary between the Legislature and the Executive is as critical as our duty to respect that between the Judiciary and the Executive. . . . We do not leave it to the agency to decide when it is in charge."[29]

Supreme Court decisions often have unintended consequences. In the case of *City of Arlington,* the unintended consequence may have been the collapse of conservative support for the *Chevron* doctrine. Within three years Justice Scalia, the great champion of the *Chevron* doctrine, had died. Justice Clarence Thomas, who authored *Brand X* and joined Justice Scalia in *City of Arlington,* did a stunning about-face and argued in a concurring opinion in 2015 that the *Chevron* doctrine may be unconstitutional.[30] The Trump Administration, taking its cues from organizations of conservative lawyers, made sure that its first two appointments to the Supreme Court—Neil Gorsuch and Brett Kavanaugh—were persons who had expressed skepticism about *Chevron.*[31] *City of Arlington* boiled down to a debate over whether to preserve a fundamental principle of separation of powers or to preserve the *Chevron* doctrine. Many conservative jurists and scholars seemingly concluded that if the price of preserving the *Chevron* doctrine was giving up on judicial enforcement of a key principle of separation of powers, they would prefer giving up on *Chevron.*

What About Step Zero?

Before turning to what lessons should be drawn from *City of Arlington,* it is worth taking a moment to consider the proposed approach to enforcing the limits on agency authority offered by Chief Justice Roberts in his dissenting opinion in the case. Under *Mead,* agencies are eligible for *Chevron* deference only if Congress has delegated power to them to act with the force of law and the agency has rendered an interpretation having the force of law.[32] Roberts argued that what the parties called agency "jurisdiction" could be reformulated in terms of whether Congress has delegated authority to the agency to act with the force of law with respect to the "specific provision" or "particular question" before the court.[33] Only if the reviewing court answers *this* question in the affirmative, in the exercise of de novo review, can the court apply the *Chevron* doctrine. In other words, by applying *Mead*'s step zero at the proper level of generality—the level that corresponds to the question of interpretation actually presented to the court—the court can ensure that *Chevron* deference applies to questions where the agency is properly acting within the scope of its delegated authority.

Justice Scalia's response to this was to insist, to the contrary, that all that is required is a general grant of rulemaking or adjudication authority to the agency. As long as there is a general grant of authority to act with the force of law, and the agency renders its interpretation in a format having the force of law, the agency is entitled to *Chevron* deference for any and all questions about whether its general authority covers the specific provision or interpretational issue before the court. The difference between Scalia and Roberts over how step zero should work was relatively narrow. Scalia argued that a general grant of authority to an agency to engage in rulemaking or adjudication is enough to trigger *Chevron*. Roberts agreed that a general grant would often be sufficient, but that courts should also consider arguments to the effect that Congress has "exempted particular provisions from that authority,"[34] in which case the general grant would not carry the agency into *Chevron* territory. So the dispute boiled down to whether courts, exercising independent judgment at step zero, should or should not entertain arguments that the particular issue in question has been carved out of a general grant of rulemaking or adjudication authority.

Chief Justice Roberts was clearly right on this point. As a matter of construing how *Mead*'s step zero should operate, Justice Scalia was in effect arguing for a superficial examination of the agency's organic statute, looking for one general grant of rulemaking or adjudication authority. Once a court discovers such a provision, and concludes that the agency's interpretation was rendered in a binding rule or adjudication, *Chevron* kicks in and the court defers to the agency on any and all issues presented under the statute. Roberts was arguing for an actual examination of the agency's organic statute, to see not only if there is a general grant of authority to act with the force of law, but also whether such a grant in fact covers the dispute before the court. It seems impossible that courts should do anything other than actually examine all relevant portions of the statute before determining whether a particular grant of authority extends to the contested provision at issue. Scalia's position about step zero was colored by his persistent hostility to the very existence of such an inquiry, and his preference, which he had hitherto insisted upon in multiple opinions, for giving *Chevron* deference to any "authoritative" agency interpretation (see Chapter 6).

Unfortunately, the Chief Justice's proposed solution to enforcing the limits Congress has imposed on agency authority does not work. Simplifying a bit, one can conceive of the question of agency authority along two dimensions. One is whether Congress has given the agency the authority to act with the force of law. The other is whether the issue in question is one that Congress wants the agency to resolve. It is quite possible to imagine an agency that is given authority to act with the force of law (e.g., issue binding regulations governing the marketing of drugs and medical devices) but is not given authority over a particular set of issues (e.g., do not regulate tobacco).[35] Conversely, it is possible to imagine an agency that is given authority over a particular set of issues (e.g., make sure employees get paid time and a half for overtime) but is not given authority to act with the force of law with respect to those issues (e.g., bring an enforcement action asking a court to determine if a violation has occurred).[36] The principle of legislative supremacy requires that *both* types of limits be enforced, not only the force of law dimension.

At a more practical level, the Chief Justice's proposed solution fails because most agencies have generally worded grants of rulemaking authority, and for many years the Court has construed such provisions as conferring authority to make rules with the force of law, without regard to the original understanding of Congress when these grants were enacted.[37] This assumption is now embedded in precedents that apply to many important agencies, including the EPA, the FDA, the National Labor Relations Board, and the Federal Reserve Board.[38] The Court, in an opinion by the Chief Justice, has even extended this assumption to a general rulemaking grant under the Internal Revenue Code which was long understood as limited to authorizing only nonbinding interpretative rules.[39] Given that general grants of rulemaking authority are now routinely interpreted as conferring authority to act with the force of law, confining the search for limits on agency authority to specific carve-outs from these grants would create a pervasive bias in favor of ever-expanding agency authority.

Perhaps the most serious objection to the Chief Justice's proposal, especially if it would devolve in practice to a search for "exceptions" to general rulemaking (or adjudication) grants, is that it tacitly accepts the assumption of the evolved *Chevron* doctrine, which is that the agency is presumed to be the primary interpreter of the statutes it administers, provided the statute requires interpretation—that is, it is unclear or ambiguous. This assumption was launched with the cryptic statement about implicit delegations in Part II of Justice Stevens's *Chevron* opinion, which was interpreted by the D.C. Circuit and Justice Scalia to mean that *any ambiguity* in a statute constitutes an implied delegation to the agency to be the primary interpreter of the statute. The assumption was made explicit in *Smiley v. Citibank (South Dakota)*, and ratified by *Mead* with a minor qualification—that the agency must act with the force of law in making its interpretation.[40] This has it backward. The question, instead, should be: Is there persuasive evidence that Congress *actually delegated* authority to the agency to interpret this particular matter? If Justice Breyer has gotten one thing right in his many quarrels with Justice Scalia and his allies over *Chevron*, it is that the presumption should be in favor of independent judicial interpretation, unless the evidence shows that Congress affirmatively intended to delegate interpretive authority to the agency. This was the baseline assumption before *Chevron*, it was the mandate of the APA, and it should be the baseline assumption in whatever follows *Chevron*.

Enforcing Limits on Agency Authority After *Chevron*

How, then, should courts proceed in enforcing the boundaries of agency authority? Under the *Chevron* doctrine, the only tools courts are given to perform this vital task are to enforce statutory directives that are clear and to invalidate agency interpretations of unclear statutes that are unreasonable. These are inadequate to the task. If faithfully applied (and, as we have seen in Chapter 10, they have been stretched out of recognition in select cases to enforce perceived limits on agency authority) they would result in a slide toward administrative government that enforces constitutional limits inconsistently and implicitly adheres at most to a weak, last-word conception of legislative supremacy. How, then, should the *Chevron* doctrine be changed in order to perform the boundary-maintenance function that is required to preserve constitutional values, including the principle of legislative supremacy?

The first and most fundamental change is to invert the baseline assumption that frames the inquiry. Under the *Chevron* doctrine, at least in its post-*Smiley* explication, agency authority to act as the primary interpreter is presumed whenever a statute is unclear or ambiguous—that is, whenever the statute requires interpretation.[41] The better baseline assumption is that questions of law must be resolved by courts, unless Congress has actually delegated authority to the agency to act as the primary interpreter with respect to the provision in question. Instead of deferring to the agency based on a *fictitious* delegation of authority of interpretive authority to agencies, grounded in ambiguity, courts should defer to agency interpretations when they conclude that Congress *actually intended* the agency is to act as the primary interpreter of the statute.[42]

There are a number of overlapping justifications for switching the default assumption to independent judicial judgment[43] and requiring evidence of an affirmative intent to delegate interpretive authority to an agency. One is that this is the traditional understanding, certainly before *Chevron* was decided, and, as we have seen in Chapter 3, it was also the understanding of Justice Stevens in writing the *Chevron* opinion itself. Another is that this is the starting point required by the APA, on any fair reading of Section 706, including the specific directive that courts are to hold unlawful and set aside agency action "in excess of statutory jurisdiction, authority, or limitations, or short of statutory right." A third is that this is more realistically what Congress desires, given that Congress undoubtedly perceives the independent judiciary as a more plausible faithful agent than executive branch agencies. Courts by tradition see their role as enforcing the instructions of the legislature. Agencies, which are subject to much greater control by the political appointees in the executive branch, are more likely to interpret statutes to further the transitory political objectives of the incumbent President. Finally, independent judicial judgment is the default most likely to preserve constitutional values, including but not limited to the principle of separation of powers and the postulate of legislative supremacy.

It must be stressed that independent judicial judgment is only a default assumption. It is quite common that Congress does in fact intend an agency to serve as the primary interpreter of a particular statutory provisions or terms. Thus, if Congress delegates authority to an agency to set "just and reasonable rates," this should be understood as delegating broad authority to the agency to determine what rate-making methodology to use in fixing rates.[44] Or if Congress delegates authority to an agency to establish air pollution standards "requisite to protect the public health," this should be understood as conferring broad authority to determine what concentrations of pollutants in the air should be regarded as safe.[45] When Congress adopts these kinds of broad delegations, the courts, in the exercise of independent judgment, should recognize that the agency has been given primary interpretational authority, and should accept the agency's interpretation (subject to the qualification about process, discussed in Chapter 12). The question, always, is whether Congress has deliberately left "space" in the statutory scheme to be filled by the agency in its discretion.

There is, unfortunately, no simple test for determining when an agency interpretation falls within the discretionary space delegated to it by Congress. Justice Scalia was right about one thing in his opinions in *Mississippi Power and Light* and *City of Arlington*: statutory provisions do not neatly sort themselves into two separate categories—"jurisdictional" and "nonjurisdictional." As was often the case, he overstated the indeterminacy of the distinction. But he was correct insofar as he was asserting that every limit imposed on agency authority by Congress is in some sense "jurisdictional." Every Justice writing in *City of Arlington* effectively acknowledged that Scalia was right about this. Where Scalia went wrong was in maintaining that if every limit is effectively jurisdictional, then the agency must be given *Chevron* deference as to all limits on the scope of its authority. The better conclusion is the opposite: If every limit is jurisdictional, every limit should be interpreted by courts as a matter of independent judgment. With the understanding, of course, that independent judgment may reveal that Congress intended to delegate interpretive authority to the agency.

There being no simple test for identifying the limits on the scope of agency authority, there is no escape from the conclusion that courts must identify those limits by considering all relevant aspects of the statutory language, structure, purpose, and the evolution of the understanding of the statute over time. To this extent, Justice Breyer has been correct in insisting that identifying an implicit congressional intent to delegate interpretational authority to an agency requires an "all-things-considered" type of inquiry. This does not mean, however, that the inquiry must proceed in a purely ad hoc or unguided fashion.

Six principles can be identified that courts should call upon in making the intent-to-delegate determination. Some of these are sufficiently fixed that they can be regarded as rule-like. Others are more in the nature of red flags, alerting the court to the need for a more searching analysis.

1. Express Delegations

One easy case for finding that Congress has delegated interpretive authority to an agency is when Congress expressly delegates authority to an agency to spell out the meaning of a particular statutory provision or term. We have seen examples of this, such as the delegation in *Batterton v. Francis*[46] to define the term "unemployment" or the delegation in *Nierotko*[47] to define the term "wages" (Chapter 2). Express preemption clauses can also include such delegations. For example, the preemption clause at issue in *Medtronic, Inc. v. Lohr*[48] expressly delegated authority to the FDA to identify certain state requirements that would be exempt from preemption.[49]

When Congress expressly delegates authority to an agency to interpret particular statutory provisions or terms, courts should accept the agency interpretation as long as it does not exceed the scope of its delegated authority. This principle is relatively rule-like.

2. Delegations to Other Institutions

Another principle that is relatively rule-like is implicated when an agency opines about the meaning of a statute over which it exercises no decisional authority. *Adams Fruit Co. v. Barrett*[50] was such a case, where the agency opined about the scope of a private right of action that could be brought in court. The Court correctly concluded that the delegation of authority to interpret went to the entity with decisional authority—in that case the court, not the agency. Cases involving the meaning of the Administrative Procedure

Act fall within this category, because the Act is designed to constrain the behavior of all agencies and is not administered by any agency.[51] Likewise, decisional authority under the criminal law is given to courts; prosecutors necessarily interpret those laws in deciding whether to bring charges, but the authority to enforce the laws and hence to interpret them is given to courts (Chapter 8).[52] The antitrust laws provide another example.[53] Perhaps the most significant instance of this principle is the understanding that courts have been given authority to make final determinations of the meaning of the Constitution. By convention, decisional authority in this context lies with the courts, and interpretational authority follows.

In *City of Arlington,* had the Court agreed to review the merits, it should have concluded that the agency acted outside the scope of its delegated authority based on this principle. The statute imposed a federal duty on local zoning authorities: They must decide applications to construct wireless transmission towers within a "reasonable period of time." But the authority to enforce this requirement was given to "courts of competent jurisdiction." This would ordinarily mean state courts, which review the decisions of local zoning boards, although it could conceivably mean a federal court acting under diversity jurisdiction or perhaps under federal question jurisdiction (the statute did not address the issue of federal court jurisdiction). Either way, the authority to enforce was given to *courts,* not to the FCC. The agency was given no authority to enforce the requirement—and therefore had not been delegated authority to interpret the provision.

3. Incontrovertible Statutory Provisions

The *Chevron* doctrine is right about one thing: Agencies have no delegated authority to interpret the statute in a way that violates its incontrovertible meaning. This constraint will rarely come into play, since agencies as well as courts can identify unambiguous limits in the statutes they administer. We nevertheless saw an example of this constraint in *Utility Air,* where the EPA sought to rewrite "250 tons" of air pollutant to mean "100,000 tons."[54] Other examples readily come to mind. In *Chevron,* the Court correctly concluded that Congress had no discernable intent as to whether "stationary source" should be defined to mean apparatus or plant. But if the agency had interpreted the term "modification" to mean any increase in pollution by more than 10%, this would incontrovertibly violate the statute, which defined modification to mean any change "which increases the amount of *any* air pollutant emitted by such source."[55] Similarly, if Congress requires that telephone companies be reimbursed for the "cost" of network elements that they must lease to competitors, the agency has discretion in determining how to measure "cost."[56] But an agency directive to lease network elements free of charge would incontrovertibly violate the directive to allow reimbursement for cost.

In describing the rule-like constraint here as an "incontrovertible" violation of the statute, the objective is to underscore that the court must perceive the conflict with a very high degree of certainty (see Chapter 5). This is necessary in order to preserve the agency's discretion to act as the primary interpreter when the alleged conflict is embedded in what is otherwise a delegation of space to the agency to establish policy (as in the examples). Given the principle of legislative supremacy, the agency cannot ignore constraints on its authority, even when it is otherwise apparent that the agency has been given significant discretion. The court must exercise independent judgment in determining whether the agency has been given space to interpret. But even within the delegated space, as determined, the court must continue to enforce incontrovertible limits on the agency's interpretation within that space.

There may be exceptions to the incontrovertible-meaning constraint, if persuasive evidence can be gathered that the statutory language was included by mistake or would result in an absurd outcome. *King v. Burwell*, considered in Chapter 10, where the Court upheld an agency interpretation that the statutory phrase "established by the state" meant "established by a state or the federal government,"[57] should probably be considered an example of a drafting error. By general consensus, however, any such exception must be narrow.[58] It too is relatively rule-like.

4. Interpretations That Violate Controlling Judicial Precedent

A fourth principle, which was discussed in Chapter 7, is that agencies should be regarded as having no delegated authority to interpret in ways that contradict controlling judicial precedent. This, of course, is contrary to the *Brand X* doctrine,[59] which holds that agencies can overturn judicial interpretations if they conclude, based on a retrospective analysis, that the agency would have been given authority to decide the matter under the *Chevron* doctrine, had that doctrine been applied. As discussed in Chapter 7, however, the prospect of re-litigating old precedents under a doctrine unknown (or not applied) when they were decided would be unworkable. It also has the potential to unravel settled expectations that have guided Congress, other courts, the agency, and private parties in orienting their behavior under the statute. If legal change is required, a better approach is to seek legislative revision of the statute, or if that is not possible, judicial modification or potentially overruling of the precedent. This principle should also be applied in a rule-like fashion.

5. Settled Expectations

Perhaps the most generally applicable principle is that agency interpretations that violate settled expectations about the scope of agency authority require closer scrutiny than do interpretations that conform to those expectations. There is little doubt that this is the primary basis on which agencies and courts have previously identified "jurisdictional" questions. A question is "jurisdictional" when the agency is proposing to deviate from the scope of its authority as previously established by convention or custom.

This principle is more in the nature of a red flag rather than a fixed rule. When agencies act in ways that are inconsistent with their prior understanding, this should alert courts to the possibility that they are exceeding the scope of their delegated authority to interpret. Closer scrutiny is required of the language, structure, purpose, and evolved understanding of the statute than would be the case if the agency interpretation falls comfortably within the scope of its prior exercises of interpretational authority. It may be that the court will ultimately conclude that the agency is properly exercising delegated interpretive authority. For example, the agency may have been under- or over-regulating in the past, once a more complete examination of its statutory authority is undertaken. Consequently, this principle merely directs the attention of the court to the need to engage in a more searching analysis of whether Congress intended to delegate interpretational authority to the agency with respect to the matter in question. It should not be regarded as a fixed rule or even a strong presumption against concluding that interpretive authority has been delegated.

6. Important Questions About the Scope of Agency Authority

A final principle, which is also in the nature of a red flag rather than a fixed rule, is that agency interpretations that have an important impact on the scope of the agency's authority should be closely scrutinized. Often this principle will overlap or be subsumed under the previous consideration of agency interpretations that conflict with settled expectations. But it is possible to imagine situations where there are no settled expectations about an issue one way or another, and an agency confronts an issue of first impression that nevertheless has major implications for the scope of its authority. An example might be the question that has arisen under virtually every one of the major civil rights statutes—namely, whether a finding of "discrimination" must rest on a finding of discriminatory intent or can also rest on a finding of discriminatory effect.[60] The agency that administers the statute may not have considered the issue on any sustained basis, or may have reached inconsistent conclusions about the matter. Thus, it may be difficult to say that there are any settled expectations about the answer, one way or another. Still, the answer will have a major effect on the scope of agency authority under the statute. The fact that the resolution of the question will have an important impact on the scope of agency authority warrants close judicial examination as to whether the agency is proposing to exceed the boundaries of its delegated authority.[61]

Illustrations

It may be helpful to consider some examples of decisions that, at least in the author's view, correctly concluded that authority to interpret had been delegated to an agency, as well as decisions that correctly concluded such authority had not been granted.

The principal example of a decision that correctly finds that authority to interpret has been delegated to the agency is, of course, *Chevron* itself. As discussed in Chapter 3, Justice Stevens engaged in a detailed examination of the Clean Air Act, establishing that Congress broadly delegated authority to the EPA to implement its provisions. He also showed that Congress had conflicting policy objectives in requiring controls on stationary sources in nonattainment areas. He further showed that Congress had failed to define "source," either in the nonattainment provisions or in related provisions, in such a way as to indicate whether either the apparatus or the plant definition had been intended. Finally, he reviewed the EPA's struggle to define the term flexibly, and the frustration of that objective by the aggressive review of the D.C. Circuit. He concluded that neither the general terms of the statute nor the legislative history revealed "an actual intent of Congress" about the correct interpretation of the term.[62] That being the case, it was appropriate to defer to the agency's interpretation, as falling within a space left by Congress for the agency to fill.

Another example of a case that correctly concludes the agency was delegated authority to interpret—or at least applied the correct approach in reaching that conclusion—is *Entergy Corp. v. Riverkeeper, Inc.*[63] At issue was whether the EPA can balance costs and benefits in promulgating regulations that govern cooling water intake structures at power plants. The environmental concern created by these structures (other than closed-cycle cooling structures) is that they can destroy large numbers of fish and other aquatic life. The relevant statutory language, which dates from the Clean Water Act of 1972, requires the EPA to set standards for the location, design, construction, and capacity of cooling water intake structures that "reflect the best technology available for minimizing adverse environmental impact."[64] The Second Circuit held that this language prohibited the EPA from using cost-benefit analysis in developing regulations setting the required standards.

Reversing in an opinion by Justice Scalia, the Court engaged in a painstaking analysis of different provisions of the Clean Water Act, both in 1972 and in subsequent amendments, that make some reference to benefits and costs. Some provisions clearly required cost-benefit analysis; others clearly precluded it; still others suggested that costs are relevant but should not be strictly balanced against benefits. Scalia concluded that the water intake provision used language ("best technology") different from than any of these other benchmarks. He also noted that the intake provision, in contrast to other benchmarks, did not list the factors the EPA should consider in setting the standards. The interpretive question boiled down to whether the statute's silence about the relationship between benefits and costs should be construed as an implied prohibition of the agency using such a tool, or left it up to the discretion of the agency whether to use such a tool. Scalia concluded that in the context of overall structure of the Act, silence conveyed "nothing more than a refusal to tie the agency's hands as to whether cost-benefit analysis should be used, and if so to what degree."[65] He also noted, as did Justice Breyer in his concurring opinion, that the agency had considered the relevance of both costs and benefits in individual permitting decisions for over thirty years.[66] The longstanding practice of the EPA should (and did) give the majority comfort in thinking that construing the discretionary space of the agency broadly was consistent with settled expectations.

The dissent, by Justice Stevens, would have triangulated more closely to other provisions in the statute that allowed costs to be considered only if disproportionate to benefits. His opinion reveals a legitimate disagreement over the size of the "space" that the statutory language left open to EPA discretion. But he, too, sought to discern the scope of the space by carefully calibrating the signals from other statutory provisions that spoke more clearly about the relationship between costs and benefits.

A third example is provided by *Verizon Communications, Inc. v. FCC.*[67] The Telecommunications Act of 1996 required incumbent local exchange carriers to lease elements of their systems to competitors, and provided that they were to be reimbursed for the "cost" of doing so. The FCC interpreted "cost" to mean "forward-looking" cost (essentially the replacement cost of these elements) rather than "historical" cost (what the local carrier had actually paid for the elements). This was challenged by the incumbents, who argued that cost, as a matter of plain meaning, had to mean actual—i.e., historical—cost.

The Court, in a lengthy opinion by Justice Souter, held that the FCC's interpretation of cost was within its discretionary authority. He noted that, historically, replacement cost had often been invoked as a permissible standard for fixing utility rates. Indeed, there were suggestions in older opinions that this measure of cost was constitutionally required. He also noted that the word "cost" appeared in connection with the statutory directive that cost was to be determined without reference to "rate-of-return or other rate-based proceeding"—terms that had been associated with the use of historical costs.[68] The conclusion was that the FCC's interpretation was "within the zone of reasonable interpretation subject to deference under *Chevron.*"[69]

We have also reviewed cases that correctly concluded that an agency interpretation would impermissibly expand or contract the scope of its delegated authority. *Dole v. Steelworkers* set aside an action by the OMB that exceeded the scope of its delegated authority under the Paperwork Reduction Act, as determined by considering all the provisions of the Act and Congress's legislated statements of purpose.[70] *FDA v. Brown & Williamson Tobacco Corp.* correctly concluded, based on an exhaustive analysis of agency disclaimers of authority and congressional responses to those disclaimers, that the FDA had not been given authority to regulate tobacco products.[71] Two decisions that invalidated agency attempts at self-deregulation also fit this description. *Maislin v. Primary Steel* overturned an attempt by the ICC to deregulate motor carrier rates, based on a conflict with prior judicial precedent.[72] *MCI v. AT&T* invalidated a similar effort by the FCC with respect to long-distance telephone service, based ultimately on the perception that the agency was moving to abandon the central regulatory mechanism of the Act.[73]

Gonzales v. Oregon[74] provides yet another illustration of a decision in which the Court engaged in a careful examination of the statute and its history and concluded that administrative authority to interpret had not been delegated. At issue was a regulation issued by the Attorney General interpreting the phrase "legitimate medical purpose" in the Controlled Substances Act. The Attorney General ruled that using controlled substances (as relevant, prescription drugs) for the purpose of physician-assisted suicide was not a legitimate medical purpose. This in turn made it a crime to use controlled substances for this purpose. The Court concluded that the Attorney General had exceeded the scope of his delegated authority. Among the factors the Court invoked in support of this conclusion were careful restrictions on the Attorney General's authority to deregister a substance,[75] the statute's more general delegation of authority to the Secretary of Health and Human Services over "scientific and medical matters,"[76] and Congress's enactment of subsequent legislation identifying HHS as the relevant agency to determine the consensus views of the medical community where that is relevant.[77] As Chief Justice Roberts later observed, the Court in *Gonzales* considered "the text, structure, and purpose of the Act" in concluding "on its own" that the Attorney General had exceeded the scope of his delegated authority.[78]

We should add that the Attorney General had never before suggested that his authority under the Controlled Substances Act included the power to regulate medical practice, so the interpretation arguably interfered with settled expectations. The regulation also expanded the scope of the Attorney General's authority in an important respect. Both features should (and presumably did) raise red flags with the Court that this assertion of interpretive authority required careful review. For good measure, the regulation also implicated federalism concerns, since the Court had previously determined that the states have discretion under the Constitution either to permit or to prohibit physician-assisted suicide.[79]

In Sum

Determining the boundaries of an agency's delegated authority is unquestionably the most difficult task assigned to courts in reviewing agency interpretations of law. Fortunately, that task is not imposed on courts as a routine matter. In most cases, it will be uncontested that the agency is operating with the sphere of its delegated authority. Cases that implicate individual constitutional rights or sharply delineated principles of federalism and separation of powers will advertise themselves as such. The primary issue in such cases is which issue to consider first: the statutory question or the constitutional question. Cases where an agency is accused of exceeding the scope of its statutorily delegated powers are more common, and more difficult, because on their face they present only a question of statutory interpretation. But such questions must be resolved as a matter of independent judgment by the courts, because the correct resolution of the statutory interpretation question implicates a constitutional principle—namely, the principle of legislative supremacy. Courts must determine, by their own lights, the best answer to the question, in order to preserve the constitutional authority of Congress.

Justice Scalia was right in *Mississippi Power & Light* and *City of Arlington* that statutory provisions that delineate and constrain agency power do not come with bright labels indicating that some are jurisdictional and others are not. But it does not follow that every ambiguous provision that arguably constrains the authority of an agency should be given over to the agency to resolve. Because every constraint is a constraint imposed by Congress, the court must interpret every constraint without deferring in a strong, *Chevron*-like fashion to the agency's interpretation of its own authority.

There is a suggestion in *City of Arlington* that deferring to agencies on all matters of ambiguity will impose much-needed discipline on Congress, forcing it to start writing clearer statutes.[80] Some lack of clarity in legislation is undoubtedly the product of careless drafting or inattention. But it is utterly unrealistic to expect Congress to anticipate every interpretational problem that will arise in the future, often in response to issues that emerge only in the future. Silences, gaps, and ambiguities are inevitable. The scope of an agency's authority, however, is at any moment in time largely fixed. It is fixed in part by statutory language, but also by practice and by convention. In order to ascertain Congress's intent with respect to the scope of an agency's authority, courts must engage in a sensitive exploration of multiple variables, taking into account not only the language and structure of the delegating statute, but also its purpose and settled expectations about the agency's authority as revealed over time. This is a delicate task, not dissimilar to the task of determining whether a federal law should be deemed to preempt state law (Chapter 9). It is a task that usually must be undertaken by higher-level appellate courts, out of respect for both the agency and the principle of legislative supremacy.

Fortunately, the task is it not left wholly to situation sense or the particularities of each case. A number of guideposts exist, many relatively rule-like: express delegations to interpret, the assignment of decisional authority, incontrovertible provisions, and issues governed by controlling precedent all establish relatively rule-like principles that can be used by reviewing courts in determining whether an agency is acting within the scope of its delegated authority. Settled expectations about agency authority and whether the issue has an important bearing on the scope of agency authority operate more in the nature of red flags that warrant further investigation. In the end, there will not always be simple answers. But that is one important reason why we have courts, and why they are given independent authority to make these critical decisions.

12

Improving the Quality
of Agency Interpretations

WHERE DO WE STAND once the various shortcomings of the *Chevron* doctrine are exposed—and hopefully corrected in whatever replaces it? We have seen that reviewing courts must continue to protect rule of law values. This means giving appropriate weight to the contemporary and longstanding interpretation canons, adhering to statutory interpretation precedent that is authoritative, and demanding a persuasive explanation from the agency if it acts in a way that deprives persons of fair notice of the requirements of the law (Chapter 7). Reviewing courts must also enforce the boundaries that define and limit the space in which the agency has discretion to interpret. This means upholding constitutional rights that are implicated by an agency interpretation (Chapter 8), resolving preemption questions independently after giving appropriate weight to agency views on issues where the agency has a comparative advantage (Chapter 9), and—most critically—determining independently that Congress has either expressly or *implicitly but actually* delegated authority to the agency to exercise discretion in interpreting the statute that establishes its authority (Chapters 10 and 11).

Notwithstanding all these qualifications and corrections, the central lesson of the *Chevron* decision—and of the entire era of jurisprudence that it eventually spawned—is that the agency, rather than the reviewing court, is the preferred institution for filling in the space that Congress has left for future interpretation in the statute under which the agency operates. This, as *Chevron* explained, is because the agency is more accountable to elected officials than the reviewing court, and the agency has more expertise in understanding the way the statute operates in its contemporary incarnation. The conclusion, which follows from the *Chevron* decision and the more than one hundred Supreme Court decisions that have applied the *Chevron* doctrine in the ensuing decades, is that once the various qualifications and corrections have been taken into account, the reviewing court should *accept* the agency interpretation. Full stop. There should be no equivocating about the possibility of the court substituting its judgment for that of the agency if the court deems the agency interpretation to be "unreasonable." This opens the door to allowing an unelected and less informed interpreter asserting its preferences in opposition to a more accountable and better informed interpreter.

An important question remains—namely, whether the mandate to accept agency interpretations that fall within the discretionary space left by Congress can be structured in such a way as to improve the quality of agency interpretations designed to fill this space. The *Chevron* doctrine arguably sought to create such an incentive by requiring at step 2 that the agency interpretation be "reasonable." But the Supreme Court has invalidated only three agency interpretations at step 2 since 1984 (Chapter 5), which provides scant guidance as to what it means for an interpretation to be unreasonable. There is a larger body of precedent in the courts of appeals, but these courts have advanced a variety of views about what unreasonable means in this context.[1] No understanding has emerged from this scattershot decisional law that is sufficiently consistent to create an incentive for improved agency interpretive practice.

In this chapter I argue that it is within the grasp of the Supreme Court to adopt a simple amendment to the doctrine of mandatory acceptance—*Chevron II* if you will—that would encourage better agency interpretations. This is to limit mandatory acceptance of agency interpretations to those adopted through notice-and-comment rulemaking or its functional equivalent.[2] Interpretations adopted through a notice-and-comment process create an opportunity for public participation and comment before the agency interpretation is adopted. As the requirements of notice-and-comment have come to be understood, such a process also requires the agency to provide an explanation for rejecting material comments made by members of the public. Notice-and-comment is not costless, and there may be reasons for an agency to forego this process in developing interpretations of the statute it administers. Courts have no authority to compel agencies to use a notice-and-comment process.[3] But they should condition their adoption of the strongest form of deference—acceptance of the agency interpretation—on the agency's use of notice-and-comment rulemaking or an equivalent procedure.

If the agency elects to use some other process such as adjudication to develop its interpretation, the court should give the agency interpretation respectful consideration and weight as appropriate (*Skidmore* deference, if you will), but not acceptance.

Conditioning acceptance on the agency's use of a notice-and-comment process has the virtue of being a simple rule, easily understood by agencies and lower courts, and thus preserves one of the advantages of the original *Chevron* doctrine. It is also the only rule that could plausibly create an incentive for agencies to make better statutory interpretations—and to do so without opening the door to allowing judges to substitute their judgment for that of the agency.

The Notice-and-Comment Process

As an initial matter, it is important to specify what exactly is entailed by a notice-and-comment process. The modern understanding of notice-and-comment grows out of the procedures for informal rulemaking set forth in Section 553 of the Administrative Procedure Act.[4] In order to adopt a substantive rule having legislative effect, the APA requires that the agency publish a notice in the Federal Register setting forth the "terms or substance of the proposed rule or a description of the subjects and issues involved"; the agency must then "give interested persons an opportunity to participate in the rule making through submission of written data, views, or arguments"; and after "consideration of the relevant matter presented" the agency must "incorporate in the rules adopted a concise general statement of their basis and purpose."[5] This bare-bones procedure is subject to a number of exceptions, including those for "interpretative rules" and "statements of policy."[6] The agency can also forego notice-and-comment when it finds "for good cause" that notice-and-comment would be "impracticable, unnecessary, or contrary to the public interest" and provides a brief statement of reasons supporting this finding.[7]

The rather minimal procedural requirements for notice-and-comment rulemaking have been significantly refined by hundreds of judicial decisions that have elaborated on the elements of APA's terse provisions. These refinements have largely been developed by the courts of appeals. "Notice" has been judicially expanded to include disclosure of studies and data relied upon by the agency in formulating a proposed rule.[8] The opportunity to comment has been expanded to require a re-opening of the comment period when the agency decides to modify the proposed rule in a way that is not the "logical outgrowth" of its initial proposal.[9] And the concise general statement of basis and purpose has been expanded to require the agency to respond to any non-repetitive, nonfrivolous comment submitted during the comment period.[10]

Attempts have been made to justify these emendations as an interpretation of language of the APA.[11] But more accurately considered, they would have to be described as a form of administrative common law.[12] A prominent justification for these judicially developed elaborations on the notice-and-comment process is that they are necessary if courts are to engage in meaningful review under the "arbitrary and capricious" standard of review of the APA. This catch-all standard has been held, by the Supreme Court, to require that the agency engage in "reasoned decision making" or provide a "reasoned explanation" for its action, including a justification for any departure from its prior policy.[13] How is the court going to determine if an agency has engaged in reasoned decision making in adopting a substantive rule using notice-and-comment procedures if the agency has not disclosed all material relevant to the rule, allowed interested parties an adequate opportunity to comment critically on the rule, and responded meaningfully to all material comments?

The Supreme Court has not explicitly endorsed the expanded understanding of notice-and-comment developed by the courts of appeals. But in a handful of significant cases it has largely accepted this understanding in bits and pieces.[14] Thus, the enhanced conception of notice-and-comment, a kind of common-law hybrid having its origins in the structure of Section 553 but significantly augmented by the perceived imperative of engaging in meaningful judicial review, appears to be securely established. Here is one recent description of the process in the context of rulemaking:

[A] central purpose of notice-and-comment rulemaking is to subject agency decisionmaking to public input and to obligate the agency to consider and respond to the material comments and concerns that are voiced. . . . "An agency's failure to respond to relevant and significant public comments generally 'demonstrates that the agency's decision was not based on a consideration of the relevant factors.'"[15]

The modern understanding of the notice-and-comment process, although rooted in the APA's procedures for substantive rulemaking, is conceptually distinct from the specific procedural requirement of the APA. This can be seen, in part, from the fact that the process as applied in substantive rulemaking is a product of judicial elaboration on what it means to provide adequate notice, a meaningful opportunity to comment, and a reasoned response to material comments that are submitted. The judicial gloss on notice-and-comment, justified largely by the enhanced conception of arbitrary-and-capricious review, goes well beyond the language of the APA. It can also be seen by the fact that agencies occasionally follow a notice-and-comment process when it is not required by the APA, and hence is not governed by the specific procedures for notice-and-comment in the APA. Agencies may do this when they issue nonbinding interpretive rules or statements of policy or when they engage in certain important adjudications that implicate the interests of more than the parties to a particular dispute. In this chapter I will speak of the notice-and-comment process or the notice-and-comment norm with the understanding that this is conceptually distinct from the specific procedures set forth in APA Section 553 for substantive rulemaking. To be sure, the most common way to comply with the notice-and-comment norm is to engage in substantive rulemaking under the APA. But it is possible to comply with the norm without issuing a substantive rule.

The evolved conception of the elements of the notice-and-comment process is relatively easy to state in the abstract. The norm requires that the agency: (a) publicly disclose its proposed rule and any data or studies that it relied upon in developing that rule; (b) allow any interested person to comment on the proposed rule, with or without presenting alternative data or studies; and (c) provide an explanation for either accepting or rejecting any material comment before it finalizes the rule.[16]

As applied to proposed statutory interpretations, the notice-and-comment norm would be modified only slightly. First, the agency should publicly disclose its proposed interpretation before it is adopted. The disclosure should explain why the agency believes the interpretation comports with the language of the statute and why the agency believes the interpretation falls within the scope of its delegated authority. It should also acknowledge whether the interpretation is either consistent with or represents a change in prior interpretations the agency has adopted, and if the agency is proposing a change, explain why the agency regards the change as justified, especially in light of any reliance interests that have been created by the previous interpretation. Second, the agency should allow interested members of the public to comment on the proposed interpretation, either supportively or critically. Finally, if and when the agency decides to adopt the interpretation as official agency policy, it should explain why it has either accepted or rejected comments that it deems material to its decision.

Conditioning acceptance of an agency interpretation on its compliance with such a notice-and-comment process would not be revolutionary. The Supreme Court has on occasion invoked similar tenets in considering agency interpretations of statutes.[17] And the previously mentioned empirical survey of courts of appeals approaches to step 2 of the *Chevron* doctrine reveals that this type of review is the most frequently given reason for rejecting an agency interpretation at step 2.[18] It is by no means the only approach—the courts of appeals cases present a variety of approaches. But review keyed to the process followed by the agency commands at least a plurality of support.

Notice-and-Comment Would Improve Agency Interpretations

As to why the notice-and-comment process would likely improve the quality of agency interpretations, the argument can be framed by considering various models of what it is that agencies seek to maximize in making their decisions.[19] The modern conception of the notice-and-comment process has been endorsed most explicitly by those who adopt a deliberative model of agency decision making. Mark Seidenfeld is the most prominent proponent of this view.[20] He envisions agencies as seeking to identify the best policy to serve the public interest by engaging in a process of deliberation that engages with all relevant stakeholders. In doing so, both the agency and the stakeholders should participate in the administrative process "with an open mind and be willing to change their policy preferences in response to discourse with diverse interests."[21]

Notice-and-comment, Seidenfeld argues, creates an incentive for agencies to conform to this deliberative model of agency behavior. The process helps ensure that the agency allows meaningful participation by the public in the process of formulating the proper interpretation of statutes. Advance disclosure, followed by public comment, followed by an agency response to material comments, establishes a dialogic process in which the agency and concerned citizens interact and share their divergent interests and perspectives. This back-and-forth process fosters better understanding and mutual respect and can lead to better interpretations, in the sense that they ultimately reflect a consensus view of the public interest.

Although Seidenfeld contrasts his deliberative model of agency government with what he calls the "pluralistic model," the pluralistic model also suggests that agencies will make better interpretations if required to comply with the notice-and-comment process. Under the pluralistic model, agencies, or at least their senior officials, make decisions in response to their perceptions of the political clout of different interest groups. The agency will worry about groups that have influence with the Congress, insofar as they may be able to trigger oversight hearings, or a movement to cut the agency's budget, or in extreme cases to curtail its authority. The agency will also worry about groups that have influence with the White House, which may impose unwelcome appointments on the agency, or recommend budget cuts, or delay its regulatory initiatives using OMB review. Even more cynically, senior officials may worry about groups that control access to revolving-door employment opportunities, such as lobbying firms, law firms, NGOs, or think tanks. The pluralistic model accepts this behavior as the logical outgrowth of the interest group model of government.[22] The goal of the agency is to forge a "deal" among competing interest groups that reflects the relative intensity and organizational capacity of the rival groups.

This is obviously a very non-idealistic view of agency behavior. But note that notice-and-comment will also help the agency make better interpretations, as defined by pluralistic assumptions. By observing which groups file comments on proposed interpretations, and with what degree of intensity, agency officials obtain information about how different interest groups line up with respect to the proposed interpretation. They can also gauge the likelihood that one or more disappointed groups will intercede with Congress or the White House if they do not get their way. In addition, the commenting process allows the agency to predict which if any groups will seek judicial review if their preferences are frustrated, and what arguments they will make. Judicial review is threatening to the agency because it creates a risk that the agency interpretation will be overturned, depriving the most powerful groups of their expected payoff. It also raises the visibility of the interpretation, which increases the risk of attracting congressional or White House attention. Thus, even under an unadulterated pluralistic view of agency behavior, notice-and-comment will improve agency interpretations, in the sense that it will lead to outcomes that strike a better balance between interest group preferences and minimize the risk that the deal struck by the agency will be upset by higher-level political intervention or judicial review.

Various other models of agency behavior can be advanced. At one time, agencies were thought to be hopelessly captured by the businesses they were charged with regulating.[23] Others have imagined that agencies are driven by a single-minded desire to maximize their budget.[24] Still others worry that agencies become over-committed to their mission, such as environmental protection for the EPA, workplace safety by OSHA, or public health for the FDA.[25] But even under these alternative theories of agency behavior, notice-and-comment can produce better interpretations, however defined, by providing the agency with better information about how to maximize whatever it is that they are imagined to want to maximize. The EPA, for example, if viewed as driven to promote environmental values, can learn what environmental groups want and can gauge the probability that the business community will seek to intercede with Congress, the White House, or the courts if the agency moves too far in the direction of what environmental groups want.

The reality is that agencies seek to advance a variety of objectives, with no agency conforming to a pure type. The basic point is that no matter how we conceptualize the preference function of agencies, they are likely to make better interpretations if they comply with the notice-and-comment process. That is because the process will generate important information through the commenting process.[26] And the process will require more deliberation among multiple offices within the agency, if only to decide how to respond to the comments.[27] If all this is true, then we can presume that notice-and-comment will improve the quality of agency interpretations, no matter how we imagine what it is that agencies are trying to accomplish.

Compliance with the notice-and-comment process will also plausibly enhance the legitimacy of agency interpretations. Notice-and-comment is understood to require advance notice of proposed interpretations and broad participation of interested members of the public through an opportunity to comment.[28] In this regard the process can be seen as a substitute for action by a representative legislature; indeed, it is in some respects arguably more truly representative than contemporary legislation.[29]

The best way to incentivize agencies to comply with the notice-and-comment process is to condition judicial acceptance of the agency's interpretation (assuming the interpretation falls within the agency's discretionary space to interpret as established by the court) on the agency's compliance with the notice-and-comment norm. In other words, courts should accept agency interpretations when the interpretation is adopted after the agency engages in a notice-and-comment process; if the agency has not done so, it would get only a lesser degree of deference such as respectful consideration. This could be done either as a matter of interpreting step 2 of the *Chevron* doctrine or under some new standard of review that replaces *Chevron*. Courts should not demand a specific procedure like rulemaking, nor should they nitpick the agency's disclosure, the length of the comment period, or the adequacy of its response to comments. The court's review should be leavened with common sense, taking account of the relative importance of the issue, the extent of reliance interests implicated by the interpretation, the possible need for expeditious action under conditions of emergency, and the APA's injunction to ignore harmless error.[30]

Counterarguments

There are two prominent counterarguments against the notice-and-comment process, both of which have been developed in the context of judicial review of agency policies adopted through substantive rulemaking.

First, the notice-and-comment process increases the costs of agency decision making. In the literature on rulemaking this is called the "ossification" problem.[31] It takes time and agency resources to spell out the arguments in support of proposed action, and to gather all the data and studies that have been relied upon in formulating the proposal. It takes more time and agency resources to wade through all the comments submitted by interested persons, which may number in the hundreds or even thousands. And it takes even more time and agency resources to develop an explanation for accepting or rejecting each material comment submitted. The more time and resources that must be devoted to any one instance of rulemaking, the less time and resources remain for other agency initiatives. Hence the charge that notice-and-comment, as interpreted in light of the reasoned decision-making norm, has resulted in an excessively encumbered or "ossified" rulemaking process.

The ossification objection is based on a straightforward argument about trade-offs. Even assuming that it improves the quality of agency decisions (however defined), notice-and-comment will reduce the number of decisions that can be made absent an expansion of agency resources. It is difficult to quantify the improvement in the quality of agency decisions, although various impressionistic accounts suggest the effect is real.[32] As to whether the number of decisions has declined, it seems plausible that the additional demand on agency time and resources would have this effect. Attempts to establish this empirically, however, have been inconclusive.[33]

Applying notice-and-comment in rendering agency statutory interpretations would arguably be less burdensome than it is in the context of adopting general agency policies through rulemaking. Generally speaking, empirical data or studies will not be relevant to the question of statutory interpretation, and comments and explanatory responses to comments will focus on legal issues rather than complex empirical claims and predictions. Also, to the extent that notice-and-comment is already required by the relevant statute for developing an agency initiative, extending it to a legal interpretation would add only marginally to the burden on the agency. Finally, if the agency is sufficiently confident in its interpretation, it can always forego the notice-and-comment process and take its chances with judicial review under the less deferential, respectful consideration standard. Failure to adhere to the notice-and-comment norm (at least in this context) should result, not in automatic invalidation of the agency interpretation, but only in a more searching form of judicial review.

The second counterargument against adopting the notice-and-comment condition is that it, like a generic requirement of "reasonableness," would create opportunities for reviewing courts to substitute their view for that of the agency on the merits. The notice-and-comment norm entails certain elements that require an exercise in judgment: Is the disclosure of the proposed interpretation adequate to provide meaningful notice to the public? When is a comment material? When has the agency given an adequate explanation for rejecting a comment? A reviewing court's answer to these questions will likely be affected by its view of the importance of the agency interpretation, and the strength of the objections to it. It is not a stretch to imagine that some courts will trim their views about whether the agency has complied with the norm in order to affirm a policy they like or vacate a policy they dislike.[34]

This concern about the potential for willful judicial behavior is present under virtually any conception of how judicial review should operate. The relevant question is whether adopting a notice-and-comment condition would increase incidence of willful behavior to an unacceptable degree relative to the benefits that might be obtained from better agency interpretations. The answer is obviously speculative. Realistically considered, the notice-and-comment requirement would open the door to some judicial meddling in what should be a domain of agency discretion. But note that the consequence of a judicial determination that the agency failed to comply with the notice-and-comment process would only change the standard of review—from acceptance to respectful consideration. This would lower the cost to the court of substituting its judgment for that of the agency, but would not make it costless. On balance it is plausible that requiring the agency to disclose its proposed interpretation, take comments on it, and give an explanation in response to comments, would result, over the large run of cases, in better agency interpretations.

The Prospectivity Bonus

An additional consideration provides further support for requiring agencies to conform to the notice-and-comment process before accepting their interpretations. This relates to the rule of law value that changes in the law should be prospective (Chapters 1 and 7). If agencies must comply with the requirements of notice-and-comment in order to gain judicial acceptance of their interpretations, the logical way to do this is to advance the interpretation in a proceeding that has prospective effect. This could, of course, include substantive rulemaking. But as previously noted, notice-and comment is conceptually distinct from substantive rulemaking. Notice-and-comment can also be used in adopting interpretive rules or policy statements, which are exempt from notice-and-comment requirements under the APA but are also rules and therefore apply only in the future.[35] Notice-and-comment can also be used when an agency enters a declaratory order, which again will operate prospectively.[36] Thus, courts can make clear that acceptance of discretionary agency interpretations is conditioned on compliance with the notice-and-comment norm, without requiring the agency to adopt any particular procedural format for implementing that norm. This will have the practical effect of incentivizing agencies to make their interpretations prospective, which from the perspective of rule of law values is independently desirable.[37]

The indirect effect of the notice-and-comment process in creating an incentive for agencies to make statutory interpretations prospective means it is unnecessary to create any per se rule against adopting the strongest form of deference (acceptance) when an agency interprets its statute in an adjudication. The Court extended the *Chevron* doctrine to agency adjudications in what can charitably be described as a fit of absentmindedness. It did it, then when an issue arose as to whether it was appropriate to do it, it answered in the affirmative, on the ground that it had done it before. Justice Souter's opinion in *Mead* effectively cemented the proposition that *Chevron* applies to interpretations rendered in an adjudication that has the force of law, again without any analysis of why this might be undesirable.[38] As we have seen, however, the notice-and-comment norm operates independently of the procedural format chosen by the agency to make its decision. Reviewing courts have no authority to order an agency to adopt a particular procedural format.[39] But the notice-and-comment process can be applied to orders that, in formal terms, are adjudications. The agency interpretation in *City of Arlington v. FCC,* for example, was issued as a declaratory order, which is a form of adjudication. The agency nevertheless solicited public comment on its proposed interpretation before it entered the order, thereby complying with the notice-and-comment norm.[40]

For the same reason, the proposed limitation on acceptance of agency interpretations would not conflict with what is known as the *Chenery* doctrine.[41] Named for a decision rendered shortly after the adoption of the APA, this says that an agency that has authority to make policy either by rulemaking or by adjudication has broad discretion to choose which mode of action in which to make policy. The doctrine has never been repudiated by the Court, although it was announced at a time when adjudication was the dominant mode of agency policymaking and the virtues of rulemaking had not yet become fully apparent. Although the proposal here would create an incentive for agencies to adopt legal interpretations in a prospective form, like rulemaking, it would not deprive agencies of the discretion to choose which format to employ in rendering an interpretation. Agencies could still announce an interpretation in an adjudication and apply it retroactively to the case in which the interpretation is announced. This would simply result in a less deferential standard of review of the interpretation by the courts.

If an agency adopts an interpretation without complying with the notice-and-comment norm, then the court should not adopt a standard of acceptance. But it should give respectful consideration to the agency interpretation, and should give it weight (or not) if it conforms to settled expectations. This, if one prefers, can be called the *Skidmore* review, which *Mead* made the general default standard to apply when the conditions for the *Chevron* doctrine are not met. It should play a similar role in whatever regime of review emerges in the future.

In Sum

Although the effort to improve agency interpretations is the last of the four values to be considered, it is by no means of least importance. Adrian Vermeule and the many academic supporters of the *Chevron* doctrine are surely correct that the locus of interpretation will inevitably shift over time to agency interpretation, given the burgeoning demands on government and the constrained capacity of Congress and the courts to keep up. So providing incentives for improved agency interpretations is of vital importance. The argument of this chapter is that the notice-and-comment process provides the best hope for improving agency interpretations. The elements of that process are simple: disclose the proposed interpretation, take comments about it from any interested party, and explain the final decision. This process can be harnessed to any type of procedural format, as long as advance notice of the proposed interpretation and an opportunity to comment are given before final adoption of the interpretation. In any event, the court cannot and should not *order* the agency to use notice-and-comment rulemaking. The proposed strategy uses the carrot rather than the stick: If the agency follows the required process, the court will accept its interpretation (provided in falls within the boundaries of agency authority as defined by constitutional values).

If the agency does not follow the notice-and-comment process, the court should give the agency respectful consideration and weight as appropriate.

The proposed condition on acceptance of the agency interpretation under the *Chevron* doctrine (or whatever succeeds it) is easily within reach of the Supreme Court. This is partly because the Court has never explained what it meant in *Chevron* by saying that an agency interpretation must be "reasonable." Partly it is because the Court has said on occasion that reasonable equates to the arbitrary-and-capricious standard of the APA, and that standard has been interpreted as incorporating a norm of reasoned decision making. Partly it is because the Court has itself invoked a failure to conform to the notice-and comment process in declining to apply the *Chevron* standard.[42] So it is well within the capacity of the deft opinion writers who populate the current Court to knit together these elements and condition acceptance of agency interpretations on compliance with the notice-and-comment norm.[43]

13

Reforming the *Chevron* Doctrine

The material canvassed in this book is designed in part to provide a basis for assessing the strengths and weaknesses of the *Chevron* doctrine, as revealed by its thirty-five-year reign as the principal legal doctrine for allocating authority between courts and administrative agencies in saying what the law is. That assessment, in turn, can provide the basis for outlining what a better doctrine might look like, whether it takes the form of a series of reforms of the *Chevron* doctrine or an entirely new start.

An Assessment of Method and Values

In assessing the *Chevron* doctrine, we can divide the discussion between the method prescribed by the doctrine for allocating interpretive authority between agencies and courts, and how well the doctrine conforms to the values we should want to see reflected in a regime of judicial review of agency interpretations of law (Chapter 1).

In terms of method, the great strength of the *Chevron* doctrine is unquestionably its adoption of a simple and readily comprehensible formula for determining, in any case, which institution is the preferred interpreter of a statute—the agency or the court. This is no small matter. The two-step doctrine is easy for judges and lawyers to grasp and provides a common vocabulary for addressing an important and recurring issue. Compared to the mix of factors invoked in the pre-*Chevron* era (Chapter 2), the two-step doctrine reduces the costs associated with resolving questions about whether deference is owed to agencies in matters of interpretation. The "attractive simplicity" of the *Chevron* doctrine is undoubtedly the primary reason for its popularity over the years with lower courts and administrative lawyers.[1] An important question going forward is whether some measure of this tractability can be retained in whatever emerges by way of replacement or modification of the *Chevron* doctrine.

The two-step approach also has the advantage of differentiating between the limits Congress has imposed on the agency and the space left by those limits for the agency to exercise discretionary authority. If the court discerns that the interpretive question has been answered by Congress, then under the principle of legislative supremacy both the court and the agency must abide by those limits. This may mean that the agency's interpretation is either forbidden or required; either way, the agency has no authority to rule otherwise. In contrast, if the court discerns that the issue falls within the space left by Congress for the agency to exercise discretion, then the agency should be allowed a significant measure of discretion in answering the question. This means, in turn, that the agency should be free to change its mind in the future, if it provides a cogent reason for modifying its interpretation. The distinction between boundaries and discretionary space is important, and also very much worth preserving.

The disadvantages of the method adopted by the *Chevron* doctrine relate to the indeterminate nature of the two standards the doctrine invokes for implementing its two steps—clarity and reasonableness. The operative standard at step 1 is clarity. As we have seen in Chapter 5, clarity refers to some degree of certainty beyond more-likely-than-not, but does not specify any particular degree of certainty. This gives judges considerable discretion in ruling at step 1, and that discretion, in turn, invites result-oriented judicial decisions. Some kind of expression of certainty is probably inevitable: judges must have a way of saying it is very certain that 250 tons does not mean 100,000 tons.[2] But having every question about the limits on agency authority reduced to a judgment about whether such limits are "clear" provides insufficient guidance to courts in determining whether the agency interpretation is permissible.

The operative standard at step 2 is reasonableness. This too is indeterminate because it is ambiguous. The vast majority of courts applying the *Chevron* doctrine have expended most of their effort at step 1, and if they conclude that the agency interpretation does not transgress the limits imposed by Congress, they have tended overwhelmingly to find the agency interpretation "reasonable" at step 2. The jurisprudence of the *Chevron* doctrine therefore provides little guidance as to what reasonable means in this context. As we have also seen in Chapter 5, reasonable could mean reasonable as a matter of the interpretive conventions developed by courts, reasonable as a matter of policy, or reasonable in terms of the process used by the agency in developing the interpretation. The failure to specify what reasonable means for purposes of step 2 has also invited result-oriented judicial decisions in the comparatively small number of cases that have declared agency interpretations unreasonable.

In short, the two-step method, as framed by the *Chevron* doctrine, wins points for its "attractive simplicity." But that simplicity was obtained by compounding two indeterminate standards. Together, the standards of step 1 and step 2 translate in practice into a very large measure of judicial discretion in accepting or rejecting agency interpretations. And they provide inadequate guidance to courts about the relevant values that are central to the process of judicial review of agency interpretations of law.

When we turn to considering how the *Chevron* doctrine stands up in terms of the values historically associated with judicial review of agency interpretations of law, summarized in Chapter 1, we again find that the *Chevron* doctrine warrants a mixed verdict, unfortunately mostly negative.

In one respect, the *Chevron* regime marks a major advance in terms of the values adumbrated in Chapter 1. Perhaps the signal achievement of Justice Stevens's opinion in *Chevron* was its recognition that if a dispute framed in terms of interpretation actually entails a discretionary policy choice, the agency is the preferred interpreter, not the court. Courts had long recognized that agency interpretations are entitled to special weight when the issue is one as to which the agency has significant experience or technical expertise. *Chevron* added that when the issue requires the reconciliation of conflicting policies, the agency is the preferred interpreter because it is more accountable to the President, who is elected by all the people.[3] The opinion should have added that agencies are also accountable to Congress. In any event, by adding political accountability to traditional concerns with expertise, the *Chevron* regime solidified the case for giving the interpretive lead to agencies on matters that involve policy choice.

In other respects, the *Chevron* doctrine has made it more difficult for courts to enforce the values historically associated with judicial review. As mentioned in Chapter 1 and considered at greater length in Chapter 7, rule of law values, understood to mean adhering to settled expectations about the law, have long been a central justification for judicial review of agency interpretations of statutes. The principal manifestation of this has been the contemporary and longstanding interpretation canons, which add or subtract weight to agency interpretations depending on whether they conform to settled expectations about the law. The twin canons have no obvious place under the two-step approach as formulated by the *Chevron* doctrine. Still, as we have seen in Chapter 7, rule of law values refuse to go away. Given the inhospitality of the *Chevron* doctrine to those values, courts have been forced to introduce them as ad hoc factors extraneous to the two-step formulation, or to develop additional qualifications of the *Chevron* doctrine, such as the understanding that Supreme Court precedents enter into and qualify the meaning of a statute or that *Chevron* deference is not warranted when an agency adopts an interpretation that deprives persons of "fair notice" of a legal change (Chapter 7).

The *Chevron* doctrine has also made it more difficult to enforce the boundaries that limit the scope of agency authority. As introduced in Chapter 1 and developed more fully in Chapters 8–11, these boundaries have a constitutional foundation, whether it be individual constitutional rights, federalism, or separations of powers. The weakness of the *Chevron* doctrine in this respect is the understanding that step 1 requires the reviewing court to identify "clear" (or "unambiguous") limits on the scope of agency authority, combined with the practice—greatly magnified by the movement promoting "textualist" interpretation—to seek clear limits in the words of the statutory provision under consideration. Boundaries do not always announce themselves clearly in the words of the relevant enactment. Sometimes, as in the *Brown & Williamson* tobacco case, they must be identified by considering a series of enactments over time.[4] Other times, as in *Dole v. Steelworkers,* the Paperwork Reduction Act case, they must be identified by considering other provisions of the statute, including relevant statements of purpose.[5] At still other times, as in *King v. Burwell,* they must be identified by considering the plan of the statute as a whole.[6] And perhaps most crucially, they must be considered in light of settled expectations, whether they be expectations about constitutional liberties, about traditional functions of state and local governments, or about trajectory of agency regulatory authority over time.

In terms of providing incentives for agencies to make better interpretations, the *Chevron* doctrine also comes up short. The key here is the indeterminacy about what it means for an agency interpretation to be reasonable. The Supreme Court could have interpreted this to mean reasonable as a matter of the decisional process followed by the agency, but it has not done so. In other contexts, the Court seems comfortable with the understanding that the Administrative Procedure Act requires reasoned decision making when an agency makes a pure policy decision, whether it be through rulemaking or adjudication. But it has failed to condition acceptance of agency interpretations of statutes by requiring agency compliance with notice-and-comment—the process most likely to result in better and more legitimate outcomes. In particular, the Court has applied the *Chevron* doctrine to interpretations announced in adjudications when there has been no advance notice or opportunity for affected persons to comment on the interpretation before it is rendered.

A Better Regime

More ambitiously, we can put the lessons learned in the *Chevron* era together to form a composite picture of what a better regime of judicial review of agency interpretations of statutes might look like. There are several justifications for outlining the elements of a better regime. First, although it is unlikely that the Supreme Court will simply overrule the *Chevron* doctrine and start afresh, it is not inconceivable. Perhaps the closest analogue would be the Court's decision in *Erie R. Co. v. Tompkins*,[7] which overruled a longstanding precedent about the allocation of authority between federal and state courts in determining the content of the common law. The Court cited new evidence about the meaning of a key statute and concerns about the constitutionality of the previous practice as grounds for a fundamental course correction.[8] Conceivably, this could serve as a model for overruling the *Chevron* doctrine. If that should happen, the Court would have to devise an alternative to put in its place. Hence the need for an outline of a better doctrine.

Second, even if the Court does not repudiate the *Chevron* doctrine, Congress could do so. Given that the *Chevron* doctrine rests on a "fiction" about congressional intent, an actual instruction by Congress about what standard should be used by courts in reviewing agency interpretations of law would seem to be entirely appropriate.[9] It is unlikely that Congress would attempt to spell out all the features of a deference doctrine. More probable is a statute requiring that courts exercise "independent judgment" on all questions of law. This might be enough to eliminate the fiction that Congress has delegated authority to an agency to interpret whenever a court finds an ambiguity in the agency's authorizing statute. Yet as discussed in Chapter 1, the phrase "independent judgment" is itself ambiguous. Such a congressional edict would not resolve whether independent judgment includes giving respectful consideration to agency interpretations or weight to agency interpretations that have elicited reliance, or whether courts can conclude that Congress has implicitly delegated interpretive authority to an agency. Again, the courts would have to resolve these ancillary questions, and having a sense of what a better deference doctrine would look like would be desirable in undertaking the task.

Third, even if, as is most likely, neither the Court nor Congress can muster the will to overturn the *Chevron* doctrine, it is useful to have a model of what a better regime might look like. This can serve as a benchmark for how the Court should go about modifying the *Chevron* doctrine, as it has in many ways in the past, and surely will continue to do so in some form in the future.

A New Three-Step Doctrine

We can describe in general terms what a better regime of judicial review might look like by expressing it in the form of a new three-step doctrine, borrowing at least the "steps" idea from the *Chevron* doctrine. To the objection that three steps is more complicated than two steps, the response might be that the *Chevron* doctrine has already mutated into three steps, with the addition of "step zero" under the *Mead* doctrine. So the reformulated three-step doctrine would be no more cumbersome than the evolved form of the *Chevron* doctrine, at least in terms of counting steps. The familiarity of the steps approach should promote acceptability of the revised approach and retain a significant measure of its simplicity and uniformity, which obviously contribute to its popularity with lower-court judges and agency lawyers. We begin with a brief description of the three steps, and then follow up with some further comments of justification and clarification.

Step One: Judicial Determination of the Boundaries of Agency Authority

The first step that the reviewing court should undertake is to determine whether the agency's interpretation falls within the boundaries of its delegated authority.[10] As we have seen, the boundaries that delineate the scope of an agency's authority to interpret are grounded in constitutional values—principles of individual rights, federalism, and separation of powers. Separation of powers principles are nearly always implicated, given the principle of legislative supremacy, which means that agencies have no authority to act unless and until they have been delegated power to do so by Congress. In order to protect the assignment of this constitutional prerogative to Congress, courts must determine whether the agency is acting within the scope of its delegated authority. Individual constitutional rights and federalism principles establish additional boundaries on agency authority. Courts should determine the boundaries of agency authority based on their best understanding about the sources of law that delineate these boundaries, without attributing any heightened degree of certainty to that judgment, such as that the boundaries are "clear" or "unambiguous." In enforcing the boundaries on agency authority, courts should give respectful consideration to the agency's view of the proper scope of its own authority. If the agency interpretation is consistent with past understandings of the scope of its authority, this should be given weight in making the judicial determination. If the interpretation represents a departure from previous understandings, the court should consider the matter more closely. Either way, the final judgment about the scope of agency authority should be the court's.

Step Two: Judicial Enforcement of Specific Statutory Requirements

If the reviewing court determines that the agency is acting within the scope of its delegated authority, the second step is to ask whether the agency interpretation violates any specific provision found in applicable legislation. Review for consistency with statutory directives again follows from the principle of legislative supremacy. Given that the agency is acting within the scope of its delegated authority, the court should set aside an agency interpretation for violation of a specific statutory directive only if it has a high degree of certainty that the agency interpretation conflicts with the statute. An appropriate articulation of the degree of certainty might be that the agency interpretation "incontrovertibly" violates the statute, although other formulations may also be acceptable. Some examples, mentioned in Chapter 11, include interpreting 250 tons to mean 100,000 tons or interpreting compensating for "cost" to mean providing no compensation.

Step Three: Judicial Review for Compliance with the Notice-and-Comment Process

If the reviewing court determines that the agency is acting within the scope of its delegated authority and that its interpretation does not violate any provision of applicable law to a high degree of certainty, the court should ask, as the third step, whether the agency interpretation is the product of a notice-and-comment process. This means the agency should have publicly announced its proposed interpretation and its rationale in advance, accepted comment from interested parties about the proposed interpretation, and given reasons for either accepting or rejecting material comments. If the agency has substantially complied with such a process, the reviewing court should accept its interpretation as a proper exercise of discretionary interpretive choice. The agency, for reasons of political accountability and expertise, is the preferred institution for resolving such issues. If an agency has failed to follow such a process, it should be entitled only to the court's respectful consideration of the agency's interpretation, and weight, depending on whether its interpretation comports with settled expectations created by past interpretations.

Some Clarifications and Justifications

Several clarifying comments about the foregoing structure are appropriate. Perhaps the first thing to note is that the structure more or less parallels the structure of the existing *Chevron* doctrine, but with modifications at each step. Step one is derivative of step zero, as developed in *United States v. Mead*

Corp. and succeeding cases (Chapter 6). Step two is similar to *Chevron*'s step 1, but with a more precise expression about the required degree of certainty. And step three adopts a version of *Chevron*'s step 2. The proposed three-step structure thus provides significant continuity with the immediate past. This is designed to promote acceptability and to capture some of the simplicity and universality associated with the existing *Chevron* doctrine, as modified by *Mead.*

That said, the proposed alternative eliminates or at least significantly reduces reliance on the two indeterminate standards—clarity and reason-ableness—employed by the *Chevron* doctrine. Clarity is eliminated at the first step, which requires instead that the court determine the best under-standing of the scope of the agency's authority. An enhanced degree of certainty returns under the second step, which requires a high degree of certainty on the part of the court before it determines that the agency's in-terpretation, advanced within its delegated space to interpret, conflicts with a particular provision of applicable statutory law. If the court applied a best understanding standard here, this might leave insufficient room for agency interpretation. The term "reasonable" has also been eliminated. The term has been interpreted by some lower courts to mean compliance with reasoned decision-making norms; here that meaning has been clarified to mean that the agency must have announced its interpretation following a notice-and-comment process that includes an explanation for why the matter falls within the agency's authority and why material comments were rejected.

The next thing to note is that there is no explicit distinction between dif-ferent tiers of deference, strong versus weak, as under current law with its sharp distinction between the *Chevron* doctrine and *Skidmore* review. Nev-ertheless, under the proposed structure, some agency interpretations must be *accepted* by the reviewing court, and others are entitled only to *respectful consideration.* This differential treatment corresponds, in a more precise for-mulation, to the *Chevron/Skidmore* dichotomy. The relevant standard of review emerges from sequentially following the three steps. An affirmative answer at each step requires the court to move on to the next step, and an affirmative answer at the last step requires the court to accept the agency in-terpretation. Conversely, a negative answer anywhere along the way requires the court to give only respectful consideration to the agency interpretation. Respectful consideration means the reviewing court must acknowledge the agency interpretation, and explain why it is rejected or accepted. If that is what *Skidmore* deference means, then the proposed structure makes *Skidmore* deference the baseline requirement applicable to all agency interpretations—and in that respect confirms the holding in *Mead*.

The reader will also note that there is nothing in the proposed structure that tracks the requirement adopted in *Mead* that *Chevron*-style deference (acceptance in the parlance used here) applies only to agency action that has "the force of law."[11] The *Mead* doctrine rests ambiguously on two distinct ideas, which the Court failed to distinguish in *Mead* or in follow-on decisions. One idea is that a delegation to the agency to act with the force of law is a signal of congressional intent to confer significant interpretational authority on the agency.[12] But authority to act with the force of law does not begin to exhaust the extent—or the limits—of an agency's delegated authority to interpret (Chapter 12). Moreover, given the Court's habit of construing any grant of rulemaking authority as conferring the power to issue rules having the force of law, this factor has been reduced to flabbiness as a guide to the scope of agency authority. The nub of the idea worth preserving is that if Congress grants relatively specific authority to the agency to act with the force of law with respect to the question presented, this is impressive evidence that the agency has been given authority to interpret within the sphere delineated by such a grant. But differentiating between agencies based on whether or not they have been given a general grant of rulemaking or adjudication authority fails as a general test for determining whether they are acting within the scope of their delegated authority.

The second idea associated with *Mead* is that agencies should get *Chevron*-style deference (acceptance) only when they advance their interpretations in a relatively formal procedural format—namely, notice-and-comment rulemaking or formal adjudication.[13] This aspect of *Mead* should be trimmed back by specifying that agency interpretations will be accepted by courts only if they are the product of a notice-and-comment process. Making acceptance of an agency interpretation conditional on compliance with the notice-and-comment norm should improve the quality and legitimacy of agency interpretations, without regard to the exact procedural format they elect to use (Chapter 12). Adopting the notice-and-comment norm will also push agencies to advance their interpretations in procedural formats that operate prospectively, because only prospective interpretations allow for public comment and a response to material comments before the interpretation is made final. But the requirements associated with notice-and-comment do not preclude issuing interpretations through interpretive rules, which are exempt from the technical requirements of notice-and-comment rulemaking, or in even in an adjudication—for example, by issuing a declaratory order.

This book has given considerable emphasis to rule of law values, under-stood to mean respecting settled expectations about the requirements of the law. In contrast to the traditional contemporary and longstanding canons, which addressed settled expectations as a freestanding element in deciding whether to accept an agency interpretation, and unlike the orthodox *Chevron* doctrine, which seems to eliminate the relevance of settled expectations, the proposed three-step structure would integrate this important value into each of the sequential inquiries.

Under the first step, which asks whether the agency is acting within the scope of its delegated authority, a departure from settled expectations should function as a red flag alerting the court to the need for a searching analysis of the issue. Conversely, if an agency can show that its action is consistent with settled expectations, this should be given weight in favor of finding that it has acted within the scope of its authority.

Under the second step, authoritative judicial precedents (other than ones that accept an agency interpretation as a matter of discretionary choice) should be regarded as having a status similar to incontrovertible statutory limitations. The primary rationale for this, again, is that such precedents will have shaped expectations about the meaning of the law, generating signifi-cant reliance interests. The *Brand X* doctrine should be limited to situations in which the prior judicial precedent was explicitly based on step 2 of the Chevron doctrine—in other words, where the court found that the statute delegated to the agency interpretational authority that the agency exercised in a permissible fashion. The Court has implicitly rejected the doctrine where the prior judicial precedent resolved an ambiguity in the statute; this rejec-tion should be made explicit (Chapter 7).

Under the third step, the court should accept the agency interpretation if it has complied with the notice-and-comment process as described in Chapter 12. One of the variables in determining whether the agency has com-plied with this norm is whether the agency has acknowledged any change relative to its past interpretations, and has explained why the change, if there is one, is justified in light of reliance interests that may have developed based on its prior interpretation. Also, in cases where the court determines that the agency has not followed the notice-and-comment norm in reaching its interpretation, the court should not accept the agency's interpretation, but should give it added weight if the interpretation is consistent with settled expectations, and reduced weight if it is not consistent settled expectations.

How the Court Should Reform the *Chevron* Doctrine

If we assume that Congress is not going to override the *Chevron* doctrine, and the Court is not going to overrule it, how then should the Court proceed in modifying or clarifying the *Chevron* doctrine to make it conform more closely to what a better regime of judicial review would look like? There are a number of pathways the Court might follow, some incremental, others more dramatic. Rather than presume to outline what an opinion or series of opinions might look like, I offer three key ideas that can be used by the Court, either singularly or in combination, to move the law of judicial review in a better direction.

1. Reaffirm the *Chevron* Decision

There is no need to overrule the *Chevron* decision. Indeed, it would be highly inappropriate to do so because there is nothing objectionable in the body of Justice Stevens's unanimous decision for the Court upholding the EPA's interpretation of "stationary source." This should be a key element of any judicial strategy for reforming the *Chevron* doctrine.[14] Continuity with the past can be preserved by reaffirming the *Chevron* decision, and providing a more qualified exposition of the two paragraphs in Part II of the opinion. These paragraphs were dicta, because they were not reflected in the body of the opinion that followed. As dicta, they should be read in context of the opinion as a whole.

The body of the opinion, as we have seen in Chapter 3, is not inconsistent with the four principal values we should want a regime of judicial review to reflect. The opinion reflects a careful exercise in de novo review of the relevant provisions of the Clean Air Act, in an effort to determine whether Congress had established any clear boundaries about the meaning of the term "stationary source" under the nonattainment program. Most notably, the Court sought to determine whether Congress had prohibited the EPA from interpreting that term to mean an entire plant as opposed to each apparatus within a plant that emits regulated pollutants. The Court accepted the EPA's interpretation only after determining that the statutory materials contained no discernable limiting principle. Thus, the *Chevron* opinion is fully consistent with—indeed, can be seen as a paradigmatic example of—the proposition that courts must decide de novo whether the agency interpretation falls within a space that Congress has left for the agency to fill in.

Here is one possible outline of how the Court might begin the process of moving toward a more satisfactory doctrine of judicial review by re-reading *Chevron,* and in so doing rewriting the *Chevron* doctrine.

As spelled out more fully in Chapter 3, most of the *Chevron* decision (Parts III–VII) can be used to support or reinforce principles about the appropriate role of judicial review of agency interpretations of its statutory authority. These elements of the decision should be reaffirmed.

First, the *Chevron* decision did not hold that settled expectations created by prior agency action are irrelevant in reviewing an agency's exercise of interpretative authority. The Court found that prior legislative and administrative action *had not created* any settled expectations. Many decisions before and after *Chevron* reaffirm that settled expectations created by contemporary or longstanding agency understanding of its statutory mandate are relevant in reviewing agency interpretations of law. Giving weight to such expectations is required by rule of law values.

Second, in speaking of implicit delegations of interpretative authority, the Court did not suggest that any silence, gap, or ambiguity in a statute automatically constitutes a delegation of interpretive authority to the agency.[15] The reviewing court must determine, using the traditional tools of statutory interpretation, whether Congress has left space for the agency to fill in the exercise of delegated authority. Only after determining that the best reading of statute is that Congress actually intended that the agency exercise discretionary interpretive authority, should the reviewing court accept the agency's interpretation. This is required by constitutional values, most prominently the anti-inherency understanding of the principle of legislative supremacy.

Third, when a reviewing court concludes that the agency interpretation is consistent with settled expectations and falls within the delegated space created by Congress, the agency interpretation should be reviewed like other exercises of delegated policymaking authority. This is required by considerations of comparative institutional analysis—namely, that the agency is a superior institution for establishing policy on grounds of political accountability and expertise.

Fourth, a critical element in reviewing such discretionary agency interpretations, as is required of any exercise if discretionary policymaking authority by an agency, is whether the agency developed its position through a process of reasoned decision making. This should be spelled out to mean that the agency should have provided notice of a proposed interpretation, an opportunity to comment, and an explanation by the agency for rejecting any comments deemed material.

The paragraphs of Part II of the *Chevron* decision are the source of the *Chevron* doctrine (Chapter 4). But like any other expression in a judicial decision, they should be read in the context of the balance of the opinion as a whole. When so read, Part II of *Chevron* can be clarified as having established two critical propositions, which are sound and should be reaffirmed.

The first proposition is that if a reviewing court determines, using the traditional tools of statutory interpretation, that a statute has highly certain meaning, that meaning must be enforced, notwithstanding any agency interpretation to the contrary. This understanding is required by rule of law values and by the separation of powers principle of legislative supremacy.

The second is that if a reviewing court determines, using the traditional tools of statutory interpretation, that Congress has expressly or implicitly delegated authority to the agency to fill a gap or space in the statute, the agency interpretation should be reviewed in a manner similar to the way courts review agency policy determinations more generally under the arbitrary-and-capricious standard of the APA. This is required by understanding that the agency, because of its political accountability and expertise, is the preferred institution for resolving questions of discretionary policy.

2. Rediscover the Administrative Procedure Act

The Administrative Procedure Act, which was ignored in *Chevron* and in most of the later cases invoking the *Chevron* doctrine, provides important support for modifying the *Chevron* doctrine. Deferring to agency interpretations of law when Congress actually intends that the agency should serve as the primary interpreter, is fully consistent with the APA's general instruction to courts to "decide all relevant questions of law."[16] As Henry Monaghan explained years ago, by deferring to the agency interpretation in such circumstances the court is following the law.[17] What is not consistent with the APA is deferring to the agency about the scope of its own authority. The APA instructs courts to "hold unlawful and set aside agency action" that is "in excess of statutory jurisdiction, authority, or limitations, or short of statutory right."[18] As Chief Justice Roberts wrote in *City of Arlington v. FCC*, "An agency cannot exercise interpretive authority until it has it; the question whether an agency enjoys that authority must be decided by a court, without deference to the agency."[19] This much is required by the APA. The discovery, if belated, of a conflict between a judge-made doctrine and a controlling statute like the APA fully justifies making appropriate qualifications to the doctrine.

3. Draw on the *Kisor v. Wilkie* Model

This does not exhaust the elements the Court should draw upon in rewriting the *Chevron* doctrine. The Court has the advantage here that *Chevron* is just one decision, and there are dozens of other Supreme Court decisions, all of equal status in formal terms, that can be called upon to qualify the unadorned propositions found in Part II of the *Chevron* opinion. A useful model here is *Kisor v. Wilkie*.[20] Prior decisions of the Court, most prominently *Auer v. Robbins*,[21] had said that courts should give "controlling weight" to an agency interpretation of their own regulations unless it is "plainly erroneous or inconsistent with the regulation." Justice Kagan's opinion for the Court in *Kisor* declined to overrule *Auer*, but recognized six qualifications to its standard of review, most drawn from prior precedent.[22] A similar strategy should be available in reaffirming the *Chevron* decision, while reforming the *Chevron* doctrine to make it better.

Some illustrations:

- The Court can draw on aspects of its pre-*Chevron* jurisprudence, most prominently the decisions that emphasize the importance of long-standing and consistent agency interpretations, to make the point that settled expectations play an important role in determining whether

Congress actually intends to delegate interpretive authority to the agency. The point can be strengthened by showing that these interpretive canons have lived on in the post-*Chevron* era, demonstrating their enduring validity.[23]

- The Court can also draw upon its decision in *Mead,* and some of its post-*Mead* decisions, for the proposition that courts must engage in an independent analysis of the statute to determine that Congress actually intended to delegate interpretive authority to the agency. The reference to implicit delegations in *Chevron* and in later decisions should be understood in light of that qualification. A delegation may be implicit—but in determining whether such a delegation was actually intended, the court must engage in a more searching analysis than assuming (fictitiously) that every ambiguity is an implied delegation.[24]

- Finally, the Court can draw upon decisions that decline to apply the *Chevron* doctrine where the agency has failed to follow a reasoned decision-making process.[25] These can be grafted onto *Chevron*'s statement that the agency interpretation must not be "arbitrary and capricious," which has been explicated in terms of compliance with the reasoned decision-making norm.

In Sum

In making a final assessment of the *Chevron* doctrine it is important not to overstate its weaknesses. Any doctrine that came out of nowhere, gained such rapid ascendency, endured for thirty-five years, and was applied by the Court in more than one hundred cases, must have something going for it. At the same time, uneasiness about the doctrine, expressed over the years by a variety of legal commentators and Justices, strongly suggests that it is possible to do better.[26] The perspective adopted here is that the *Chevron* doctrine's greatest strength is its simplicity, and its recognition that, with respect to many, if not most, legal questions resolved by agencies and reviewed by courts, the agency is the preferred interpreter. Its greatest weakness is that it oversimplifies, and thereby ignores variables as to which we would prefer to have courts serve as the principal interpreter—namely, in protecting rule of law values and determining the limits on agency authority established by the Constitution, including the principle of legislative supremacy.

When the *Chevron* doctrine is seen in this more balanced perspective, it should be clear that it can be reformed in ways that preserve what is valuable, while making room for adjustments to correct its shortcomings. This chapter has offered one view of what a better deference doctrine might look like, and has offered some suggestions about how the Court might modify the *Chevron* doctrine to bring the law of judicial review more closely in line with what a better doctrine would look like. Other pathways are also surely possible. Change has been constant throughout the history of the *Chevron* doctrine, and will surely persist in the future.

Concluding Thoughts

As this is written, the fate of the *Chevron* doctrine is unknown. The Court may continue to ignore it until some kind of consensus emerges about what to do next. When and if that happens, the Court may overrule it, or may reaffirm it. Most likely the Court will modify it in some fashion, either piecemeal or in one grand revision. Chapter 13 offered some specific suggestions regarding how the *Chevron* doctrine should be modified.

A larger reason for writing this book has been to highlight a set of issues that will always and inevitably arise in calibrating the proper allocation of authority between agencies and courts to say what the law is. From this perspective, the saga of the *Chevron* doctrine can be viewed as an extended case study revealing the issues that are likely to come to the fore in managing any division of authority between courts and agencies in interpreting the law.

The overriding issue is one of comparative advantage: On what sorts of issues do courts have a comparative advantage, and on what sorts of issues are agencies likely to do better? This book has argued that courts hold the advantage in protecting rule of law values, enforcing the boundaries of agency authority, and creating incentives for agencies to make better interpretations. Agencies have the advantage in resolving questions of law that Congress has expressly or implicitly but actually left for the agency to resolve in light of conflicting policies. The *Chevron* doctrine broke new ground in terms of understanding why agencies should take the lead in resolving questions that entail conflicting policies. But its appealing simplicity made it more difficult for courts to perform the functions where courts have a comparative advantage. A challenge for any judicial review doctrine is to direct the attention of courts to the types of considerations where they have the advantage, while preserving for agencies the space in which they should be allowed to exercise discretion.

Even if the Court overrules the *Chevron* doctrine or Congress overturns it, the underlying problem of defining the appropriate sphere of authority of agencies and courts will endure, and will almost certainly grow in importance. This is because the administrative state will continue to expand, given the complexity of modern society and the need for coordination of its many interacting parts. And given the limited capacity of Congress and the federal courts to resolve the multitude of issues that will arise, the legal system will inevitably be forced to draw upon legal interpretations advanced by administrative agencies in bringing some order to the administrative state.

Whatever its fate, it is worth considering in broad terms what effect the *Chevron* doctrine has had on our legal system, given its thirty-five-year reign. Perhaps the safest conclusion is that the *Chevron* doctrine has contributed to power seeping away from Congress, the "keystone" of the constitutional order as originally designed and for most of our history.[1] In matters that do not excite judicial attention, the *Chevron* doctrine has facilitated the transfer of power from Congress to the administrative state. When cases present technical questions under complicated statutory regimes, busy lower-court judges can invoke the *Chevron* doctrine and simply ratify whatever the agency proposes to do. In matters that judges find more compelling, it has facilitated the transfer of power to the courts by manipulating the nebulous standards of clarity and reasonableness. There are, of course, other reasons for the decline of Congress and the concomitant increase in executive and judicial assertiveness to fill the vacuum.[2] But the transfer of power that has taken place has been facilitated by the *Chevron* doctrine, and especially by the ambiguities of step 1 and step 2.

The story of the *Chevron* doctrine also provides material for more general reflections about the nature of lawmaking by the Supreme Court. The Court is not solely responsible for the *Chevron* doctrine. As we have seen in Chapter 4, the *Chevron* decision was initially regarded by the Justices as just another case. It was the D.C. Circuit that seized on two paragraphs in the opinion to declare a new standard of review for agency legal interpretations. Still, if the Court had not acquiesced in this reading, thereby validating it, the *Chevron* doctrine would not have spread to other courts of appeals, and would not have become entrenched. Eventually the Court took full owner-ship of the doctrine and began offering qualifications, as in the *Mead* deci-sion. By and large, therefore, the *Chevron* story is about the Supreme Court and how it acknowledged, applied, and revised a new legal doctrine in a case-by-case fashion. The *Chevron* doctrine is quintessential common law, meaning a form of law created by courts by reasoning from one judicial pre-cedent to another. The ups and downs of the *Chevron* doctrine tell us much about the promise and the perils of making law by the Supreme Court in this case-by-case fashion.

The promise of lawmaking by courts in the common-law mode is that it allows for experimentation and trial and error as the law is refined over time. Consider in this regard the question whether agency interpretations that qualify for *Chevron* deference should effectively override previous judicial in-terpretations of the same question (Chapter 7). The Court's initial instinct was to reject the idea that agencies could overrule judicial interpretations. Then an aggressive opinion by Justice Thomas reached the opposite conclu-sion with respect to interpretations by the courts of appeals.[3] On further reflection, the Court reverted to its initial response to the question.[4] This back-and-forth is perhaps not very edifying in the abstract. But it can be viewed as an example of the Court mulling over a novel and potentially diffi-cult question, until it finally comes to rest about the correct answer. Other examples of the virtues of incremental decision making might be the Court's cautious approach in deciding whether the *Chevron* doctrine should replace other standards of review like the *Skidmore* doctrine, and its gradual adop-tion of limiting principles, such as the understanding that *Chevron* applies only to agencies that exercise decisional authority and its rejection of ex post rationalizations of counsel as a basis for *Chevron* deference (Chapter 6).

A great peril of the common-law approach is its path dependency. In de-veloping a judge-made rule over time, the courts often come to a fork in the road, and when they decide to go either to the west or the east, it may not be possible to go back. This is because of the strong presumption against over-ruling precedents once they have been decided. The biggest path dependency considered in this book is the *Chevron* doctrine itself. It became clear over time that the doctrine failed to account for settled expectations created by agency interpretations, and failed to acknowledge the importance of a con-textual examination of the scope of the agency's delegated authority. Yet the

Court plunged ahead, periodically seeking to vindicate these values either as extraneous add-ons or by describing step 1 or step 2 in an expansive fashion allowing for their consideration. As the precedents applying the two-step approach piled up, it became increasingly difficult to contemplate a different approach. Similarly, when the Court first confronted the question whether the *Chevron* doctrine had displaced the *Skidmore* standard, the answer was that *Skidmore* continues to apply if an agency lacks the authority to interpret in a manner that has the "force of law."[5] This notion was reaffirmed in *Christensen* and then in *Mead* (Chapter 6), by which time it was too late to go back and consider whether acting with the force of law is an adequate basis for delineating the sphere of an agency's delegated authority to interpret.

With respect to both its strengths and its weaknesses, it is instructive to compare the common-law *Chevron* doctrine to legislation. Legislative action typically lacks the capacity for trial and error and adaptive change that we associate with common-law decision making. At least at the federal level, Congress can be induced to intervene—and to surmount the hurdles of the bicameral approval and overcoming a Presidential veto—only rarely. Certainly this is true with respect to standards of review of agency questions of law. Section 706 of the Administrative Procedure Act, which addresses this question explicitly, has not been amended since 1946. At the same time, legislation holds at least the potential for escaping from the clutches of path dependency. If and when Congress can be convinced to intervene, legislation holds the promise of making major course corrections, in a way that is much more difficult to achieve under the common-law method. And precisely because legislation is difficult to achieve, a statute, once enacted, has much more stability than administrative policy or administrative common law like the *Chevron* doctrine.

Other features of common-law decision making have also contributed to the less-than-satisfactory performance of the Supreme Court in formulating and refining the *Chevron* doctrine. There is an inherent tension when any high-level appeals court engages in lawmaking in the common-law fashion. On the one hand, the high-level court is aware that the legal doctrine it is formulating will be applied by lower-level courts in a large number of cases, many of them quite routine. This awareness inclines the high-level court toward formulating rules of decision that are clear and easy to follow. On the other hand, the high-level court will also want to reach results that it regards as correct or just in the cases that come before it. This impulse may require it to bend or stretch the rules it has previously articulated in order to get the right outcome. But in doing so, of course, the clarity and binding nature of the rules of decision become murkier. This "crystals and mud" phenomenon has been documented in other areas of the law,[6] and it helps explain some of the dynamics we have seen in the history of the *Chevron* doctrine.

Another part of the problem is that the *Chevron* doctrine concerns a question of *legal method*—a doctrine that courts use in resolving disputes as opposed to primary rules of decision that govern the behavior of parties outside the court. Courts, at least in the United States, tend to regard precedents that speak to legal method as relatively weak, or in some contexts as having no binding force at all.[7] For example, the controversy over the use of legislative history in interpreting statutes, spawned by Justice Scalia and the textualist movement, did not generate a norm binding on other judges. The use of legislative history as a tool of interpretation varies from one judge to another; although it has diminished overall, it has not disappeared. The many canons of interpretation have a somewhat similar status. They are regarded as legitimate tools of interpretation, but judges are not obligated to use them in any particular case. The *Chevron* doctrine involves a method for courts to use in reviewing agency interpretations of law, and thus unsurprisingly has a somewhat weaker status as a precedent, at least at the level of the Supreme Court. This helps explain why the *Chevron* doctrine, at least as reflected in the behavior of the Supreme Court, has oscillated between being considered as something like an interpretive canon and something like a rule of law, and why it has generated multiple course corrections.

The relatively weak status of the *Chevron* doctrine as a matter of precedent also accounts for the persistent disagreement among the Justices about its proper scope and application. Justice Stevens—the author of *Chevron*—was never comfortable with the *Chevron* doctrine, and frequently dissented from decisions in which it was applied. Yet he was sufficiently proud of his progeny that he could not bring himself to condemn the doctrine outright. Justice Scalia, the most consistent proselytizer for the *Chevron* doctrine, conceived of it as having a very broad application, operating to the exclusion of any other deference doctrine. But he could never convince his fellow Justices to embrace this view. Justice Breyer thought that the *Chevron* doctrine oversimplifies the variables relevant in deciding whether to accept an agency interpretation.

Although he wrote majority opinions that reflected this view, it is not clear that this perspective was fully supported by a majority his colleagues either. Justice Thomas started out as an enthusiastic exponent of a pure version of the doctrine, but has now apparently decided that it is unconstitutional. Justice Gorsuch may share this view, or some version of it. These divergent perspectives inevitably find their way into majority opinions written by different Justices, with the result that the doctrine has taken on different hues on different occasions. This is undoubtedly a characteristic of common-law decision making more generally (including most of constitutional law). But the authorial effect seems particularly pronounced in the cases invoking the *Chevron* doctrine.

The weak status of precedents about legal interpretation, and the ambivalence of many of the Justices about the *Chevron* doctrine, may also account for one of the odder aspects of the *Chevron* story. We have seen that on several occasions, a sharp disagreement emerged about the *Chevron* doctrine, only to be left to fester unresolved for a significant period of time. When Justices Stevens and Scalia clashed over whether the *Chevron* doctrine should apply to pure questions of law (Chapter 4), the Court never offered a definitive answer. When Justices Brennan and Scalia clashed over whether the *Chevron* doctrine should apply to questions about the scope of agency authority, twenty-five years elapsed until Justice Scalia finally prevailed on this critical point in *City of Arlington* (Chapter 11). And when Justices Thomas and Breyer clashed in *Christensen* over the conditions for identifying an agency action eligible for review under the *Chevron* doctrine (Chapter 6), Justice Souter sought to paper over the disagreement in *Mead*, but Breyer continued to advance his individual view in subsequent opinions for the Court. This unwillingness to confront and resolve internal conflicts—or to abide by a collective resolution when one is seemingly reached—unquestionably sows uncertainty in lower courts and agency lawyers and undermines the stability of the conventions governing the division of authority between agencies and courts.

Without regard to how we measure the costs and benefits of the *Chevron* doctrine, Justice Stevens's decision must be regarded as a landmark, if only because it gave us the doctrine. Most landmark decisions—such as *Brown v. Board of Education* or *Roe v. Wade*—are recognized as being landmarks the moment they are decided. Perhaps the strangest thing about the *Chevron* decision is that it was not recognized as being a landmark decision when it was decided, and became one only sometime later. This happened due to the cumulative effect of a series of fortuitous events, among them Justice Stevens's creative restatement of certain principles of judicial review in Part II of his opinion, Judge Patricia Wald's quick embrace of the two-step formula in the D.C. Circuit, Justice Scalia's elevation to the Supreme Court from the D.C. Circuit and his decision to aggressively defend the D.C. Circuit's *Chevron* doctrine, the rapid growth in the appeal of the two-step approach among lower-court judges as a more streamlined way to process challenges to agency interpretations of law, and the Justice Department's campaign to make the *Chevron* doctrine the universal standard for judicial review of agency interpretations of law. Individually, each of these events is readily explicable; cumulatively, they would have to be described as a legal accident.

The wonder of it all is that the Court that rendered this decision had utterly no intention of producing the *Chevron* doctrine. Indeed, the Court did not even realize it had produced such a doctrine until other key actors in the legal system determined to make selected passages in the opinion into a landmark doctrine. *Chevron* became a powerful precedent because the paragraphs that became "the *Chevron* doctrine" embody a principle that resonates strongly with lawyers and especially judges—namely, that judges enforce the law but do not meddle with policy. The simplicity of the two-step doctrine, relative to the jumble that preceded it, appealed to lower-court judges, and its rule-like structure meant that it gained a powerful advocate on the Supreme Court in the form of Justice Antonin Scalia. Once it became entrenched, the *Chevron* doctrine took on a life of its own. The Court came to regard it as a rule of law, and other judges took note and followed suit.

Perhaps equally remarkable is the sudden collapse of support for the doctrine. As the doctrine became encrusted with exceptions, most notably with the *Mead* decision and its step zero, it lost much of its appealing simplicity. When it was applied with ruthless logic, as in *Brand X* and *City of Arlington*, it came to be seen as a form of overreach, threatening other important jurisprudential commitments. With the passing of Justice Scalia, its great champion, a new school of thought, committed to the idea that courts have an unflagging duty in every case to "say what the law is," surged to the fore, and identified the *Chevron* doctrine as the enemy. The new appointments to the Supreme Court during the Trump presidency, and the new commitments they bring to that role, mean that the *Chevron* doctrine, as it existed at the peak of its power in *Brand X* and *City of Arlington,* will almost certainly be replaced by something different, even if it is still called "*Chevron.*" The exact form the new doctrine will take is unknown, as is the future more generally. The hope of this book is that whatever emerges will be informed by the lessons of the past, of which the strange saga of the *Chevron* doctrine offers many.

Notes

Introduction

1. James O. Freedman, Crisis and Legitimacy: The Administrative Process and American Government 8, 35 (1978).

2. It is not entirely clear why the Obama Administration's aggressive interpretations of existing regulatory authority triggered a round of hand-wringing about the legitimacy of the administrative state, whereas the Bush II Administration's War on Terror and the Trump Administration's immigration policies did not, at least not to the same degree. Part of the reason may be that the perceived executive overreach of the Bush II and Trump Administrations was seen more as a power grab by the White House than as an expansion of the administrative state. Indeed, in the case of the Trump Administration's unilateral initiatives, the administrative state was often perceived (by both Trump and his opponents) as a source of resistance, rather than an instrument working in alignment with the administration.

3. *See generally* Gillian E. Metzger, *Foreword: 1930s Redux: The Administrative State Under Siege*, 131 Harv. L. Rev. 1, 8–17, 24–28 (2017).

4. 467 U.S. 837 (1984).

5. For studies that examine judicial review in the courts of appeals before *Chevron*, see David H. Willison, *Judicial Review of Administrative Decisions: Agency Cases Before the Court of Appeals for the District of Columbia, 1981–84*, 14 Am. Pol. Q. 317, 320–21 (1986) (win rate of 66% in 1981–84); Martha Anne Humphries & Donald R. Songer, *Law and Politics in Judicial Oversight of Federal Administrative Agencies*, 61 J. Pol. 207, 215 (1999) (win rate of 57% in 1969–88); Peter H. Schuck & E. Donald Elliott, *To the* Chevron *Station: An Empirical Study of Federal Administrative Law*, 1990 Duke L.J. 984, 1008 (win rate of 60.6% in 1975). For studies after *Chevron*, see Schuck & Elliott at 1008 (win rate of 76.6% in 1984–85); Orin S. Kerr, *Shedding Light on* Chevron: *An Empirical Study of the* Chevron *Doctrine in the U.S. Courts of Appeals*, 15 Yale L.J. on Reg. 1, 31 (1998) (win rate of 73% in 1995 and 1996 when *Chevron* was applied); Jason J. Czarnezki, *An Empirical Investigation of Judicial Decisionmaking, Statutory Interpretation, and the*

Chevron *Doctrine in Environmental Law,* 79 U. Colo. L. Rev. 767 (2008) (win rate of 69% in EPA cases in 2003–05); Kent Barnett & Christopher J. Walker, Chevron *in the Circuit Courts,* 116 Mich. L. Rev. 1, 28 (2017) (win rate of 77.4% in 2003–13 when *Chevron* was applied).

6. Compare Thomas W. Merrill, *Judicial Deference to Executive Precedent,* 101 Yale L.J. 969, 980–93 (1992) (finding a decline in deference after *Chevron*), with Thomas W. Merrill, *Textualism and the Future of the* Chevron *Doctrine,* 72 Wash. U. L.Q. 351, 354 (1994) (finding an uptick in deference in the 1991–1992 Terms); *see also* William N. Eskridge, Jr. & Lauren E. Baer, *The Continuum of Deference: Supreme Court Treatment of Agency Statutory Interpretations from* Chevron *to* Hamdan, 96 Geo. L.J. 1083 (2008) (finding that the Supreme Court applies *Chevron* in only a small number of the cases in which it reviews agency interpretations of law); Connor N. Raso & William N. Eskridge, Jr., Chevron *as a Canon, Not a Precedent: An Empirical Study of What Motivates Justices in Agency Deference Cases,* 110 Colum. L. Rev. 1727 (2010) (concluding that the Supreme Court applies *Chevron* so inconsistently that it is better characterized as a canon of statutory construction rather than as binding precedent).

7. King v. Burwell, 576 U.S. 473, 485–86 (2015) (discussed further in Chapter 10).

8. *See* studies cited in note 5 *supra.*

9. Kent Barnett & Christopher J. Walker, Chevron *in the Circuit Courts,* 116 Mich. L. Rev. 1 (2017).

10. Pereira v. Sessions, 138 S.Ct. 2105, 2120 (2018) (Kennedy, J., concurring).

11. *See* Philip Hamburger, Chevron *Bias,* 84 Geo. Wash. L. Rev. 1187 (2016) (highlighting the potential for bias when an agency acts as both enforcement agent and interpreter of the law).

12. E. Donald Elliott, Chevron *Matters: How the* Chevron *Doctrine Redefined the Roles of Congress, Courts and Agencies in Environmental Law,* 16 Vill. Env. L.J. 1 (2005).

13. Christopher J. Walker, Chevron *Inside the Regulatory State: An Empirical Assessment,* 83 Fordham L. Rev. 703 (2014).

14. Marbury v. Madison, 5 U.S. 137, 177 (1803).

15. Peter J. Wallison, Judicial Fortitude: The Last Chance to Rein in the Administrative State (2018). Wallison was a senior lawyer in the Reagan Administration and is currently a senior fellow at the American Enterprise Institute.

16. Adrian Vermeule, Law's Abnegation (2016). Vermeule is Professor of Law at Harvard Law School.

17. *Id.* at 200.

18. City of Arlington v. FCC, 569 U.S. 290 (2013).

19. Vermeule, *supra* note 16, chapter 3.

20. Jeffrey A. Pojanowski, *Neoclassical Administrative Law,* 133 Harv. L. Rev. 852 (2020). The skeptics include not just Wallison but also Philip Hamburger, Is Administrative Law Unlawful? (2014), and Richard A. Epstein, The Dubious Morality of Modern Administrative Law (2020). Pojanowski says that Vermeule embodies the supremacist approach "in almost platonic form," *supra* at 861, and lists Gilliam Metzger, see note 3, and Jon D. Michaels, Constitutional Coup: Privatization's Threat to the American Republic (2017), as falling in the same camp, with qualifications.

21. *See, e.g.,* Jack M. Beermann, *End the Failed* Chevron *Experiment Now: How* Chevron *Has Failed and Why It Can and Should be Overruled,* 42 Conn. L. Rev. 779 (2010) (anti-*Chevron*); Nicholas R. Bednar & Kristin E. Hickman, Chevron's *Inevitability,* 85 Geo. Wash. L. Rev. 1392 (2017) (pro-*Chevron*); Cass R. Sunstein, Chevron *as Law,* 107 Geo. L.J. 1613 (2019) (pro-*Chevron*).

22. *See* Gregory A. Elinson & Jonathan S. Gould, *The Politics of Deference,* 75 Vand. L. Rev. (forthcoming 2022) (detailing the relationship between fluctuating support for the *Chevron* doctrine and partisan control of the executive and judicial branches).

23. Elena Kagan, *Presidential Administration,* 114 Harv. L. Rev. 2245 (2001).

24. *See* Kristin E. Hickman, *To Repudiate or Merely Curtail? Justice Gorsuch and* Chevron *Deference,* 70 Ala. L. Rev. 733 (2019) (reviewing Justice Gorsuch's opinions on the Tenth Circuit critical of the *Chevron* doctrine); Brett M. Kavanaugh, *Fixing Statutory Interpretation,* 129 Harv. L. Rev. 2118 (2016) (book review) (criticizing "clarity" as a threshold requirement for independent judgment under the *Chevron* doctrine).

25. *See* Jonathan R. Siegel, *The Constitutional Case for* Chevron *Deference,* 71 Vand. L. Rev. 937, 951 n.90 (2018) (reporting that in 2016, 239 Republicans and 1 Democrat voted in favor and 171 Democrats voted against; in 2017, 233 Republicans and 5 Democrats voted in favor and 183 Democrats voted against).

26. H.R. Rep. No. 114-622, at 4 (2016).

27. The last successful invocation of the *Chevron* doctrine to uphold an agency interpretation appeared in *Cuozzo Speed Technologies, LLC v. Lee,* 136 S. Ct. 2131, 2142–44 (2016). The case was argued and decided after the death of Justice Scalia but before Justice Gorsuch joined the Court. For details about collapsing support for the *Chevron* doctrine among the Justices after 2016, see Nathan Richardson, *Deference Is Dead (Long Live* Chevron*),* 73 Rutgers U. L. Rev. 441 (2021).

28. Pereira v. Sessions, *supra* note 10 at 2121(Alito, J., dissenting).

29. *See* Kristin E. Hickman & Aaron L. Nielson, *Narrowing* Chevron's *Domain,* 70 Duke L.J. 931, 1000–04 (2021) (listing 107 Supreme Court decisions applying the *Chevron* doctrine between 1984 and 2019).

30. United States v. Mead Corp., 533 U.S. 218 (2001).

31. Kisor v. Wilkie, 139 S. Ct. 2400 (2019).

32. Vermeule, *supra* note 16, at 13.

33. RONALD DWORKIN, LAW'S EMPIRE (1986).

1. Judicial Review of Agency Interpretation—Four Values

1. For a discussion of different meanings of the rule of law over time, see BRIAN Z. TAMANAHA, ON THE RULE OF LAW: HISTORY, POLITICS, THEORY (2004). The version advanced here, which emphasizes the importance of courts and executive officers complying with settled law, is most closely associated with the work of Friedrich Hayek. *See* F.A. HAYEK, THE ROAD TO SERFDOM 112–123 (1944).

2. *See, e.g.,* LON L. FULLER, THE MORALITY OF LAW 33–94 (2d ed. 1969); JOSEPH RAZ, *The Rule of Law and Its Virtue, in* THE AUTHORITY OF LAW: ESSAYS ON LAW AND MORALITY 210 (2d ed. 2009). Fuller's account of the morality of law is similar to what is here called the rule of law and has played a central role in recent debates about the *Chevron* doctrine and administrative law. Cass R. Sunstein and Adrian Vermeule argue in a recent book that modern administrative law effectively embodies the features of the rule of law outlined by Fuller. CASS R. SUNSTEIN & ADRIAN VERMEULE, LAW & LEVIATHAN: REDEEMING THE ADMINISTRATIVE STATE (2020). Richard Epstein counters that the modern administrative state flunks Fuller's criteria for a regime governed by the rule of law. RICHARD A. EPSTEIN, THE DUBIOUS MORALITY OF MODERN ADMINISTRATIVE LAW (2020).

3. *See* U.S. Const. art. VI.

4. Sunstein & Vermeule, *supra* note 2, at 136.

5. *See* Arthur Chaskalson, *From Wickedness to Equality: The Moral Transformation of South African Law,* 1 INT'L J. CONST. L. 590, 594, 598 (2003).

6. Thomas W. Merrill, *Legitimate Interpretation—Or Legitimate Adjudication?,* 105 CORNELL L. REV. 1395, 1402–07 (2020).

7. *See* THE FEDERALIST No. 78 (Alexander Hamilton) (arguing that the independence of federal judges would allow them to exercise "judgment" rather than "will" in resolving disputes that come before them).

8. *See* Abbe Gluck & Richard A. Posner, *Statutory Interpretation on the Bench: A Survey of Forty-Two Judges on the Federal Courts of Appeals,* 131 HARV. L. REV. 1298 (2018).

9. The duty of lower federal courts to follow Supreme Court precedent is generally understood to be quite strong. *See generally* Richard M. Re, *Narrowing Supreme Court Precedent from Below,* 104 GEO. L.J. 921 (2016) (citing authorities supporting the strict rule of vertical *stare decisis* and discussing examples of lower courts narrowing or extending Supreme Court precedent). Horizontal *stare decisis* within the same court is considered less strong, but nonetheless the Supreme Court adheres to a presumption against overruling its precedents. The importance of respecting controlling precedent was common ground among the Justices in a recent wide-ranging debate about whether it is more important to adhere to the rationale of a prior precedent or to the outcome reached by the precedent.

Compare Ramos v. Louisiana, 140 S. Ct. 1390, 1404 (2020) (opinion of Gorsuch, J.) (arguing that the rationale is what matters), with *id.* at 1429–30 (Alito, J., dissenting) (maintaining that the outcome is what matters).

10. *See* Samuel Estreicher, *Policy Oscillation at the Labor Board: A Plea for Rulemaking,* 37 ADMIN. L. REV. 163, 171 (1985) (noting that "[t]he [NLRB's] behavior—abrupt changes in policy appearing to rework in wholesale major areas of Board law, often undone three or four years later—sows disrespect for the agency," with the result that "courts are reluctant to pay little more than lip service to the doctrine of deference to agency policymaking . . . given the agency's apparently cavalier view of its own established rules").

11. *See* Jonathan S. Masur & Eric A. Posner, *Chevronizing Around Cost-Benefit Analysis,* 70 DUKE L.J. 1109, 1114–36 (2021) (discussing several environmental policy reversals by the Trump EPA, including rules addressed to climate change).

12. *See, e.g.,* Department of Homeland Security v. Regents of the University of California, 140 S.Ct. 1891, 1910–15 (2020) (remanding a decision to rescind a prior policy statement for failure to consider alternatives and reliance interests); Kisor v. Wilkie, 139 S.Ct. 2400, 2417–18 (2019) (stating that the Court has rarely given deference to an agency interpretation of its regulations "conflicting with a prior one"); Encino Motorcars, LLC v. Navarro, 136 S. Ct. 2117, 2126 (2016) (declining to give weight to an agency's regulation because it "was issued without the reasoned explanation that was required in light of the Department[of Labor]'s change in position and the significant reliance interests involved").

13. Fuller, *supra* note 2, at 51–62.

14. The framers of the Constitution clearly shared the view that changes in the law should be made prospectively. The Constitution explicitly prohibits ex post facto criminal laws and bills of attainder. U.S. Const. art. I, §§ 9, 10. States are prohibited from enacting laws impairing the obligation of contracts. *Id.* § 10. Persons cannot be deprived of life, liberty or property without due process of law, *id.* amends. V & XIV, understood to mean (in part) in a manner not in accordance with law. These provisions do not completely cover the waterfront. But even when these specific constraints do not apply, courts require a special justification to uphold a statute that applies retroactively, and statutes that are unclear on this point will be construed as applying only prospectively. *See* Usery v. Turner Elkhorn Mining Co., 428 U.S. 1, 16–18 (1976) (holding that due process requires a separate justification for making a statute retroactive); Landgraf v. USI Film Prods., 511 U.S. 244, 266 (1994) (holding that statutes otherwise unclear on the matter should be presumed to operate only prospectively).

15. *See* Harper v. Virginia Dept. of Taxation, 509 U.S. 86, 97 (1993). ("When this Court applies a rule of federal law to the parties before it, that rule . . . must be given full retroactive effect in *all* cases still open on direct review and as to all events, regardless of whether such events predate or postdate our announcement of the rule.") (Emphasis added.)

16. *See* Bowen v. Georgetown Univ. Hosp., 488 U.S. 204, 208 (1988). ("[A] statutory grant of legislative rulemaking authority will not, as a general matter, be understood to encompass the power to promulgate retroactive rules unless that power is conveyed by Congress in express terms.").

17. Peter L. Strauss, *Publication Rules in the Rulemaking Spectrum: Assuring Proper Respect for an Essential Element*, 53 ADMIN. L. REV. 803 (2001).

18. This last point is in some tension with SEC v. Chenery Corp., 332 U.S. 194 (1947), which is usually read as holding that agencies have broad discretion to make policy through adjudication (where the agency acts like a court) and apply it retroactively, even if they have authority to engage in rulemaking. Justice Jackson in dissent charged that this was contrary to the values associated with the rule of law. *Id.* at 210. For an argument that this type of review is consistent with *Chenery,* see Chapter 12.

19. Cooper v. Aaron, 358 U.S. 1, 18 (1958).

20. *See* KEITH E. WHITTINGTON, POLITICAL FOUNDATIONS OF JUDICIAL SUPREMACY 1–13 (2007) (tracing the emergence of judicial supremacy in constitutional interpretation); Larry Alexander & Frederick Schauer, *On Extrajudicial Constitutional Interpretation,* 110 HARV. L. REV. 1359 (1997) (endorsing judicial supremacy as promoting a "settlement function").

21. Obergefell v. Hodges, 576 U.S. 644 (2015).

22. *See* Campbell Robertson, *Roy Moore, Alabama Chief Justice, Suspended over Gay Marriage Order,* N.Y. TIMES, Sept. 30, 2016, https://www.nytimes.com /2016/10/01/us/roy-moore-alabama-chief-justice.html ("Nine months after instructing Alabama's probate judges to defy federal court orders on same-sex marriage, Roy S. Moore, the chief justice of the Alabama Supreme Court, was suspended . . . for violating the state's canon of judicial ethics."); Alan Blinder & Tamar Lewin, *Clerk in Kentucky Chooses Jail over Deal on Same-Sex Marriage,* N.Y. TIMES, Sept. 3, 2015, http://nytimes.com/2015/09/04/us/kim-davis-same-sex-marriage.html ("A Kentucky county clerk . . . was jailed . . . after defying a federal court order to issue [marriage] licenses to gay couples.").

23. RICHARD H. FALLON, JR., LAW AND LEGITIMACY IN THE SUPREME COURT 68 (2018).

24. For example, other than impeachment, the Constitution says nothing about who has the authority to remove federal officials from office. *See* Seila Law LLC v. Consumer Financial Protection Bureau, 140 S.Ct. 2183, 2226–29 (2020) (Kagan, J., concurring in part and dissenting in part).

25. *See generally* Henry P. Monaghan, *Constitutional Fact Review,* 85 COLUM. L. REV. 229 (1985) (considering when courts should closely review factual determinations that bear on the protection of constitutional rights).

26. *See, e.g.,* Michigan v. EPA, 576 U.S. 743, 761–62 (2015) (Thomas, J., concurring); Guedes v. Bureau of Alcohol, Tobacco, Firearms and Explosives, 140 S.Ct. 789 (2020) (statement of Gorsuch, J., respecting denial of certiorari). The most promi-

nent academic inspiration is PHILIP HAMBURGER, IS ADMINISTRATIVE LAW UN-LAWFUL? 315–21 (2014).

27. U.S. Const. art. I, §§ 1–4, 7–8.

28. U.S. Const. art. II, §§ 1, 2, 3. *See, e.g.,* Zivotofsky ex rel. Zivotofsky v. Kerry, 576 U.S. 1 (2015) (holding that the President has exclusive authority under the Constitution to recognize a foreign sovereign).

29. *See* Thomas W. Merrill, *Rethinking Article I, Section 1: From Nondelegation to Exclusive Delegation,* 104 COLUM. L. REV. 2097, 2117–18 (2004) (detailing the three conceptions based on different readings of the Constitution).

30. Thomas W. Merrill, *The Disposing Power of the Legislature,* 110 COLUM. L. REV. 452, 454 (2010).

31. Lest the "last word" conception be regarded as fanciful, it should be noted that this is the understanding that has sometimes been adopted by the Supreme Court in authorizing courts to employ federal common law to resolve particular kinds of disputes. For discussion, see Thomas W. Merrill, *The Judicial Prerogative,* 12 PACE L. REV. 327, 329–31 (1992).

32. *See, e.g.,* Whitman v. Am. Trucking Ass'ns, 531 U.S. 457, 472 (2001) ("Article I, § 1, of the constitution vests '[a]ll legislative Powers herein granted . . . in a Congress of the United States.' This text permits no delegation of those powers. . . ."); Loving v. United States, 517 U.S. 748, 758 (1996) ("The fundamental precept of the delegation doctrine is that the lawmaking function belongs to Congress and may not be conveyed to another branch or entity."); Marshall Field & Co. v. Clark, 143 U.S. 649, 692 (1892) ("That congress cannot delegate legislative power to the president is a principle universally recognized as vital to the integrity and maintenance of the system of government ordained by the constitution.").

33. The invalidations occurred in Panama Refining Co. v. Ryan, 293 U.S. 388 (1935), and A.L.A. Schechter Poultry Corp. v. United States, 295 U.S. 495 (1935). Both involved provisions of the National Industrial Recovery Act, a New Deal–era statute that promoted extensive self-regulation by industry trade groups.

34. *See, e.g.,* Merrill, *supra* note 29 at 2103–09.

35. Gundy v. United States, 139 S.Ct. 2116, 2148 (2019) (Gorsuch, J., dissenting, joined by Roberts, C.J., and Thomas, J.) ("[W]hile Congress can enlist considerable assistance from the executive branch in filling up details and finding facts, it may never hand off to the nation's chief prosecutor the power to write his own criminal code. That 'is delegation running riot.'") (quoting *Schechter Poultry,* 295 U.S. at 553 (Cardozo, J., concurring)). Justice Alito filed a concurring opinion indicating that he too was open to reconsidering the contours of the nondelegation doctrine in a proper case. *Id.* at 2131.

36. *See* United States v. Grimaud, 220 U.S. 506 (1911) (upholding delegation to the Forest Service of authority to promulgate regulations the violation of which was punishable as a crime). The definitive history of the rise of legislative rulemaking

29029

290029

290029

290029

290029

290029

29029

29029

29029

29029

29029

2902

by agencies has yet to be written. For aspects of that history, see Thomas W. Merrill & Kathryn Tongue Watts, *Agency Rules with the Force of Law: The Original Convention*, 116 HARV. L. REV. 467 (2002).

37. Youngstown Sheet & Tube Co. v. Sawyer (Steel Seizure Case), 343 U.S. 579 (1952).

38. *Id.* at 585.

39. The most famous being the concurrence of Justice Jackson, who posited a "zone of twilight" where the President asserts his own authority when Congress has not spoken on the issue. *Id.* at 634–55.

40. *See, e.g., Bowen v. Georgetown Univ. Hosp., supra* note 16 at 208 ("It is axiomatic that an administrative agency's power to promulgate legislative regulations is limited to the authority delegated by Congress."); Mistretta v. United States, 488 U.S. 361, 386 n.14 (1989) ("[R]ulemaking power originates in the Legislative Branch and becomes an executive function only when delegated by the Legislature to the Executive Branch."); Louisiana Pub. Serv. Comm'n v. F.C.C., 476 U.S. 355, 374 (1986) ("an agency has no power to act . . . unless and until Congress confers power upon it"); Chrysler Corp. v. Brown, 441 U.S. 281, 302 (1979) ("The legislative power of the United States is vested in the Congress, and the exercise of quasi-legislative authority by governmental departments and agencies must be rooted in a grant of such power by the Congress and subject to limitations which that body imposes.").

41. For a recent example, by a unanimous Court, see AMG Capital Management, LLC v. Federal Trade Commission, 141 S.Ct.1341 (2021) (holding that the FTC's claim of authority to secure restitution or disgorgement of funds obtained through unfair trade practices was foreclosed by the history and structure of the Federal Trade Commission Act).

42. *See generally* Henry P. Monaghan, *The Protective Power of the Presidency,* 93 COLUM. L. REV. 1, 61 (1993) (concluding, based on a wide-ranging review of the relevant history, that "[o]ur tradition is that no official—from the President on down—can invade private rights unless authorized by legislation").

43. *See* Daphna Renan, *Pooling Powers,* 115 COLUM. L. REV. 211 (2015).

44. *See* Adam B. Cox & Cristina M. Rodriguez, *The President and Immigration Law Redux,* 125 YALE L.J. 104 (2015) (discussing the Deferred Action for Childhood Arrivals, or DACA, program and its foundation in a theory of enforcement discretion); Memorandum from Eric Holder, Att'y Gen., to United States Attorneys and Assistant Attorney General for the Criminal Division, Re: Department Policy on Charging Mandatory Minimum Sentences and Recidivist Enhancements in Certain Drug Cases (Aug. 12, 2013), https://www.justice.gov/sites/default/files/oip /legacy/2014/07/23/ag-memo-department-policypon-charging-mandatory -minimum-sentences-recidivist-enhancements-in-certain-drugcases.pdf.

45. The Trump Administration, denied an appropriation from Congress to construct a border wall between the United States and Mexico, diverted money for

this purpose using an obscure law that allows retransfer of Defense Department funds for military purposes. A district court decision in the Ninth Circuit enjoining the diversion of funds as unlawful was stayed by the Supreme Court, Trump v. Sierra Club, 140 S.Ct. 1 (2020); see also id. at 140 S.Ct. 2620 (2020), allowing construction to go forward until it was suspended by the Biden Administration. For its part, the Obama Administration, unable to secure legislation establishing a cap-and-trade program to reduce greenhouse gas emissions, devised a "Clean Power Plan" to accomplish something similar using a little-used provision of the Clean Air Act. This was rescinded by the Trump Administration, and the rescission was in turn vacated and remanded by the D.C. Circuit. See American Lung Assn. v. EPA, 985 F.3d 914 (D.C. Cir. 2021).

46. *See, e.g.*, Cass R. Sunstein, *Nondelegation Canons*, 67 U. CHI. L. REV. 315, 316 (2000) ("Rather than invalidating federal legislation as excessively open-ended, courts hold that federal administrative agencies may not engage in certain activities unless and until Congress has expressly authorized them to do so.").

47. United States v. Southwestern Cable Co., 392 U.S. 157, 168 (1968) (upholding the FCC's assertion of authority "despite its inability to obtain amendatory legislation").

48. *See* Dalton v. Spector, 511 U.S. 462, 472 (1994) ("[O]ur cases do not support the proposition that every action by the President, or by another executive official, in excess of his statutory authority is ipso facto a violation of the Constitution."). *But see* Larry Alexander & Evan Tsen Lee, *Is There Such a Thing as Extraconstitutionality?: The Puzzling Case of* Dalton v. Spector, 27 ARIZ. ST. L. REV. 845, 852 (1995) ("When a federal official acts beyond legal authority, she violates the limited powers doctrine, which is itself a constitutional violation.").

49. This proposition seems to suggest that some form of judicial review to ensure that agencies act within the scope of their authority is required by the Constitution. For some of the difficulties in sustaining such an argument, see Thomas W. Merrill, *Delegation and Judicial Review*, 33 HARV. J.L. & PUB. POL'Y 73 (2010). As long as Congress is jealous to preserve its constitutional prerogative to decide who decides, Congress will presumably continue to provide for judicial review of agency action in order to hold the executive in check. If Congress decides to acquiesce in allowing the executive branch to become the primary source of policy initiatives, Congress may lose interest in ensuring that judicial review is available.

50. *See generally* WILLIAM E. SCHEUERMAN, LIBERAL DEMOCRACY AND THE SOCIAL ACCELERATION OF TIME (2004).

51. *See* PAUL C. LIGHT, THICKENING GOVERNMENT: FEDERAL HIERARCHY AND THE DIFFUSION OF ACCOUNTABILITY 69 (1995) (noting that the average tenure of a political appointee in the executive branch is roughly two years).

52. *See, e.g.*, Thomas H. Hammond & Jack H. Knott, *Who Controls the Bureaucracy? Presidential Power, Congressional Dominance, Legal Constraints, and*

Bureaucratic Autonomy in a Model of Multi-Institutional Policymaking, 12 J.L. Econ. & Org. 119 (1996).

53. For sources of congressional control, see Jack M. Beermann, *Congressional Administration,* 43 San Diego L. Rev. 61 (2006) ("Congress is deeply involved in the day to day administration of the law. . . . Formally, Congress attempts to control the administration of the law legislatively. . . . Informally, Congress uses the threat of legislative action . . . to control or at least influence the administration of the law in myriad ways. . . .").

54. *See* Eloise Pasachoff, *The President's Budget as a Source of Agency Policy Control,* 125 Yale L.J. 2182, 2203–04 (2016).

55. For OMB oversight of significant regulations, see Cass R. Sunstein, *The Office of Information and Regulatory Affairs: Myths and Realities,* 126 Harv. L. Rev. 1838 (2013). For sources of presidential control of agencies, see generally Elena Kagan, *Presidential Administration,* 114 Harv. L. Rev. 2245 (2001). Then-Professor Kagan concluded that "the most important [extrajudicial] development in the last two decades in administrative process, and a development that also has important implications for administrative substance[,] . . . is the presidentialization of administration—the emergence of enhanced methods of presidential control over the regulatory state." *Id.* at 2383.

56. *See* 28 U.S.C. § 566(a) (2018) ("It is the primary role and mission of the United States Marshals Service to provide for the security and to obey, execute, and enforce all orders of the United States District Courts, the United States Courts of Appeals, the Court of International Trade, and the United States Tax Court, as provided by law.").

57. *See* Henry Paul Monaghan, *Jurisdiction Stripping Circa 2020: What the Dialogue (Still) Has to Teach Us,* 69 Duke L.J. 1, 23–26 (2019).

58. For an overview of the political constraints that tend to align the Supreme Court with the general wishes of the public, see generally Barry Friedman, The Will of the People (2009).

59. *See* Jerry L. Mashaw, *Prodelegation: Why Administrators Should Make Political Decisions,* 1 J.L. Econ. & Org. 81, 95 (1985) ("Strangely enough it may make sense to imagine the delegation of political authority to administrators as a device for improving the responsiveness of government to the desires of the electorate.").

60. For the social background, values, and attitudes of the progressives, see generally Richard Hofstadter, The Age of Reform 131–73 (1955). See also Thomas K. McCraw, Prophets of Regulation: Charles Francis Adams, Louis D. Brandeis, James M. Landis, Alfred E. Kahn (1984) (offering a portrait of Charles Francis Adams, Jr., a leading advocate of regulatory reform during this era).

61. *See* Anne Joseph O'Connell, *Actings,* 120 Colum. L. Rev. 613 (2020).

62. *See* Congressional Research Service, *Statutory Inspectors General in the Federal Government: A Primer* 2–3 (2019), https://crsreports.congress.gov/product /pdf/R/R45450 (discussing inspectors general); Bethany A. Davis Noll & Richard L. Revesz, *Regulation in Transition,* 104 Minn. L. Rev. 1 (2019) (discussing rationale and history of the Congressional Review Act).

63. *See* Richard J. Pierce, Jr., Chevron *and Its Aftermath: Judicial Review of Agency Interpretations of Statutory Provisions,* 41 Vand. L. Rev. 301 (1988) (arguing that the resolution of ambiguous statutes should be regarded as policy decisions); Ilan Wurman, *The Specification Power,* 168 U. Penn. L. Rev. 689 (2020) (arguing that the resolution of general statutes should be characterized as specification).

64. Peter L. Strauss, *"Deference" Is Too Confusing—Let's Call Them "*Chevron *Space" and "Skidmore Weight,"* 112 Colum. L. Rev. 1143 (2012).

65. Gary Lawson, *Outcome, Procedure, and Process: Agency Duties of Explanation for Legal Conclusions,* 48 Rutgers L. Rev. 313, 316 (1996).

66. *See* Motor Veh. Mfrs. Assn. v. State Farm Mut. Auto. Ins. Co., 463 U.S. 29 (1983).

67. *Department of Homeland Security v. Regents, supra* note 12 at 1910–15 (holding that rescission of a policy statement was arbitrary and capricious because it failed to consider alternatives and reliance interests of beneficiaries); Dept. of Commerce v. New York, 139 S.Ct. 2551 (2019) (holding that a memorandum issued by the Secretary of Commerce instructing the department staff to include a citizenship question on the 2020 census form was arbitrary and capricious because it rested on a contrived rationale).

68. The proposition that courts lack authority to require procedures beyond those mandated by the APA was announced in Vermont Yankee Nuclear Power Corp. v. Natural Resources Defense Council, Inc., 435 U.S. 519, 524 (1978), and reaffirmed in Little Sisters of the Poor v. Pennsylvania, 140 S.Ct. 2362, 2385–86 (2020), and Perez v. Mortgage Bankers Assn., 575 U.S. 92, 100 (2015).

69. For a proposal that moves in this direction, see Kristin E. Hickman & Aaron L. Neilson, *Narrowing* Chevron's *Domain,* 70 Duke L.J. 931 (2021) (arguing that the Court should either refuse to apply *Chevron* deference to agency interpretations adopted in an adjudication or should limit *Chevron* to formal adjudications).

2. Before *Chevron*

1. 323 U.S. 134, 140 (1944).

2. *See, e.g.,* Edward's Lessee v. Darby, 25 U.S. (12 Wheat.) 206, 210 (1827) (contemporaneous interpretation); United States v. Vowell, 9 U.S. (5 Cranch) 368, 371 (1809) (longstanding interpretation).

3. Aditya Bamzai, *The Origins of Judicial Deference to Executive Interpretation,* 126 YALE L.J. 908 (2017).

4. *See, e.g.,* Watt v. Alaska, 451 U.S. 259, 272–73 (1981) (refusing to defer to agency interpretation "in conflict with its initial position").

5. *See* ANTONIN SCALIA & BRYAN G. GARNER, READING LAW: THE INTERPRETA-TION OF LEGAL TEXTS (2012) (devoting the majority of their treatise on legal inter-pretation to various canons); WILLIAM N. ESKRIDGE, JR., INTERPRETING LAW: A PRIMER ON HOW TO READ STATUTES AND THE CONSTITUTION (2016) (also de-voting substantial coverage to different canons).

6. United States v. Moore, 95 U.S. 760, 763 (1877) (hypothesizing agency par-ticipation in drafting); SEC v. Sloan, 436 U.S. 103, 126 (1978) (Brennan, J., concur-ring) (positing shared assumptions).

7. NLRB v. Bell Aerospace Co. Div. of Textron, Inc., 416 U.S. 267, 274–75 (1974). *See also* Red Lion Broadcasting Co. v. F.C.C., 395 U.S. 367, 382 (1969); Zemel v. Rusk, 381 U.S. 1, 11–12 (1965); Allen v. Grand Central Aircraft Co., 347 U.S. 535, 544–45 (1954).

8. Power Reactor Development Company, Petitioner, v. Int'l Union of Elec., Radio & Mach. Workers, AFL-CIO, 367 U.S. 396, 409 (1961).

9. United States v. Hill, 120 U.S. 169, 182 (1887).

10. Udall v. Tallman, 380 U.S. 1, 17 (1965) (quoting *United States v. Midwest Oil Co.,* 236 U.S. 459, 472–73 (1915)).

11. Bamzai, *supra* note 3, at 938.

12. *See, e.g.,* A.L.A. Schechter Poultry Corp. v. United States, 295 U.S. 495 (1935) (invalidating the National Recovery Act); United States v. Butler, 297 U.S. 1 (1936) (striking down the Agricultural Adjustment Act).

13. Bamzai, *supra* note 3, at 959–62.

14. Thomas W. Merrill, *Article III, Agency Adjudication, and the Origins of the Appellate Review Model of Administrative Law,* 111 COLUM. L. REV. 939 (2011). The leading case generally cited as ratifying the appellate review model is Crowell v. Benson, 285 U.S. 22 (1932), decided at the threshold of the New Deal.

15. Gray v. Powell, 314 U.S. 402 (1941), which deferred to the agency's application of the term "producer" on the facts presented, *id.* at 413, but resolved the meaning of the word "disposal" de novo, *id..* at 414–17, is often characterized this way. But the Court offered no explanation for its different treatment of the two issues.

16. 322 U.S. 111 (1944).

17. The Act unhelpfully provided that "[t]he term 'employee' shall include any employee. . . ." 29 U.S.C. § 152 (1940).

18. *Hearst,* 322 U.S. at 129.

19. *Id.* at 130.

20. *Id.* at 131 (citations omitted).

21. 330 U.S. 485 (1947).

22. *Id.* at 488.

23. 327 U.S. 358, 369 (1946).

24. *Id.* at 366–67.

25. *Id.* at 369–70.

26. Gary Lawson & Stephen Kam, *Making Law out of Nothing at All: The Origins of the* Chevron *Doctrine,* 65 ADMIN. L. REV. 1 (2013); *see also* GARY LAWSON, FEDERAL ADMINISTRATIVE LAW 593-605 (8th ed. 2019).

27. As we will see in Chapter 4, the Court briefly revived the distinction in Immigration and Naturalization Service v. Cardozo-Fonseca, 480 U.S. 421, 445–47 (1987), only to have it disappear again. Lawson counts O'Leary v. Brown-Pacific-Maxon, Inc., 340 U.S. 504 (1951), as adopting the distinction between pure questions of law and mixed questions of law and fact. But the question in the case was whether a worker who drowned while attempting to rescue two men in distress did so in the course of his employment. However implausibly, the Court treated the issue as a simple question of fact, rather than a mixed question of law and fact. *Id.* at 507–08.

28. *See* Lawson & Kam, *supra* note 26, at 24 ("To be sure, courts very seldom expressly identified the legal questions involved as being either pure or mixed. The classifications are ours, not theirs. . . .").

29. Lawson & Kam, *supra* note 26, at 17.

30. 323 U.S. 134 (1944).

31. *Id.* at 137.

32. *Id.* at 139–40.

33. *Id.* at 140.

34. *See generally,* Kristin E. Hickman & Matthew D. Krueger, *In Search of the Modern* Skidmore *Standard,* 107 COLUM. L. REV. 1235 (2007).

35. Most questions involving judicial review of an agency interpretation of law takes place in the regional courts of appeals or district courts. The regional courts of appeals can render rulings that have precedential force only in their own circuit. Thus, a court of appeals that adopts a persuasive brief or article cannot guarantee that another court of appeals will do the same. Most agencies, in contrast, have nationwide jurisdiction, which means that following their interpretations holds the promise of achieving national uniformity. *See* Peter L. Strauss, *One Hundred Fifty Cases per Year: Some Implications of the Supreme Court's Limited Resources for Judicial Review of Agency Action,* 87 COLUM. L. REV. 1093 (1987).

36. This paragraph and ensuing paragraphs draw on George B. Shepherd, *Fierce Compromise: The Administrative Procedure Act Emerges from New Deal Politics,* 90 NW. U. L. REV. 1557 (1996).

37. *Id.* at 1643.

38. TOM C. CLARK, U.S. DEP'T OF JUSTICE, ATTORNEY GENERAL'S MANUAL ON THE ADMINISTRATIVE PROCEDURE ACT 93 (1947).

39. Shepherd, *supra* note 36, at 1662–63.

40. 5 U.S.C. § 706 (2018).

41. *Id.* § 706(2)(A), (E).

42. *Id.* § 706(2)(C).

43. *See* NLRB v. Bell Aerospace, *supra* note 7 at 274–75; Udall v. Tallman, *supra* note 10 at 16; Zemel v. Rusk, *supra* note 7; Power Reactor Dev. Co. v. Int'l Union *supra* note 8 at 293; U.S. v. Allen-Bradley Co., 347 U.S. 535 (1954); *see also* Anita S. Krishnakumar, *Longstanding Agency Interpretations,* 83 FORDHAM L. REV. 1823, 1888–93 (2015) (collecting Supreme Court decisions from 1976 to 1983).

44. Henry P. Monaghan, Marbury *and the Administrative State,* 83 COLUM. L. REV. 1, 27–28, 34 (1983).

45. Shepherd, *supra* note 36, at 1594–98.

46. *See* WALTER GELLHORN AND CLARK BYSE, ADMINISTRATIVE LAW 506–577 (1954) (reproducing multiple judicial decisions including *Hearst* and *Skidmore* in a section devoted to "Application of Statutory Terms to Facts and Interpretation of Statutory Terms" but not mentioning the APA); 4 KENNETH CULP DAVIS, ADMINISTRATIVE LAW TREATISE 189–270 (1958) (quoting the APA once and then ignoring it in a lengthy chapter devoted to showing that the Supreme Court oscillates between a "reasonableness" approach and a "rightness" approach to agency interpretations by manipulating the distinction between law and fact).

47. 432 U.S. 416 (1977).

48. 42 U.S.C. § 607(a) (1970).

49. *Batterton,* 432 U.S. at 424–25.

50. *Id.* at 430.

51. Schweiker v. Gray Panthers, 453 U.S. 34 (1981); Herweg v. Ray, 455 U.S. 265 (1982).

52. United States v. Vogel Fertilizer Co., 455 U.S. 16, 24 (1982); Rowan Cos. v. United States, 452 U.S. 247, 253 (1981).

53. Courts would reject the inference provided by these factors if outweighed by other considerations. *See, e.g.,* National Muffler Dealers Assn., Inc. v. United States, 440 U.S. 472, 485–86 (1979) (rejecting contemporary interpretation, in part because the petitioner could not show reliance on it).

54. 454 U.S. 27 (1981).

55. *Id.* at 37–38.

56. 436 U.S. 103 (1978).

57. *Id.* at 121.

58. Pittston Stevedoring Corp. v. Dellaventura, 544 F.2d 35, 49 (2d Cir. 1976).

59. Cynthia R. Farina, *Statutory Interpretation and the Balance of Power in the Administrative State,* 89 COLUM. L. REV. 452, 473–74 (1989) (discussing the several attempts by Senator Dale Bumpers to amend the Administrative Procedure Act to reaffirm the duty of courts to exercise independent judgment in reviewing agency determinations of questions of law).

3. The *Chevron* Decision

1. 42 U.S.C, §§ 7401-7671q (2018). I will follow convention in citing to the section numbers of the Act as they appear in the Statutes at Large. Thus, CAA § 111(a)(3), the definition of stationary source under Section 111 of the Act, corresponds to 42 U.S.C. § 7411(a)(3) in the United States Code.

2. CAA § 111(a)(2).

3. *Id.* § 111(a)(3).

4. *Id.* § 111(a)(4).

5. *See* 36 Fed. Reg. 24,875, 24,977 (Dec. 23, 1971).

6. 40 Fed. Reg. 58,416 (Dec. 16, 1975).

7. *Id.* at 58,418 (amending 40 CFR § 60.2) (emphasis added).

8. *Id.* at 58,419 (adding 40 CFR § 60.14).

9. ASARCO Inc. v. Environmental Protection Agency, 578 F.2d 319, 325 (D.C. Cir. 1978).

10. *See* Thomas W. Merrill, *Capture Theory and the Courts: 1967–1983,* 72 CHI-KENT L. REV. 1039, 1065–66 (1997) (citing judicial and extrajudicial writings of Judge Wright exhibiting preoccupation with agency capture).

11. *ASARCO,* 578 F.2d at 328.

12. *Id.* at 329 n.40.

13. CAA § 302(j).

14. *Id.* § 169(2)(C) (PSD); *id.* § 171(4) (NAP).

15. 43 Fed. Reg. 26380 (June 19, 1978).

16. *Id.* at 26394.

17. *Id.* at 26403.

18. 636 F.2d 323 (D.C. Cir. 1980).

19. The panel consisted of Judges Leventhal, Robinson, and Wilkey.

20. *Id.* at 397.

21. *Id.* at 400.

22. *Id.*

23. The Alabama Power panel issued an order with a summary of its ruling in June 1979, but released its full opinion only December, which was then further revised in April 1980.

24. 44 Fed. Reg. 51924, 51934 (Sept. 5, 1979).

25. 45 Fed. Reg. 52676 (Aug. 7, 1980).

26. *Id.* at 52746.

27. For general background, see Joseph D. Kearney & Thomas W. Merrill, *The Great Transformation of Regulated Industries Law,* 98 COLUM. L. REV. 1323 (1998).

28. 46 Fed. Reg. 16280, 16281 (March 12, 1981). The EPA did not propose to revisit the definition of source under the NSPS, apparently on the ground that this would contravene the judgment in *ASARCO.*

29. 46 Fed. Reg. 50766 (Oct. 14, 1981).

30. *Id.* at 50767.

31. Natural Resources Defense Council v. Gorsuch, 685 F.2d 718 (D.C. Cir. 1982).

32. *Id.* at 726.

33. *Id.*

34. *Id.* at 726–27.

35. *Id.* at 727 n.39. Indeed, the opinion "express[ed] no view on the decision we would reach if the line drawn in *Alabama Power* and *ASARCO* did not control our judgment." *Id.* at 720 n.7.

36. *Id.* at 727 n.41.

37. Courts frequently respond to agency deviations from prior policy by requiring an explanation or new evidence in support of the change, a requirement sometimes called the "swerve doctrine." *See, e.g.,* Shaw's Supermarkets, Inc. v. NLRB, 884 F.2d 34 (1st Cir. 1989).

38. The author has previously written a detailed account of the course of decision at the Supreme Court based on the briefs, the transcript, and Justice Blackmun's papers. The interested reader is directed to Thomas W. Merrill, *The Story of Chevron: The Making of an Accidental Landmark,* 66 ADMIN. L. REV. 253 (2014). Earlier versions of the same "story" appear in STATUTORY INTERPRETATION STORIES (WILLIAM N. ESKRIDGE ET AL. eds. 2011) and ADMINISTRATIVE LAW STORIES (PETER L. STRAUSS ed. 2006). All citations herein are to the ADMINISTRATIVE LAW REVIEW version.

39. Merrill, *supra* note 38, at 272.

40. The Court has never conclusively resolved whether precedents established by a 4–3 or 4–2 vote are binding in later cases. Jonathan Remy Nash, *The Majority That Wasn't: Stare Decisis, Majority Rule, and the Mischief of Quorum Requirements,* 58 EMORY L.J. 831, 832–35 (2009).

41. The internal communications between Chief Justice Burger, Justice Brennan, and Justice Stevens can be found in Paul J. Wahlbeck, James F. Spriggs, & Forrest Malzman, The Burger Court Opinion Writing Database, available at http://supremecourtopinions.wustl.edu/files/opinion_pdfs/1983/82-1005.pdf. These letters are not found in Justice Blackmun's files, since he was not copied on any of these communications.

42. The footnote appears in *Chevron,* 467 U.S. at 849 n.22, and is otherwise inexplicable absent this background information.

43. *Chevron* was part of an avalanche of opinions handed down at the end of the 1983 Term—a total of thirty-nine decisions from June 25 (when *Chevron* was released) to July 5 (when the Term finally ended).

44. *Chevron,* 467 U.S. at 864.

45. Justice Blackmun recorded no reaction to the characterization of judicial review as entailing two-steps or to the passages in the final section of the opinion about the illegitimacy of judges resolving contested policy questions.

46. Merrill, *supra* note 38, at 274.

47. *See* Chapter 2, *supra.*

48. 467 U.S. at 863–64.

49. *Id.* at 856, 864.

50. *Id.* at 864.

51. *Id.* at 860.

52. *Id.* at 861 ("[T]he meaning of a word must be ascertained in the context of achieving particular objectives, and the words associated with it may indicate that the true meaning of the series is to convey a common idea."). The first canon is known as *noscitur a sociis. Noscitur a sociis,* Black's Law Dictionary (2d ed. 1910). The second is more obscure, but Stevens cited Russell Motor Car Co. v. United States, 261 U.S. 514, 519 (1923), as having adopted it.

53. *Chevron,* 467 U.S. at 861.

54. This reading is consistent with an opinion filed by Justice Stevens seven years later in Rust v. Sullivan, 500 U.S. 173, 220 (1991). Dissenting from the majority's invocation of *Chevron* in upholding an agency regulation, he wrote: "The new regulations did not merely reflect a change in a policy determination that the Secretary had been authorized by Congress to make. *Cf.* [*Chevron* at 865]. Rather, they represented an assumption of policymaking responsibility that Congress had not delegated to the Secretary." *See id.,* at 842–43. *Id.* at 222 (Stevens, J., dissenting).

55. Brief for the Administrator of the EPA at 62–72, *Chevron,* 467 U.S. 837 (Nos. 82-1005, 82-1247, and 82-1591) (developing the argument that the bubble concept was designed to increase state flexibility in attaining the national ambient air quality standards).

56. 467 U.S. at 859–60, 866.

57. *Id.* at 864.

58. *Id.* at 836–37, quoting United States v. Shimer, 367 U.S. 374, 383 (1961); *id.* at 866, quoting *Shimer,* 367 U.S. at 383.

59. *Id.* at 865–66.

60. *Id.* at 853.

61. The Court did not describe the comments the agency received, but the government's brief made clear that comments were filed. *See* Brief for the Administrator of the EPA at 69–70, *Chevron,* 467 U.S. 837 (Nos. 82-1005, 82-1247, and 82-1591).

62. The EPA apparently took the position that the regulation at issue in *Chevron* had not been adopted under provisions of the Act that require the use of the full-scale process review norm as codified by Section 307(d) of the Clean Air Act. *See* Requirements for Preparation, Adoption and Submittal of Implementation Plans and Approval and Promulgation of Implementation Plans, 46 Fed. Reg. 50766-01. Pursuant to this understanding, it did not respond to any of the comments that had been filed.

63. *Id.* at 865 (emphasis added).

64. *Id.* at 842–43. Footnotes to this paragraph proved to be important. *See, e.g.,* INS v. Cardoza-Fonseca, 480 U.S. 421, 446–48 (1987) (quoting *Chevron,* 467 U.S. at 843 n.9) ("The question whether Congress intended the . . . standards to be identical is a pure question of statutory construction for the courts to decide. . . . In *Chevron* . . . we explained: 'The judiciary is the final authority on issues of statutory construction and must reject administrative constructions which are contrary to clear congressional intent.'").

65. *Id.* at 843–44.

66. *Ruiz* was concerned with the merits of an agency interpretation and did not discuss the standard of review. *See Ruiz,* 415 U.S. at 209–10 ("We are confronted . . . with the issues whether the geographical limitation placed on general assistance eligibility by the BIA is consistent with congressional intent and the meaning of the applicable statutes, or, to phrase it somewhat differently, whether the congressional appropriations are properly limited by the BIA's restrictions, and, if so, whether the limitation withstands constitutional analysis.").

67. Batterton v. Francis, 432 U.S. 416, 424–26 (1977).

68. Antonin Scalia, *Judicial Deference to Administrative Interpretations of Law,* 1989 DUKE L.J. 511, 517 (1989) ("And to tell the truth, the quest for the 'genuine' legislative intent is probably a wild-goose chase anyway. In the vast majority of cases I expect that Congress . . . didn't think about the matter at all. If I am correct in that, then any rule adopted in this field represents merely a fictional, presumed intent, and operates principally as a background rule of law against which Congress can legislate.").

69. Prominent examples are SOPRA, mentioned in the Introduction, *see* Separation of Powers Restoration Act, S. 909, 116th Cong. (2019); and the Bumper Amendment, which came close to enactment in the years before *Chevron, see* S. 1080, 97th Cong. § 5, 128 Cong. Rec. 5302 (1982).

70. 5 U.S.C.§ 706 (2018). There is ample evidence that Congress prefers that ambiguities be resolved by its faithful agent—the courts—rather than by agencies subject to greater influence by its great institutional rival—the executive. *See* n. 69 *supra.*

71. For other examples of creativity from Justice Stevens during his early years on the Court, some of which proved consequential and others that did not, see Hampton v. Mow Sung Wong, 426 U.S. 88 (1976) (requiring a clear statement from Congress before upholding a regulation barring non-U.S. citizens from civil service employment); Indus. Union Dep't v. American Petroleum Inst., 448 U.S. 607 (1980) (interpreting the OSH Act as incorporating a threshold requirement of "significant risk" before the agency could set safety standards for workplace exposure to carcinogens).

72. Brief for the Administrator of the EPA at 41, *Chevron,* 467 U.S. 837 (Nos. 82-1005, 82-1247, and 82-1591).

73. *Id.* at 41, quoting INS v. Wang, 450 U.S. 139, 144 (1981).

74. Jeffrey Rosen, *The Dissenter: Justice John Paul Stevens,* N.Y. Times, Sept. 23, 2007, available at https://www.nytimes.com/2007/09/23/magazine/23stevens-t .html.

75. The correspondence is reproduced in Wahlbeck et al., *supra* note 41. Note that Stevens in the second letter quite skillfully plays on what he perceives to be Brennan's reluctance to undertake the "chore" of writing a dissenting opinion. He alludes to this again in the final paragraph of the letter: "In all events, I thought I should let you know that you probably will have to be writing a dissent in this fascinating case unless what I put on paper is more persuasive than my threat to make you undergo the punishment of the hurdle." *Id.* (The reference to the "fascinating case" was probably intended as sarcasm; the Justices generally regarded the prospect of untangling complicated regulatory cases as tedious.) At this point (May 23) Stevens knows that Brennan's previous letter raising a concern about a contradiction in the EPA's regulations was based on a mistake. He can thus infer that the task of unraveling the details about the bubble policy in a dissenting opinion would entail a great deal of effort on the part of Brennan (or more likely his law clerk), which would be especially unwelcome with the end-of-term crunch rapidly approaching. Stevens's hunch proved to be correct. When Stevens agreed to add a face-saving footnote alluding to the supposed contradiction raised by Brennan—*see supra* at note 42—the latter quickly capitulated and joined Stevens's opinion.

4. The Rise of the *Chevron* Doctrine

1. Thomas W. Merrill, *Judicial Deference to Executive Precedent,* 101 Yale L.J. 969, 981 (1992) (collecting data for the Supreme Court from the 1984 term to the 1990 term).

2. 470 U.S. 116 (1985).

3. *Id.* at 125. For overall data on the 1984 Term, see Merrill, *supra* note 1, at 1038–39.

4. *Chem. Manuf'rs* at 152 (Marshall, J., dissenting).

5. *See* Merrill, *supra* note 1, at 981.

6. *See, e.g.,* Board of Governors of Financial Reserve System v. Dimension Financial Corp., 474 U.S. 361, 368 (1986) (quoting Chevron U.S.A. Inc. v. Natural Resources Defense Council, Inc., 467 U.S. 837, 843 (1984)).

7. 478 U.S. 833 (1986).

8. *See* Merrill, *supra* note 1, at 992 (concluding that the rate at which the Court accepted agency interpretations actually declined in the years after *Chevron*). There was an uptick in the 1991–92 terms, but the numbers nonetheless remained small. Thomas W. Merrill, *Textualism and the Future of the* Chevron *Doctrine,* 72 Wash. U. L.Q. 351, 360 (1994). More comprehensive reviews of the impact of *Chevron* on the Supreme Court find little evidence of increased deference to agencies.

William N. Eskridge & Lauren E. Baer, *The Continuum of Deference: Supreme Court Treatment of Agency Statutory Interpretations from* Chevron *to* Hamdan, 96 Geo. L.J. 1083, 1121 (2008).

9. 476 U.S. 974 (1986).

10. *Id.* at 975–76.

11. *Id.* at 980.

12. *Id.* at 979.

13. Merrill, *supra* note 1, at 981 tbl.1. (The table shows Supreme Court decisions by term; most of the 1989 Term cases were decided in 1990.)

14. *See* Connecticut Dep't of Income Maintenance v. Heckler, 471 U.S. 524, 528 (1985) (Stevens, J.) ("[T]he State's position is foreclosed by the plain language of the statute, by the Secretary's reasonable and longstanding interpretation of the Act, and by the Act's legislative history."); Aluminum Co. of Am. v. Central Lincoln People's Util. Dist., 467 U.S. 380, 402–03 n.3 (1984) (Stevens, J., dissenting) (objecting that the agency had not been a "model of consistency" and its interpretation was not entitled to "so much deference as to override the plain import of the words Congress enacted.").

15. *See* GARY LAWSON, FEDERAL ADMINISTRATIVE LAW 593-605 (8ᵗʰ ed. 2019); Gary Lawson & Stephen Kam, *Making Law out of Nothing at All: The Origins of the* Chevron *Doctrine,* 65 ADMIN. L. REV. 1, 39 (2013).

16. 742 F.2d 1561 (D.C. Cir. 1984); *see* Lawson & Kam, *supra* note 15, at 39.

17. 42 U.S.C. §7541(c)(1) (1982) (cross-referencing 42 U.S.C. §7521(d) (1982)).

18. *See* General Motors Corp. v. Ruckelshaus, 742 F.2d 1561, 1565 n.7 (D.C. Cir. 1984) (en banc).

19. General Motors Corp. v. Ruckelshaus, 724 F.2d 979 (D.C. Cir. 1983). Judge Wald dissented from the panel decision.

20. General Motors Corp. v. Ruckelshaus, 742 F.2d 1561 (D.C. Cir. 1984) (en banc).

21. *Id.* at 1566.

22. *Id.* at 1566–67. Judge Antonin Scalia, then relatively new to the court, joined Judge Wald's opinion.

23. *Id.* at 1574–75 (Bazelon, J., dissenting).

24. 744 F.2d 133, 150–51 (D.C. Cir. 1984).

25. *Id.* at 140–41.

26. Lawson & Kam, *supra* note 15, at 39.

27. *See* Gregory A. Elinson and Jonathan Gould, *The Politics of Deference,* 75 VAND. L. REV. (forthcoming 2022) (draft at 24–28).

28. *Rettig,* 744 F.2d at 155.

29. Lawson & Kam, *supra* note 15, at 41.

30. *See* Pennsylvania Public Utility Comm'n v. United States, 749 F.2d 841 (D.C. Cir. 1984) (Wald, J.). Lawson observes that despite several brief mentions of *Chevron,* "the decision could have been written precisely the same way, in both

substance and form, if *Chevron* (and *General Motors* and *Rettig*) had never existed." Lawson & Kam, *supra* note 15, at 49–50.

31. For an extensive discussion of the D.C. Circuit's decisional law during this period, see Lawson & Kam, *supra* note 15, at 44–50.

32. Thomas W. Merrill, *The Story of* Chevron: *The Making of an Accidental Landmark,* 66 ADMIN. L. REV. 253, 278 (2014).

33. The D.C. Circuit citations represent about 40% of all citations to *Chevron* at the court of appeals level during the first three years. The percentage is only slightly lower today: D.C. Circuit citations to *Chevron* represent 37% of all court of appeals cases citing to *Chevron* in the past three years. (There were 2,655 cases citing *Chevron* in the D.C. Circuit versus 7,245 cases citing to *Chevron* in the courts of appeals overall, based on a Westlaw search conducted on June 1, 2021).

34. *See* Natural Resources Defense Council v. Thomas, 805 F.2d 410, 420 (D.C. Cir. 1986) (Wald, C.J.) ("dictates"); Int. Brotherhood of Teamsters v. ICC, 801 F.2d 1423, 1426 (D.C. Cir. 1986) (Starr, J.) ("familiar two-step"); Transbrasil S.A. Linhas Aereas v. DOT, 791 F.2d 202, 205 (D.C. Cir. 1986) (Wald, C.J.) ("always"); Investment Co. Institute v. Conover, 790 F.2d 925, 932 (D.C. Cir. 1986) (Starr, J.) ("familiar framework").

35. For evidence that Democratic and Republican judges on the D.C. Circuit respond differently to cases in ways that match the party affiliation of the President who appointed them, see Richard L. Revesz, *Congressional Influence on Judicial Behavior? An Empirical Examination of Challenges to Agency Action in the D.C. Circuit,* 76 N.Y.U. L. REV. 1100, 1106–09 (2001) (summarizing studies). Interestingly, one study finds less partisan influence in *Chevron* cases than in cases presenting procedural challenges to agency decisions. Richard L. Revesz, *Environmental Regulation, Ideology, and the D.C. Circuit,* 83 VA. L. REV. 1717 (1997).

36. Merrill, *supra* note 32, at 279.

37. *Id.*

38. *Id.* at 280.

39. *Id.* at 280–81.

40. *See, e.g., Rettig,* 744 F.2d at 156 (Wald, C.J.) (reversing agency interpretation as unreasonable at step 2 of *Chevron*); FAIC Secur., Inc. v. United States, 768 F.2d 352 (D.C. Cir. 1985) (Scalia, J.) (reversing agency interpretation as contrary to statute at step 1 of *Chevron*).

41. *See* Kenneth W. Starr, *Judicial Review in the Post-*Chevron *Era,* 3 YALE J. ON REG. 283 (1986); Abner Mikva, *How Should the Courts Treat Administrative Agencies?,* 36 AM. U. L. Rev. 1 (1986); Antonin Scalia, *Judicial Deference to Administrative Interpretations of Law,* 1989 DUKE L.J. 511; Laurence H. Silberman, Chevron— *The Intersection of Law & Policy,* 58 GEO. WASH. L. REV. 821 (1990). Although this confirms that the D.C. Circuit judges attributed great significance to *Chevron,* it would be difficult to characterize these efforts as advocacy pieces. Judge Starr's article presented a carefully balanced view of *Chevron,* and Justice Scalia's

article took pains to point out that the *Chevron* standard did not necessarily mean more deference to agencies.

42. 480 U.S. 421 (1987).

43. *Id.* at 445 & n.29. Curiously, a review of the government's briefs and the transcript of oral argument reveals that it did not place "heavy reliance" on *Chevron*, as opposed to general principles of deference. The footnote was probably written after Justice Scalia circulated his concurrence, which of course was all about *Chevron*.

44. *Id.* at 446.

45. *Id.* at 448.

46. 322 U.S. 111 (1944).

47. *Cardozo-Fonseca* at 453–54 (Scalia, J., concurring in the judgment).

48. *Id.* at 454 (Scalia, J., concurring in the judgment).

49. *Id.* at 454–55 (Scalia, J., concurring in the judgment).

50. *Id.* at 455 (Scalia, J., concurring in the judgment).

51. Scalia, *supra* note 4, at 521.

52. *Id.* at 521, 517.

53. *Id.* at 517.

54. *Cardozo-Fonseca*, 480 U.S. at 445–46 n.29. The lengthy verbatim quotation from *Chevron* in the footnote is one of the stranger aspects of the byplay between Justices Stevens and Scalia in *Cardozo-Fonseca*. The author's view is that the footnote was probably added after Scalia circulated his concurrence, charging Stevens with eviscerating *Chevron*. By reproducing all of Part II of *Chevron*, Stevens was effectively inviting the reader to draw her own conclusions as to whether there was any incompatibility between the pure question of law/law application distinction and *Chevron*. A better response would have been to acknowledge that Part II was merely a condensed summary of the deference doctrine and that there was no intent to modify the traditional understanding of court–agency relations, as confirmed by reading the *Chevron* opinion in its entirety.

55. Justice Stevens was a graduate of Northwestern Law School, where I formerly served as the John Paul Stevens Professor of Law. In that capacity, I was occasionally invited to attend public events at which Stevens agreed to speak when he came to Chicago. I recall at least two occasions when someone in the question-and-answer session asked a version of the "What did you intend when you wrote *Chevron*?" question. The answer was always that he regarded it as simply a restatement of existing law, nothing more or less.

56. 484 U.S. 112 (1987).

57. *Id.* at 124 n.20.

58. *Id.* at 133 (Scalia, J., concurring).

59. *Id.* at 134.

60. 484 U.S. at 123.

61. *See* Adams Fruit Co. v. Barrett, 494 U.S. 638, 649–50 (1990) (holding that *Chevron* does not apply to legal issues concerning the scope of private rights of action in court because in these circumstances it is the court, not the agency, that is charged with administration of the statute).

62. Lawson & Kam, *supra* note 15, at 72.

63. *See* Negusie v. Holder, 555 U.S. 511, 531, 534, 538 (2009) (Stevens, J., concurring in part and dissenting in part); *see also* Republic of Austria v. Altman, 541 U.S. 677, 701–02 (2004) (Stevens, J.).

64. *See* Cass R. Sunstein, *Law and Administration After* Chevron, 90 COLUM. L. REV. 2071, 2105–09 (1990).

65. K Mart Corp. v. Cartier, 486 U.S. 281, 291 (1988) (Kennedy, J.).

66. *See* Rust v. Sullivan, 500 U.S. 173, 184 (1991) (Rehnquist, C.J.); Pension Benefit Guarantee Corporation v. LTV Corp., 496 U.S. 633, 647–48 (1990) (Blackmun, J.); Sullivan v. Everhart, 494 U.S. 83 (1990) (Scalia, J.); Mead Corp. v. Tilley, 490 U.S. 714 (1989) (Marshall, J.); Young v. Community Nutrition Institute, 476 U.S. 974 (1986) (O'Connor, J.).

67. United States v. Alaska, 503 U.S. 569, 575 (1992) (White, J.).

68. Dole v. United Steelworkers, 494 U.S. 26, 35 (1990) (quoting NLRB v. Food and Commercial Workers, 484 U.S. 112, 123 (1987)).

69. *See, e.g.,* Massachusetts v. E.P.A., 549 U.S. 497, 553 (2007) (Scalia, J., dissenting) ("[Justice Stevens's majority opinion] nowhere explains why [the EPA's] interpretation is incorrect, let alone why it is not entitled to deference under *Chevron.* . . ."); I.N.S. v. St. Cyr, 533 U.S. 289, 320 n.45 (2001) (Stevens, J.) ("The INS argues that we should extend deference under *Chevron*[,] . . . [but] there is, for *Chevron* purposes, no ambiguity in [the] statute for an agency to resolve.").

70. Babbitt v. Sweet Home Chapter of Communities for a Greater Oregon, 515 U.S. 687, 703–04 (1995) (Stevens, J.).

71. *See* Kent Barnett & Christopher J. Walker, Chevron *in the Circuit Courts,* 116 MICH. L. REV. 1, 45 (2017) ("The D.C. Circuit led the way [in the study] by applying the *Chevron* standard to 88.6% of [statutory] interpretations [by agencies], followed by the First (87.9%), Eighth (85.7%), Federal (84.6%), and Fourth (80.6%) Circuits. The Sixth Circuit, by contrast, applied *Chevron* the least frequently, only 60.7% of the time. Five other circuits were below 70%.").

72. Justice Scalia predicted in 1989 that courts would come to embrace the *Chevron* doctrine in part because "it represents a rule that is easier to follow and thus easier to predict." Scalia, *supra* note 41, at 521.

73. From 1987 to 1990 I served as Deputy Solicitor General in the Justice Department, overseeing appeal authorizations and Supreme Court litigation in civil cases. After only a few months on the job, I joked to friends that I was the Deputy Solicitor General for *Chevron,* because it seemed that virtually every request from

the Civil Division for appeal authorization or for Supreme Court participation was based on the need to expand or defend the *Chevron* doctrine.

74. The classic study of the advantages of being an institutional litigant is Marc S. Galanter, *Why the "Haves" Come Out Ahead: Speculations on the Limits of Legal Change,* 9 L. & Soc'y Rev. 95 (1974).

75. *See* United States v. Mead Corp., 533 U.S. 218, 240–41 (2001) (Scalia, J., dissenting) ("The Court has largely replaced *Chevron* . . . with that test most beloved by a court unwilling to be held to rules[:] . . . th'ol' 'totality of the circumstances' test."); National Cable & Telecommunications Ass'n v. Brand X Internet Services, 545 U.S. 967, 1020 (2005) (Scalia, J., dissenting) ("It is a sadness that the Court should go so far out of its way to make bad law.").

76. *See* Kent Barnett & Christopher J. Walker, Chevron *Step Two's Domain,* 93 Notre Dame L. Rev. 1141 (2018).

77. *See* City of Arlington v. FCC, 569 U.S. 290 (2013), discussed in Chapter 10.

78. *See* National R.R. Passenger Corp v. Boston and Maine Corp., 503 U.S. 407, 420 (1992) (deferring under *Chevron* to an interpretation not explicitly advanced by the agency but which the Court characterized as "a necessary presupposition of the ICC's decision.").

5. The Indeterminacies of the *Chevron* Doctrine

1. Preemption doctrine is discussed in Chapter 9. The standards for determining whether procedural due process is met and whether a regulation is a taking are both discussed in Gary Lawson, Katharine Ferguson, & Guillermo A. Montero, *Oh Lord, Please Don't Let Me Be Misunderstood! Rediscovering the* Mathews v. Eldridge *and* Penn Central *Frameworks,* 81 Notre Dame L. Rev. 1 (2005).

2. For the proposition that the doctrine is "well settled," see United States v. Alaska, 503 U.S. 569, 575 (1992). On the high incidence of decisions ignoring the *Chevron* doctrine, see Thomas W. Merrill, *Judicial Deference to Executive Precedent,* 101 Yale L.J. 969, 982 (1992); William N. Eskridge & Lauren E. Baer, *The Continuum of Deference: Supreme Court Treatment of Agency Statutory Interpretations from* Chevron *to* Hamdan, 96 Geo. L.J. 1083, 1121–29 (2008). For the argument that the *Chevron* doctrine is best explained as a canon of interpretation, see Cass R. Sunstein, *Law and Administration After* Chevron, 90 Colum. L. Rev. 2071, 2105–09 (1990). For a decision treating the doctrine as a rule of law, see, e.g., United States v. Haggar Apparel Co., 526 U.S. 380, 395 (1999) (vacating and remanding a lower-court decision for failing to apply the *Chevron* doctrine).

3. The quoted sentences appear in Chevron U.S.A. Inc. v. Natural Resources Defense Council, Inc., 467 U.S. 837, 842–43 & n.9 (1984).

4. *See* Cuomo v. Clearing House Ass'n, L.L.C., 557 U.S. 519, 525 (2009) ("There is necessarily some ambiguity as to the meaning of the statutory term 'visitorial powers,' especially since we are working in an era when the prerogative writs—through which visitorial powers were traditionally enforced—are not in vogue.").

5. *See* Bostock v. Clayton County, 140 S.Ct. 1731, 1738–43 (2020).

6. *Chevron,* 467 U.S. at 851–53, 862–64.

7. A parallel argument is that "ambiguous" is ambiguous—meaning either that a text requires interpretation in order to determine its meaning or that the text has no ascertainable meaning. Ryan Doerfler, *The "Ambiguity" Fallacy,* 88 GEO. WASH. L. REV. 1110 (2020).

8. Richard M. Re, *Clarity Doctrines,* 86 U. CHI. L. REV. 1497, 1510–16, 1531–40 (2019).

9. Gary Lawson, *Proving the Law,* 86 Nw. U. L. REV. 859, 890–91 (1992) (concluding that the baseline standard of proof for legal interpretations is "better than its available alternatives").

10. Brett M. Kavanaugh, *Fixing Statutory Interpretation,* 129 HARV. L. REV. 2118, 2134–44 (2016) (reviewing ROBERT A. KATZMANN, JUDGING STATUTES (2014)).

11. *Id.* at 2139.

12. Ryan D. Doerfler, *Going "Clear"* (Univ. of Chi., Pub. Law Working Paper No. 720, 2019), https://papers.ssrn.com/sol3/papers.cfm?abstract_id=3326550 [https://perma.cc/K62K-FTW5].

13. *See* King v. Burwell, 576 U.S. 473 (2015) (considering the issue of subsidies on federal exchanges); FDA v. Brown & Williamson Tobacco Corp., 529 U.S. 120 (2000) (considering FDA jurisdiction over tobacco). Both decisions are discussed in Chapter 10.

14. *See* Yellow Transp., Inc. v. Michigan, 537 U.S. 36 (2002).

15. Doerfler, *supra* note 12 at 21–22.

16. The FDA devoted an entire rulemaking proceeding, consuming nearly 700 pages in the Federal Register, to the jurisdictional question. *See* Nicotine in Cigarettes and Smokeless Tobacco FDCA Jurisdictional Determination, 61 Fed. Reg. 44619–45318 (1996).

17. The relevant interpretation was contained in an IRS regulation, 26 CFR §1.368-2, which in turn adopted a definitional provision contained in regulations issued by the Department of Health and Human Services. *See* Rules and Regulations: Patient Protection and Affordable Care Act: Exchange, SHOP and Eligibility Appeals: Final Rule, 78 Fed. Reg. 54069, 54134 (Aug. 20, 2013) codified at § 45 CFR 155.20. There was no discussion of the issue that eventually reached the Supreme Court in the agency proceedings, evidently because no one raised it in comments.

18. Doerfler, *supra* note 12 at 31–32.

19. Colin S. Diver, *The Optimal Precision of Administrative Rules,* 93 YALE L.J. 65, 67–76 (1983).

20. The survey examined all Supreme Court decisions identified as applying the two-step *Chevron* standard of review between 1984 and 2019, as identified in an appendix to Kristin E. Hickman & Aaron L. Nielson, *Narrowing* Chevron's *Domain,* 70 DUKE L.J. 931, 1000-04 (2021). Overall, 39.4% of the decisions referenced

the "precise question" formulation, 50.9% omitted it, and 9.4% were too difficult to classify one way or the other. If the too difficult to classify decisions are excluded, 43% of the decisions reference the "precise question" language and 56% omit it (out of a revised sample of 96 cases).

21. Michigan v. EPA, 576 U.S. 743, 751 (2015).

22. Entergy Corp. v. Riverkeeper, Inc., 556 U.S. 208, 218 n.4 (2009); *see id.* at 241 n.5 (Stevens, J., dissenting).

23. United States v. Home Concrete & Supply, LLC, 566 U.S. 478, 493 n.1 (2012) (Scalia, J., concurring in part and concurring in the judgment).

24. *See* Matthew Stephenson & Adrian Vermeule, Chevron *Has Only One Step*, 95 Va. L. Rev. 597 (2009). This was endorsed by Justice Scalia in a footnote in *Home Concrete & Supply,* supra note 23 at 493 n.1 (Scalia, J., concurring in part and concurring in the judgment).

25. Caleb Nelson, *Stare Decisis and Demonstrably Erroneous Precedent*, 87 Va. L. Rev. 1, 5–8 (2001).

26. *See* Kenneth A. Bamberger & Peter Strauss, Chevron's *Two Steps*, 95 Va. L. Rev. 611 (2009).

27. *See* William N. Eskridge, Jr., *The New Textualism*, 37 UCLA L. Rev. 621, 650–56 (1990) (describing Justice Scalia's early campaign).

28. *See* U.S. Dept. of Justice, Office of Legal Policy, Using and Misusing Legislative History: A Re-Evaluation of the Status of Legislative History in Statutory Interpretation 20–26 (1989); Frank H. Easterbrook, *The Role of Original Intent in Statutory Construction*, 11 Harv. J. L. & Pub. Pol'y 59 (1988).

29. Thomas W. Merrill, *Textualism and the Future of the* Chevron *Doctrine*, 72 Wash. U. L.Q. 351, 370–71 (1994).

30. *See* K Mart Corp. v. Cartier, Inc., 486 U.S. 281, 291–92 (1988) (opinion of Kennedy, J.); National R.R. Passenger Corp. v. Boston & Me. Corp., 503 U.S. 407, 417 (1992).

31. Linda Jellum, Chevron's *Demise: A Survey of* Chevron *from Infancy to Senescence*, 59 Admin. L. Rev. 725, 761 (2007).

32. When Professor Jellum sought a decision in which the choice of textualism versus intentionalism made a difference in whether the court deferred to the agency interpretation, she chose an en banc decision of the Court of Appeals for the Fifth Circuit, evidently because no Supreme Court case fit the bill. *Id.* at 730–37 (discussing Mississippi Poultry Ass'n v. Madigan, 992 F.2d 1359 (5th Cir. 1993), aff'd on reh'g, 31 F.3d 293 (5th Cir. 1994) (en banc)).

33. Antonin Scalia, *Judicial Deference to Administrative Interpretations of Law*, 1989 Duke L.J. 511, 521 (1989).

34. Merrill, *Textualism, supra* note 29, at 368–70.

35. *See id.* at 372.

36. *See* John F. Manning, *The New Purposivism*, 2011 Sup. Ct. Rev. 113 (2012).

37. *See, e.g.,* Antonin Scalia & Bryan A. Gardner, Reading Law: The Interpretation of Legal Texts 56 (2012) ("Of course, words are given meaning by their context, and context includes the purpose of the text.").

38. Antonin Scalia, *Common-Law Courts in a Civil-Law System: The Role of United States Federal Courts in Interpreting the Constitution and Laws, in* A Matter of Interpretation: Federal Courts and the Law 17 (1997). *See generally* John F. Manning, *What Divides Textualists from Purposivists?,* 106 Colum. L. Rev. 70, 70–78 (2006); Caleb Nelson, *What Is Textualism?,* 91 Va. L. Rev. 347, 347–53 (2005).

39. FDA v. Brown & Williamson Tobacco Corp., 529 U.S. 120, 126; 143–159 (2000) (O'Connor, J.).

40. This is known by the Latin phrase *ejusdem generis* (of the same kind or class). Black's Law Dictionary 556 (8th ed. 2004).

41. To cite one illustration, in INS v. St. Cyr, 533 U.S. 289 (2001), the Court refused to give *Chevron* deference to the Attorney General's interpretation applying certain restrictive amendments of the immigration laws to pending cases. The Court noted that the interpretation was contrary to the substantive canon that ambiguous statutes will be interpreted to apply prospectively. The canon was labeled a traditional "tool[] of statutory construction," and consequently, "there is, for *Chevron* purposes, no ambiguity in such a statute for an agency to resolve." *Id.* at 320–21 n.45.

42. *See* Scalia, *supra* note 33, at 516 (*Chevron* "if it is to be believed, . . . [adopted] an across-the board presumption, that, in the case of ambiguity, agency discretion is meant.").

43. *Chevron, supra,* 467 U.S. at 865.

44. Smiley v. Citibank (South Dakota), N.A., 517 U.S. 735, 740–41 (1996) ("We accord deference to agencies under *Chevron,* not because of a presumption that they drafted the provision in question, or were present at the hearings, or spoke to the principal sponsors; but rather because of a presumption that Congress, when it left ambiguity in a statute meant for implementation by an agency, understood that the ambiguity would be resolved, first and foremost, by the agency, and desired the agency (rather than the courts) to possess whatever degree of discretion the ambiguity allows.").

45. Scalia, *supra* note 33 at 517.

46. *Chevron, supra,* 467 U.S. at 843–45 & n.11.

47. *See, e.g.,* Connecticut Light & Power Co. v. Fed. Power Comm'n, 324 U.S. 515, 537 (1945) (stating that an agency interpretation should be accepted if it has a "reasonable basis in law"); NLRB v. Hearst Publ'ns, Inc., 322 U.S. 111, 131 (1944) (same).

48. *See, e.g.,* Federal Election Comm'n v. Democratic Senatorial Campaign Committee, 454 U.S. 27, 39 (1981) (framing the question as whether the agency interpretation was "sufficiently reasonable" to be accepted by the reviewing court);

Zenith Radio Corp. v. United States, 437 U.S. 443, 450 (1978) (same); Train v. Natural Resources Defense Council, Inc., 421 U.S. 60, 75 (1975) (same); United States v. Shimer, 367 U.S. 374, 383 (1961) (upholding the agency interpretation as a "reasonable accommodation of conflicting policies").

49. 5 U.S.C. § 706(2)(A) (2018).

50. As then-Judge Breyer remarked in an early critique of the *Chevron* doctrine: "It is difficult, after having examined a legal question in depth with the object of deciding it correctly, to believe both that the agency's interpretation is legally wrong, and that its interpretation is reasonable." Stephen Breyer, *Judicial Review of Questions of Law and Policy*, 38 Admin. L. Rev. 363, 379 (1986).

51. *See infra* notes 61–66 & accompanying text.

52. *See* Greater Boston Television Corp. v. FCC, 444 F.2d 841, 851–52 (1970) (Leventhal, J.) ("[A]gencies and courts together constitute a 'partnership' in furtherance of the public interest, and are 'collaborative instrumentalities of justice.' The court is in a real sense part of the total administrative process, and not a hostile stranger to the office of first instance."); *see also* Christopher P. Banks, Judicial Politics in the D.C. Circuit Court 40 (1999) ("Judge Leventhal thought that courts and agencies should work as 'partners' . . . in the administrative process. . . . Other legal experts, though, . . . scoffed. . . . Judge Henry Friendly, for example, sniffed, 'There is little doubt who is considered to be the senior partner.'").

53. 5 U.S.C. § 706(2)(A) (2018).

54. *Chevron*, 467 U.S. at 844 & n.12 (citing, inter alia, Batterton v. Francis, 432 U.S. 416, 424–26 (1977)).

55. *Id.* at 844 ("Sometimes the legislative delegation to an agency on a particular question is implicit rather than explicit. In such a case, a court may not substitute its own construction of a statutory provision for a reasonable interpretation of an agency.").

56. *See* Judulang v. Holder, 565 U.S. 42, 52–53 n.7 (2011); Mayo Found. for Med. Educ. v. United States, 562 U.S. 44, 53 (2011); United States v. Mead Corp., 533 U.S. 218, 229 (2001).

57. *See* Ronald M. Levin, *The Anatomy of* Chevron *Step Two Reconsidered*, 72 Chi.-Kent L. Rev. 1253 (1997).

58. Levin thought it was "too late in the day" to adopt the former option and instead appeared to endorse the latter option. *Id.* at 1296.

59. Gary Lawson, *Outcome, Procedure, and Process: Agency Duties of Explanation for Legal Conclusions*, 48 Rutgers L. Rev. 313 (1996). Lawson's third option—procedural review—refers to a style of review that emerged in the D.C. Circuit in the 1960s and early 1970s in which the reviewing court would review the procedures (such as written versus oral proceedings) followed by the agency. The Court in Vermont Yankee Nuclear Power Corp. v. Natural Resources Defense Council,

Inc., 435 U.S. 519 (1978), held that this type of review violates the APA. By common consensus, however, process review is distinct from procedural review, and continues to be enforced under the arbitrary-and-capricious standard of the APA. *See* Motor Vehicle Manf. Ass'n v. State Farm Mutual Auto. Ins. Co., 463 U.S. 29, 43 (1983) ("Normally, an agency rule would be arbitrary and capricious if the agency has relied on factors which Congress has not intended it to consider, entirely failed to consider an important aspect of the problem, offered an explanation for its decision that runs counter to the evidence before the agency, or is so implausible that it could not be ascribed to a difference in view or the product of agency expertise.").

60. *See* William N. Eskridge, Jr., & Lauren E. Baer, *The Continuum of Deference: Supreme Court Treatment of Agency Statutory Interpretations from* Chevron *to* Hamdan, 96 Geo. L.J. 1083, 1154 tbl.20 (2008) (ranking Justice Scalia as one of the least likely Justices to affirm agency interpretations of statutes).

61. 525 U.S. 366 (1999).

62. With the emergence of widespread cellular telephony, the FCC's effort to stimulate competition in local land-line markets became largely irrelevant. Not for the first time, technological change rendered economic regulation obsolete.

63. 573 U.S. 302 (2014).

64. *Id.* at 324.

65. 549 U.S. 497 (2007).

66. 576 U.S. 743 (2015).

67. Kent Barnett & Christopher J. Walker, Chevron *Step Two's Domain*, 93 Notre Dame L. Rev. 1441 (2018).

6. The Domain of the *Chevron* Doctrine

1. Antonin Scalia, *Judicial Deference to Administrative Interpretations of Law*, 1989 Duke L.J. 511, 516 (1989).

2. *Id.*

3. 533 U.S. 218 (2001).

4. *Chevron*, 467 U.S. at 843, 844.

5. A partial exception to this generalization is Martin v. Occupational Safety and Health Review Comm'n, 499 U.S. 144 (1991), where one entity promulgated regulations and another brought enforcement actions. The Court concluded that *Chevron* authority followed the entity given rulemaking authority. This might have led to a more general conclusion limiting the *Chevron* doctrine to interpretations adopted through rulemaking, but it did not. As discussed *infra*, the Court almost casually applied the *Chevron* doctrine to interpretations adopted in adjudications of various sorts, as well as those announced through rulemaking.

6. One survey of Supreme Court decisions reports that the Court invoked *Chevron* in five majority opinions (out of twenty-one cases) after 1984 involving review of the NLRB. James J. Brudney, Chevron *and* Skidmore *in the Workplace: Unhappy Together,* 83 FORDHAM L. REV. 487, 507 n.52 (2014). Interestingly, the article also reports that the Court has been noticeably less deferential to the NLRB in the post-*Chevron* era than it was in the pre-*Chevron* era, *id.* at 509 tbl.2, although multiple factors, including hostility to the NRLB by increasingly conservative Justices, may explain this.

7. John F. Coverdale, *Court Review of Tax Regulations and Revenue Rulings in the* Chevron *Era,* 64 GEO. WASH. L. REV. 35, 57–63 (1995).

8. Mayo Found. for Med. Educ. and Research v. United States, 562 U.S. 44 (2011); *see id.* at 53–56 (overruling National Muffler Dealers Assn., Inc. v. United States, 440 U.S. 472 (1979)); *id.* at 56–57 (disapproving decisions from the 1980s applying the distinction between specific and general rulemaking grants).

9. *See* United States v. Mead Corp., 533 U.S. 218, 230–31 n.12 (2001) (citing eight cases applying the *Chevron* doctrine to an interpretation rendered in an adjudication); *id.* at 231 (citing NationsBank of North Carolina, N.A. v. Variable Annuity Life Ins. Co., 513 U.S. 261, 257 (1995) as a case applying the *Chevron* doctrine to an informal adjudication in the form of a letter of the Comptroller of the Currency granting the request of a national bank to act as an agent selling annuities).

10. INS v. Aguirre-Aguirre, 526 U.S. 415 (1999).

11. *Id.* at 425 (quoting INS v. Cardozo-Fonseca, 480 U.S. 421, 448–49 (1987)).

12. United States v. Haggar Apparel Co., 526 U.S. 389, 390–91 (1999).

13. *Id.* at 391.

14. 494 U.S. 638 (1990).

15. *Id.* at 649–50 (citations omitted).

16. *Id.* at 650, quoting Federal Maritime Comm'n v. Seatrain Lines, Inc., 411 U.S. 726, 745 (1973).

17. 488 U.S. 204 (1988).

18. *Id.* at 212–13 (citations omitted).

19. Thomas W. Merrill & Kristin E. Hickman, Chevron's *Domain,* 89 GEO. L.J. 833, 849–52 (2001). This was an undercount—the article failed to include the question whether *Chevron* applies to agency interpretations of the preemptive effect of a statute, an issue that took on prominence later.

20. 323 U.S. 134 (1944). *See supra* Chapter 2.

21. *See, e.g.,* United States v. Pennsylvania Indus. Chem. Corp., 411 U.S. 655, 674 (1973) (citing *Skidmore* and *Federal Maritime Board v. Isbrandtsen Co.,* 356 U.S. 481, 499 (1958) in deferring to the agency's interpretation); Fed. Land Bank of Wichita v. Bd. of Cty. Comm'rs of Kiowa Cty., State of Kan., 368 U.S. 146, 155 (1961) (citing *Skidmore,* the APA, and Unemployment Comp. Comm. v. Aragon, 329 U.S. 143, 153 (1946) in declining to review the agency's interpretation); T.I.M.E. Inc. v. United States, 359 U.S. 464, 490 & n.25 (1959) (Black, J., dissenting) (citing

Skidmore and *Fawcus Machine Co. v. United States,* 282 U.S. 375, 378 (1931) in support of the proposition that "interpretations of statutes by agencies charged with their administration are entitled to very great weight").

22. 429 U.S. 125 (1976).

23. Geduldig v. Aiello, 417 U.S. 484 (1974).

24. *Gilbert,* 429 U.S. at 141.

25. *Id.* at 143.

26. Pregnancy Discrimination Act of 1978, 92 Stat. 2076 (codified at 42 U.S.C. § 2000e(k) (2018)).

27. Scalia, *supra* note 1, at 517 (stating that after *Chevron* "there is no longer any justification for giving 'special' deference to 'long-standing and consistent' agency interpretations of law").

28. 499 U.S. 244 (1991).

29. *Id.* at 258.

30. Civil Rights Act of 1991, Pub. L. No. 102–166, 105 Stat. 1075, 1078, 1079.

31. *Id.* at 260 (Scalia, J., concurring in part and concurring in the judgment).

32. *Id.*

33. Justice Marshall, joined by Justices Blackmun and Stevens, dissented. *Id.* at 260. Marshall found the EEOC interpretation worthy of deference but did not suggest that *Chevron* supplied the relevant standard of review. *Id.* at 275–78.

34. Reno v. Koray, 515 U.S. 50, 61 (1995).

35. Martin v. Occupational Safety and Health Review Comm'n, 499 U.S. 144, 157 (1991).

36. Merrill & Hickman, *supra* note 19, at 836; *see* Cass R. Sunstein, Chevron *Step Zero,* 92 Va. L. Rev. 187, 207–11 (2006).

37. 529 U.S. 576 (2000).

38. Stephen Breyer, *Judicial Review of Questions of Law and Policy,* 38 Admin. L. Rev. 363, 372–82 (1986).

39. *Id.* at 373.

40. *Christensen,* 529 U.S. at 587.

41. *Id.* at 591 (Scalia, J., concurring in part and concurring in the judgment).

42. *Id.* at 596–97 (Breyer, J., dissenting).

43. *Id.* at 595 n.2 (Stevens, J., dissenting).

44. 533 U.S. 218 (2001).

45. The statute authorized the Secretary of the Treasury to promulgate regulations "providing for the issuance of binding rulings prior to the entry of the merchandise concerned," 19 U.S.C. § 1502(a) (2000), but the regulations specified that the rulings were binding only on "Customs Service personnel." 19 C.F.R. 177.9(a).

46. *See* Garcia v. San Antonio Metro. Transit Auth., 469 U.S. 528, 531 (1985) (overruling *National League of Cities v. Usery,* 426 U.S. 833 (1976)). Three Justices remained on the Court from *Garcia,* which had overruled *National League*

of Cities. Chief Justice Rehnquist dissented in *Garcia,* joined by Justice O'Connor, and he had been the author of *National League of Cities;* Justice Stevens joined the majority in *Garcia.* Rehnquist and O'Connor joined the Thomas opinion in *Christensen;* and Stevens dissented.

47. 533 U.S. at 226–27.

48. *Christensen,* 529 U.S. at 587.

49. *Mead,* 533 U.S. at 227.

50. *Id.* at 230.

51. *Id.* at 230–31.

52. *Id.* at 245 (Scalia, J., dissenting).

53. *Id.* at 233–34 (majority opinion).

54. *See* Thomas W. Merrill, *The* Mead *Doctrine: Rules and Standards, Meta-Rules and Meta-Standards,* 54 ADMIN. L. REV. 807, 814 (2002).

55. *Mead,* 533 U.S. at 244 (Scalia, J., dissenting).

56. *Id.* at 243 (Scalia, J., dissenting).

57. *Id.* at 230 ("It is fair to assume generally that Congress contemplates administrative action with the effect of law when it provides for a relatively formal administrative procedure tending to foster the fairness and deliberation that should underlie a pronouncement of such force.").

58. *Id.* at 239 (Scalia, J., dissenting).

59. *Id.* at 241 (Scalia, J., dissenting).

60. 535 U.S. 212 (2002).

61. *Id.* at 217.

62. *Id.* at 220, citing North Haven Bd. of Ed. v. Bell, 456 U.S. 512, 522 n.12 (1982).

63. *Id.* at 222 (citations omitted).

64. Justice Breyer evidently forgot the following lines from *Mead:* "[C]lassification rulings are best treated like 'interpretations contained in policy statements, agency manuals, and enforcement guidelines.' [*Christensen.*] They are beyond the *Chevron* pale." *Mead,* 533 U.S. at 234.

65. *Id.*

66. *Id.* at 226 (Scalia, J., concurring in part and concurring in the judgment).

67. *Id.*

68. *See* Lisa Schultz Bressman, *How* Mead *Has Muddled Judicial Review of Agency Action,* 58 VAND. L. REV. 1443 (2005); Adrian Vermeule, Mead *in the Trenches,* 71 GEO. WASH. L. REV. (2003).

69. *See generally,* Kristin E. Hickman, *Three Phases of* Mead, 83 FORDHAM L. REV. 527 (2014).

70. *See* United States v. Eurodif S.A., 555 U.S. 305, 314–19 (2009) (binding adjudication); Household Credit Services, Inc. v. Pfennig, 541 U.S. 232, 238–39 (2004) (notice-and-comment rulemaking); SEC v. Zandford, 535 U.S. 813, 819–20 (2002) (formal adjudication).

71. *See* Wos v. E.M.A. ex rel. Johnson, 568 U.S. 627, 643 (2013) (enforcement guideline); Alaska Dep't of Envtl. Conservation v. EPA, 540 U.S. 461, 487–88 (internal guidance); Wis. Dep't of Health & Family Servs. v. Blumer, 534 U.S. 473, 485 (2002) (proposed regulation).

72. 551 U.S. 158 (2007).

73. *Id.* at 173–74.

74. *See* Coeur Alaska, Inc. v. SE Alaska Conservation Council, 557 U.S. 261, 296 (2009) (Scalia, J., concurring); National Cable & Telecommunications Ass'n v. Brand X Internet Services, 545 U.S. 967, 1014–20 (2005) (Scalia, J., dissenting); Smith v. City of Jackson, 544 U.S. 228, 244–45 (2005) (Scalia, J., concurring); Raymond Yates M.D., P.C. Profit Sharing Plan v. Herndon, 541 U.S. 1, 24 (2004) (Scalia, J., concurring).

75. 569 U.S. 290 (2013).

76. *See* Thomas W. Merrill, *Step Zero After* City of Arlington, 83 FORDHAM L. REV. 753, 776–79 (2014).

77. United States v. Mead Corp., 533 U.S. 218, 227 n.6 (citations omitted).

78. *Id.* at 229.

79. *See, e.g.,* Vill. of Barrington, Ill. v. Surface Transp. Bd., 636 F.3d 650, 658–59 (D.C. Cir. 2011) (concluding that *Mead*'s step zero was satisfied despite the absence of notice-and-comment rulemaking or formal adjudication because the procedures employed "create further opportunities for public participation" and are "far more formal—and thus much more likely to 'foster . . . fairness and deliberation'—than those at issue in *Mead*") (quoting *Mead*, 533 U.S. at 230); *see also* Bressman, *supra* note 68, at 1443, 1458–59 (2005) ("After *Mead*, courts diverge as to what evidence demonstrates that Congress intended an agency to issue an interpretation with the force of law. . . . [S]ome courts . . . ask whether, in addition to binding effect, the interpretation reflects public participation. . . .").

7. Rule of Law Values

1. William N. Eskridge, Jr., & Lauren E. Baer, *The Continuum of Deference: Supreme Court Treatment of Agency Statutory Interpretations from* Chevron *to* Hamdan, 96 GEO. L.J. 1083, 1148–49 (2008); Connor N. Raso & William N. Eskridge, Jr., Chevron *as a Canon, Not a Precedent: An Empirical Study of What Motivates Justices in Agency Deference Cases,* 110 COLUM. L. REV. 1727, 1781–82 (2010).

2. Anita S. Krishnakumar, *Longstanding Agency Interpretations,* 83 FORDHAM L. REV. 1823 (2015).

3. *See* David Zaring, *Reasonable Agencies,* 96 VA. L. REV. 135, 169 (2010) (concluding that agencies prevail on judicial review 60–70% of the time without regard to the doctrine employed by the reviewing court).

4. *See* Entergy Corp. v. Riverkeeper, Inc., 556 U.S. 208, 207 (2009) (Scalia, J.) ("While not conclusive, it surely tends to show that the EPA's current practice is

a reasonable and hence legitimate exercise of its discretion to weigh benefits against costs that the agency has been proceeding in essentially this fashion for over 30 years.")

5. Thompson v. North American Stainless, LP, 562 U.S. 170, 179 (2011) (Ginsburg, J., concurring).

6. *See, e.g.,* Bragdon v. Abbott, 524 U.S. 624, 545 (1998).

7. K Mart Corp. v. Cartier, 486 U.S. 281, 312 (1988) (Brennan, J., concurring in part and dissenting in part).

8. This is common ground among the Justices. See the wide-ranging discussion in Ramos v. Louisiana, 140 S.Ct. 1390 (2020).

9. Thomas W. Merrill, *Legitimate Interpretation—Or Legitimate Adjudication?,* 105 CORNELL L. REV. 1395, 1422–25 (2020).

10. *See* Neal v. United States, 516 U.S. 284, 295–96 (1996) ("Our reluctance to overturn precedents derives in part from institutional concerns about the relationship of the Judiciary to Congress . . . Congress, not this Court, has responsibility for revising its statutes.").

11. *See* Philip Hamburger, Chevron *Bias,* 84 GEO. WASH. L. REV. 1187 (2016).

12. Baldwin v. United States, 140 S.Ct. 690 (2020) (Thomas, J., dissenting from denial of certiorari).

13. 497 U.S. 116 (1990).

14. Motor Carrier Act of 1980, Pub. L. 96-296, 94 Stat. 793.

15. *Id.* at 130, 131, 135, quoting Square D Co. v. Niagara Frontier Tariff Bureau, Inc., 476 U.S. 409, 420 (1986).

16. Pub. L. No. 103–180, 107 Stat. 2044 (1993). For post-*Maislin* decisions dealing with the fallout, see Reiter v. Cooper, 507 U.S. 258 (1993); I.C.C. v. Transcon Lines, 513 U.S. 138 (1995); Security Services, Inc. v. K Mart Corp., 511 U.S. 431 (1994).

17. 502 U.S. 527 (1992).

18. *Id.* at 537.

19. 516 U.S. 284 (1996).

20. *Id.* at 295–96.

21. 545 U.S. 967 (2005).

22. *Id.* at 982–83.

23. *Maislin,* 497 U.S. at 131; *see also Lechmere* at 536–37; *Neal* at 295.

24. Caleb Nelson, *Originalism and Interpretive Conventions,* 70 U. CHI. L. REV. 519 (2003).

25. In previous writing (before *Brand X* was decided), the author and Kristin Hickman proposed that even if the matter is viewed from the perspective of the *Chevron* doctrine, the Court should adopt a conclusive presumption that all pre-*Chevron* judicial decisions were adopted at step 1, in order to avoid the litigation-over-litigation problem. *See* Thomas W. Merrill & Kristin E. Hickman, Chevron's *Domain,* 89 GEO. L.J. 833, 917–20 (2001).

26. *Brand X, supra* note 21 at 1016 (Scalia, J., dissenting).

27. *Id.* at 1003 (Stevens, J., concurring).

28. The Court's decision in *Brand X* had the effect of validating and in turn encouraging an almost laughable set of flip flops by the FCC concerning the proper classification of internet service providers under the Telecommunications Act of 1996. See Telecommunications Act of 1996, 110 Stat. 56, codified at 47 U.S.C. § 153(46) (2000) (definition of "telecommunications" service); *id.* at § 153(20) (definition of "information service"). The Commission initially classified the internet as a telecommunications service in 1998, then changed its mind in 2002 and decided it was an information service—in the order upheld by *Brand X*. The Commission changed its mind again in 2015 and reclassified the internet as a telecommunications service, in a decision upheld in United States Telecommunications Assn. v. FCC, 825 F.3d 674 (D.C. Cir. 2016), only to change its mind once again in 2018 and call it an information service, also largely upheld in Mozilla Corp. v. FCC, 940 F.3d 1 (D.C. Cir. 2019). The Biden Administration is reported to want to reclassify it once more as a communications service. The yin and yang corresponds to changing attitudes about the need for "net neutrality" regulation of the internet, which in turn appears to be associated with the political party of the individual appointed to be the chair of the FCC. This history vividly illustrates the instability associated with the failure of Congress to enact legislation addressing important questions of public regulation, exacerbated by the instability of agency policy encouraged by the *Chevron* doctrine.

29. 566 U.S. 478 (2012).

30. 357 U.S. 28 (1958).

31. 26 CFR § 301.6501(e) -1(a)(1)(iii) (2011).

32. *Home Concrete,* at 487.

33. *Id.* at 488–89, 490.

34. *Id.* at 493–95 (Scalia, J., concurring in part and concurring in the judgment).

35. *Id.* at 496 (Scalia J. concurring in part and concurring in the judgment).

36. *Id.* at 494 (Scalia, J., concurring in part and concurring in the judgment).

37. 138 S. Ct. 1612 (2018).

38. *Home Concrete,* 566 U.S. at 495 (Scalia, J., concurring in part and concurring in the judgment).

39. 567 U.S. 142 (2012).

40. Bowles v. Seminole Rock & Sand Co., 325 U.S. 410, 414 (1945).

41. 519 U.S. 452 (1997).

42. For the original critique, see John E. Manning, *Constitutional Structure and Judicial Deference to Agency Interpretations of Agency Rules,* 96 COLUM. L. REV. 612 (1996) (arguing that *Auer* deference violates the separation of powers principle that the power to make and interpret rules should not be lodged in the same body).

43. Perez v. Mortgage Bankers Ass'n, 575 U.S. 92, 108–112 (2015) (Scalia, J., concurring in the judgment).

44. 139 S.Ct. 2400 (2019).

45. Fair Labor Standards Act of 1938 13(a), 52 Stat. 1067, codifed at 29 U.S.C. § 213 (a)(1) (1940).

46. *Smithkline Beecham, supra* note 39 at 155–56.

47. *Id.* at 158–59. Because no deference was due under *Auer,* Justice Alito proceeded to interpret the regulations de novo, and concluded that the detailers were properly classified as "outside salesmen" and hence were exempt from the overtime pay requirement. Justice Breyer, writing for four dissenters, agreed that no deference to the Department's *amicus* brief was appropriate. He put this on the ground that the government had offered inconsistent theories in its *amicus* filings, not on the ground of the industry's justifiable reliance on seventy years of inaction. Undertaking his own de novo review of the regulations, Breyer concluded that the detailers should have been classified a "promotional employees" rather than salesmen, and thus should have been allowed to recover overtime pay.

48. *Id.* at 158, quoting Dong Yi v. Sterling Collision Centers, Inc., 480 F.3d 505, 510–11 (7th Cir. 2007).

49. *Kisor,* 139 S.Ct. at 2417–18.

50. 29 U.S.C. § 213(b)(10)(A) (2018).

51. 136 S.Ct. 2117 (2016).

52. *Id.* at 2124.

53. *Id.* at 2125–26.

54. *Id.* at 2126.

55. *Id.* at 2127.

56. Justice Ginsburg, joined by Justice Sotomayor, concurred, noting that the Department was free on remand to adopt the position that service representatives are not exempt, provided it supplied a better explanation for this outcome. Justice Thomas, joined by Justice Alito, dissented on the ground that the Court should have proceeded to decide the merits, and held that service representatives are exempt.

57. Guedes v. Bureau of Alcohol, Tobacco, Firearms, and Explosives, 140 S.Ct. 789 (2020) (statement of Gorsuch, J., regarding denial of certiorari).

8. Constitutional Avoidance

1. *See* United States v. Bass, 404 U.S. 336 (1971) (rule of lenity); Landgraf v. USI Film Produs., 511 U.S, 244 (1994) (presumption against retroactivity); Gregory v. Ashcroft, 501 U.S. 452 (1991) (requiring a clear statement by Congress before a general federal statute will be applied to traditional state functions).

2. *See* EEOC v. Arabian Am. Oil Co., 499 U.S. 244 (1991) (presumption against extraterritorial application of general statutes); WILLIAM N. ESKRIDGE, JR., INTERPRETING LAW: A PRIMER ON HOW TO READ STATUTES AND THE CONSTITUTION 442–43 (2016) (listing canons designed to protect Indian tribal sovereignty).

3. FCC v. Pacifica Found., 438 U.S. 726 (1978). The sanction consisted in a demerit that could be taken into account when the broadcasting license of the station came up for renewal. When the Commission tightened its policy years later, extending it to "fleeting expletives" in live broadcasts, the Court assessed the new policy under the arbitrary and capricious standard of the APA. *See* FCC v. Fox Television Stations, Inc., 566 U.S. 502 (2009).

4. 18 U.S.C. § 1464 (1976).

5. *Pacifica,* 438 U.S. at 760 (Powell, J., concurring).

6. 497 U.S. 547 (1990).

7. *Id.* at 569.

8. *Id.* at 569, quoting Columbia Broadcasting System, Inc. v. Democratic National Committee, 412 U.S. 94, 103 (1973).

9. *See* Adarand Constructors, Inc. v. Peña, 515 U.S. 200, 227 (1995).

10. 500 U.S. 173 (1991).

11. *Id.* at 179 (quoting 42 U.S.C. § 300a–6 (1988)).

12. It was also challenged as violating the principle of reproductive autonomy recognized in Roe v. Wade, 410 U.S. 113 (1973). *See Rust,* 500 U.S. at 201–03. This was a more difficult challenge to mount, given that the Court had held it was permissible not to fund abortions while funding other reproductive choices. *See id.* at 202 ("It similarly would strain logic, in light of the more extreme restrictions [upheld in other cases], to find that the mere decision to exclude abortion-related services from a federally funded pre-conceptual family planning program, is unconstitutional."). To simplify the discussion, I ignore this claim here.

13. *Id.* at 190, 191.

14. 535 U.S. 467 (2002).

15. 485 U.S. 568 (1988).

16. National Labor Relations Act § 8(b)(4), 29 U.S.C. § 158(b)(4) (1982).

17. *DeBartolo,* 485 U.S. at 576.

18. *Id.* at 582 (quoting 29 U.S.C. § 158(b)(4) (1982)).

19. 531 U.S. 159 (2001).

20. 33 U.S.C. § 1344(a) (2000); *id.* § 1362(7) (2000).

21. United States v. Riverside Bayview Homes, Inc., 474 U.S. 121 (1985).

22. *E.g.,* United States v. Lopez, 514 U.S. 549 (1995) (adopting a somewhat restrictive three-part classification of Congress's power under the Commerce Clause).

23. *SWANCC,* 531 U.S. at 172–73 (quoting *DeBartolo,* 485 U.S. at 575).

24. *Id.* at 172.

25. 547 U.S. 715 (2006).

26. *Id.* at 732.

27. *Id.* at 776 (Kennedy, J., concurring in the judgment).

28. *Id.* at 787, 788 (Stevens, J., dissenting).

29. *Id.* at 757–59 (Roberts, C.J., concurring). The Chief Justice refrained from blaming Congress, which had also failed to clarify the law in the wake of the *SWANCC* decision.

30. Adrian Vermeule, *Saving Constructions,* 85 Geo. L.J. 1945, 1949 (1997).

31. There is a third version of constitutional avoidance, which Vermeule labels "procedural" avoidance. Vermeule, *supra* note 30, at 1948–49. This says that if a matter can be resolved as a matter of statutory interpretation, the constitutional question should not be considered at all. *See* Ashwander v. Tennessee Valley Auth., 297 U.S. 288, 347 (1936) (Brandeis, J., concurring). The sequencing in *Rust* and *Verizon* can also be characterized as procedural avoidance, in that if the agency or the reviewing court determines that the statute does not permit the challenged action, the constitutional issue is avoided.

32. Richard A. Posner, *Statutory Interpretation—in the Classroom and in the Courtroom,* 50 U. Chi. L. Rev. 800, 816 (1983); *see also* William K. Kelley, *Avoiding Constitutional Questions as a Three-Branch Problem,* 86 Cornell L. Rev. 831 (2001); Vermeule, *supra* note 30, at 1960–63; Frederick Schauer, Ashwander *Revisited,* 1995 Sup. Ct. Rev. 71.

33. Charlotte Garden, *Avoidance Creep,* 168 U. Pa. L. Rev. 331, 333 (2020) ("[A]voidance decisions have tended to creep beyond their stated boundaries, as decisionmakers either treat them as if they were constitutional precedent, or extend them into new statutory contexts while disregarding key aspects of their original reasoning.").

34. In other words, it represents a form of classical avoidance. *See* text after note 30 *supra.*

35. As emphasized by Kelley, *supra* note 32.

36. For examples of agencies considering constitutional rights in the course of setting agency policy, see Syracuse Peace Council Against TV Station WTVH Syracuse, 2 FCC Rcd 5043, 5043 (1987) ("[B]ased upon this record, our experience[,] . . . fundamental constitutional principles, and the findings contained in our comprehensive 1985 Fairness Report, we conclude that the fairness doctrine, on its face, violates the First Amendment. . . ."); Religious Exemptions and Accommodations for Coverage of Certain Preventive Services Under the Affordable Care Act, 83 Fed. Reg. 57,536, 57,536 (Nov. 15, 2018) ("These rules expand exemptions to protect religious beliefs for certain entities and individuals whose health plans are subject to a mandate of contraceptive coverage through guidance issued pursuant to the Patient Protection and Affordable Care Act."). For contrasting views about whether agencies should take greater account of constitutional values in their decision making, compare Gillian E. Metzger, *Administrative Constitutionalism,* 91 Tex. L. Rev. 1897 (2013), with David E. Bernstein, *Antidiscrimination Laws and the Administrative State: A Skeptic's Look at Administrative Constitutionalism,* 94 Notre Dame L. Rev. 1381 (2019).

37. *See* United States v. Wiltberger, 18 U.S. (5 Wheat.) 76, 95 (1820); 1 WILLIAM BLACKSTONE, COMMENTARIES ON THE LAWS OF ENGLAND *88.

38. Marinello v. United States, 138 S.Ct. 1101, 1108–09 (2018); United States v. Bass, 404 U.S. 336, 348 (1971).

39. *See generally* Paul J. Larkin, Jr., Chevron *and Federal Criminal Law,* 32 J. L. & POL. 211, 222–30 (2017) (reviewing the history).

40. 494 U.S. 152, 177 (1990) (Scalia, J., concurring in the judgment).

41. Dan M. Kahan, *Is* Chevron *Relevant to Federal Criminal Law?,* 110 HARV. L. REV. 469 (1996); Sanford N. Greenberg, *Who Says It's a Crime?* Chevron *Deference to Agency Interpretations of Regulatory Statutes That Create Criminal Liability,* 58 PITT. L. REV. 1 (1996).

42. United States v. Apel, 571 U.S. 359, 369 (2014); *see also* Abramski v. United States, 573 U.S. 169, 191 (2014). It is possible that the Court assumes it would violate Article III of the Constitution to confer authority on an administrative agency to adjudicate criminal charges. *See* Gomez v. United States, 490 U.S. 858, 864 (1989) (relying in part on the canon of constitutional avoidance in holding that a federal magistrate as opposed to an Article III judge may not supervise voir dire in selecting a jury in a criminal case over the objection of the defendant).

43. *See, e.g.,* Clark v. Martinez, 543 U.S. 371, 380–81 (2005).

44. United States v. Mead Corp., 533 U.S. 218, 233–34 (2001).

45. Clark v. Martinez, *supra* note 43, at 382.

46. 504 U.S. 505, 518 n.10 (1992) (plurality opinion); *id.* at 519 (Scalia, J., concurring in the judgment).

47. 515 U.S. 687, 704 n.18 (1995).

48. Clark v. Martinez, *supra* note 43, at 380–81 (2005); Leocal v. Ashcroft, 543 U.S. 1, 11 n.8 (2004).

49. *See* Carter v. Welles-Bowen Realty, Inc., 736 F.3d 722, 729–36 (6th Cir. 2013) (Sutton, J., concurring); Gutierrez-Brizuela v. Lynch, 834 F.3d 1142, 1149–58 (10th Cir. 2016) (Gorsuch, J., concurring).

9. The Preemption Puzzle

1. *See, e.g.,* Hughes v. Talen Energy Marketing, LLC, 136 S.Ct. 1288, 1297 (2016), quoting Altria Group, Inc. v. Good, 555 U.S. 70, 76 (2008) ("the purpose of Congress is the ultimate touchstone in every pre-emption case"); La. Pub. Serv. Comm'n v. FCC, 476 U.S. 355, 369 (1986) ("The critical question in any preemption analysis is always whether Congress intended that federal regulation supersede state law.").

2. U.S. Const. art. VI, cl. 2. *See, e.g.,* Lorillard Tobacco Co. v. Reilly, 533 U.S. 525, 540–41 (2001) (identifying the Supremacy Clause as the "relatively clear and simple mandate" that allows Congress to "pre-empt[] state action in a particular

area"); Nw. Cent. Pipeline Corp v. State Corp. Comm'n, 489 U.S. 493, 509 (1989) (referring to Congress's "power under the Supremacy Clause . . . to preempt state law").

3. *See generally* Thomas W. Merrill, *Preemption and Institutional Choice*, 102 Nw. U. L. Rev. 727, 730–38 (2008).

4. *See generally* Arizona v. United States, 567 U.S. 387, 398–400 (2012) (listing the four categories with citations, but treating frustration of purpose as a subset of conflict preemption). Individual Justices have attacked one or more of the categories of preemption as unsound, the most common targets being frustration preemption and field preemption. For a critique of the Court's categorical approach on the ground that it fails to direct attention to the important variables in determining whether federal law preempts state law, see Thomas W. Merrill, *Preemption in Environmental Law: Formalism, Federalism Theory, and Default Rules*, in Federal Preemption: States' Powers, National Interests 166 (Richard A. Epstein & Michael S. Greve, eds., 2007).

5. *See* Ernest A. Young, *"The Ordinary Diet of the Law": The Presumption Against Preemption in the Roberts Court*, 2011 Sup. Ct. Rev. 253 (2012).

6. Compare Cipollone v. Liggett Group, Inc. 505 U.S. 504, 518 (1992) (Stevens, J.) (presumption of preemption applies in construing an express preemption clause); with *id.* at 554-47 (Scalia, concurring in part and dissenting in part) (presumption does not apply in construing an express preemption clause).

7. Rice v. Santa Fe Elevator Co., 331 U.S. 218, 230 (1947).

8. *Cf.* Antonin Scalia & Bryan A. Garner, Reading Law: The Interpretation of Legal Texts 291–92 (2012) (making a similar argument about the willingness of courts to infer field preemption).

9. *See* Watters v. Wachovia Bank, N.A., 550 U.S. 1, 38 & n.21 (2007) (Stevens, J., dissenting) (citing three federal statutes expressly delegating authority to agencies to preempt state law). In the Medical Device Amendments of 1976, Congress enacted a general preemption clause but expressly authorized the FDA to exempt particular state requirements from preemption. 21 U.S.C. §360k(b) (2018).

10. *E.g.,* Fidelity Fed. Sav. & Loan Ass'n v. De La Cuesta, 458 U.S. 141 (1982).

11. *E.g.,* Wyeth v. Levine, 555 U.S. 555 (2009) (regulatory preamble); Geier v. Am. Honda Motor Co., 529 U.S. 861 (2000) (government *amicus* brief).

12. For a discussion of how agency legal interpretations should be regarded when an agency has been explicitly delegated authority to preempt state law, or when a legislative regulation promulgated by an agency is claimed as the basis for preemption of state law, see Merrill, *supra* note 3, at 766–69.

13. 517 U.S. 735 (1996).

14. Marquette National Bank of Minneapolis v. First of Omaha Service Corp., 439 U.S. 299 (1978). In *Marquette Bank,* the complaint was that a national bank chartered in Nebraska could charge a higher rate of interest than was allowed under Minnesota law, which meant it could issue credit cards without an annual

fee, which national banks chartered in Minnesota felt obliged to do given the more restrictive usury laws in Minnesota.

15. *Smiley,* at 740–41.

16. *Id.* at 744.

17. *Marquette Bank, supra* note 14.

18. *Smiley,* 517 U.S. at 744.

19. 550 U.S. 1 (2007).

20. *Id.* at 20–21.

21. *Id.* at 41 (Stevens, J., dissenting) (quoting Geier v. Am. Honda Motor Co., 529 U.S. 861, 883, 908 (2000)).

22. 557 U.S. 519 (2009).

23. *Id.* at 534. In hindsight, one can see the decision as a step in Scalia's evolution toward using the "reasonableness" requirement of step 2 of the *Chevron* doctrine as the sole rubric for reviewing agency interpretations of law. See Chapter 5 *supra,* discussing Scalia's view late in his tenure on the Court that the *Chevron* doctrine has only one step—asking whether the agency interpretation is "reasonable."

24. *Clearing House,* 557 U.S. at 537 (Thomas, J., dissenting).

25. 505 U.S. 504 (1992).

26. 529 U.S. 861 (2000).

27. *Id.* at 883.

28. 518 U.S. 470 (1996).

29. *Id.* at 485.

30. *Id.* at 495.

31. *Id.* at 496. *See supra* note 9, on the FDA's authority to exempt state law from preemption under the Act.

32. *See generally* Nina A. Mendelson, Chevron *and Preemption,* 102 Mich. L. Rev. 737 (2004); Catherine M. Sharkey, *Preemption by Preamble: Federal Agencies and the Federalization of Tort Law,* 56 DePaul L. Rev. 227 (2007).

33. 552 U.S. 312 (2008).

34. *Id.* at 326–27.

35. 555 U.S. 555 (2009).

36. *Id.* at 575, quoting 71 Fed. Reg. 3922, 3934–35 (2006).

37. *Id.* at 576.

38. *Id.* at 577.

39. Requirements for Prescription Drug Product Labels, 65 Fed. Reg. 81082, 81082 (Dec. 22, 2000).

40. *Wyeth,* 555 U.S. at 578.

41. *Id.* at 577.

42. *See, e.g.,* Mutual Pharmaceutical Co. v. Bartlett, 570 U.S. 472 (2013); PLIVA, Inc. v. Mensing, 564 U.S. 604 (2011); Bruesewitz v. Wyeth, 562 U.S. 223 (2011).

43. Since 2016, the Court has declined to consider the relevance of the *Chevron* doctrine in preemption cases, on the ground that the statute in question is "clear."

See Coventry Healthcare of Missouri, Inc. v. Nevils, 137 S.Ct. 1190, 1198 n.3 (2017) (Ginsburg, J.); FERC v. Electric Power Supply Ass'n, 577 U.S. 260, 277 n.5 (2016) (Kagan, J.).

44. *See* Merrill, *supra* note 3, at 746–59.

10. The Principle of Legislative Supremacy

1. *See* Michigan v. EPA, 576 U.S. 743, 760–62 (2015) (Thomas, J., concurring); Perez v. Mortgage Bankers Assn., 575 U.S. 92, 119 (2015) (Thomas, J., concurring in judgment); *see also* Baldwin v. United States, 140 S.Ct. 690 (2020) (Thomas, J., dissenting from denial of certiorari); County of Maui v. Hawaii Wildlife Fund, 140 S.Ct. 1462, 1482 (Thomas, J., joined by Gorsuch, J., dissenting) ("[D]eference under [*Chevron*] likely conflicts with the Vesting Clauses of the Constitution."); Gutierrez-Brizuela v. Lynch, 834 F.3d 21149-58 (10th Cir. 2016) (Gorsuch, J., concurring). *See also* Kisor v. Wilkie, 139 S.Ct. 2400, 2437–2440 (2019) (Gorsuch, J., joined by Thomas, J., Kavanaugh, J., and Alito, J.) (suggesting that *Auer* deference to an agency's interpretation of its regulation may violate the original understanding of the judicial power established by Article III).

2. The constitutional objection to the *Chevron* doctrine based on Article III is new. *See* Craig Green, Chevron *Debates and the Constitutional Transformation of Administrative Law*, 88 Geo. Wash. L. Rev. 654, 695–704 (2020). Conservative judges and commentators were generally enthusiastic about the *Chevron* doctrine when it was first established, and never raised the Article III objection. *Id.* at 665–72. Indeed, some went so far as to maintain that *Chevron*-style deference was *required* by principles of separation of powers. *See, e.g.,* Douglas W. Kmiec, *Judicial Deference to Executive Agencies and the Decline of the Nondelegation Doctrine*, 2 Admin. L. Rev. 269 (1988). That an argument is new does not necessarily mean that it is wrong; but it at least warrants treating it with skepticism.

3. Philip Hamburger, Law and Judicial Duty (2008). Hamburger subsequently concluded that the *Chevron* doctrine is inconsistent with this conception of judicial duty. *See* Philip Hamburger, Is Administrative Law Unlawful? 316 (2014); Philip Hamburger, Chevron *Bias*, 84 Geo Wash. L. Rev. 1187 (2016).

4. Marbury v. Madison, 5 U.S. (1 Cranch) 137, 177 (1803).

5. *Id.*

6. *Id.* at 170.

7. *See* Steven G. Calabresi, *The Originalist and Normative Case Against Judicial Activism: A Reply to Professor Randy Barnett*, 103 Mich. L. Rev. 1081, 1092 (2005) ("There is simply no way to read the bare-bones language of Article III . . . and conclude that the Framers meant the Court to be a powerful institution. . . . Nor does the bare text of the Constitution suggest that the federal courts have a distinct role as the defenders and protectors of the federal Constitution."). There is

a near-universal consensus that executive actors have a duty to comply with judicial judgments to which they are a party. *See* William Baude, *The Judgment Power*, 96 GEO. L.J. 1807, 1821–26 (2008); Richard H. Fallon, Jr., *Executive Power and the Political Constitution*, 2007 UTAH L. REV. For the functional significance of this and possible exceptions, see Thomas W. Merrill, *Legitimate Interpretation—Or Legitimate Adjudication?*, 105 CORNELL L. REV. 1395, 1412–17 (2020).

8. *See* Thomas W. Merrill, *Judicial Opinions as Binding Law and as Explanations for Judgments*, 15 CARDOZO L. REV. 43 (1993) (weighing the various arguments, pro and con, in support of a duty of executive officers to obey the understanding of law reflected in judicial opinions). For collections of various historical views about whether judicial opinions are binding on the executive and legislative branches, including the views of Presidents Madison, Jackson, and Lincoln (all of whom said no), see LOUIS FISHER & NEAL DEVINS, POLITICAL DYNAMICS OF CONSTITUTIONAL LAW (1992); THE FEDERALIST SOCIETY, WHO SPEAKS FOR THE CONSTITUTION? THE DEBATE OVER INTERPRETIVE AUTHORITY (Occasional Paper No. 3, 1992).

9. Cooper v. Aaron, 358 U.S. 1 (1958).

10. Crowell v. Benson, 285 U.S. 22, 45–47 (1932).

11. *See* Abbott Labs. v. Gardner, 387 U.S. 136, 140–41 (1967) (interpreting the APA as creating a presumption in favor of judicial review).

12. *See* Larry Alexander & Frederick Schauer, *On Extrajudicial Constitutional Interpretation*, 110 HARV. L. REV. 1359 (1997); Dan T. Coenen, *The Constitutional Case Against Intracircuit Nonacquiescence*, 75 MINN. L. REV. 1339 (1991); Daniel A. Farber, *The Supreme Court and the Rule of Law:* Cooper v. Aaron *Revisited*, 1982 U. ILL. L. REV. 387.

13. For a recent statement reaffirming this point, see Merck Sharp & Dohme Corp v. Albrecht, 139 S.Ct. 1668, 1679 (2019) (quoting in part New York v. FERC, 535 U.S. 1, 18 (2002)): "'[A]n agency literally has no power to act . . . unless and until Congress confers power upon it.' . . . [W]hatever the means the FDA uses to exercise its authority, those means must lie within the scope of the authority Congress has lawfully delegated."

14. Thomas W. Merrill, *The Disposing Power of the Legislature*, 110 COLUM. L. REV. 452, 454 (2010).

15. *See, e.g.*, Social Security Bd. v. Nierotko, 327 U.S. 358, 364–70 (1946); ICC v. Cincinnati, New Orleans & Texas Pacific Ry. Co., 167 U.S. 479 (1897).

16. The APA recognized that Congress could explicitly or implicitly make agency action unreviewable. 5 U.S.C. § 701(a) (2018). But Congress has rarely done so where important private rights are at stake.

17. 494 U.S. 26 (1990).

18. *Id.* at 32. The Paperwork Reduction Act is codified at 44 U.S.C. § 3501 et seq. (2018).

19. 29 CFR § 1910.1200 (1984).

20. 44 U.S.C. § 3502(11) (2012). The term "information collection requests" was defined to include "collection of information" requirements. "Collection of information" was defined in turn to include "obtaining or soliciting of facts by an agency through . . . reporting or recordkeeping requirements." *Id.* § 3502(4).

21. *Dole,* 494 U.S. at 44–46 (White, J., dissenting).

22. *Id.* at 54 (White, J., dissenting).

23. 576 U.S. 473 (2015).

24. The Patient Protection and Affordable Care Act, 124 Stat. 119 (2010).

25. 42 U.S.C. § 18031 (2012).

26. *See* 26 CFR § 1.36B-2 (2013), making credits available to persons purchasing insurance on "an Exchange." "Exchange" was defined in turn as "an exchange serving the individual market . . . regardless of whether the Exchange is established and operated by a State . . . or by HHS." 45 CFR § 155.20 (2014).

27. King v. Burwell, 759 F.3d 358, 376 (4th Cir. 2014).

28. *King,* 576 U.S. at 485–86 (citations omitted) (quoting FDA v. Brown & Williamson Tobacco Corp., 529 U.S. 120, 147 (2000)).

29. *See, e.g.,* Mila Sohoni, King's *Domain,* 93 NOTRE DAME L. REV. 1419 (2018); Jonas J. Monast, *Major Questions About the Major Questions Doctrine,* 68 ADMIN. L. REV. 445 (2016); Note, *The Rise of Purposivism and the Fall of* Chevron: *Major Statutory Cases in the Supreme Court,* 130 HARV. L. REV. 1227 (2017).

30. *King,* 576 U.S. at 498:

> In a democracy, the power to make the law rests with those chosen by the people. Our role is more confined—"to say what the law is." Marbury v. Madison, 1 Cranch 137, 177 (1803). That is easier in some cases than in others. But in every case we must respect the role of the Legislature, and take care not to undo what it has done. A fair reading of legislation demands a fair understanding of the legislative plan.

31. The dissent in *King,* authored by Justice Scalia, insisted that the plain meaning of "established by a state" does not mean "established by a state or the federal government." *King,* 576 U.S. at 499–500 (Scalia, J., dissenting). The dissent also hypothesized that Congress could have limited tax credits to state-established exchanges in order to create an incentive for states to establish their own exchanges. *Id.* at 513. But burying the limitation on tax credits to exchanges "established by a state" in an obscure definitional provision dealing with how to determine the amount of the credit would be a bizarre way to create such an incentive scheme. And there was no discussion in the legislative deliberations suggesting such an objective, and no mention of the possible implications of the definitional provision in the administrative implementation of the Act. The most logical explanation for the definition is that it was a drafting error not caught by the congressional staff given the compressed time in which to produce an enrolled bill for the President's signature.

32. 512 U.S. 218 (1994).

33. 47 U.S.C. § 203(b)(2) (1988).

34. *MCI,* 512 U.S. at 242.

35. *See generally* Linda Jellum, Chevron's *Demise: A Survey of Chevron from Infancy to Senescence,* 59 ADMIN. L. REV. 725 (2007); Thomas W. Merrill, *Textualism and the Future of the* Chevron *Doctrine,* 72 WASH. U. L.Q. 351 (1994).

36. *MCI,* 512 U.S. at 229–31.

37. *Id.* at 231–32.

38. *Id.* at 244 (Stevens, J., dissenting).

39. *Id.* at 243 (Stevens, J., dissenting).

40. *Id.* at 231 n.4.

41. 47 U.S.C. § 160(a) (2012) ("[T]he [FCC] shall forbear from applying any regulation . . . of this Act to a telecommunications carrier . . . if [it] determines that—(1) enforcement . . . is not necessary to ensure that the . . . regulations . . . are just and reasonable[;] . . . (2) enforcement . . . is not necessary for the protection of consumers; and (3) forbearance from applying such . . . regulation is consistent with the public interest.").

42. 529 U.S. 120 (2000).

43. 21 U.S.C. §§ 321 (g)(1), 321(h)(3) (1988).

44. FDA v. Brown & Williamson Tobacco Corp., 529 U.S. 120, 186 (2000) (Breyer, J., dissenting) (quoting *Chevron,* 467 U.S. at 863).

45. *Id.* at 126 (emphasis added).

46. *Id.* at 177 (Breyer, J., dissenting).

47. *Id.* at 156.

48. *Id.* at 189 (Breyer, J., dissenting) (quoting Helvering v. Gregory, 69 F.2d 809, 810–11 (2d Cir. 1934) (L. Hand, J.)).

49. *Id.* at 159. It is not clear that this is what Justice Stevens meant when he spoke of "implicit delegations" in Part II of his *Chevron* opinion. The equation of ambiguity with implicit delegation was promoted by Justice Scalia, and entered the U.S. Reports with his opinion in Smiley v. Citibank (South Dakota), N.A., 517 U.S. 735, 740–41 (1996). Justice O'Connor's endorsement of the idea in the quoted sentence helped cement the notion that this was the basis for *Chevron* deference, at least for "non-extraordinary" purposes.

50. *Id.*

51. 576 U.S. 473, 486–86 (2015).

52. *See* Nora Freeman Engstrom & Robert L. Rabin, *Pursuing Public Health Through Litigation: Lessons from Tobacco and Opioids,* 73 Stan. L. Rev. 285, 302–05 (2021) (summarizing the tobacco litigation and settlement).

53. Family Smoking Prevention and Tobacco Control Act, Pub. L. No. 111-31, 123 Stat. 1776–1852 (2009) (codified as amended in scattered sections of 21 U.S.C.).

54. 549 U.S. 497 (2007).

55. 42 U.S.C. 7602(g) (2000). The definition, which was added in 1977 (91 Stat. 770), reads:

> The term "air pollutant" means any air pollution agent or combination of such agents, including any physical, chemical, biological, radioactive (including source material, special nuclear material, and byproduct material) substance or matter which is emitted into or otherwise enters the ambient air. Such term includes any precursors to the formation of any air pollutant, to the extent the Administrator has identified such precursor or precursors for the particular purpose for which the term "air pollutant" is used.

56. National Climate Program Act of 1978, Pub. L. No. 95–367, 92 Stat. 601 (1978) (codified as amended at 15 U.S.C. §§ 2901–08 (1982)).

57. Global Climate Protection Act of 1987, Pub. L. No. 100–204, 101 Stat. 1407 (1987) (codified as amended at 15 U.S.C. 2901 (1988)).

58. Clean Air Act Amendments of 1990, Pub. L. No. 101–549, 104 Stat. 2468 (1990) (codified as amended at 42 U.S.C. §§ 7401–7671q (1994)).

59. *See* 42 U.S.C. § 7403(g) (1994). Subdivision (1) authorized the EPA to conduct research into developing "[i]mprovements in nonregulatory strategies and technologies for preventing or reducing multiple air pollutants," including "carbon dioxide." Lest the limitation to "nonregulatory strategies" was missed, subsection (g) cautioned that "[n]othing in this subsection shall be construed to authorize the imposition on any person of air pollution control requirements."

60. Energy Policy and Conservation Act, Pub. L. No. 94–163, 89 Stat. 871 (1975) (codified as amended in scattered sections of 15 U.S.C.).

61. *See* Control of Emissions from New Highway Vehicles and Engines, 68 Fed. Reg. 52922, 52928 (Sept. 8, 2003) ("EPA is urged on . . . by . . . Brown & Williamson. . . . In light of Congress' attention to the issue[,] . . . and the absence of any direct or even indirect indication that Congress intended to authorize regulation . . . to address global climate change, it is unreasonable to conclude that the CAA provides the Agency with such authority.").

62. *Massachusetts,* 549 U.S. at 532–33 (quoting Clean Air Act, Pub. L. No. 89–272, §101(8), 79 Stat. 992 (1965) (codified as amended at 42 U.S.C. §7521(a)(1) (1994)).

63. *Id.* at 558–59 (Scalia, J., dissenting).

64. *Id.* at 552–53 (Scalia, J., dissenting).

65. *See* Thomas W. Merrill, *Justice Stevens and the* Chevron *Puzzle,* 106 Nw. U. L. Rev. 551, 561–62 (2012) (hypothesizing that Justice Stevens in *Massachusetts* was engaging in "a nudging function—forcing the administration and Congress to reconsider apparent underregulation of a problem of global dimensions.").

66. Bryan Walsh, *Why the Climate Bill Died,* Time, July 26, 2010, https://science .time.com/2010/07/26/why-the-climate-bill-died.

67. 573 U.S. 302 (2014).

68. *Id.* at 319.

69. *Id.* at 316–20. Justice Scalia's reliance on the EPA's longstanding constructions was, of course, inconsistent with his repeated insistence in earlier opinions that this canon had been rendered an "anachronism" by *Chevron.*

70. *Id.* at 310 (quoting THE CLEAN AIR HANDBOOK (Julie R. Domike & Alec C. Zacaroli eds., 3d ed. 2011)); *id.* at 321–22.

71. *Id.* at 315.

72. *Id.* at 324 (quoting 75 Fed. Reg. 31514, 31555 (June 3, 2010) ("Tailoring Rule")).

73. *Id.* at 327.

74. *Id.*

75. *Id.* at 339 (Breyer, J., concurring in part and dissenting in part). The material in quotation marks in the text is a condensation of what Breyer said, but I believe an accurate one.

76. For a reprise of sorts, although not couched in terms of the *Chevron* doctrine, see Alabama Assn. of Realtors v. Dept. of Health and Human Services, 141 S.Ct. 2485 (2021). Acting on emergency motions seeking a stay of a nationwide moratorium on evictions by the Centers for Disease Control, the majority (speaking per curiam) held that the moratorium almost certainly exceeded the scope of the CDC's authority and stayed the moratorium. A dissenting opinion by Justice Breyer argued that the moratorium was consistent with the broad purpose of the statute—to prevent the spread of disease—and the moratorium was in the public interest.

77. *See* Thomas W. Merrill, *Interpreting an Unamendable Text,* 71 VAND. L. REV. 547 (2018) (discussing the challenges to interpretation when the enacting body no longer updates relevant sources of authority).

11. Discerning the Boundaries of Agency Authority to Interpret

1. 487 U.S. 354 (1988).

2. 16 U.S.C. §§ 824(a) & (b)(1) (1982).

3. *Id.* at 377 (Scalia, J., concurring).

4. *Id.* at 387 (Brennan, J., dissenting) (citations omitted).

5. *Id.* at 388 (Brennan, J., dissenting).

6. *Id.*

7. *Id.* at 381 (Scalia, J., concurring).

8. *Compare* Nathan Alexander Sales & Jonathan H. Adler, *The Rest Is Silence:* Chevron *Deference, Agency Jurisdiction and Statutory Silence,* 2009 U. ILL. L. REV. 1497, and Thomas W. Merrill and Kristin Hickman, Chevron's *Domain,* 89 GEO. L. REV. 833, 909–14 (2001) (*Chevron* should not apply to questions about the scope of agency authority), *with* Cass R. Sunstein, *Law and Administration After* Chevron, 90 COLUM. L. REV. 2071, 2099–2100 (1990) (cautioning that the distinction is

"elusive"), and Quincy M. Crawford, *Comment,* Chevron *Deference to Agency Interpretations that Delimit the Scope of the Agency's Jurisdiction,* 61 U. CHI. L. REV. 957 (1994) (agreeing with Justice Scalia).

9. 569 U.S. 290 (2013).

10. Telecommunications Act of 1996, Pub. L. No. 104-104, 110 Stat. 56 (1996) (codified as amended in relevant part at 47 U.S.C. § 332(c)(7)(B)(ii) (2012)).

11. 47 U.S.C. § 332(c)(7)(B)(v) (2012).

12. City of Arlington v. FCC, 668 F.3d 229, 237 (5th Cir. 2012).

13. *City of Arlington,* 569 U.S. at 295. It is a testament to *Chevron*'s iconic status that the petitioners saw no need to provide a citation to the case in the question presented.

14. It was arguably unwise for the Court to limit its consideration to the abstract question whether the *Chevron* doctrine applies to questions of agency jurisdiction and to decline to review the other questions potentially presented. A consideration of the merits would have illuminated why the decision had been identified without any difficulty by both the FCC and the Fifth Circuit as being "jurisdictional." This in turn would have deflated much of the rhetorical force in Justice Scalia's opinion about the "false dichotomy" between jurisdictional and nonjurisdictional decisions. *Id.* at 304.

15. *Id.* at 295–300.

16. *Id.* at 304 (citations omitted).

17. William N. Eskridge, Jr., & Lauren E. Baer, *The Continuum of Deference: Supreme Court Treatment of Agency Statutory Interpretations from* Chevron *to* Hamdan, 96 GEO. L.J. 1083, 1154 tbl.20 (2008) (ranking Justice Scalia as one of the least likely Justices to affirm agency interpretations of statutes).

18. 5 U.S.C. § 706 (2012).

19. Henry P. Monaghan, Marbury *and the Administrative State,* 83 COLUM. L. REV. 1, 27 (1983).

20. 5 U.S.C. § 706(2)(C) (emphasis added).

21. *City of Arlington,* 569 U.S. at 297.

22. *Id.* at 297–98.

23. *Id.* at 310–12 (Breyer, J., concurring in part and concurring in the judgment).

24. *Id.* at 312 (Roberts, C.J., dissenting).

25. *Id.* at 316 (Roberts, C.J., dissenting). Speaking in defense of the "amici" (the author filed an *amicus* brief in the case on behalf of the National Governors' Conference), the question presented spoke in terms of agency "jurisdiction" and it is hazardous to insist that the Court should consider a different question than the one it has agreed to hear.

26. *Id.* (Roberts, C.J., dissenting).

27. *Id.* at 323 (Roberts, C.J., dissenting).

28. *Id.* at 323–24.

29. *Id.* at 327 (citations omitted).

30. Michigan v. EPA, 576 U.S. 743. 761–62 (2015) (Thomas, J., concurring).

31. *See* Introduction.

32. United States v. Mead Corp., 533 U.S. 218, 226–27 (2001).

33. *Id.* at 318 (Roberts, C.J., dissenting).

34. *Id.* at 323 (Roberts, C.J., dissenting).

35. *See* FDA v. Brown & Williamson Tobacco Corp., 529 U.S. 120 (2000).

36. *See* Skidmore v. Swift & Co., 323 U.S. 134 (1944).

37. For the unedifying story of how the Supreme Court gradually and without explicit consideration came to regard every grant of rulemaking as conferring authority on the agency to make rules having the force of law, see Thomas W. Merrill and Kathryn Tongue Watts, *Agency Rules with the Force of Law: The Original Convention,* 116 HARV. L. REV. 467, 493–528 (2002). This development is a greater deviation from the system of separation of powers as originally conceived than *Chevron* doctrine, because it sanctions a massive transfer of legislative power to agencies, whether or not actually intended by Congress. *Chevron* at least acknowledges the principle of legislative supremacy when Congress enacts clear or unambiguous statutes.

38. *See* Household Credit Servs., Inc. v. Pfennig, 541 U.S. 232, 238 (2004) (Federal Reserve Board); Am. Hosp. Ass'n v. NLRB, 499 U.S. 606, 616 (1991) (NLRB); Chevron U.S.A. Inc. v. Natural Res. Def. Council, Inc., 467 U.S. 837, 843 (1984) (EPA). The Court first recognized the FDA's legislative rulemaking authority in a group of pre-*Chevron* cases known as the *Hynson* Quartet. *See generally* USV Pharm. Corp. v. Weinberger, 412 U.S. 655 (1973); Weinberger v. Bentex Pharms., Inc., 412 U.S. 645 (1973); Ciba Corp. v. Weinberger, 412 U.S. 640 (1973); Weinberger v. Hynson, Westcott & Dunning, Inc., 412 U.S. 609 (1973).

39. Mayo Found. for Med. Educ. & Research v. United States, 562 U.S. 44, 54-58 (2011).

40. Smiley v. Citibank (South Dakota), N.A., 517 U.S. 735, 740–41 (1996) (discussed in Chapter 9); United States v. Mead Corp., 533 U.S. 218, 226–27 (2001) (discussed in Chapter 6).

41. *Smiley supra* note 40 at 740–41 ("We accord deference to agencies under *Chevron* . . . because of a presumption that Congress, when it left ambiguity in a statute meant for implementation by an agency, understood that the ambiguity would be resolved, first and foremost, by the agency, and desired the agency (rather than the courts) to possess whatever degree of discretion the ambiguity allows.").

42. As Jeffrey Pojanowski, reasoning from rule of law and legislative supremacy assumptions, has written: "[T]he scope of the agency's authority is a question of law . . . for the court to decide. The scope may be broad, such as requiring the agency to act in the public interest, and in those cases there may be very little law to apply. But . . . the agency cannot expand or narrow its authority beyond the court's best interpretation of what the legislature delegated." Jeffrey A. Pojanowski, *Neoclassical Administrative Law,* 133 Harv. L. Rev. 852, 902 (2020).

43. As spelled out more fully in Chapter 13, by referring to "independent judgment" as opposed to de novo review here, I think the reviewing court should give respectful consideration and weight as appropriate to an agency's legal judgment about the scope its authority. But the court should not accept the agency's interpretation as long as the question is unclear, as the Court seemingly held in *City of Arlington*.

44. *E.g.,* Federal Power Comm'n v. Hope Natural Gas Co., 320 U.S. 591 (1944).

45. *See* Whitman v. American Trucking Ass'ns, 531 U.S. 957 (2001).

46. Batterton v. Francis, 432 U.S. 416 (1977).

47. Social Security Board v. Nierotko, 327 U.S. 358 (1946).

48. 518 U.S. 470 (1996).

49. 21 U.S.C.§ 360k(b) (2000).

50. 494 U.S. 640, 640 (1990).

51. Metro. Stevedore Co. v. Rambo, 521 U.S. 121, 137 n.9 (1997).

52. Crandon v. United States, 494 U.S. 152, 177 (1990) (Scalia, J., concurring).

53. *See* Margaret H. Lemmos, *The Other Delegate: Judicially Administered Statutes and the Nondelegation Doctrine,* 81 So. CAL. L. REV. 405 (2008).

54. Utility Air Regulatory Group v. Environmental Protection Agency, 573 U.S. 302, 325 (2014) (Chapter 10).

55. *See supra* Chapter 3.

56. *See* Verizon Communications, Inc. v. FCC, 535 U.S. 467 (2002), discussed *infra.*

57. King v. Burwell, 576 U.S. 473, 489–90, 497–98 (2015).

58. *See, e.g.,* John F. Manning, *The Absurdity Doctrine,* 116 HARV. L. REV. 2387 (2003).

59. National Cable & Telecommunications Association v. Brand X Internet Services, 545 U.S. 967 (2005).

60. *See, e.g.,* Texas Dept. of Housing & Community Affairs v. the Inclusive Communities Project, Inc., 576 U.S. 519 (2015) (considering the issue under the Fair Housing Act); Smith v. City of Jackson, 544 U.S. 228 (2005) (considering the issue under the Age Discrimination in Employment Act); Griggs v. Duke Power Co., 401 U.S. 424 (1971) (considering the issue under Title VII of the Civil Rights Act of 1964). Justice Scalia cast the controlling vote in *Smith,* where he deferred to the agency's interpretation of the question under the *Chevron* doctrine.

61. This does not necessarily exhaust the circumstances that can be described as red flags requiring closer judicial scrutiny. Another principle might be that an agency assertion of authority which seems discordant in light of the plain language of the statute under which it operates requires closer scrutiny. *See, e.g.,* AMG Capital Management, LLC v. FTC, 141 S.Ct. 1341 (2021) (concluding that the FTC's practice of seeking recoupment of funds under a statute authorizing the agency to obtain "injunctions" in court exceeded the scope of its delegated authority).

62. *Chevron,* 467 U.S. at 861.

63. 556 U.S. 208 (2009).

64. 33 U.S.C. § 1326(b) (2012).

65. *Riverkeeper,* 556 U.S. at 222.

66. *Id.* at 224; *id.* at 234–35 (Breyer, J., concurring in part and dissenting in part).

67. 535 U.S. 467 (2002).

68. 47 U.S.C. § 252(d)(1) (2006).

69. *Verizon,* 535 U.S. at 501.

70. 494 U.S. 26 (1990).

71. 529 U.S. 120 (2000).

72. 497 U.S. 116 (1990).

73. 512 U.S. 218 (1994).

74. 546 U.S. 243 (2006).

75. *Id.* at 262–63.

76. *Id.* at 265.

77. *Id.* at 266.

78. City of Arlington v. FCC, 569 U.S. 290, 321 (2013) (Roberts, C.J., dissenting) (emphasis omitted).

79. Washington v. Glucksberg, 521 U.S. 702, 705–06 (1997).

80. As Justice Scalia wrote in *City of Arlington:* "[*Chevron*] provides a stable background against which Congress can legislate: Statutory ambiguities will be resolved within the bounds of reasonable interpretation, not by the courts but by the administering agency. Congress knows how to speak in plain terms when it wishes to circumscribe, and in capacious terms when it wishes to enlarge, agency discretion." 569 U.S. at 296 (citation omitted).

12. Improving the Quality of Agency Interpretations

1. Kent Barnett & Christopher J. Walker, Chevron *Step Two's Domain,* 93 NOTRE DAME L. REV. 1441 (2018).

2. For a sustained argument that *Chevron* deference should be limited to interpretations adopted through notice-and-comment rulemaking, see Kristin E. Hickman & Aaron L. Nielson, *Narrowing* Chevron's *Domain,* 70 DUKE L.J. 931 (2021). The proposal in this chapter is similar to, and draws inspiration from, their article.

3. Perez v. Mortgage Bankers Ass'n, 575 U.S. 92, 100–02 (2015); Vermont Yankee Nuclear Power Corp. v. Natural Resources Defense Council, Inc., 435 U.S. 519, 543–44 (1978).

4. 5 U.S.C. § 553 (2018).

5. 5 U.S.C. §§ 553(b) & (c) (2018).

6. 5 U.S.C. §§ 553(b)(A), 553(d) (2018). Other exceptions are provided for rules respecting military or foreign affairs functions, for matters relating to agency personnel and management, and for matters concerning "public property, loans, grants, benefits, or contracts." *Id.* § 553 (a).

7. *Id.* at §§ 553(b)(B), 553(d) (2018).

8. *E.g.,* Portland Cement Ass'n v. Ruckelshaus, 486 F.2d 375, 393 (D.C. Cir. 1973).

9. *E.g.,* Chocolate Manfr's Ass'n v. Block, 755 F.2d 1098 (4th Cir. 1985).

10. *E.g.,* Amoco Oil Co. v. EPA, 501 F.2d 722, 739 (D.C. Cir. 1974).

11. *See* J. Skelly Wright, *The Courts and the Rulemaking Process: The Limits of Judicial Review,* 59 CORNELL L. REV. 375 (1974) (arguing that the modern conception of notice-and-comment can be derived from the text of § 553).

12. *See* American Radio Relay League, Inc. v. FCC, 524 F.3d 227, 248 (D.C. Cir. 2008) (Kavanaugh, J., concurring in part, concurring in judgment in part, and dissenting in part) ("Courts have incrementally expanded those procedural requirements well beyond what the text [of § 553] provides."). *See generally* Gillian E. Metzger, *Embracing Administrative Common Law,* 80 Geo. Wash. L. Rev. 1293 (2012) (distinguishing statutory and common law in administrative law).

13. *See* Pension Benefit Guaranty Corp. v. LTV Corp., 496 U.S. 633, 654–55 (1990); Merrick B. Garland, *Deregulation and Judicial Review,* 98 HARV. L. REV. 505, 530 (1985). The arbitrary-and-capricious standard applies to all forms of agency action. *See, e.g.,* Department of Homeland Security v. Regents of the University of California, 140 S.Ct. 1891 (2020) (invoking the arbitrary-and-capricious standard to remand a decision to revoke a policy statement for failure to consider alternatives and not addressing reliance interests); FCC v. Fox Televisions Stations, Inc., 556 U.S. 502 (2009) (ruling that arbitrary-and-capricious review requires an explanation for a change in agency policy adopted in an FCC adjudication); Citizens to Preserve Overton Park, Inc. v. Volpe, 401 U.S. 402 (1971) (applying an enhanced conception of arbitrary-and-capricious review to an informal adjudication).

14. *See* Encino Motorcars, LLC v. Navarro, 136 S.Ct. 2117, 2125 (2016) (declining to defer to an agency regulation because of inadequate notice); Wyeth v. Levine, 555 U.S. 555, 578 (2009) (similar); Perez v. Mortgage Bankers Ass'n, 575 U.S. 92, 96 92015) ("An agency must consider and respond to significant comments received during the period for public comment."); Motor Vehicle Manf. Assn. v. State Farm Mut. Auto. Ins. Co, 463 U.S. 29, 46–51 (1983) (holding that an agency must explain its reasons for rejecting a material alternative proposed during the rulemaking process); Dep't of Commerce v. New York, 139 S.Ct. 2551, 2575 (2019) (holding that an agency acts in an arbitrary and capricious fashion when its explanation "is incongruent with what the record reveals about the agency's priorities and decisionmaking process").

15. Make the Rd. N.Y. v. Wolf, 962 F.3d 612, 634 (D.C. Cir. 2020) (quoting Lilliputian Sys., Inc. v. Pipeline & Hazardous Materials Safety Admin., 741 F.3d 1309, 1312 (D.C. Cir. 2014)).

16. For a decision often regarded as the paradigmatic example of the notice-and-comment norm in the context of rulemaking, see United States v. Nova Scotia Food Products Corp., 568 F.2d 240 (2d Cir. 1977).

17. *See, e.g., Encino Motorcars,* 136 S.Ct. at 2125; Wyeth v. Levine, 555 U.S. 555, 578 (2009).

18. Barnett & Walker, *supra* note 1, at 1466 fig.3.

19. *Cf.* Richard A. Posner, *What Do Judges and Justices Maximize? The Same Thing as Everybody Else,* 3 Sup. Ct. Econ. Rev. 1 (1993).

20. Mark Seidenfeld, *A Syncopated* Chevron: *Emphasizing Reasoned Decisionmaking in Reviewing Agency Interpretations of Statutes,* 73 Tex. L. Rev. 83 (1994).

21. *Id.* at 125–26.

22. For citations to the literature on pluralist and interest group theory, see Thomas W. Merrill, *Chief Justice Rehnquist, Pluralist Theory, and the Interpretation of Statutes,* 25 Rutgers L.J. 621, 625–31 (1994).

23. *See* Thomas W. Merrill, *Capture Theory and the Courts: 1967–1983,* 72 Chi.-Kent L. Rev. 1039 (1997).

24. William Niskanen, Bureaucracy and Representative Government (1971).

25. *See* Serge Taylor, Making Bureaucracies Think 12–140 (1984) (describing the mission-oriented mentality of government agencies and their resistance to recognizing factors or problems that do not relate to their own mission).

26. *See* Hickman & Nielson, *supra* note 2, at 966 ("[A]ll else being equal, a process that solicit comments and forces agencies to engage with the views of the public should generally lead to better policy outcomes.")

27. *Cf.* William F. Pedersen, Jr., *Formal Records and Informal Rulemaking,* 85 Yale L.J. 38, 59–60 (1975) (describing how the prospect of judicial review improves internal collaboration in agencies).

28. *See* Hickman & Nielson, *supra* note 2, at 967 ("A process that requires an agency to interact with broad segments of society and explain why it has acted in view of concerns raised by the general public, all else being equal, typically should yield more legitimate outcomes.")

29. *See* Jerry L. Mashaw, *Prodelegation: Why Administrators Should Make Political Decisions,* 1 J. L & Econ. Org. 81 (1985); Richard B. Stewart, *The Transformation of American Administrative Law,* 88 Harv. L. Rev. 1669 (1975).

30. 5 U.S.C. § 706 (2018) ("In making the foregoing determinations[,] . . . due account shall be taken of the rule of prejudicial error.").

31. *See, e.g.,* Richard J. Pierce, Jr., *Seven Ways to Deossify Agency Rulemaking,* 47 ADMIN. L. REV. 59 (1995); Thomas O. McGarity, *Some Thoughts on "Deossifying" the Rulemaking Process,* 41 DUKE L.J. 1385 (1991).

32. *See, e.g.,* Elizabeth Fisher, Pasky Pascual, & Wendy Wagner, *Rethinking Judicial Review of Expert Agencies,* 93 TEX. L. REV. 1681 (2015); Patricia M. Wald, *Judicial Review of Complex Administrative Agency Decisions,* 462 ANNALS AM. ACAD. POL. & SOC. SCI. 72, 76–77 (1982).

33. *See* Jason Webb Yackee & Susan Webb Yackee, *Is Federal Rule-Making "Ossified"?,* 20 J. Pub. Admin. Res. & Theory 261 (2009); Stephen M. Johnson, *Ossification's Demise? An Empirical Analysis of EPA Rulemaking from 2001–2005,* 38 ENVTL. L. 767 (2008).

34. For this reason, I would not go further, and charge the reviewing court with taking a "hard look" at the agencies' reasons for choosing one particular interpretation rather than another. *Cf.* Catherine M. Sharkey, *Cutting in on the* Chevron *Two-Step,* 80 FORDHAM L. REV. 2359 (2018) (advocating the addition of hard look review to the *Chevron* framework). This poses too much risk of courts substituting their judgment for that of the agency on matters of discretionary choice. Requiring advance notice, public comment, and reasons for accepting or rejecting comments about a proposed interpretation should create enough of an incentive for improved agency interpretation efforts. Inviting courts to engage in a more intrusive form of oversight increases the risk of courts substituting their judgment about policy for that of the agency.

35. Rules under the APA are defined as agency action having future effect. 5 U.S.C. § 551(4) (2018). Interpretive rules and policy statements are exempt from notice-and-comment requirements under 5 U.S.C. § 553(d)(2) (2018), but agencies are free to use a version of notice-and-comment in developing these rules if they wish.

36. 5 U.S.C. § 551(6) (2018) (defining "order" of an agency to include an order "declaratory in form").

37. *See* Hickman & Nielson, *supra* note 2, at 971–77 (discussing the retroactivity of interpretations rendered in adjudication as raising due process concerns).

38. United States v. Mead Corp., 533 U.S. 218, 230–31 & n.12 (2001).

39. *See* note 3 *supra.*

40. *See* City of Arlington v. FCC, 668 F.3d 229, 235 (5th Cir. 2012), aff'd, 569 U.S. 290 (2013).

41. SEC v. Chenery Corp., 332 U.S. 194 (1947).

42. *See, e.g.,* Encino Motorcars, LLC v. Navarro, 136 S.Ct. 2117, 2125 (2016) (refusing to give *Chevron* deference to an agency interpretation that failed to explain its departure from previous interpretations, and describing this as a failure "to follow the correct procedures").

43. As to whether considerations of *stare decisis* preclude the Court from denying the strongest form of deference to agency interpretations adopted through

adjudication, see Hickman & Nielson, *supra* note 2, at 982–96. They argue that applying *Chevron* to adjudications is inconsistent with *Chevron*'s justifications in terms of public participation, accountability, and legitimacy, and that the Court has in fact applied *Chevron* in only a relatively small number of adjudications, as opposed to rulemakings that follow the notice-and-comment procedure.

13. Reforming the *Chevron* Doctrine

1. *See* Stephen Breyer, *Judicial Review of Questions of Law and Policy*, 38 ADMIN. L. REV. 363, 373 (1986).

2. Utility Air Regulatory Group v. Environmental Protection Agency, 573 U.S. 302 (2014).

3. *Chevron*, 467 U.S. at 865.

4. FDA v. Brown and Williamson Tobacco Corp., 529 U.S. 120 (2000).

5. Dole v. United Steelworkers of America, 494 U.S. 26 (1990).

6. King v. Burwell, 576 U.S. 473 (2015).

7. 304 U.S. 64 (1938).

8. *Id.* at 72–73, 77–80. For the reasons discussed in Chapter 2, it is unlikely that "new evidence" about the meaning of the Administrative Procedure Act will be discovered that sheds light on *Chevron*. Discovering the plain text of that statute is another matter, although admittedly it will be hard for the Court to explain why it ignored that text throughout the period dominated by the *Chevron* doctrine.

9. *See, e.g.,* Kent Barrett, *Codifying Chevmore*, 90 N.Y.U. L. REV. 1 (2015); Elizabeth Garrett, *Legislating* Chevron, 101 MICH. L. REV. 2637 (2003). For a wide-ranging discussion of the issues presented by the prospect of Congress enacting legislation that directs courts how to interpret statutes, see Nicholas Quinn Rosenkranz, *Federal Rules of Statutory Interpretation,* 115 HARV. L. REV. 2085 (2002).

10. To distinguish the steps in this three-step process from the *Chevron* steps, these steps are spelled out (step one, step two, step three), whereas, except for step zero, the *Chevron* steps are designated with numerals (step 1, step 2).

11. In this respect, the proposed reformulation differs from the author's endorsement of the "force of law" criterion in Thomas W. Merrill & Kristin E. Hickman, Chevron's Domain, 89 GEO. L.J. 833, 874–82 (2001).

12. United States v. Mead Corp., 533 U.S. 218, 229 (2001).

13. *Mead,* 533 U.S. at 230.

14. Thomas W. Merrill, *Re-Reading* Chevron, 70 DUKE L.J. 1153 (2021).

15. The idea that any ambiguity in a statute should be presumed to be an implicit delegation to the agency to function as the primary interpreter was introduced by Justice Scalia in his 1989 Law Review article, Antonin Scalia, *Judicial Deference to Administrative Interpretations of Law,* 1989 DUKE L.J. 511, 516 (1989), and was written into decisional law in Smiley v. Citibank (South Dakota), N.A., 517 U.S. 735, 740–41 (1996) (Scalia, J.).

16. 5 U.S.C. § 706 (2018).

17. *See* Henry Monaghan, Marbury *and the Administrative State,* 83 COLUM. L. REV. 1, 27 (1983).

18. 5 U.S.C. § 706(2)(C) (2018).

19. 569 U.S. 290, 313 (2013) (Roberts, C.J., dissenting).

20. 139 S.Ct. 2400 (2019).

21. 519 U.S. 452 (1945).

22. *Kisor,* 139 S.Ct. at 2415–18.

23. *See generally* Chapter 7; Anita S. Krishnakumar, *Longstanding Agency Interpretations,* 83 FORD. L. REV. 1823 (2015).

24. Justice Breyer's opinions for the Court in Long Island Care at Home Ltd. v. Coke, 551 U.S. 158, 173–74 (2007), and Barnhart v. Walton, 535 U.S. 212, 222 (2002), can be cited as underscoring that finding an implicit delegation entails more than identifying a source of rulemaking or adjudication authority to act with the force of law. Although United States v. Mead Corp., 533 U.S. 223, 226–27 (2001), instructed that the *Chevron* doctrine should apply only when an agency had made its interpretation pursuant to delegated authority to act with the force of law, this is inadequate to ensure that the agency is acting within the scope of its delegated authority. As explained in Chapter 10, the question of agency authority exists along two dimensions. One is whether Congress has given the agency the authority to act with the force of law. The other is whether Congress has given the agency the authority to decide the particular question presented. The principle of legislative supremacy requires that both types of limits be enforced.

25. *See, e.g.,* Encino Motorcars, LLC v. Navarro, 136 S.Ct. 2117, 2125 (2016) (refusing to give *Chevron* deference to an agency interpretation that failed to explain its departure from previous interpretations); Wyeth v. Levine, 555 U.S. 555, 578 (2009) (refusing to apply the *Chevron* doctrine in part because the agency had not provided any notice of its interpretation before it was adopted).

26. Among the Justices who have expressed reservations about the *Chevron* doctrine, from a variety of perspectives, the materials in this book would identify Justices Brennan, Stevens, and Breyer, and more recently, Justices Thomas, Gorsuch, and Kavanaugh. Recall too that Chief Justice Roberts and Justices Kennedy and Alito dissented from the proposition in *City of Arlington* that the *Chevron* doctrine should apply in determining the scope of the agency's authority.

Concluding Thoughts

1. *Cf.* MORRIS FIORINA, CONGRESS: KEYSTONE OF THE WASHINGTON ESTABLISHMENT (1989) (arguing that Congress continued to be the "keystone" through the 1980s).

2. Some commonly cited reasons for the decline of Congress: (1) The realignment of the southern conservatives from the Democratic to the Republican Party

skewed the two parties toward increased ideological homogeneity. This makes it harder to forge compromises across party lines. *See, e.g.,* Richard H. Pildes, *Why the Center Does Not Hold: The Causes of Hyperpolarized Politics in America,* 99 CALIF. L. REV. 273 (2011). (2) Americans have increasingly sorted themselves into ideologically homogeneous regions, which means that primary elections matter a great deal in determining who becomes a member of Congress. This, in turn, pushes members to avoid compromise with the opposing party, in order to protect their flank against a primary challenge. See BILL BISHOP, THE BIG SORT: WHY THE CLUSTERING OF LIKE-MINDED AMERICA IS TEARING US APART (2009). (3) Election and reelection are highly dependent on fundraising and constituent services, which leaves less time for traditional legislating. *See* Fiorina, *supra* note 1. (4) Internal reforms have weakened the seniority system, which makes it harder for longer-serving members to secure passage of their favored legislative projects. (5) Members increasingly leave their families in their home districts and commute to Washington for shortened work weeks when in session, leaving little time for social interaction and forging friendships across party lines, and offering less time for legislating. For an overview of the fallout created by the inability of Congress to perform its role as the principal engine of federal law and policy, see Abbe R. Gluck, Anne Joseph O'Connell & Rosa Po, *Unorthodox Lawmaking, Unorthodox Rulemaking,* 115 COLUM. L. REV. 1789 (2015).

3. National Cable & Telecommunications Association v. Brand X Internet Services, 545 U.S. 967 (2005).

4. United States v. Home Concrete & Supply, LLC, 566 U.S. 478 (2012).

5. E.E.O.C. v. Arabian Am. Oil Co. (Aramco), 499 U.S. 244 (1991).

6. The classic study is Carol M. Rose, *Crystals and Mud in Property Law,* 40 STAN. L. REV. 577 (1988).

7. *See generally,* Abbe R. Gluck, *Intersystemic Statutory Interpretation: Methodology as "Law" and the* Erie *Doctrine,* 120 YALE L. J. 1898, 1908–1918 (2011).

Acknowledgments

This book reflects a long engagement with the Supreme Court's "*Chevron* doctrine," including briefs filed as a practicing lawyer starting in the late 1980s, and articles and workshops presented at the law schools with which I have been affiliated over the years (Northwestern, Yale, and Columbia). It would be impossible to thank every client and institution that has made this engagement possible, but the book is very much a distillation of what I have learned (or thought I have learned) from these repeated opportunities to ponder the implications of the doctrine. Special thanks should be given to Columbia University, which awarded me a sabbatical in the spring of 2020 that fortuitously coincided with a self-imposed exile to avoid the novel coronavirus. This gave me the time and freedom from distractions to undertake the book.

Two former students deserve a special note. Kristin Hickman and Katherine Tongue Watts produced yearlong research projects under my supervision on aspects of the *Chevron* doctrine during my days at Northwestern University Law School. Their work advanced my understanding in many ways, and resulted in co-authored articles in top journals. I am pleased to report that they are now highly regarded professors of Administrative Law, at the University of Minnesota and Washington University, respectively.

A number of colleagues were gracious enough to read all or parts of the manuscript and provide helpful comments, including the aforementioned Kristin Hickman and Jeremy Kessler, Ron Levin, Gillian Metzger, Chuck Sable, and Peter Strauss. Henry Monaghan deserves special thanks for providing detailed suggestion on the entire text. He is an inspiration to all who know him and his work. Two veterans of the *Columbia Law Review,* Lefteri Christodulelis and Sara Tofighbakhsh, provided outstanding research assistance before heading off to judicial clerkships.

Portions of Chapters 1, 3, and 13 were first published as "Re-Reading *Chevron,*" 70 *Duke Law Journal* 1153 (2021). Chapters 2 and 4 advance discussions first presented in "Judicial Deference to Executive Precedent," 101 *Yale Law Journal* 969 (1992). Chapter 3 includes text first published in and Chapter 4 builds on ideas first introduced in "The Story of *Chevron:* The Making of an Accidental Landmark," 66 *Administrative Law Review* 253 (2014).

Index